The Army is My Calling

The Army is My Calling

The Life and Writings of
Major John Rogers Vinton
1801-1847

by
John & Mary Lou Missall

Florida Historical Society Press

The Army is My Calling

The Life and Writings of Major John Rogers Vinton, 1801-1847

Cover: *John Rogers Vinton*, possibly by Joseph Greenleaf Cole
Frontispiece: *John Rogers Vinton*, artist unknown
All maps by John Missall

ISBN: 978-1-886104-91-4

The Florida Historical Society Press
435 Brevard Avenue
Cocoa, FL 32922
http://myfloridahistory.org/press

For Frank and Dale Laumer:
Dear Friends;
Everlasting Inspirations.

Other Works by John & Mary Lou Missall

The Seminole Wars: America's Longest Indian Conflict

Elizabeth's War: A Novel of the First Seminole War (*From the Florida Historical Society Press*)

Hollow Victory: A Novel of the Second Seminole War (*From the Florida Historical Society Press*)

This Miserable Pride of a Soldier: The Letters of Journals of Col. William S. Foster in the Second Seminole War (editors)

This Torn Land: Poetry of the Second Seminole War (editors)

Just Havin' Fun: Adventures of an Oil Well Firefighter (with Boots Hansen)

An Ancient Tale New Told: The Stories of Shakespeare (by John Missall)

Contents

Illustrations

Color Plates

Located between Chapters 10 & 11, page 154

* Painted by John Rogers Vinton

Maps

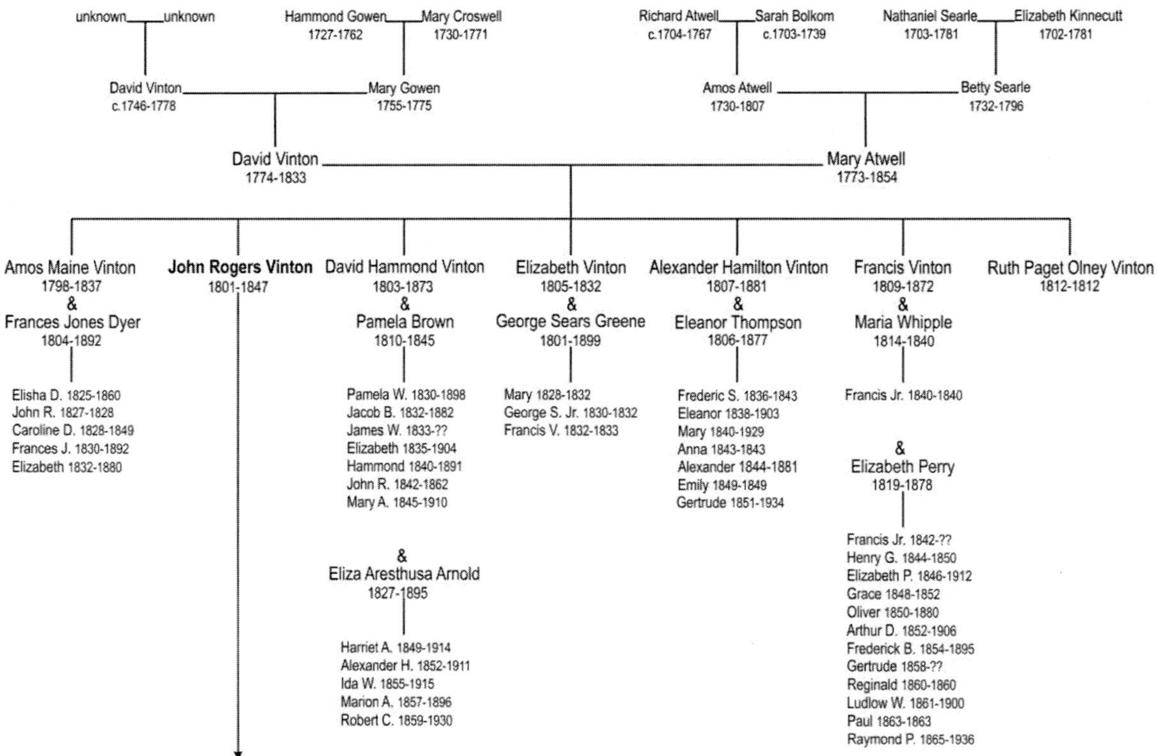
unknown
unknown
Hammond Gowen
1727-1762
Mary Croswell
1730-1771
Richard Atwell
c.1704-1767
Sarah Bolkom
c.1703-1739
Nathaniel Searle
1703-1781
Elizabeth Kinnecutt
1702-1781
David Vinton
c.1746-1778
Mary Gowen
1755-1775
Amos Atwell
1730-1807
Betty Searle
1732-1796
David Vinton
1774-1833
Mary Atwell
1773-1854
Amos Maine Vinton
1798-1837
&
Frances Jones Dyer
1804-1892
Elisha D. 1825-1860
John R. 1827-1828
Caroline D. 1828-1849
Frances J. 1830-1892
Elizabeth 1832-1880
John Rogers Vinton
1801-1847
David Hammond Vinton
1803-1873
&
Pamela Brown
1810-1845
Pamela W. 1830-1898
Jacob B. 1832-1882
James W. 1833-??
Elizabeth 1835-1904
Hammond 1840-1891
John R. 1842-1862
Mary A. 1845-1910
&
Eliza Aresthusa Arnold
1827-1895
Harriet A. 1849-1914
Alexander H. 1852-1911
Ida W. 1855-1915
Marion A. 1857-1896
Robert C. 1859-1930
Elizabeth Vinton
1805-1832
&
George Sears Greene
1801-1899
Mary 1828-1832
George S. Jr. 1830-1832
Francis V. 1832-1833
Alexander Hamilton Vinton
1807-1881
&
Eleanor Thompson
1806-1877
Frederic S. 1836-1843
Eleanor 1838-1903
Mary 1840-1929
Anna 1843-1843
Alexander 1844-1881
Emily 1849-1849
Gertrude 1851-1934
Francis Vinton
1809-1872
&
Maria Whipple
1814-1840
Francis Jr. 1840-1840
&
Elizabeth Perry
1819-1878
Francis Jr. 1842-??
Henry G. 1844-1850
Elizabeth P. 1846-1912
Grace 1848-1852
Oliver 1850-1880
Arthur D. 1852-1906
Frederick B. 1854-1895
Gertrude 1858-??
Reginald 1860-1860
Ludlow W. 1861-1900
Paul 1863-1863
Raymond P. 1865-1936
Ruth Paget Olney Vinton
1812-1812

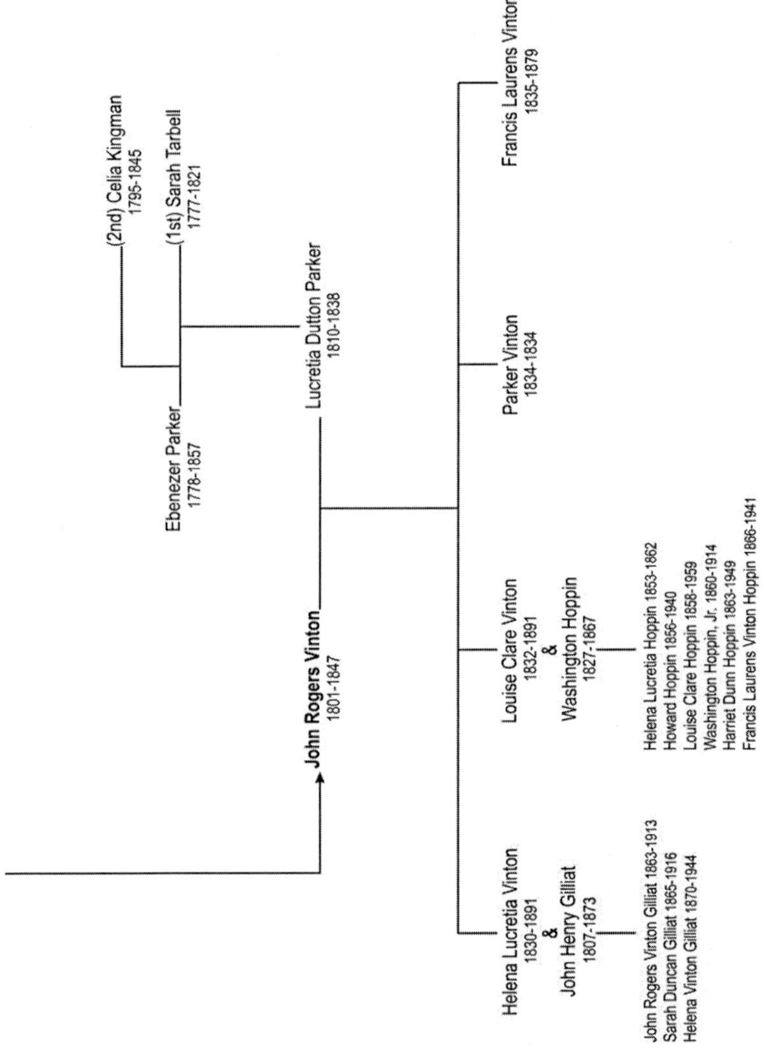

(2nd) Celia Kingman
1795-1845
(1st) Sarah Tarbell
1777-1821
Ebenezer Parker
1778-1857
Lucretia Dutton Parker
1810-1838
John Rogers Vinton
1801-1847
Helena Lucretia Vinton
1830-1891
&
John Henry Gilliat
1807-1873
John Rogers Vinton Gilliat 1863-1913
Sarah Duncan Gilliat 1865-1916
Helena Vinton Gilliat 1870-1944
Louise Clare Vinton
1832-1891
&
Washington Hoppin
1827-1867
Helena Lucretia Hoppin 1853-1862
Howard Hoppin 1856-1940
Louise Clare Hoppin 1858-1959
Washington Hoppin, Jr. 1860-1914
Harriet Dunn Hoppin 1863-1949
Francis Laurens Vinton Hoppin 1866-1941
Parker Vinton
1834-1834
Francis Laurens Vinton
1835-1879

Preface

After twenty-five years in the army, John Rogers Vinton came to the realization that he wanted to be a soldier. Up until that point his military career had been one of chance or convenience and not the true focus of his ambition. He was like many of us, satisfied with the work he did, but always believing that there had to be something better.

Vinton spent his entire adolescence and adult life in the army, entering West Point in 1814, just prior to his thirteenth birthday, and, like the true soldier he came to be, giving his life on the battlefield in Mexico at age forty-six. During those thirty-three years the army provided him with the opportunity to touch his civilian dreams, but never did he take the chance and truly embrace them. Within a military context he was a surveyor and engineer, a political operative, an artist, and even a preacher. Yet for the first twenty-three years of his career he was never a "warrior." No campaigns, no battlefields, and no enemy intent on taking his life. It took personal tragedy and a hopeless war to make him realize that the life of a soldier, in peacetime as well as wartime, was truly his calling.

Within that long career, there is surprisingly little battlefield glory in the life of John Rogers Vinton. The total of his combat experience amounted to one siege and two battles, and someone might wonder why we should find his life interesting. Simply put, life is made up of much more than a few deadly days, and when we look at Vinton we can see ourselves, whether it be making a home, learning a trade, or following our dreams. His trials, triumphs, disappointments, and accomplishments are the same as ours, simply in a different context.

What makes Vinton appealing as a subject is the amount of detail we have from his life and the familiarity we feel for the associations he formed. His family background can be traced to the *Mayflower* and the battles of Lexington and Concord. Two of his brothers became prominent churchmen, while another also made a career of the army and served into the Civil War. In short, his family made a lasting mark on their community. It was a close-knit clan that wrote numerous letters, many of which have been preserved. Vinton also kept daily journals and although some have not survived, we do have those that pertain to the most significant portions of his life. Overall, we have a surprisingly complete record of his life from the day he left the Military Academy to the day he died.

It is also a record of the place and time in which he lived. Many of his letters concern the sort of family matters most of us eventually face: Financial hardships, the loss of loved ones, long separations, the upbringing of children, and domestic arrangements. If nothing else, it is a detailed, personal look into the life of an army officer and the nation in general during an important period of our history. That in itself makes this work valuable.

Vinton was also a talented artist, well known today for his depictions of the Second Seminole War. Much of his surviving work is reproduced in this book, but not all of it was obtainable. Several pieces were so similar that it seemed a waste to include both versions. Most tantalizing were those works that were mentioned in letters but which have not survived or could not be located. Foremost among those are portraits of his two daughters. We know he painted their pictures, for in one letter he tells his daughter Louise, "Your likeness & Sister Helena's, that I painted, hang up in our bedroom so we can be reminded of you at least every morning & night." We'll always feel that those pictures are hanging on the wall or sitting in the attic of some descendant we failed to locate.[1]

We first became interested in John Rogers Vinton through our work with the Seminole Wars Foundation. The organization had obtained access to two of his journals from the Second Seminole War, and it was thought a transcription might prove useful for scholarship into the conflict. Our good friend Jackson Walker, an accomplished artist who specializes in Florida history, originally took on the task, hoping to gain some insight into Vinton's artwork. Unfortunately, artistry was a leisure pastime for Vinton, and he rarely mentioned it. There was simply nothing for Jackson to discover in the journal, and he passed the project on to us, more specifically to Mary, who enjoys transcribing works from the period.

As often happens when doing research, questions were raised that prompted us to look for answers. We ultimately located other journals, correspondence, letter books, and artworks at various repositories in different parts of the country. All these places thought Vinton's legacy was important, but no one had ever taken the time to bring it all together to tell the complete story. That became our mission.

After Mary completed the painstaking task of deciphering and transcribing all the handwritten documents, the task of editing the work fell to John. All told, Mary transcribed about a thousand single-spaced pages, of which perhaps a quarter ended up in this book. If we believed something was of any historical significance or provided personal insight into someone, we did our best to include it. We felt that tedious passages dealing with personal finances, astronomical observations (for surveying), obscure friends and relatives, and mundane domestic or military matters were best left out of the final product.

The question then arose as to how best to present the material. We could have published the entire collection of transcriptions with a minimum of commentary, but that would have been a very large, dry work devoid of the great humanity we found in Vinton's life. We could have done a very detailed biography, examining the whys and wherefores of every decision he made, but in the end, we didn't feel Vinton warranted that sort of attention. He wasn't an Andrew Jackson or a Zachary Taylor; he just didn't occupy that high a position in the scheme of things.

Vinton's story is important because of its humanity. He doesn't do great things, but he's there when they happen. He goes through the experiences we all go through, and his writings give us an insight into his mind and, when we reflect upon it, our own minds as well. What we, as authors/editors, decided to do was help Vinton tell his own story. His writings and those of his family would provide the window into his world. We would provide background information and historical context. We fully understand that some of his contemporaries saw things in a completely different light, but that's their story to tell. This is John Roger's Vinton's life through his eyes, and we should listen to it much the same as we should listen to our parents or grandparents telling us theirs.

Due to the more personal nature of the work, a "silent" style of editing was adopted, wherein the changes are hidden, with the exception of ellipses and minimal bracketed comments. As noted above, the majority of the manuscript material did not become part of this work, and large portions of some letters have been removed from what is presented here. The overall goal was to produce a narrative that flowed smoothly yet remained true to Vinton's character. To achieve this, we selected only those passages that gave us insight into Vinton's personality or the events that were important to his life.

We also attempted to eliminate redundant passages, but the reader will find there are times when we felt the historical significance of the matter required the inclusion of letters that varied only in minor details. The most notable of these are in the chapters that cover the Battles of Lake Monroe and Monterrey.

These were both significant events in their respective wars, and we felt it important to add the extra detail to the historical literature for those conflicts.

There were generally three types of manuscript material we used: journals, personal correspondence, and letter books. The nomenclature of the journals needs some explanation. The first journal we worked on was labeled Journal One and covered much of Vinton's time in Florida (1839-1841, Special Collections, Providence Public Library). We also had Journal Three, which he kept during the Mexican-American War (1846-1847, Special Collections, Providence Public Library). Obviously, we wanted Journal Two, which appeared to cover the final months of the war in Florida. We never found it. What we did find was his first journal (1817-1818), which he started soon after he left West Point (Rubenstein Library, Duke University). There was also a journal from a lengthy trip he made in 1827, followed by a journal he kept while serving in Washington in 1827-1828 (Special Collections, University of Delaware Library). This last book was labeled Journal Five, but predates Journal One of the Seminole War. In addition, there was a short, unnumbered journal from April to June of 1838 (Rubenstein Library, Duke University). These journals are not necessarily diaries, and it does not appear he maintained a running log of his entire military career. Instead, he seems to have kept the journals when on special missions or deployed in a war zone, possibly as a reference should anyone question his actions or inquire into his accounts. When he was comfortably stationed at some military post in peacetime, there was little reason to keep a daily record of events or observations.

For those who are unfamiliar with them, letter books may need some explanation. In the days before scanners, photocopiers, and even carbon paper, if an individual wanted to keep a record of his or her correspondence, the only way to do it was to make a handwritten copy. To avoid the problem of keeping and organizing hundreds of loose sheets of paper, these copies were usually written in a bound, blank book. At a time when letters often got lost in the mail and printed receipts were rare, letter books were very important. A record of what a person wrote and who he wrote it to could preserve a career or save a considerable amount of money.

The problem with letter books is that they were rarely intended to be read by anyone other than the author. This leads to all sorts of difficulties in interpretation. For one thing, Vinton often used the letter book as a first draft, with insertions crammed between the lines in impossibly small handwriting, and deletions crossed out with a thick, dark line that probably covered a bit more than he intended. Likewise, if it was obvious to Vinton when and to whom the letter was written, he chose not to include that information. Little could he have imagined that almost two hundred years later, someone would really like to know those things. There is also the possibility that he never actually sent the letter he was drafting, or what he sent was substantially different from the version in the letter book. Perhaps after reading his first draft he decided that what he *wanted* to say was better left unsaid, or at least needed to be toned down.

Vinton was a highly educated, well-read man, but his use of punctuation is at times confusing. The placement of commas is particularly daunting. He often puts one where least expected, or leaves them out when really needed. As editors, we had to resist the temptation to simply delete them all and put them where we felt they belonged. Vinton also seemed in love with the dash, frequently putting them in after commas and periods. For the most part we kept the punctuation as he wrote it, except to occasionally insert or delete a comma when the meaning of the sentence would be altered with or without it.

Modern readers may find the language a little intimidating. This was the Romantic Age, when over-wrought prose laced with five-syllable words was in fashion. Vinton was proud of his command of the language. Indeed, he faced a problem when writing to his small children: "It was a new relation for me to enter on and I confess I felt diffident as to my ability to address them with that plainness & perspicuity which was necessary for their young minds. I find it the most difficult thing I ever undertook in the matter of writing, to reduce my style to that necessary simplicity & yet maintain it in consistency & uniformity—Ideas that start up for utterances seem to flow only in the phraseology most natural to me, & that, you know, is notoriously too ornate & turgid for juvenile understandings."[2]

For the most part, Vinton's handwriting was legible and easy to understand, though not every word could be deciphered. These documents are almost two centuries old, and time has done its damage. There were also problems associated with reproductions. Most documents were on microfilm, and we used either printouts or scanned images. Some of the documents had been scanned or photographed very cleanly, others in a more hap-hazard fashion. Margins were at times cut too close or pages overlapped, obscuring words along the edge of the sheet. On many of the letters, it appeared as if instead of breaking the sealing wax, someone tore or cut around it to open the letter, leaving a few words unreadable.

There are, of course, words we simply could not decipher, though surprisingly few, considering the amount of material. These are indicated by four dots enclosed in brackets [. . . .]. Occasionally there would be a word we couldn't read but the context suggested what it should be, so we included out best guess in brackets with a question mark. Vinton was fond of abbreviations, and we transcribed them as he wrote them. Most are easy to understand and used frequently, such as *sh'd* for *should*, *w'd* for *would*, and *yr.* for *your.* If we felt the meaning was unclear, we put the full word in brackets following the abbreviation. We will also be the first to admit that there are no doubt errors in our interpretations.

Correct spelling was important to Vinton, and he even went as far as pointing out errors in letters from his children. He used the old style for words such as *honour* or *favour*, and we saw no reason to mark them with [*sic*]. We added [*sic*] following words like *connexion, waggon,* and *mispelt* to avoid confusion, even though they were acceptable spellings in Vinton's time. There were also several compound words that everyone uses today, but that were not always joined at the time, such as *every one* or *to day.* Unless a word was so misspelled as to make its meaning questionable, we left spellings as they were written.

Capitalization posed its own challenges. Rules of capitalization were not firmly set at the time, and people tended to use capitals more than we do today. Whatever rules Vinton used, he generally stuck to them. The most annoying deviation from modern usage was the word *Indian*, which almost always begins with a small *i*, though there were a few times when he wrote it both ways in the same letter. Most of our troubles came from instances where lower and upper case letters at the beginning of a word were nearly indistinguishable from each other, especially the letters *S* and *C.* A small *s* was only slightly smaller than a capital *S*, but significantly larger than the rest of the lower case letters in the remainder of the word. To make matters more confusing, he occasionally threw in a completely different shaped upper case *S*.

Personal correspondence was usually the easiest thing to read. After all, they were intended for another person's eyes. Still, even these occasionally proved challenging. Vinton was usually careful in his penmanship, but at times he was rushed or writing under difficult conditions. The quality of pen and ink could make quite a difference, both in the darkness and sharpness of the characters. There were also a few occasions when he had a bit more to say but had run out of room on the paper, so he wrote cross-ways across the first page, right over the existing text.

In presenting these letters we usually omitted the dateline, salutation, and closing signature. These are almost always revealed in the introductory paragraph, understood, or of no real value to the narrative. This practice saves considerable space in the finished product and allows the narrative to flow smoothly. Still, there were exceptions, such as in the final letter Vinton received from his daughter Louise, shortly before his death. At such a poignant moment, the words "My dear Father" and "your affectionate daughter" carried too much emotional weight to be left out.

A work of this scope could not be accomplished without the aid of many others. First of all, we'd like to thank Jackson Walker for passing the project on to us, Joe Knetsch for reviewing the initial manuscript, and the Board of Directors of the Seminole Wars Foundation for encouraging us to take on the project.

Because the manuscript material was housed at widely scattered institutions, there were a number of people who assisted us in obtaining copies of Vinton's correspondence, journals, and letter books. Foremost among them was Pam Cooper, Supervisor of the Archive Center & Genealogy Department at the Indian River County (FL) Public Library, who gave us access to the library's sizable collection of Vinton papers. We also received considerable assistance from Dr. Samuel Watson, Suzanne Christoff, Alicia Mauldin-Ware, and Susan Lintelmann at the U.S. Military Academy. Others include Karen DePauw, Sierra Dixon, and Diana McCain of the Connecticut Historical Society; Kelly Wooten and Megan O'Connell at the Rubenstein Rare Book & Manuscript Library, Duke University; James M. Denham, Florida Southern College; Richard J. Ring, Providence Public Library; and Laurie Rizzo, University of Delaware Library.

Locating Vinton's artwork proved much harder than gathering his manuscripts, due to the fact that there was no one catalog that listed their locations. Foremost, we'd like to thank the several anonymous Vinton family members and other individuals who supplied pictures of relations or allowed us to use images from their private collections, including Samuel and Roberta Vickers and Dr. Samuel Smith. Among those helping us find artwork were Dr. James Cusick, Special Collections, George A. Smathers Library, University of Florida; Yvette Yurubi, Special Collections, University of Miami Libraries; Gary Hood and Marlana Cook of the West Point Museum; Jackie Penny, American Antiquarian Society; Jocelyn Wilk, Columbia University; the staff at the New York Public Library; Kim Cumber, North Carolina State Archives; J. D. Kay, Rhode Island Historical Society; Deborah Sisum and Kay Peterson, Smithsonian Institution.

As part of our research we visited numerous places associated with Major Vinton and were extended every courtesy wherever we went. Among those welcoming us were Carol Cross of Augusta State University, who gave us a tour of the home Vinton occupied as commanding officer of the Augusta Arsenal, and

Rev. David M. Carter, Rector of Christ Church of Pomfret, who took time to show us a backpack that belonged to Vinton's brother Alex.

We also wish to thank our editor Ben Brotemarkle and the staff at the Florida Historical Society Press, and our many friends and relations who have always given us the most heartfelt encouragement.

1

Young, Active, & Naïve

> *"My confidence in the overruling Providence of God is unqualified, so that I go to the field of action fully assured that whatever may befall me will be for the best. I feel proud to serve my country in her time of appeal,—and should even the worst,—death itself,—be my lot, I shall meet it cheerfully. … I have hitherto lived mostly for others. … But my children will reap some of the fruits of my self-denial by the means I shall leave them, of living independently & securing a good education. I commit them in full reliance to the parental care of their Heavenly Father, and I hope their trust in Him will ever be at least as firm & increasing as has been my own."*[1]

GOD. COUNTRY. FAMILY. The life of John Rogers Vinton was shaped by a firm belief in these three entities, sometimes working in concert to gently guide him along, while at other times driving him in opposing directions. For him, God was ever-present in the form of a Divine Providence that would carry a person from cradle to grave, much like the steady current pushing a canoe downriver. A person could divert his course in life much the same as a paddler might work his canoe against the flow, stop on shore, or explore interesting tributaries, yet like a paddler caught in the river's current, a person could never truly escape God's plan.

Love of country was also an important factor in Vinton's life, which led to a belief that building a better life went hand-in-hand with building a better nation. He was a Rhode Islander by birth and always "expressed the greatest regard and affection for his native state."[2] For Vinton, the founding of the republic was the stuff of recent memory. Thomas Jefferson wasn't some glorious icon from a mythic past; he was President of the United States when Vinton was born. Revolutionary heroes weren't long-dead legends; they were people who walked the streets in his own hometown. Indeed, his paternal grandfather had been one of the legendary Minutemen and had faced the British at Lexington and Concord. Like many Americans, Vinton believed he lived in a nation that afforded limitless possibilities. "Our country," he later remarked, "is affluent of resources, all within ourselves, and needing only the occasion to be developed, when we shall step forth the most potent & glorious nation on the face of the globe."[3]

Yet it was family, more than anything else, that made John Rogers Vinton who he was. America may have cast off the old English aristocracy, but the notion of "great families" had not been completely discarded, especially by members of what often appeared to be a new aristocracy. For people like the Vintons, whose lineage could be traced back to the *Mayflower*, social standing was to be cultivated and protected.[4]

Vinton's ancestor Thomas Rogers had fled England in 1617 with his wife Alice and their four children, taking up residence in Leiden in the Netherlands, where they hoped to freely practice their Puritan religious beliefs. In 1620 Thomas and his eighteen year old son Joseph boarded the *Mayflower*, leaving Alice and the three younger children behind, presumably to join them after a new home was established in America. Unfortunately, Thomas was one of the many Pilgrims to succumb during that first brutal winter in the New World, leaving Joseph to fend for himself. In 1630 Joseph's brother John Rogers joined him at the Plymouth colony.[5]

Several generations later John's descendant Betsey Searle would marry Amos Atwell, a wealthy merchant and ship owner of Providence. During the course of his life, Atwell would be a Lieutenant Colonel in the Providence Militia, justice of the peace, town councilman, and member of the General Assembly. The couple would produce a daughter, Mary Atwell, who would become John Rogers Vinton's mother.[6]

Vinton's paternal lineage is more difficult to trace. There were Vintons in Lynn, Massachusetts as early as 1648, French Huguenots who had sought refuge in England and then migrated to America. Whether or not Vinton's grandfather, David, was descended from this line isn't known. We do know that he was born around 1746 in Sutton, Massachusetts, and that in 1772 he purchased half a dwelling house in Medford, was employed as a cordwainer (a maker of fine leather shoes), and married Mary Gowen, the daughter of a sea captain from Charlestown, near Boston. Their first son, David Jr., was born in January 1774.[7]

The course of the family's life, and world history in general, changed on 19 April 1775, when David Sr. took up arms at Lexington and Concord. Several months later he faced double tragedies when both his wife and a newborn son died within the span of two weeks. Leaving David Jr. with brother-in-law William Gowen, the elder Vinton enlisted as a seaman aboard the Massachusetts privateer *True Blue*. Captured by the British, Vinton was held as a prisoner of war for nearly two years, until he was exchanged in 1777. Once again he took to the sea, this time serving until late May 1778. He died in December of that year at the age of thirty-two from unknown causes, leaving David Jr. an orphan.[8]

Fortunately, the five year old child was not uncared for. His uncle William, a gold and silversmith in Medford, was appointed the boy's guardian, and he later apprenticed young David in the same trade with David Tyler of Boston. After finishing his apprenticeship at the age of eighteen, David moved and opened his own business in Providence, Rhode Island, located at the "northeast corner of Market parade" on the east side of the Providence River. It was an excellent location in the heart of the city's commercial district.[9]

When David Vinton arrived in Providence in 1792, both the town and state were undergoing a period of expansion and development. New bridges were being constructed or existing ones enlarged, and Rhode Island was experiencing a "turnpike era," with the extension of land routes, greatly improved stage facilities, and shortened transportation times. In nearby Pawtucket the first textile mills were being constructed by Samuel Slater, ushering in the Industrial Revolution and bringing growth to the area. Possessing one of the nation's finest harbors, Rhode Island flourished in the areas of shipbuilding, international commerce, and whaling. Providence could boast of having "more navigation than any of its size in the Union; and there is a greater number of vessels belonging to this port than to New York." Between 1790 and 1800, the population of Providence would increase from 6,380 to 7,614, and David Vinton's business was growing with it.[10]

From 1792 to 1795 Vinton advertised himself in the *Providence Gazette* as a goldsmith and jeweler from Boston, making and selling an assortment of goldsmith's wares. His reputation as a skilled silversmith has endured, and some of his exquisite handicraft has been exhibited at the Fowler Museum at UCLA and the Metropolitan Museum of Art in New York. A silver arm band with his stamp "DV," presented to a Creek Indian leader by the United States government, was found among artifacts at the excavation of Fort Benning in Georgia.[11]

By 1796 Vinton had become more of a "general merchant," making ink and selling cards, books, and music, in addition to "spoons and bracelets, etc." When and how David met Mary Atwell is unknown, but on 17 May 1797, the couple was married by Rev. Enos Hitchcock, a Congregationalist minister who had served as a chaplain in Washington's army during the Revolution.[12]

On 30 October 1798 Mary gave birth to their first child, Amos Maine,[13] named after her older brother. A year later David expanded his business, selling "bonnets, wigs, butter, sheet music and miscellaneous musical instruments."

Also expanding was the family, and on 16 June 1801, John Rogers Vinton came into the world. Additional brothers and sisters followed every other year for the remainder of the decade. The couple's third son, David Hammond,[14] was born in 1803, Elizabeth in 1805, Alexander Hamilton[15] in 1807, and the last son, Francis[16] (no middle name), in 1809.[17]

David Vinton was a respected citizen in the community and considered "not rich but moderately thriving."[18] With the help of families like the Vintons, Providence continued to grow at a brisk rate, reaching a population of more than 10,000 in 1810. The increase in potential customers must have been welcomed by Vinton, whose business may have suffered during President Jefferson's Embargo Act of 1807-1809, which cut off much of the trade with Europe, the source of many of the goods he sold.

In 1811 David was proposed for membership in Providence's Mt. Vernon Masonic Lodge No. 4, whose Master was brother-in-law Amos Atwell.[19] Vinton received his first Masonic degrees in March and April of that year and was appointed to a committee for procuring a book of songs for the Lodge's use. For a man who loved music it was the perfect assignment, and one that would lead him down an unexpected path several years later.[20] Becoming a Mason was also an important social advancement for Vinton, as the fraternity was a powerful and influential group in early America. Many of the Founding Fathers, including Washington, Franklin, and Hamilton, were Masons. Membership in the society could open doors of opportunity that outsiders might not know existed.

On 24 January 1812, Mary gave birth to her final child, Ruth Paget Olney Vinton, but the girl died less than four months later.[21] Matters were made worse when the United States declared war against Great Britain in June of 1812. As far as the people of Rhode Island were concerned, war was not the solution to the troubles with England. With an economy that depended on free trade and ocean-going commerce, a confrontation with the massive Royal Navy could only bring trouble. Rhode Islanders feared their shipping interests would be devastated worldwide and the entrance to the harbor blockaded. Protesting against the war, the people of Rhode Island sent petitions, proclamations, and resolutions to the government, calling the conflict a "public calamity." A day of mourning was declared and church bells rang for most of the day. Many shops and stores were closed, and the town flags on the Great Bridge and shipping wharves were displayed at half-mast.[22]

The people of Rhode Island may not have been happy about the war, but their independent, patriotic spirit still remained. Two months after the declaration of war townsmen pledged to "aid in the support and complete execution of the laws," to fend off any invasions, and to recommend that everyone capable of bearing arms be prepared on a moment's notice to defend themselves, families, and country.[23]

Life in Providence took on an air of uncertainty. Merchant ships still sailed from the city, but many foreign ports were closed to American vessels, and a number were captured by British warships or privateers. Whenever possible, businessmen turned their attention from commerce to manufacturing or engaged in privateering during the "state of stagnation." The worst hit industry was whaling, and many people had to find other ways to make a living. A writer recalled that, "The cotton, woolen, iron, and other metallic industries, together with the manufacture of jewelry, that have since made our city a hive of activity and caused its rapid development," suffered during this period.[24]

With a wife and six children to provide for, David Vinton may have been facing hard times. The eldest son, Amos Maine (who went by his middle name), had probably completed his education and may have been working, perhaps in the family business. Then, in mid-July 1814, a British fleet appeared off Newport, blockaded the entrance to the harbor, and captured several small merchant ships traveling from Providence to New York. A state of emergency went up and defense preparations were enacted. Ninety-four people, including David and Maine Vinton, tendered their services to erect fortifications for the defense of Providence.[25]

If indeed hard times had come to the family, Mary Vinton did whatever was necessary to hold things together. Years later John would remember his mother's sacrifices and "the sums laid out for the education of the children, when, often, upon the dinner table, a little rice was made to serve for our repast."[26] Watching her earnestly seeking "divine aid and guidance," he often saw her "kneeling at her bedside, imploring help and direction from above."[27]

Then there was a day in church when he saw the "keen pang of mortification" on her face as "her flock of little children were ignominiously driven from a pew because it had been mortgaged to a creditor." The practice of selling pews was common at the time, and a pew's location within the church signified a person's standing in the community. The shame was only temporary, however, for Mary's "upbearing resolution" was soon rewarded when an "*equally respectable* pew" was secured in another church. Those who knew Mary Vinton described her as a "lady of uncommon powers of mind, and of great dignity and force of character." Her devotion to her children, "aspiring spirit," and "intrepid heart" left a lasting impression on young John. "Deep & sharp the suffering my Mother endured during that long trial," he recalled, "before the dawn of better things."[28]

Yet it would be unrealistic to picture the home as being filled with doom and gloom. With five or six children in the house there was probably little time to dwell on unfortunate circumstances. On his fortieth birthday John wrote to his mother, "Forty years!! This sounds like a ripe and full period. Can you still imagine your boy John, young, active, & naïve. … And yet the temper of my mind & tastes, is still youthful. I love more the simple pleasures that took my fancy, most when a boy."[29]

Nothing is known about John's early education. He may have attended one of the free schools established in Providence or received private instruction at home. Whatever the case, there can be little doubt he received the finest schooling the family could afford. That was fortunate, because he was about to put that education to work.

On 4 May 1814, more than a month before John's thirteenth birthday, an appointment to the United States Military Academy at West Point was obtained through the "unsolicited kindness" of family friend Gen. Joseph G. Swift, Chief Engineer of the army and Superintendant of the Academy.[30] A week and a half later his father wrote to Secretary of War John Armstrong, acknowledging receipt of the appointment and accepting it "agreeably to the tenor of the order contained in his commission."[31] John was still two years short of the minimum age of fifteen, but it was wartime, rules were bent, and the requirement waived.

Nowhere is it mentioned why the Vinton's chose West Point. Besides the fact that there was a war going on and patriotic feelings were running high, financial considerations may have played a part in the decision. Sending John to a boarding school to complete his education would have been expensive, and there were four younger children to think about. The army, on the other hand, would educate John for free, there would be one less mouth to feed at home, and the young man would be guaranteed a job after graduation. It was an opportunity that would have been difficult to ignore.

When Vinton entered West Point the Academy was still in its infancy, having graduated only 101 cadets since its inception in 1802. It was certainly not the storied institution it is today. Indeed, it had nearly died of neglect in the years before the war, with no graduating class in 1810. The approach of war with Great Britain changed Congress and the Administration's attitude, and "An Act Making Further Provision for the Corps of Engineers," signed into law on 29

April 1812, placed the Academy on firm footings.[32] New instructors were hired, buildings that had been in place since the Revolution were either refurbished or replaced, and a large number of cadets recruited. Vinton was one of 149 young men who began their studies in 1814.

Cadets were required to be "well versed in reading writing, and arithmetic," and would have to master the higher mathematics needed to become a competent engineer. During the period John was in attendance the curriculum expanded, and by the time he graduated a cadet's stay at the school grew from two years to four years. Still, because of wartime exigencies, some cadets were pushed through in only a year or two.[33]

Figure 1: West Point, circa early 1820s. Painting by W. G. Wall, engraving by John Hill.

These were years of change at West Point, but the most important of those modifications took place under Superintendant Sylvanus Thayer, who assumed his position soon after Vinton graduated. None of the massive stone buildings that exist today were there in Vinton's time. A new barracks, mess hall, and classroom building were under construction with plans for an additional barracks and quarters for professors and officers. Indeed, conditions were so uncomfortable that the school closed from the first of December to mid-March. Classroom time was also interrupted by a mandated three-month summer camp, where the young men would learn the duties of a field officer.[34]

Although discipline was not as strict as it would be a few years later, the life of a cadet was still very regimented and difficult. Accommodations were fittingly Spartan, with two or three students sharing one small, bare room. There was no plumbing in the barracks, and water had to be brought in buckets, a job usually given to the lower classmen. Each room had a fireplace, and it was the junior cadets' responsibility to fetch and split firewood. As one of the younger cadets, Vinton probably did more than his share of menial tasks in his first year at the Academy. If a cadet wanted a cot, a desk, or a chair, he was expected to purchase it himself, along with uniforms, books, and paper. Many cadets slept on the floor. The students were fed simple fare in a bare mess hall devoid of tablecloths. The army was providing food, shelter, an education, and little else.[35]

Engineering was the core of the curriculum, but it was not the civil engineering that the school would soon become famous for. The nation was fighting what was an often embarrassing war, and Vinton and his fellow cadets were taught military engineering, with little thought of how such knowledge would be useful in a rapidly expanding nation entering the industrial age. Nonetheless, proficiency in surveying and the skills required to construct forts, roads, and bridges could be easily adapted to civilian life.

Training officers to be competent engineers was the primary mission of West Point, but other valuable subjects were also taught. Because all military correspondence was handwritten, proper penmanship and spelling were stressed, and classes in English grammar were added. On the expanding frontier, army officers were often the only representatives of the government, so they were expected to be gentleman of the highest order. To that end, a chaplain was appointed, who taught Geography, History, and Ethics. Other classes included French (thanks to Napoleon, the "language" of military science), Fencing (swords were still very useful in close combat or when mounted), Astronomy (a necessity for surveyors), Natural and Experimental Philosophy (the sciences), Drawing (which Vinton excelled at), Mathematics, Greek, and Latin. It was a lot of information for a young mind to absorb.[36]

While John was at West Point learning to be a soldier, life in Providence continued for the Vinton family. For the remainder of 1814 and into the following year, the British fleet continued its blockade, stifling commerce in Rhode Island and the rest of New England. The residents of Providence could do little but wait, getting by as best they could. Then, on 13 February 1815, news was received that the war was over. Watching the reaction, a resident remarked, "One can scarcely realize how much our townsmen were opposed to, and suffered from this war, till he knows the details of their rejoicing over its termination."[37] Nearly two weeks later the Providence *Gazette* published, "The noise of the axe and the hammer begins again to be heard in our workshops and on our wharves, and the busy note of preparation presages the return of those halcyon days from which we have been too long and unnecessarily estranged. Already are a number of our best ships fitting up with every possible degree of dispatch, confidently expecting that no intervening cloud will obscure the bright prospect of free and uninterrupted commerce throughout the globe."[38]

Sadly, there was an "intervening cloud," and it arrived on the morning of 23 September 1815 in the form of a devastating hurricane, the first major hurricane to strike New England since 1635. The twelve-foot-high storm surge flooded central Providence, reaching as far as Benefit Street, where the Vintons lived. An East India Company ship, the largest in the harbor, broke free of her moorings, hurtled across the bridge, wrecked the upper story of an insurance building, and landed in the cove. Other boats and wreckage poured through the gap the ship had made, forcing nearly all of the vessels from their moorings. Wharves and bridges were washed away, streets were strewn with "ruins of chimneys, trees, fences, and houses," and five hundred buildings destroyed. Within two hours, Providence was crippled, with the loss falling mostly on the "enterprising and active members of the community." The financial loss was estimated at one and a half million dollars or about "one-fourth of the total valuation of the town." As people always do, the townspeople "rallied under the shock" and began rebuilding the city.[39]

To what extent, if any, the Vintons suffered from the storm isn't recorded. Vinton's shop, close to the waterfront, probably sustained severe damage, if not total destruction. The home may also have been affected, depending upon its elevation above the street. Many years later John recalled, "I remember when the house in which we were all born, was abandoned, and how precarious afterwards became our chance for a suitable shelter elsewhere." Although he would have been at West Point at the time, he would have remembered the loss, especially when he returned home in December. For all the residents of Providence it must have been a discouraging time. Just as business was returning to normal, much of it was swept away.[40]

During this period, other changes were taking place in the Vinton household. Whether by choice or necessity, David Vinton closed his business, thereby depriving the family of a steady income. Perhaps it had been washed away in the hurricane and the entire inventory lost; perhaps he'd found something more promising. By 1816 Vinton had become a prominent member in the Masonic fraternity and had begun traveling the nearby area as a paid lecturer.[41] After compiling musical material for five years, as requested by the Lodge, he published *The Masonic Minstrel*, a book of Masonic music and poetry. The volume proved successful, selling over 12,000 copies by subscription. It included *Pleyel's Hymn*, a funeral dirge composed by Ignatz Joseph Pleyel (a student of Franz Joseph Haydn), but with poetic lyrics written by David Vinton. The piece became a Masonic standard, sung by Freemasons in lodges and at gravesites throughout America. In 1880 Robert Morris described Vinton as the "sweet poet and Masonic songster of the period."[42]

Vinton also published *Tablets of Masonry,* a volume that included his written lectures and transcripts of those provided by others. His lecturing and publishing efforts brought Vinton fame and income, but they also embroiled him in controversy. Problems first arose in nearby Connecticut, where the state lodges had appointed their own lecturer. Whether it was for personal reasons or philosophical differences, some of the Connecticut lodges began to take measures to prevent Vinton from lecturing in the state. They were also opposed to his publishing Masonic lectures, and later ordered copies of *Tablets of Masonry* burned as a security measure.[43]

Having been partially frozen out of his home area, Vinton decided to take his books and lectures south, mainly to the Carolinas and Georgia. Many years later, Mary reminisced in a letter to her son Frank, "I am much pleased & interested in the acct. you give of yr. meeting with yr. father's friends: You will probably hear more of him, he remained some time in N.C. & wrote often from there. From some seaport, wh. I do not remember, in that state, he sent me a barrel of Shad, the finest I ever saw."[44]

As the family struggled to adjust to their new circumstances, John was completing his education at West Point. Unfortunately, the expanding curriculum was outpacing the ability of the students to grasp it all. When examinations were held in December 1816, no one passed and for the second time in the Academy's history, there was no graduating class. By the following spring John Rogers Vinton was ready to take his exams. The army had taken him in and given him a quality education. What he would do with that education was up to him.[45]

2

Here is the Beginning of a Service

On 17 July 1817 sixteen year old John Rogers Vinton, graduate number 168, left the United States Military Academy as a Third Lieutenant in the Corps of Artillery. There was no class ranking at the time, so we can't say how well he did compared to his fellow graduates. Vinton did have the distinction of being the first graduate from Rhode Island, but few followed in his path. Indeed, the Vinton clan seemed to be one of the few families in Rhode Island inclined toward a career in the army. The second and third Rhode Island residents to graduate from West Point were his brother Hammond in 1822, followed by future brother-in-law George Greene in 1823. The trend continued, with his brother Frank being graduate number 590 in 1830, but only the fifth Rhode Islander.[1]

Vinton's parents had instilled a love of learning in the young man, something that remained with him throughout his life and was passed on to his children. A friend would later remember Vinton's accomplishments, saying he was "a scholar in the Greek, Latin and Hebrew languages … extensively read in theology, well versed in metaphysics, ethics, constitutional and international law … master of Mathematics … deeply interested in astronomy, chemistry and most of the physical sciences." He also loved drawing and was "so skillful and so tasteful with his pencil" that his pictures would "rank among the works of professed artists."[2]

Although he had no way of knowing it, Vinton was entering an army in transition. Before the War of 1812 the nation had been unsure whether or not it even wanted a standing army. Most people, nurtured on the myth of the Minutemen and other volunteer fighters, felt the state militias were all that was needed to defend the nation. Major Indian uprisings and the threat of war with France in the 1790s had necessitated temporary buildups in the army, but the numbers had always been reduced when the emergency ended. Organization was lacking and few officers made the army their career.

Early defeats in the War of 1812 had shown how deficient the system was. Invasions of Canada were repulsed, forts in the west were lost, and at the Battle of Bladensburg the militia broke and ran, allowing the British to burn Washington. The purchase and distribution of supplies and equipment was inefficient, and the officer corps was either old or inexperienced. By the end of the war lessons had been learned and a new group of young, professional officers had risen to positions of leadership. Americans were now willing to accept a standing army, albeit a very small one.

The core of this new army would be a well-educated, professional officer corps. There would also be permanent Supply, Quartermaster, Ordnance, Commissary, and Medical Departments. It was intended to be an expandable army, with a strong framework in place to accommodate a rapid increase in troop strength should an emergency arise. In peacetime the army would build and maintain coastal fortifications, map the coastlines, explore new territories in the West, and handle Indian relations. Men like Vinton would have to be diplomats, engineers, peace officers, and, once in a great while, warriors.

Few of those changes had taken place by the time Vinton graduated, and some had not even been thought of yet. Some of the changes, such as the proficiency of West Point officers on the battlefield, would not be appreciated for decades, while others would never be fully implemented. Adaptation and evolution are never straight-forward, and there will always be setbacks. Yet for young men like Vinton, the army was now a viable, respected career path.

After graduating from the Academy, Vinton began to keep a journal of his activities. The first portion of it, from 17 July 1817 to 26 April 1818, was done from memory. After that he kept it as a day-to-day diary, though near the end the entries became more sporadic. The journal provides an interesting insight into his life during the first two years of his military career, and because he was involved in topographical survey work during this period, the journal opens a unique window into life along the thinly settled northern frontier.[3]

The first few pages of the journal show us a young man eager to start his career, not afraid to assert himself, but still a little homesick. The first challenge he faced was in determining where he was supposed to be stationed. His orders assigned him to the Southern Division, headquartered in Nashville, but he was without the funds necessary to get there. He applied to the Quartermaster for an advance, but the Quartermaster turned him down, perhaps feeling the orders were in error. For the most part, the army tried to keep their officers in a region close to home, and even Vinton thought it odd that he was being sent to the South. A pair of classmates who were also ordered to Nashville offered to lend him the money, but after receiving a letter from his mother, he did something that would probably be a Court Martial offense today: He wrote to the War Department and asked for a posting in the Northeast and then went home to Providence.

Vinton was happy to be home and enjoyed the opportunity to visit friends and family, but he soon became bored:

> I read plays and some novels at home and made frequent sorties in the streets; attended the reading room & in the evenings visited the ladies or played the flute, an amusement always productive of great pleasure.—I might here have been happy enough but the continual anxiety, the hope & fear, & my igno-

> rance of my destined goal, which my orders would reveal were enough to almost counteract the causes for happiness.[4]

After two months at home, Vinton received orders to report to Major John J. Abert[5] at Newark, New Jersey, as part of the United States Coast Survey. As he noted in his diary:

> Here is the beginning of a service which to me will always be beneficial when compared with many into which I might as well have enter'd.—It is a situation which was proposed to me by Mr. Zoeller[6] at West Point (& teacher of Drawing there) and with which I always thought I should be pleased.—I delight in the study of the Sciences & am very fond of drawing & Surveying in general, this situation therefore could not fail to please me. …
>
> Thus flush'd with new hopes of happiness & improvement combined, I longed to depart, even from the place of my nativity—not because I disliked it at all, but because I disliked idleness.[7]

Vinton received a promotion to Second Lieutenant and began work with the Coast Survey in October 1817, serving under the direction of Dr. Ferdinand Hassler,[8] one of the nation's leading astronomers. Part of the work involved determining the precise geographic locations of fire signals near the mouth of the Hudson River. Today this portion of the country is a densely-packed urban area with many easily-recognized landmarks that can be seen for miles. In the early nineteenth century a shoreline might stretch for miles with no distinguishing features. A fire signal, on the other hand, would be an easily identifiable point that could be observed from miles away, especially on a clear night.

For the teenaged Vinton, working on the Coast Survey was an excellent opportunity to learn the use of astronomical instruments and study the art of surveying. The work was exacting and required the careful observation of celestial objects and distant landmarks, often in nearly inaccessible locations. For astronomical objects the precise horizontal position, elevation, and time of observation had to be recorded. To triangulate the position of landmarks, the exact angle between them had to be determined. These figures were then turned into latitudes and longitudes using pre-calculated tables and complex mathematical formulas. Even the slightest error in measurement or computation could cause positional errors in hundreds of feet or up to several miles.

One of the fire signals was located on Staten Island, close to the home of the sitting Vice President, Daniel Tompkins. Tompkins was a former Governor of New York, which explains why Vinton referred to him as "Gov'r Tompkins" in his journal. Governor was seen as the more prestigious position, and to have addressed him as "Vice President Tompkins" would have been a minor insult.[9] The Tompkins family occasionally welcomed the officers into their home, which afforded Vinton and his companions a respite from the long hours of tedious observations and mind-numbing calculations. As Vinton noted, "We all passed a pleasant afternoon & evening at dinner at Gov'r Tompkin's which brought to remembrance again a little civilization. In the evening we had a dance, for there were about 5 or 6 ladies present, 3 of them his daughters."[10]

Guesswork was not allowed in their calculations, and if obstacles to observation got in the way they had to be removed. "Notwithstanding the increase of cold & approach of winter we decamped & commenced our jaunt to Gravesend, a sandy, barren, bleak place within 2 yds of the high tide. Here we commenced our observations and work, but found that it was impossible to see the Light House on Sandy Hook for a hill of hard sand which obstructed the view. The Lighthouse is a main point of one of the triangles therefore we found it necessary to commence cutting away the sand hill, which took two days."[11]

The arrival of cold weather made further work impossible, so the survey crew took up winter quarters in Newark, New Jersey. For various reasons the other officers soon departed, leaving Vinton alone for the latter part of December. "I was rather lonesome during all this time but was satisfied with study & mental improvement. I went out very seldom & endanger'd my health for I was often troubled with bilious complaints. I learned the use of the reflecting circle [an instrument similar to a sextant, used to measure the angular altitude of a celestial object] &c &c during this time & made some very good observations. ... My whole thoughts were directed on my duty & improvement & visiting was seldom, my amusement my flute which always proves a happy companion."[12]

By January 1818 Vinton's fellow officers had returned, and he was being tempted by the social life of the city. At first he resisted, but the studious young man's resolve didn't last long. "A rumour now flew about the town (for Newark is remarkable for tale bearers) that a Mr. Whale, a dancing master in New York, intended opening a dancing school here for the winter." The instructor was also planning a weekly "Public" or "practicing ball," but the idea did not appeal to Vinton. "I foresaw it would divert too much of my attention to Study on the Ladies & the Dancing, however, McNeill & Adams soon join'd & after the first *Public* I join'd myself."[13]

A few attempts were made to take observations when the winter weather was clear, but little came of the effort. Then, in April, Hassler received word that the project was to be suspended because the money had run out. Feeling it would be a great waste to halt the project just as the weather was becoming agreeable, Hassler immediately went to Washington to argue for a continuance. In the meantime, Vinton could do little but sit around Newark and wait. Not that he was completely idle: "I rode to Elizabethtown with the ladies & there visited the Governor's lady & saw the place. This was certainly a very pleasant excursion."[14]

He also had time to travel to New York City. While there he paid a visit to two young ladies from Newark, Catherine and Maria Camman,[15] and spent time with Capt. Alden Partridge, who had been Acting Superintendant at West Point while Vinton was a student. Vinton was also surprised to learn that his father was in the city, visiting from the South. It took two days to find him, but it was worth the effort, for they had not seen each other for two years. Considering that the elder Vinton would soon return to the South, this may have been the last time John saw his father.[16]

In May 1818 Vinton received word from Hassler that the Coastal Survey was finished for the year. Hassler had been offered several other government jobs, so the young lieutenant was forced to continue waiting in Newark for further orders. In the meantime, Vinton and his crew were dispatched to dismantle some of the fire signals that had been used during the survey. It was a day and age when settlements were few and far between, and accommodations were hard to find. In such remote places travelers were forced to rely on the local inhabitants for a place to spend the night and take a meal. Most people were happy to see strangers; it was a good way for isolated families to socialize and get the latest news. Some people, on the other hand, were not very welcoming:

> We were treated very inhospitably by the people, owners of the land we were upon, for some reason or other, but such degraded, debased & savage wretches, I never before have seen. After the wife had boil'd us some eggs, (which was not until we paid & persuaded her), she bid us, eat them & begone quick.[17]

A trip out to Long Island a few days later proved just as frustrating, though not without some amusement:

> We were proceeding toward Bath but as it happen'd, we turned off the wrong road & arrived suddenly on the Beach where was seen only a few straggling huts.—We saw nobody but a little boy—asked him what his father's name was?—he replied, "Daddy."[18]

Vinton was soon assigned as an assistant to Dr. Hassler on the Northern Boundary Survey. This was an important duty, and was an indication of Hassler's and the army's respect for the young Vinton's abilities. The Boundary Survey was a stipulation of the Treaty of Ghent, which had ended the War of 1812. One of the unresolved issues of the war was the exact location of the border between the United States and Canada. The 1783 Treaty of Paris had been very vague about certain portions of the border, most notably in northern Maine.

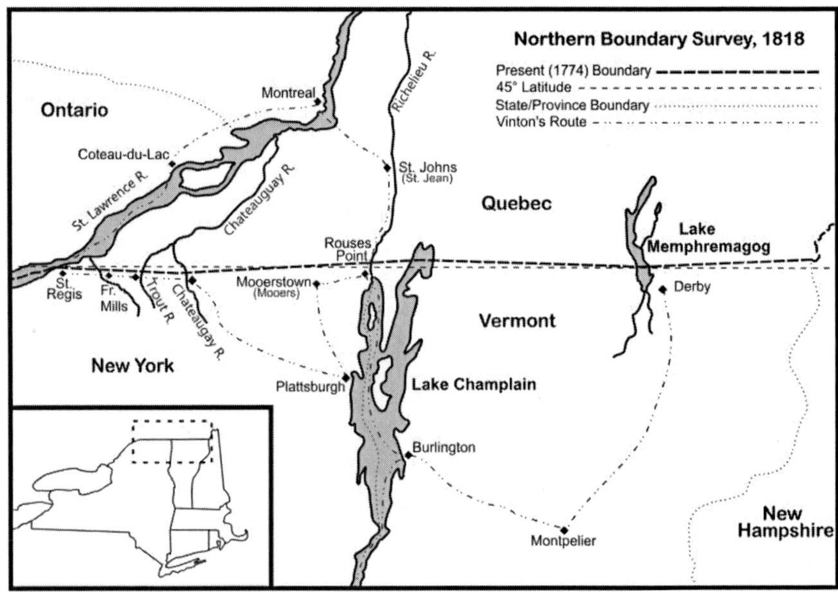

Even some boundaries that were clearly defined on paper still needed to be delineated on land. The latest treaty had called for a set of surveyors from both nations to work alongside each other to determine the precise borderline. One section of the boundary included the northern borders of New York and Vermont, which were designated on paper as being the forty-fifth parallel of latitude. A survey had been done in 1774, before the Revolution, but was not considered accurate, and several points were in dispute. This was the section to which Vinton and Hassler were assigned. With the exception of a few small settlements, the entire 155-mile stretch was a virtual wilderness.[19]

Vinton now began to keep a day-by-day record of his travels. Although Hassler left immediately for the northern border, Vinton remained in Newark a few days longer, closing out some last-minute business. The intention was for the two to reunite at Burlington, Vermont. Hassler may have had a head start, but he was travelling primarily by road. Vinton would go most of the distance by that new modern marvel, the steamboat.

Journal of the Northern Boundary Survey[20]

> Newark, May 14th, Friday [Ed.: Friday was the 15th]: This Morning I have been round bidding the ladies all farewell. Oh what a parting will it be this afternoon for at 3 o'clock I start for New York.—My duty calls me away & I give up every thing nor will I now complain. …
>
> May 21st Thursday [at West Point]: This day I received two letters from the City of Washington, one from the Paymaster who tells me where to get my pay & the other from the Hon. Secy of War, who gives me a direct order to join & conform to the instructions of Mr. Hassler.—He tells me I am allow'd $1.50 per day & all transportation paid. This is good news & tomorrow's Steam boat will carry me to Albany. …
>
> May 23rd at Albany, NY: To my great disappointment & mortification I learn that I am obliged to wait at this city until next Tuesday morn'g when the Stage will start for White Hall [Whitehall] or Skeensboro [Skenesborough] at the Head of Lake Champlain, from thence I must take the Steam boat to Burlington where I hope to meet the Commissioners. …
>
> Tuesday, May 26th: I awoke this morning very early & then layed [*sic*] waiting for the driver to call me which he did about 4 o'clock A.M. We were able soon to start & arrived at Troy about 6, a very pleasant little village & full of Trojans. …
>
> On the Way to Whitehall—May 27th: After having rode 5 miles, the Stage was clog'd in up to the hubs of the wheels in the mud with which the roads were full. I took a large rail to pry the wheels out & fell in the mud myself.—With us was an old Quaker who sympathized in my distress but I was disposed to laugh. … We succeeded in getting the Stage out of the mire & arrived at Whitehall in time for our breakfast. … We lounged our time until 2 o'clock P.M. when we started in the Steam boat Phenix.

Vinton met up with Dr. Hassler and other members of the survey at Burlington. They continued north by steamboat, crossing the border into Canada and arriving at St. John's on the Richelieu River on 28 May.

> May 28th, Thursday, St. Johns: … We concluded that the best way Mr. Hassler was to go to St. Regis was by taking his carriages on board the Steam boat to Plattsburgh, there being a direct road from thence to St. Regis. I however came with Messrs. Van Ness & Bradley for Montreal & find some transportation from that place to St. Regis where we all are to meet. So we started in a stage & travelling over bad roads, through 20 miles of flat open country we arrived at La Prairie a small place situated on the opposite bank of the St. Lawrence to Montreal & about 19 miles over. … Took dinner & cross'd over the huge St. Lawrence & landed at Montreal. … After passing through a narrow street (though one of the best) I arrived at the Mansion House Hotel where we put up.
>
> The Roman Catholic is the chief religion here & from the great church I saw marching out, about 30 small white dress'd Nuns, following about 10 or 15 young lads,—then came about 25 old Nuns in black & Holy Fathers & Mothers, all going back to the Nunnery to which they belong, for there are several convents here & pretty well filled.—A Military Garrison is kept up here & centinels [*sic*] placed along the streets. Two British sub officers came along & stopp'd, stared and gap'd at me full in my face after finding by my pantaloons buttons that I was an American officer.

Vinton left Montreal on 30 May, heading south in a two-wheeled carriage along bad roads until he reached Coteau-du-Lac, a small settlement forty-five miles west of Montreal. Early the following morning he went down to the St. Lawrence River and hired two men in a sailing canoe to take him the thirty-six miles to St. Regis (the point where the survey would commence), arriving there at 6:00 P.M.

At St. Regis he met up with Dr. Johann Ludwig Tiarks (the British astronomer) and the rest of the British survey crew. Unfortunately, Hassler and the other American surveyors had yet to arrive. Later in the day most of the American team showed up, with the exception of Hassler. After waiting a few days, "It was concluded that I should take the Barge & go to the French Mills [near Fort Covington, New York] to learn information from Mr. Hassler so with 4 [. . . .] Canadian boat men & one indian I embark'd for a distance of 16 miles by water but 9 by land. About eleven o'clock A.M. we started & arrived at the Mills in 2 ½ hours after a very pleasant ride in a fine large boat."

> Wednesday June 3rd at French Mills: … The people had seen no signs of Mr. Hassler but an old soldier who had just come

from Plattsburgh hearing me inquire, declared he saw Mr. Hassler with his carriages, one of which was broken a little & he himself so *sick* as to be hardly able to alight from his carriage. … The soldier said he was at the best inn on the road & 40 miles from the French Mills. I waited in hopes of hearing more information & in the meantime visited the mills & walked around the place. …

View of our Station, not our Station but a part of the Village of
French Mills

Figure 2: View of the Village of French Mills, New York. Sketch by John Rogers Vinton.

Thursday, June 4th at the French Mills: I heard more accounts this morning relating to Mr. Hassler who was so unwell as to be obliged to send to Plattsburgh for a Doctor. I of course gave up the idea of staying any longer here & order'd the boat to be ready, but waited until the mail had arrived in which I found a letter from Mr. Hassler to Mr. Van Ness. I took it & started for St. Regis again. … I landed at St. Regis but found the people all gone to dinner with Col. Ogilvie[21] to keep up the birthday of His Royal Majesty George. …

Saty 13th: Mr. Bradley went to the French Mills this morning in a canoe to meet Mr. Hassler who after numerous misfortunes expects to arrive there this morning. Mr. Hassler arrived in better health than was expected, but not well—two days were spent in forming plans for the operations of the Summer Campaign & today June 17th we pitched our camp on the greatest elevation near St. Regis. …

June 25th: We have had as long a spell of fine weather for this fortnight almost as I have ever seen any where & we have taken many observations. We sent some men down to the French Mills last evening to elevate a tar barrel on fire so as to answer for a fire signal but no light was seen from our camp so that attempt was unsuccessful. —I think since we have encamped that I like the indians much better than before. The younger ones visit me often & I have from them & their squaws, plenty of strawberries. I am particularly partial to a young chief whom they call St. Jean Baptiste.

June 26th St. Regis: This evening by consent of all the young indians, & especially by desire of the chief, they all assembled around me to give me a *name*. I readily consented for I was told by some of them who could speak English, that in case of war or any emergency whatever if I should be forgotten by them I was still safe by mentioning the name which at least they would all remember. … My name which was, Shakorontha kaitats, & which was pronounced by them Sakorontagaituts. The last syllable but one being pronounced very <u>long</u> & the very last, but with a breath & very lightly. …

St. Regis, July 19th: The men commenced some days ago to cut a line through the woods in the direction of the French Mills where Mr. Hassler expects soon to make his next station. … Today we finished our terrestrial observations and packed up the Theodolite, but expect to make a small station on the Island opposite the villages, tomorrow.

July 23rd St. Regis: … Scipio Hassler [Dr. Hassler's son] & myself being uncomfortably warm about 1 o'clock today went to bathe in the cool & pleasant waters of the St. Lawrence. While we yet were in the water it clouded & soon the sky was almost black & thunder rolled & lightning played across the Firmament although with such threatening aspects, we had no idea of any serious storm at hand. However seeing it increase fast we began to dress immediately & before we had started from the Bank of the River, a very violent wind accompanied with rain & hail stones half as large as an egg fell thick & with more fury than I could have had an idea of. … I remained under the tree until the storm had in a small degree subsided & then ran to the camp where I found all confusion. The great Repeating

Circle [an instrument used to determine a precise angular separation between two terrestrial objects, not to be confused with a Reflecting Circle] had fallen from its stand & broke so as to be unfit for further use. The dinner tent & table with all the dinner & those sitting by the table all all [*sic*] overthrown. No material injury was done here except the dinner destroyed for I wanted mine. Nearly a half pint of Mercury was spilled & some little misfortune happed otherwise, but the destruction of the Repeating Circle was truly serious. ... Scipio Hassler went in the afternoon up the country to Mr. Adams' camp where he obtained another Repeating Circle not used by him and equally good with ours.

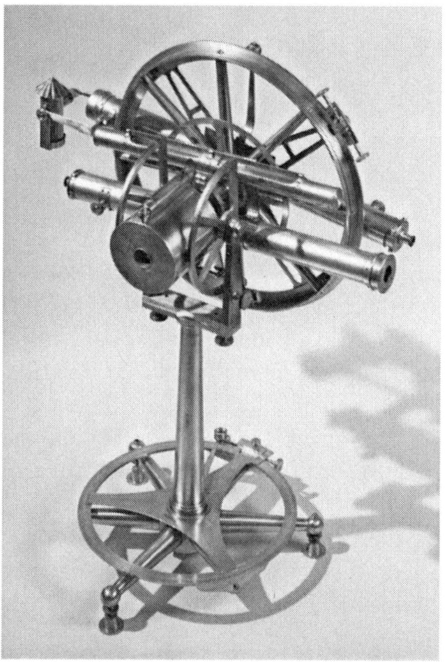

Figure 3: Repeating circle owned by Dr. Ferdinand R. Hassler, possibly used by John Rogers Vinton.

Aug. 3rd: We are now encamped on a rising ground near the Village of Fort Covington at French Mills. The situation is pleasant enough but some of our men having behaved disorderly, we discharged them which caused among them great discontent.—And have now not enough to send in the woods to cut. Before we started from St. Regis a short time, one of the

> men a very unruly quarrelsome Scotchman, having been drunk & very saucy came to such a pitch of impudence as to raise his hand to strike Mr. Hassler, which his son Scipio seeing immediately gave the man the first blow & with one or two more settled him on the ground. Still the man was very impertinent & we discharged him, but he having some Friends near him of his own stamp, they all joined against us & a little more & we should have had a grand battle but they seeing we were rather too strong for them they excused themselves & have not troubled us since.

The survey work could now begin, but it would not be easy. Latitude was determined by precise observations of the stars. In order to see the stars and to travel along the line through the woods, trees needed to be felled. Unfortunately, many of the laborers who had been hired to cut the trees had been dismissed. There was also the problem of having to stay up all night making astronomical observations. After three weeks at French Mills, Vinton noted, "I grow rather fatigued by setting up every night as is now necessary to observe the Stars & it is not until the Sun causes the east to be so much enlightened as to cause the stars to vanish, that we cease our work."

Exhaustion often leads to accidents, and on 25 August Vinton wrote, "The other day having taken an axe for the purpose of exercise in cutting a stick of wood, the axe slipped from the gap & came with considerable force against my foot, through the boot & made a considerable wound in my foot, but by care & the application of Goldbeater's skin, in 4 days I could walk quite well."

> September 4th, Station at Trout River: Having packed up the Reflecting Circle & Artificial Horizon together with whatever necessaries we should need, we started from the Camp at Fort Covington. … Quite contrary to our expectations, on our arrival we found no house nor habitation, except a small hut which was temporarily erected for the workmen who were about to build a saw mill on the river. The only provision we had with us were some tongue & bread.—We therefore sent to the houses round (the nearest of which was two miles) for provisions but meat was not to be found nor could we procure either butter or cheese, and with difficulty we found some potatoes. So we contented ourselves, with tongue & potatoes one day & potatoes & tongue the next. … Thus we lived hard 4 days when our provisions were about exhausted & the clamp screw of the Circle broke we decamped & arrived at the Camp of Mr. Hassler Saturday Sept. 12th near Noon. …

The surveyors were now encamped near the Chateaugay River. Although the camp was similar to what they had just left, Vinton noted, "We live better & are supplied with better provisions with much more regularity. The people are of a better nature, more generous & richer. … Our camp is render'd quite pleasant & sociable by our new company, the weather being fine & affairs in good order. During Mr. Hassler's absence I observed with the Reflecting Circle as usual, & gave to him on his arrival about 20 observations of Sun & Stars."

Figure 4: "View of our Station at Chateaugay River." Sketch by John Rogers Vinton.

> 30th Sept: We have been quite pleased with this Station indeed, & leave with all our observations completed tomorrow. … Mr. Bradley arrived here last evening from Burlington & was pleased with the Camp & prospects. He proposed to Mr. Hassler to send me with my Reflecting Circle to a locality near Lake Memphremagog to determine the Latitude of that point, he having heard that a variance of some miles has been discovered from the true parallel.

To send the young officer to a far-away station to make critical observations showed that Hassler and the others were confident of the skill Vinton had acquired in a relatively short time. There were other observations that needed to be made before he left, and part of the team went with Hassler to the north end of Lake Champlain, while Vinton went with Dr. Tiarks to Mooers, New York. After the observations were complete at Mooers, Vinton and Dr. Tiarks moved on to Odell Town. After five days of observing, they headed for Lake Champlain, where they caught up with Hassler. It was now early October, and Vinton was ready to head out by himself.

The trip did not start out well. Vinton arrived by steamboat in Burlington late in the evening, only to find that the stage for Montpelier departed at 2:00 A.M. "In the morning, I was awakened according to expectations by the Stage driver & in a very easy carriage & good horses & driver we enjoyed a very pleasant ride, notwithstanding we all had rather been in bed." When he arrived in Montpelier he was greeted by another member of the expedition who advised him the road to Derby and Lake Memphremagog was impassible. Stymied, Vinton and his companion caught a ride back to Burlington in a light wagon, and then hopped aboard a steamboat headed north, where they would rejoin the two astronomers.

Upon arriving at his destination, Vinton found Hassler and Tiarks ready to depart for Montreal. Saying his farewell, he crossed Lake Champlain and joined other members of the expedition at the surveyor's camp. The season was getting late, and he noted, "It is now the 22nd of October & for the first time this morning we had a light snow storm & the keen wind & cold gives token of the approaching cold weather. I sincerely hope we shall discontinue operations soon."

A week later, his plans changed again:

> Oct. 30th: This day, by the request of Mr. Bradley, who is again here, I am to start again for Lake Memphremagog. … Accordingly I started as usual in the Steam boat with Mr. B. & in two days was in Montpelier—there he took cold & in 3 or 4 more days, I took a man & one horse waggon & went alone to Derby, the town near Lake Memphremagog.—Dismal were some of my thoughts on the road & dismal my spirits, when after staying 4 or 5 days at Derby, I had not yet been able to get an observation. Flushed with the idea of so soon going in the land of the civilized again I was doubly impatient & therefore doubly felt the irksomeness of the hours that I was obliged to pass, idly & unimproved. Not until the sixth day could I succeed in taking an observation. …

Not only was Vinton frustrated with the weather delay, when the skies finally cleared and he did get an observation, his assistant failed to record one of the readings, forcing him to repeat the process. By this point he was ready to go home, even though he wasn't confident in the readings he'd taken. "I departed that afternoon & after having arrived at Montpelier, (64 miles) I calculated both my observations & to my utter astonishment & joy they agreed with each other to a few tenths of a second."

Winter was at hand, and work on the survey was about to be suspended until spring. Vinton had worked hard and had gained valuable skills and experience. Unfortunately, all his work was for naught. He and his companions often discovered the original 1774 survey was in error. This had been expected, but proved especially embarrassing when an American fort at the northern end of Lake Champlain was discovered to be just north of the border, clearly in Canadian territory. Situations such as this created an impasse between the two nations which was not resolved until 1842, when the Webster-Ashburton Treaty declared that the 1774 boundary would be made official.[22]

After spending some time in Burlington, Vinton caught a steamer heading south to New York City. With his return to the city, Vinton's time with the Northern Boundary Survey was over. After spending two weeks at home in Providence, the young lieutenant worked his way down to Washington, where he spent a few days touring the city, had a pleasant interview with the Secretary of War, and was ordered back to Newark to complete his calculations from the survey work.

Vinton returned to Newark, a place he truly loved, but felt adrift. Unsure of where his life was headed, the seventeen year old seems to have fallen into a state of depression. On 15 January 1819, he made the following entry into his journal:

> Having spent the past winter at this place & enjoyed many a blissful hour with friends ... I felt a natural desire to take up my residence here once more.—For, having to lead almost a wanderer's life, being in my country's service & a citizen of the U. States, where would my inclinations more naturally lead me? Home? No, home is past for me, & therefore, it would be fruitless & unreasonable, to create more, or augment those ties of love & regard I already possess for many in Providence—but which are now I hope, sufficiently weakened or even alienated, to erase the idea of home-sickness. ...
>
> Sometimes a fit of the *Azures Demons* [the "blues"], over spreads my thoughts & creates a gloomy succession of ideas and reflections, by no means injurious to my welfare or happiness.—One thought seems however to take the lead of all the rest. My duty has a great deal of *sameness* & *repetition* of the same thing, & when I reflect & consider the frailty of all our sublunary enjoyments I can but lament that I live. So far have my reflections carried me away at times that I have thought I would be willing almost to commit suicide, were it not sinful. But even in the most calm & composed moments I have concluded

> that life is not to be desired by me, could my friends be as willing to part with me, as I am with myself.
>
> For, if (for instance) I should all at once determine to make a bold effort, & be either something or nothing in the world, I would risk my life at a great hazard, in battle or otherwise.—Now the contempt of life would create a courageous mind, & if I should happen to survive, great credit would be due to great bravery—this would be gain. But if on the contrary I was killed, this certainly would be the thing I most desired, therefore, also a gain.[23]

One of the things that may have contributed to his dark mood was a dispute with Dr. Hassler. For some reason Hassler appears to have wanted to be rid of Vinton. Perhaps the young officer was outshining Hassler's own son, Scipio. Perhaps Vinton's observations and calculations were *too* good. Why did the government need a high-priced astronomer if a low-paid officer could do just as well? At any rate, by 20 March Vinton had discarded his melancholy mood and was on the offensive:

> Day before yesterday a conclusion was made to all the affairs relating to the concern of Mr. Hassler & myself.—A Warfare. A Paper War was declared some days before & no war was ever conducted with so much fierceness before—Diamond cut Diamond—He accused me of assurances & Presumption—I him, of Hypocrisy & Malice—I told I would not pretend more to dissimulation & therefore must proclaim my sentiments, assert my rights, maintain my dignity & bear the consequences.
>
> Extreme, insulting contumely, on his side & too much imprudence for a subordinate, on mine—The case being laid before the War Dept. however, they thought as I did.—The Secy at War, said, "Since Mr. H. & the Lieut. cannot agree, it is best they separate." I received accordingly, those orders I applied for in Washington.—I joined Major Abert again [on the Coast Survey].[24]

It was now April, and Vinton was ready to move on. He was still smarting from the fight with Hassler, but was looking upon it more philosophically. He had learned important lessons and made good friends. True, a military career would always be one of uncertainty, but he was willing to accept that:

> Suffice it to say, I have been universally pleased this last winter & am perfectly satisfied and at times even anxious to recom-

mence active operations. No situation I think in life, is more liable to a change of circumstances than mine. One year ago I was informed of the duty of last year, & this information came to my knowledge so unexpectedly I determined never more to make my calculations of more than a month to come, so universally have I been disappointed & so very precarious have I found the circumstances of our situation & existence.[25]

3

Dispatched on a Special Mission

Precisely where John Rogers Vinton was stationed and what he was doing between 1818 and 1821 is unclear. If he kept a journal for this period it has not survived, nor has much in the way of family correspondence. The records show he remained with the Northern Boundary Survey through 1821, but due to the falling out with Dr. Hassler, that is doubtful. He had mentioned returning to duty with Major Abert, so in all likelihood he returned to the Coast Survey, which Abert was in charge of. The Boundary Survey and the Coast Survey were both under the auspices of the Topographical Engineers, so there may have been no distinction as far as the army was concerned. If Vinton was under Abert's command, he would have been on the move often and could have been found anywhere along the Eastern Seaboard. The dispute with Hassler doesn't seem to have affected his career to any degree, for he received a promotion to First Lieutenant on 30 September 1819.[1]

On 5 September 1821 his mother wrote to him at Marblehead, Massachusetts, worried about a possible transfer John might soon receive. Up until this time Vinton's military career had kept him relatively close to home at postings in the Northeast. Now the army was talking of sending him far south, to Fort St. Marks (near the Gulf Coast, south of Tallahassee) in the recently acquired Florida Territory, a place that was considered very unhealthy:

> Were almost any situation short of St. Mark's to be obtained, I sh'd not hesitate, but I *know* it is utterly impossible for me to enjoy a moment's happiness, while you are there—when you depart for that post I shall feel as if I had parted with you forever, & knowing my own feelings, & frailty, I fear I c'd not survive it … This subject must be dropped—it will engross all my thoughts & my paper.[2]

The letter also indicated that Mother was having financial problems. She had "engaged lodgings" and would "break up housekeeping by the first of October in the hope of lessening our expenses." She also mentioned that, "I have to pay grandma 30 dolls at the end of this month." If nothing else, Mother could depend on her sons for a portion of her support. Hammond was still at West Point, but eager to do his part. "He says I must not be discouraged by present poverty; in one year more, he shall be able to take his turn & he is 'sure, both of us' (you & he) can support the family, & hopes neither I, or his sister, shall ever be put to the anxiety of raising our hands for support."[3]

So where was Father? Earlier in the year David Vinton had been dealt a serious personal blow when he was expelled by the Grand Lodge of North Carolina "for un-Masonic conduct."[4] When news of the expulsion reached his home lodge in Rhode Island, a committee was appointed to investigate the allegations. The lodge declared that the North Carolina proceedings were "wholly unwarranted" and denied rumors that Vinton had "left his family and that they were being supported by the Lodge."[5]

In 1821, in an effort to cut costs, Congress down-sized and reorganized the army. On 1 June Vinton was placed in the 4th Artillery, but was transferred on 5 December to the 3rd Artillery at Charleston, South Carolina. He remained in that regiment for the rest of his life. The next three years are some of the least documented of his career. With no journal and very little family correspondence, there is little to go on but monthly post returns, which only show his presence at various posts. From December 1821 until August 1822, he appears to have been second in command at Charleston Harbor.[6]

The following year Vinton was on ordnance duty at Bellona Arsenal, several miles west of Richmond, Virginia, along the James River. The arsenal stored and maintained cannon and muskets for the army, along with stockpiles of gunpowder and ammunition. Ordnance duty was considered a temporary assignment, and in August 1823 Vinton rejoined his company, which was then stationed at Fort Nelson, near Portsmouth, Virginia.[7]

In April 1824, Vinton was again transferred, this time to Fortress Monroe, a massive new fortification being constructed outside Hampton, Virginia, on a barrier island called Old Point Comfort. Upon its completion in 1834, it would be the largest stone fortress ever constructed in the United States. With the 1814 burning of Washington still in everyone's memory, the government was determined not to let another enemy fleet sail into Chesapeake Bay.[8]

Fortress Monroe was also the location of the army's new Artillery School of Practice, which had been set up to teach artillery officers the finer points of their trade. Vinton served as adjutant to the school's commanding officer, Col. Abraham Eustis, and while the duties of an adjutant were mostly clerical, it was also a position of trust and responsibility. A good adjutant was someone who could be depended upon to keep things running smoothly, allowing the commanding officer to focus on more important tasks.[9]

While John was advancing his career, other members of the family were also making their way in the world. Older brother Maine was an established merchant and auctioneer with a business on South Main Street. After returning from a trading voyage to Canton, China in 1824, he married Frances Jones Dyer, a member of one Rhode Island's most prominent families. Hammond had graduated from West Point in 1822 and was serving as an ordnance officer at Fort Atkinson, Iowa, while younger brother Alex was attending Brown University in Providence. After deciding to become a physician, Alex transferred to Yale and earned his medical degree in 1828. Still at home were nineteen year old Elizabeth and fifteen year old Frank.[10]

Changes in the lives of the children meant changes in the life of Mary Vinton, who celebrated her fiftieth birthday on 10 May 1823. During the summer of 1824 she travelled to Pomfret, Connecticut, about forty miles west of Providence, to visit her niece and other family members.[11] Pomfret must have appealed to Mary, for she decided to move there. Situated in the "most picturesque regions of Connecticut," Pomfret had "charms of its own" and offered "what is best in rural life, either for visiting or settlement."[12] It was an agricultural village of about 2,000 people, not insignificant when compared with Providence, which had a population of only around 12,000 at the time.[13] Temporarily leaving Elizabeth and Frank with Maine and Frances, she purchased a small farm called *La Plaisance*. She thought of the farm as a retreat for the entire family and also an investment, or as Frank once remarked, "the home and refuge of us all."[14]

No matter where she was, Mother continued to offer advice and guidance to her children. She lectured fifteen year old Frank on the difference between wants and needs, reminding him that having sufficient food, shelter, and clothing would supply his "*real* wants," while the rest were "*imaginary*" desires that "may be resisted & controlled." She told him to aim towards feeling "an indifference for self indulgence," and be like his brother John, "to whom self denial has become no cross, you will bear with cheerful submission, the vicissitudes & disappointments" that all human beings are subject to.[15]

On 1 March 1825 Vinton left Fortress Monroe and began duty as aide-de-camp to Major General Jacob Brown,[16] commanding general of the army and the highest ranking officer in the United States military. Vinton's new position was a prestigious one and would not have been given to just anyone, and although it was not a promotion, it was certainly a step up. In addition to his normal pay, Vinton would receive a bonus for being an aide, plus allowances for extra rations and the services of a personal servant.[17] The assignment would provide Vinton with important experience, introduce him to valuable friends, and allow him to participate at the highest levels of social life in the nation's capital.[18]

Vinton wasn't the only one moving into new quarters in Washington. President John Quincy Adams was inaugurated into office on 4 March, and with him came a new set of cabinet officers and numerous bureaucrats. Along with those names and faces came a host of new policies the Adams Administration hoped to carry out in addition to the usual set of unforeseen crises that would have to be dealt with. Vinton had a lot to learn.

Figure 5: Maj. Gen. Jacob Jennings Brown, by John Wesley Jarvis.

Jacob Brown had been one of the foremost military heroes to come out of the War of 1812. He had started the war as a general in the New York State Militia, a position acquired more through political connections than any military experience or expertise. Brown soon proved himself a courageous, intelligent, and tenacious leader and was given a major general's commission in the regular army. Put in charge of the northern frontier, he was able to hold off the British when he appeared to be the underdog, and defeat them when the odds were more equal. In the military downsizing of 1821, the position of commanding general was created and given to Jacob Brown.

By the time Vinton came to serve as Brown's aide in Washington, the general's health was already deteriorating. In October 1821, before assuming his new duties, Brown had suffered a severe stroke at his home in Brownville, New York, at the eastern end of Lake Ontario. The stroke had left him unable to speak and without the use of his right arm and leg. Within a month he had recovered his speech and was able to walk with some assistance, but it would be a full year before he was well enough to assume his duties at Washington. Another stroke in 1826 would weaken the general even more.[19]

If Brown needed physical assistance from Vinton in the months after the lieutenant's arrival, he wasn't going to get it. Indeed, it was Vinton who needed the assistance. In April he had broken one of his legs, and in a July letter to Mother he described how he got around and why he wasn't coming home that summer:

> I sit & sleep on my sofa bedstead (the one I had from Maine) with my leg in splints, suspended nearly horizontally from a little frame work in front of me. When I wish to go from one room to the other for dinner or for music, a servant takes my leg, frame & all, and I with my crutches march forward to my new seat without any other inconvenience than calling for the waiter—Thus my situation is absolutely as agreeable as it can be under these circumstances and so Dr. Hubbard says time will cure me, but time is patience. ... As to visiting home this summer, it seems to be distinctly ordained that I should not—for never hath the hand of prevention been so plainly visible.[20]

He then commented on the news that Elizabeth was engaged to Lt. George Sears Greene, a West Point acquaintance of Hammond's. Having seen the hardships many army wives endured, he offered Elizabeth some brotherly advice:

> You know or ought to know that by marrying a Military Officer, you subject yourself to a multitude of privations,—must endure a multitude of hardships—must leave all those endearments of your parental roof which have always heretofore been identified with your happiness & every thing you hold dear—must launch into the cold & friendless world, depending chiefly on yr. own resources & the vigour of yr. character for a support against its dangers—open or concealed.—Bear up against these & you do well to marry. But in marrying do not forget, that, although you are the wife & the dependent, you have much of yr. husband's character to support—For the world will appreciate to its full value the aid or the detriment con-

ferred on the husband by the character & ability—of the wife. She is to sustain him in all those delicate relations which fill up the routine of social life, & it is in her power to do him essential good or essential evil.[21]

Vinton had broken his leg in April, and it must have been an extremely serious fracture, for he was still on crutches in November. In a short letter to Mother, he told her he had finally recovered to the point where he could rejoin society and had even received an invitation to the White House:

> I went to Church yesterday for the first time since my disaster in April last.—It was refreshing to hear once more the eloquent prayers of our incomparable liturgy, & the [. . . .] peal of praise poured forth to the Glory of our Heavenly Father—My appearance was greeted by the congratulations of all my friends—By an invitation rec'd today to dine with the President, I suppose my reentrance in Society must be acknowledged—But my crutches will prevent much of the social pleasure which I might promise myself were I forced from [dependence?] on them.[22]

A year had passed since Vinton's arrival in Washington, and now that he was back on his feet he was able to enjoy the social life of the city. Society, of course, meant the mixing of eligible young men and women, and it was not only politicians and military men who were taking notice of Lt. John Rogers Vinton. As always, Mother was quick to give advice. In late March 1826, Vinton merrily responded to one of her letters:

> I have written frequently of late, but I cannot longer refrain from acknowledging with many thanks, your excellent letter of the 10th, in which I read so clear, so sensible & so beautiful an argument on the subject of Belles & Matrimony. I showed the letter … to the Genl. & to Mrs. B. and I have never seen them more pleased with anything of the kind, than they were with this.—A rumour was afloat that I was rather "attentive" to one of the said Belles, and their friendship for me & care for my reputation so great that their remonstrances & caveats became as animated as if I had been their own Son. The Genl. bade me express to you with what exalted satisfaction he perused your lines, & Mrs. Brown could only add how happy & proud she should be to accept your invitation & cultivate in Pomfret that

> acquaintance with you personally which she now values so highly by reputation.[23]

Vinton was maturing as an officer, and in 1827 he was selected for a delicate mission that concerned the very existence of the Union. Two years earlier a treaty had been signed with the Creek Indians in which all their land in Georgia was ceded to the government, leaving them only a small reservation in Alabama. The treaty had breezed through Senate confirmation, and newly-elected President Adams had seen little reason not to sign it. The Creek Nation, on the other hand, saw plenty of reasons. The treaty had been negotiated by two Georgians (working with the state's interests in mind) and wealthy Creek leaders who were very friendly to the whites. Among those leaders was the mixed-blood William McIntosh, who received a $25,000 payment for his part in the negotiations. As far as most of the Creek Nation was concerned, McIntosh and his cohorts lacked the authority to sell tribal land, and they asked the federal government to intervene. In the meantime, the legitimate Creek leadership ordered McIntosh's death, and his home was subsequently attacked and McIntosh executed.[24]

Adams was in a tough position. For the better part of two years, the state, the Indians, and the federal government argued and postured. The army was sent in to keep the peace, but a war of words erupted between Georgia Governor George Troup[25] (a cousin of the slain McIntosh) and Maj. Gen. Edmund P. Gaines,[26] the officer in charge. Troup, facing a tough reelection fight, was fanning the flames of "states' rights," while Gaines, fed up with the corruption and greed of the Georgians, defended national sovereignty in dealing with the Indians. In the meantime, a delegation of Creek leaders came to Washington to negotiate a new treaty. The resulting Treaty of Washington was acceptable to the Creeks, but not to Troup and the State Legislature. Contrary to orders from the War Department, Georgia began to survey the Indian land, even portions that had not been included in the new treaty, and set up a lottery to distribute the land. Adams threatened to call out the army to enforce the new treaty and remove any settlers from the disputed land. Governor Troup threatened to call out the state militia to stop the army. The situation was a tense and delicate, and if not handled properly, civil war might erupt.[27]

Hoping to avoid conflict Adams had to come to some sort of understanding with Governor Troup, but wanted the negotiations to be done discreetly. The task would require an anonymous courier to carry the sensitive documents from Washington to the Georgia capital at Milledgeville. Secretary of War James Barbour selected Vinton for the job, confident in his "zeal, capacity and discretion." Even at the young age of twenty-six, Vinton was well-qualified. He was an officer with ten year's experience and was familiar with the workings of national politics.[28]

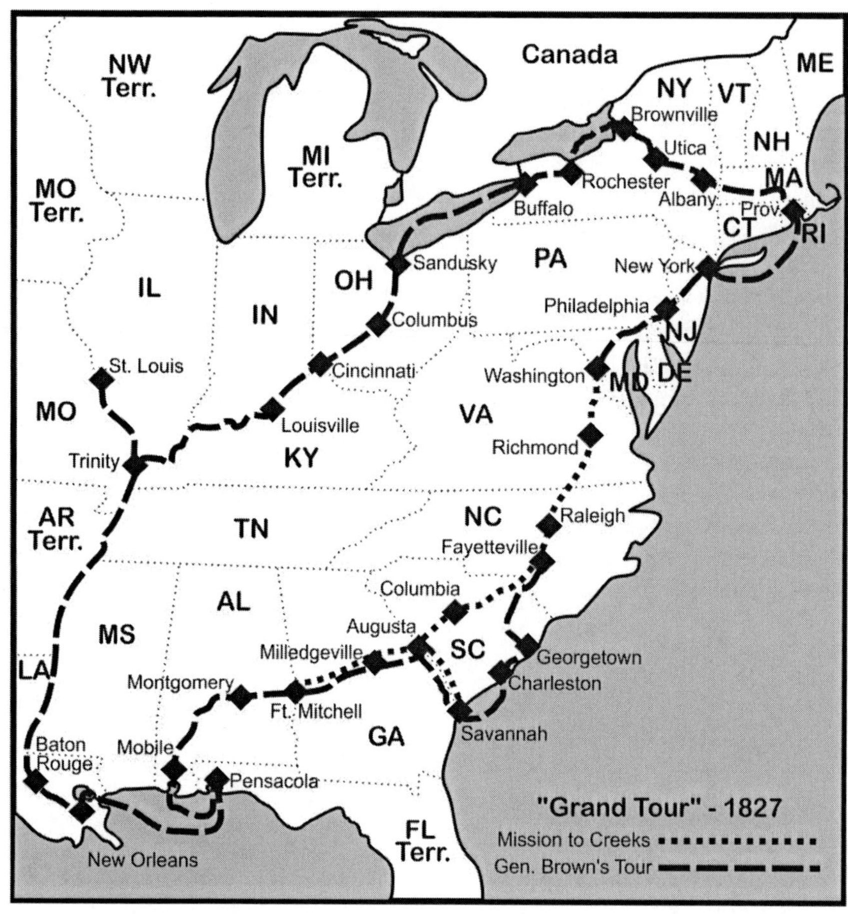

Using an army officer for such internal diplomatic missions was not unusual. The officer corps was learning to stay out of politics and was gaining respect for working in the best interests of the nation, not whoever happened to be in power at the time. Before the War of 1812, officers were often political appointees, frequently without much military experience. They also tended to stay in the same state or region for much of their careers, which gave them little opportunity to form a truly national allegiance. The war had forged a more "national" army with officers often stationed far from home. West Point also served to encourage this nationalism by mixing cadets from different states and sections of the country. Even the Indians trusted the soldiers to an extent, knowing the army was often the only force standing between them and land-hungry frontiersmen eager to remove the natives by any means available.

In a way, Vinton was traveling as a "secret" agent, wearing civilian clothes and under orders not to divulge his mission. During his trip he kept a journal in which he recorded impressions of the people and places he encountered and a record of expenditures. He would have to reconcile his accounts when he returned to Washington, and he needed to have all his paperwork in order. What he did not know was that General Brown was soon to depart on an inspection tour of military installations in the Southern and Western states and territories. All in all, it would be six months before Vinton returned to Washington.[29]

While in Georgia, Vinton would be travelling through a rapidly expanding frontier. Atlanta would not be founded for another ten years and would not become the capital until after the Civil War. To reach the Creek Agency, he would pass through the future city of Columbus, a ferry crossing in the wilderness that did little to impress him. Yet in less than ten years Columbus would be a major town where Vinton would invest heavily in property and where he dreamed of someday retiring. Roads, accommodations, and the means of conveyance in this part of the nation were very rudimentary. Travel would be difficult and strenuous, as Vinton was about to find out.

Journal of an Expedition from Washington to Georgia & the Creek Nation – 1827[30]

> Milledgeville, 11th Feby 1827: I write from my chamber at the LaFayette Hotel (Mr. Scott's) where I have lodged two days & find my first leisure to record the circumstances of my journey hither.
>
> On Monday, the 29th of Jany the messenger of the Secy of War called at my office in Washington announcing the Secretary's wish to see me immediately.—I waited on him without delay and learned that I had been selected as a Special Agent & bearer of dispatches to Georgia.—On Tuesday I received my instructions and on Monday my last dispatch and set out in the afternoon of that day for Alexandria where I slept in order to take the Richmond stage early the next morning.—On Thursday the 1st of February I was awakened at 3 A.M., and in this disagreeable summons, experienced a foretaste of what I was obliged to undergo for the nine succeeding days without intermission—except when I slept not at all.
> In order to present, in a single view the route of my journey hither, the time required in the performance of it, the number of miles travelled & the expense incurred, I preface with the following sketch.

Thursday, Feby 1st.: Set out from Alexandria at 3 A.M.—slept a few hours at Fredricksburgh that night.

Friday, Feby 2d.: Left Fredricksburgh at 3 A.M., joined the Mail Cart which overtook our stage 40 miles before we arrived at Richmond,—joined the Mail Stage there and arrived at Petersburgh to supper.—Rode all night, towards Fayetteville.

Saty., Feby 3d.: Breakfasted on the road 3 A.M. from Petersburgh. Rode all day and all the next night.

Sunday, Feby. 4th.: Arrived at Raleigh at 11 A.M. and at Fayetteville at 10 P.M.—Rested 3 hours but did not retire to sleep.

Monday, Feby. 5th.: Left Fayetteville at 1 o'clk A.M.—Supped at Cheraw and some 12 or 15 miles beyond, slept 4 hours at a tavern on the road.

Tuesd'y, Feby. 6th.: Took stage again at 8 A.M. and arrived at Camden, S.C. at 2 P.M. Rested half an hour in Camden & at 2 ½ P.M. took stage again & arrived at Columbia (the Capital) about 11 P.M.

Wednesday 7th Feby.: Set out from Columbia at 3 A.M. for Augusta (Geo.) supped at Edgefield & arrived at Hamburgh [Hamsburg] at 11 & Augusta ½ past 11 o'clk P.M.

Thursday 8th Feby.: At 3 A.M. we left Augusta—travelled all day & gained only 55 miles—Lodged 3 hours at Powelton.

Friday, 9th Feby.: Awakened at 3 A.M. & proceeded on our journey—& arrived at Milledgeville at 12 M. passing through Sparta, a pretty town some 20 miles N.E. of the Capital.

From Wash'n to Alex'a	6 miles	Dolls 1.00
Alex'a to Fredrbg	69	6.00
Fr. to Richmond	60	5.00
Rich'd to Petersbg	22	2.00
Petersbg to Fayettev.	90	18.00
Fay. to Camdem	125	12.50
Camd. to Columb.	35	3.50
Colum. to Augusta	85	9.00
Augusta to Milledgeville	95	10.00
	Total miles 687	Stage Fare $67.00

20.00 Subsistence on road

> My journey, on the whole was marked by very few incidents of a peculiar nature—One night we broke the tongue of the Stage which delayed us 3 hours in replacing it. On another occasion we broke the spring bolt, but soon supplied its place with a new one & were enabled to proceed—and lastly, between Edgefield & Augusta one of the leaders fell off a small bridge as we were crossing a ravine, some 10 feet down, snapped the tackling and lodged himself in a sandy gully, on his back, totally helpless and unmanageable. We left him & rode on with 3 horses to Augusta. These were our only accidents—None were very serious though they might have occasioned unpleasant delay had we not always been so fortunate as to find means at hand to repair our injuries. …
>
> Excepting on the immediate margins of the rivers I saw no land of any tolerable degree of excellence—No plantations under high culture,—No habitations of convenience or comeliness, no hope of future settlement & prosperity. A wide expanse of pine barren overspreads all the country south of the Roanoke (generally speaking) and the character of the population which a traveler is likely to see in passing through it (the lower order of whites) is miserable, vulgar and ignorant in the extreme.

Vinton had arrived in Milledgeville, but Governor Troup wasn't there. Having been told the governor was expected to return any day, there was nothing for him to do but sit and wait. Days passed, and after reading every available book and newspaper, boredom set in. Due to the secret nature of his mission, even his social interactions were limited. "I take my meals at the public table,—overhear the conversation of the boarders & visitors, and sometimes chat upon general topics with my next neighbour—But further than this I do not suffer myself to indulge. My name is known to the landlord of course, & to such others as have sufficient curiosity to inquire it, but my profession, my business or my destination is known to none."[31]

The primary topic of conversation in town was "the Great Land Lottery" that had been devised to sell off much of the disputed land supposedly ceded by the Creeks. Everyone, it seemed, had a ticket. The fact that the Federal Government and the State of Georgia were still at odds over the matter didn't seem to bother anyone. Vinton could see the early signs of disunion, and the growing tensions between North and South. The whole affair was "well calculated to cooperate with the original feeling of hostility against the northern ascendancy which prevailed very generally through these states."

Each day spent in Milledgeville lowered his opinion of the place and its inhabitants. "I am heartily sick of Milledgeville however—whatever course the great concerns of the nation may take—I pray that His Excellency will be graciously pleased to make his appearance very soon—or I shall never find myself in humour to speak well of his Capitol again." He hoped "the Gov'r would return and release me from this worse than tedious metropolis."

Vinton also began to worry that he was bungling his mission:

> As each day passes by I think the argument against me grows stronger & the question, "Why did you not follow the Gov'r to the place where he had gone?" becomes hourly more unanswerable.—But why? I was told positively by the officers in the Exec. Depts & by his landlady that the Gov'r would not delay beyond Tuesday or Wednesday and had I attempted to pursue him or send express to the Cherokee Corner, neither myself nor messenger could have returned so soon as either of these days, and much useless expense would have been incurred for which I had no authority.

Eight days had passed, and Governor Troup had yet to return. When the Washington newspapers arrived on 17 February, Vinton was appalled to discover that his identity and the contents of his "secret" dispatches had been leaked to the press. "This places the business in a ridiculous light, & the laugh is against me. I'm no longer the 'mysterious stranger' here, but then I am no longer compelled to my unnatural reserve—People I find are civil enough and polite, if I will be affable—and that is the way of the world in most places."

Anxious that the governor see the official dispatches before reading them in the papers, Vinton decided he would leave Milledgeville and go off in search of Governor Troup. Before he could leave, however, "my good landlord tapped at my door & announced the arrival of Gov'r Troup!—Thus there was an end to all my anxiety.—My heart was lightened of a grievous burthen and I leaped from my lethargy (i.e. my chair) with perfect delight."

> I waited but a minute or so before Gov'r Troup made his appearance, just returned & fatigued as he was from his long journey—His figure was of the middle size & rather spare—His face homely & uncouth, but his manners and address those of a well bred gentleman. "I announce myself to your Excellency," said I, "as Lieut. Vinton of the Army recently from Wash'n City from whence I have been dispatched on a Special Mission hither, under orders from the Secy of War, by whom I am instructed to place these documents into your Excellency's

> own hands & to receive your Excellency's reply." The Governor received them with all courtesy, but his manner was still sedate & equable as it continued in fact throughout the reading of the Secy's letter (which was of a different temper from my address) and so continued afterwards, I had the polite offer of a glass of wine & an invitation to visit His Excellency, &c. …

Now that his business was public knowledge, Vinton became a minor celebrity in Milledgeville. "Since the disclosure of all my secrets by the publication of my dispatches, I find myself much more the object of public curiosity & regard. … An ordinary share of tact however will ensure me general popularity for all seem to be reasonable, and far less disposed to faction & violence than I had supposed."

The people of Georgia may not have been hostile toward Vinton, but Governor Troup was taking a hard line against the Adams Administration. Citing the fact that Vinton was an army officer, an aide to the commanding general, and had been dispatched by the Secretary of War, Troup took the position that the dispatches constituted a military threat to the sovereignty of Georgia. In his response, addressed to Secretary Barbour, Troup declared, "From the first decisive act of hostility, you will be treated as a public enemy …" The situation appeared volatile, but Vinton sensed it was all politics as usual and that he was little more than a pawn in the game:[32]

> Monday, 19th Feby 1827, Milledgeville: The newspapers of today are rife with messages, documents, orders & editorial squibs—Gov'r Troup has caused his reply to the Secy of War to be published, & has issued orders not only to civil officers to prevent the process directed to be served by the U.S. Marshal, but has also called on the military to be held in readiness, & designated depots for arms & ammunition with orders to resist any steps the U.S. might take to enforce the measures which the Executive has declared. This looks like civil war!!
>
> The Gov'r reaps popularly from such a course as this, at least gains notoriety, and therefore he chooses to pursue it. His Excellency has the art too of imparting some of his notoriety to all such as have to do with him & poor humble Lt. Vinton is dragged in throughout his fiery letter, & presented in the midst of this blazonry to the curious world. … Since the formation of our Government we have never had a conjuncture so pregnant with threatened evil as the present.—Yet it would be folly to suppose that anything really serious is to grow out of it.

Vinton had delivered his dispatches to the governor, but his mission wasn't over. He also had messages for U. S. District Attorney Richard Habersham[33] and Creek Indian Agent Col. John Crowell.[34] Arriving in Savannah on 24 February after a thirty-hour stage ride, Vinton handed Habersham orders to instruct the local U. S. Marshall to enforce the law by removing white settlers from Creek land. Not wanting to be caught between Adams and Troup, Habersham resigned his office.

Vinton immediately retraced his path back to Milledgeville, where he saw the contents of the "sealed letter" he was carrying to Colonel Crowell printed in the local papers. The mission was becoming a farce, but orders were orders, and he was forced to carry on. Boarding yet another stage, he started on his way toward the Creek Indian Agency at Fort Mitchell in eastern Alabama. The journey took forty-eight hours, "resting a few hours at Clinton the first night & a few also at Wall's Stand, half way between the Chattahoochee & Flint—A miserable hovel; scarcely a shelter from the weather,—dirty beds well animated, or perhaps, no bed at all,—Still I jogged on contently and made my journey with good spirits and no serious jeopardy of health."

Vinton delivered his message to Crowell on 2 March. While there, he took time to become acquainted with several of the Creek leaders:

> I saw the Little Prince[35] and had some conversation with him through an interpreter Paddy Carr.[36] The old man has long been acknowledged first Chief of the Nation, but I imagine that his virtues, whatever they may have formerly been, are paralyzed by extreme age, not least so weakened as to impair the general firmness & efficiency of his character and make him the sure victim of extraneous intrigue & sinister practice.

His mission at last complete, Vinton was ready to go home. "How joyously did I recross the Chattahoochee knowing that every step now, was an approximation to Washington!"

Vinton may have thought the mission was over, but there was a surprise in store. "Arrived at Augusta at 8 P.M. on Wednesday, the 7th March & there found new instructions from the Secy of War to return to the Creek Nation on matter of a new character connected with the Agent & the Little Prince. … So, back again to the Agency I travelled—the journey becoming truly irksome by the frequency with which the same objects were presented to my wearied view." He arrived at the agency on 12 March and met with Little Prince, who convinced Vinton to remain for the Council meeting:

> The grand Rendezvous for Council house of the Nation, is at Broken Arrow, about 2 miles north of the Agency and adjoin-

> ing the land of the Little Prince. This is a square—on each side of which is a barrack or shed under which the indians sit, smoking & deliberating or attending to the orator of the occasion. One of their rites while assembled here is to take "black drink" as they term it, a decoction of the putrefied leaves of some shrub which resembles the Yapan [*sic*] tea of N. Carolina. I found its taste bitter but not disagreeable nor in any respect intoxicating though sensibly soporific. The indians however have a resource against the effects of this quality of the plant, which else might impair the efficiency of their judgment in Council. It is handed round by 2 or 3 waiters of their own body, in gourds, from which the chiefs commence their potations and each warrior follows the example, thus set.—In less than half an hour, they commence their eructations [belching] and vomit forth by small quantities all that they have drunken. Whatever impression I had formed of the dignity by which this grave assembly might have been characterized, it was cancelled entirely after witnessing the disgusting operation which I have described. Yet with them no revolting sentiment arises from the spectacle or the practice—So powerful is education that even sights which I had imagined would create natural aversion, with them is associated with the august idea of Legislative Council and Religious devotion. …

For four days Vinton waited for the Creek chiefs to come to a decision and respond to the Secretary of War. What he finally received wasn't what he expected, but it did provide a lesson in how the government dealt with the Indians:

> After much procrastination, the Little Prince gave me on the 17th the paper he had spoken of as a letter addressed by the Chiefs to the Secy of War. But in this character I did not receive it, as it was entirely without signature, and (as I had found out) drawn up by one Blake,[37] whom I knew to be a devoted friend of Col. Crowell's & therefore an unfair depositor of the chiefs ideas. To satisfy the old man however I wrote his name to it, and that of Tuskanaehah,[38] of Tuckabatchee Micco or Mad Tyger[39] & Tustennuggee Emarlo[40].

Having gotten the chiefs' response, Vinton was once again ready to head home. "At 6 P.M. on Wednesday 21st March, I arrived at Augusta, having passed over the road now for the sixth time!" He arrived at Fayetteville, North Carolina, on 27 March, "extremely fatigued with this incessant Stage travelling over so monotonous a road."

In the end, it was President Adams who blinked in the standoff over the Creek lands. In the early days of the republic, the federal authorities simply didn't have the power or the will to enforce Indian treaties without the cooperation of the states. The Creeks, knowing they were fighting a losing battle, eventually agreed to cede the disputed land to Georgia.[41]

The mission was over, but the trip wasn't. Vinton now joined General Brown for the inspection tour of the South and West. Why Brown was even undertaking such an arduous trip, given his poor state of health, is hard to imagine. He may have sensed that his time on Earth was limited and wanted to conduct a "farewell tour" to visit the troops and see friendly old faces. It may also have been a political mission. The authority of the national government had been tested; perhaps it was time for a hero of the late war with Britain to remind Southerners they were still part of the Union. There may have been other, less obvious reasons for the trip, but for Lieutenant Vinton, it was a great opportunity. He was about to tour the nation, something few Americans could afford to do.

Vinton and Brown met at Fayetteville on 29 March and started for Charleston the following day. "The Genl's health was evidently low but by moderate journeys we hoped still to encounter successfully whatever was yet before us in the shape of difficulty." It was not going to be a pleasure trip, as the first leg of the journey showed:

> On Saty 31st March we set out from Lumberton in the morning, & by nightfall came to the Great Pedee [Pee Dee River] which we crossed in a canoe—the rain pouring at the same time, & a wretched craft bedaubed with mud & in danger of upsetting constantly. This with some other difficulties & riding all night, before we reached Georgetown gave a severe trial to the Genl's ability to bear fatigue & privation, but he succeeded, & over the next day we concluded to rest at Georgetown. That was Sunday the 1st of April—On the 2d—we rode in to Charleston—rainy & boisterous day. We all got wet crossing the ferry to the City, & much of our baggage quite drenched.

The party spent six days in Charleston, and Vinton noted how the days were spent. "On Wednesday the Genl received calls from various individuals, &c—On Thursday inspected the troops of the harbour at Fort Moultrie. Friday, received a call of ceremony, from the Mayor & City Council,—highly complemented in a neat address from his honor, & returned a short & suitable reply. Took fruit & wine at Col. Haynes [Hayne's][42] —The Genl has determined to dine out nowhere. Saturday visited the Arsenal. … The Genl was also invited to the Theater & to the Museum to dine with the Corporation &c &c. He accepted only the Museum."

On 10 April 1827, Brown and Vinton boarded a steamboat for Savannah. "Savannah I found full of hospitality & good feeling as usual. The Genl was much pleased also—He visited the Cantonment at Oglethorpe Barracks under Capt. Ervin [Erving].[43] I dined every day with Col. Fenwick,[44] and on the whole passed a week there as pleasantly as one in his infirm state of health could have expected."

Leaving Savannah on 18 April, Vinton again found himself headed for Augusta and Milledgeville. This time, at least, he was making the trip to Augusta by steamer instead of stage coach. "Twenty four hours on the Savannah River—pleasant excursion—good company."

It was not the route Vinton would have chosen. "The Genl had deliberated much on the expediency of taking water conveyance from Charleston round Cape Florida to New Orleans or Pensacola, in which route we sh'd probably have seen Havana, but that plan was abandoned and the great enterprise of traveling Georgia & the Creek Nation was at length undertaken. I trembled for the Genl in his weak state of health, but he loved land scenes, so much better than the sea."

On 22 April they arrived at Milledgeville, "a town where I had already passed many tedious hours." After paying a call on Governor Troup, they boarded the mail stage making its way toward Alabama. They got as far as the Flint River, "which we found so much swelled as to prevent the passage of the mail or anything else. Two days we stayed at Crowell's, on the left bank of the Flint & played chess with the Genl & beguiled his time as well as I could, until the 26th, when we passed over the angry flood & proceeded on to Chattahoochee."

On 27 April they set out from the Creek Agency at Fort Mitchell and stopped at the next Stage house, a place called Spain's Stand. "Here we found ourselves in the midst of the Creek Nation. The Genl felt too much overcome with fatigue to pursue his journey with this mail so he stayed over two days until the next. His sufferings were very severe. A less energetic man would have given up the enterprise, but he struggled on."

By the first of May the exhausted pair had reached Montgomery, Alabama, "hailed by us as the long promised land. … A delegation of the citizens of Montgomery came out to meet the Genl on his approach and took him in another carriage, with martial escort & pageantry to his quarters." After resting the night, the journey continued:

> On the 2d May we embarked on Steam boat and after various delays, taking in cotton from the banks &c, we arrived at Mobile on the 5th —weather cold enough for a fire. On the 7th May, went to Mobile Point,—inspected the fortifications there, & remained three days the guests of Lt. Ogden.[45] On the 10th we took passage in that officer's schooner for Pensacola, and after a somewhat eventful passage, anchored in the beautiful bay at twilight. There are no wharves or docks in Pensacola so we were taken from our boats by the sailors *a la mode de pigback*, to the dry beach. Pensacola is a poor place, & but for its fine harbour w'd be insignificant. We passed ten days as guests of Col. Clinch[46] and a very pleasant time it was.

On 24 May they left Pensacola for New Orleans and arrived after two days' passage. They visited the French theatre, various military installations, and the battleground where Andrew Jackson had defeated the British twelve years earlier. Vinton was impressed with the city, but not the climate. "New Orleans is a City so unique in its character, & so interesting in its mercantile importance that I found much to occupy my attention, but the weather was excessively hot and I longed for the hour when I should commence our ascent to more Northern latitudes. The Genl here enjoyed better health than usual. … The Mississippi was in its high state, the water some four feet above the level of the town, and bearing on its bosom huge ships without number that seemed almost suspended above our heads."

Now began the pleasant journey up the Mississippi by steamboat. Two days were spent in Baton Rouge, and by 20 June they were at St. Louis and Jefferson Barracks, the largest army installation in the West. "Here we found ourselves surrounded by friends. Genl Atkinson[47] & his charming lady insisted on our becoming their guests and for six days we revelled [*sic*] in all the enjoyments of social & friendly communion."

Leaving St. Louis, they proceeded up the Ohio River. The 4th of July was celebrated in Cincinnati, where a public dinner was held in honor of General Brown and Postmaster General (later Supreme Court Justice) John McLean.[48]

The trek continued, this time overland, and with much more company. "On the 6th July, accompanied by Judge McLean, we took Stage for Sandusky, through Xenia, Big Springs, Urbana, Zanesfield, Springfield, & Upper Sandusky. Mrs. McLean, her sister, son & niece, all joined the party. … Here again we had 250 miles to travel by land, through a new & in some parts unimproved country & over bad roads. The General had another trial of his fortitude but, the country was so fertile and luxuriant, the party so pleasant & the weather so agreeable that he had much to entertain his mind and beguile his griefs." There was no such thing as luxury travel on the frontier, even for the nation's leading citizens.

The party reached Sandusky on 11 July and boarded a steamer the next day, arriving in Buffalo on the 14th. "Visited Niagara falls on the 15th—Genl too sick to accompany me.—Not so well pleased with the cataract as I expected to be." Of more interest were the battlegrounds along the Niagara frontier where General Brown and his compatriots had done their fiercest fighting against the British during the War of 1812.

For General Brown, the trip was drawing to a close. "On the 16th July took canal boat at Buffalo, for Rochester—Much pleased with that village. … Took Steam boat … on the 18th and set out for Sacket's Harbour. Here we arrived the next day (19th July) and proceeded immed'y to Brownville." The general had reached his hometown. "The Genl was very much excited—All his friends delighted to meet him."

Vinton was ready to go home. It had been a once-in-a-lifetime trip, but it had also been a grueling six-month journey. He left Brownville the following day and by the end of July 1827, he was at home with Mother in Pomfret. He had made the Grand Tour of the nation and had learned to negotiate the turmoil of American sectional politics. It was now time for him to negotiate the political and social turmoil of the nation's capital.

4

The General was Dying

By late summer 1827 Lieutenant Vinton and General Brown had both returned to Washington and were settled back into the social and political life of the city. For Vinton, the next six months would prove an emotional rollercoaster, taking him to both the highest and lowest points in his life thus far.

The foremost subject of conversation in the capital was the next year's presidential election, which would prove one of the dirtiest and most divisive in the nation's history. The animosity connected with the approaching contest had been engendered by the outcome of the 1824 election. Andrew Jackson had won the popular vote over John Quincy Adams, but when the Electoral College met, neither man could muster a majority. According to the Constitution, the decision fell to the House of Representatives, which was as equally divided as the Electoral College. In the end, Speaker Henry Clay put his support behind Adams, who was awarded the presidency. When Clay was subsequently appointed secretary of state, the Jacksonians cried foul, calling Clay's support for Adams a "corrupt bargain." Feeling they had been robbed of the presidency, Jackson and his supporters were determined to win the next time around.

Thus it was that in late September 1827, Vinton entered his thoughts on the political situation into his journal:

> Rarely has it been that our Nation, yet young in the experience of political vicissitude, has been so agitated with any single topic as with this of the next Presidency. It is indeed a question which ought to challenge the serious interest of a great people on whose suffrages alone it is to turn. Yet it is somewhat surprising that the great excess of sympathy or animosity which is evinced in almost every parlour & kitchen in the country, should be felt by men whose interests are so remotely affected by the pair that it might almost be termed a question of pure abstraction with them. But so it is. Farmers quit their plough or their sickle, mechanics throw by their tools, & merchants neglect their books to become *politicians*—and panegyrize or vilify the Presidential Candidate who to them is as the man in the moon. ...[1]

In considering the upcoming election, Vinton looked to the opinions of men he respected, one of which was Postmaster General McLean. Like many people, Vinton was concerned about electing a military hero to the presidency. The lessons learned from the rise of military dictators like Napoleon were still fresh in American minds:

> Grave men like Clinton & McLean cannot be influenced by the éclat [radiance] of martial exploits. But in Jackson, it is evident they see the *lesser evil.* While they acknowledge the awful precedent which this election would create,—the portentous *imitation* of all former Republics whose liberties have fallen a sacrifice to popular enthusiasm in favor of successful mil'y leaders, these politicians join with the popular voice in tolerating the alternative & encountering the hazard rather than endure that coalition of office which at least, *resembles* corruption, and as such, *more seriously threatens* the purity & the permanency of our institutions than would the open election of a Military Chieftain.[2]

Vinton was still a young man, but his accomplishments had not gone unnoticed by the people of Rhode Island. Sometime during 1827 Brown University awarded him an honorary Master of Arts degree, though exactly why he received it is not recorded. The arts of all kinds were important to him, but he certainly didn't consider himself a "master" of any of them, and was continually trying to improve his skills:

> I have recently taken a great fancy to painting likenesses & drawing heads. Mr. Wood, of this place is quite an artist in this branch of water colouring. Knowing that a little instruction would be of great service to me, I took 2 or 3 lessons of Wood some weeks since & have profited so much by them that my style is altogether improved & my knowledge of the art greatly enlarged. These exercises are very agreeable to me, but they consume so much time that I am unable to decide whether I do rightly in devoting my hours to so subordinate a branch of accomplishment. It is very pleasant however to have portraits of our friends and I feel that the possession of the skill requisite to take them is at least a valuable acquisition.[3]

In October 1827 Vinton temporarily assumed a position of great importance in the army. The Adjutant General, Col. Roger Jones,[4] decided to take a vacation, and Vinton was chosen to assume the duties of the office while

Jones was away. In a sense, the Adjutant General was responsible for the day-to-day operation of the army. Routine correspondence and requests from the field came to the Adjutant General's office, and unless the matter required consultation with some higher authority, the Adjutant General would make a decision and send out a reply. In theory, twenty-six year old Lieutenant Vinton could tell a battle-hardened general where to go and what to do. If the responsibility weighed heavily on Vinton's shoulders, he certainly didn't show it. Instead, he seemed more concerned with an ugly blemish on his face:

> Col. Jones, who has long been promising himself the luxury of a country excursion, took horse today, and left me in charge of his Office. In this transient assumption of Official dignity I feel more practically aware of the prerogatives which attach to my situation, the law authorizing Aides de Camp to serve as Acting Asst. Adjt. Genl's when so ordered by their Chiefs.
>
> I slide into the routine of the office with a good deal of ease and should like to discharge its duties a long time. En avant [forward]—however—is my motto.—My biles [boils] have not left my face yet. So—alas! to my beauty! I scarcely dare appear before decent people my cheek is so disguised—Sulphur & Salts—diet and exercise—Constant crosses and no indulgences—Such is life! life!![5]

The weight of his temporary authority soon began to be felt when the War Department issued orders rotating the artillery regiments manning the nation's coastal fortifications. Companies that were situated in comfortable (and supposedly "healthy") posts near the pleasures of major population centers would soon find themselves stationed at remote forts in the more "sickly" parts of the nation. Many people were not going to be happy with the forced relocations, and Vinton feared they might adopt a "kill the messenger" attitude. After all, it was his signature at the bottom of the order, and to make matters worse, he had been given the responsibility of deciding precisely who got transferred where. Yet he shrugged it off, saying, "Such things are more pregnant with blame than praise because the querulous are noisy and the satisfied, quiet. However my name has gone forth in an imposing attitude, and if distinction consists in notoriety, I shall not have labored in vain."[6]

From his position at the War Department, Vinton was able to watch the slow disintegration of the Adams Administration. A year before the election was to take place, people were already counting votes. In a journal entry dated 9 November 1827, Vinton noted that an election in New York promised to foretell which way the national vote would go. "We shall hear from the election in New York in a day or two, and then learn more to warn us of the final issue of the Presidential Question than has yet appeared. If Jackson gets 10 of the Electoral Votes of that State his election is almost certain, and the general opinion now is that he will even have a majority of them. If so farewell to the Adams School, and all the Cabinet of the present Administration." Postmaster General McLean was leaning toward Jackson, and even General Brown, a staunch supporter of Adams, was starting to speak warmly of Old Hickory.[7]

When the results from New York came in, Vinton noted the rise of Martin Van Buren, but was not overly impressed with the man:

> I can scarcely suppose it possible that Mr. Van Buren possesses individually such influence with his party as to guide or control their votes on a question like this, but rather that by watching the current & shaping his course with it, he manages to ride along the surface of the stream, & this at least gains the credit of a Leader.[8]

Politics may have been the lifeblood of Washington, but high society was the heart that kept it pumping. One event on the social calendar was of particular importance to Vinton, and showed how petty that society could be:

> The approaching nuptials of Miss [Eveline Aurilla] McLean [daughter of the Postmaster General] & Capt. [Joseph Pannell] Taylor[9] cause no small excitement with us, as Pamela [Gen. Brown's daughter] is to be Bridesmaid and my brother [Hammond] one of the groomsmen. New dresses and fashions are therefore the order of the day within doors, and calls of ceremony the business of the morning hours abound. Poor Eveline was in quite a dilemma as to her third Bridesmaid. Having lately arrived at womanhood and possessing few intimate acquaintances in the city she had no one after Pamela, on whom she could call for this service, without incurring those little remarks from the gossiping world which anything singular is sure to excite. So when it was known that Sophia Ramsay was the chosen attendant, I heard it frequently asked, "Is it not strange that Miss R. should have been invited as Miss McL's Bridesmaid? Why I heard they never visited more than once or twice and no intimacy or particular friendship ever subsisted between them!"—All this was accompanied by the congenial sneers, which caring spirits love to exhibit and so it falls out with our pretty, frank, ingenious & thoughtless Eveline. May she be happy,—still![10]

The romantic notions brought on by the wedding were not lost on Vinton. One young lady in particular caught his eye, though his assessment of her seemed more logical than loving:

> On Tuesday evening Capt. Taylor's marriage with Miss McLean was celebrated at the Judge's Mansion and in the evening a large party assembled to offer the customary congratulations. … Yesterday (Friday) we were also invited to dine at Judge McLean's where the bridal party were to be present. The feast was very pleasant and productive of high social enjoyment. Miss Haskins, who came from Philadelphia to attend Miss Eveline, proves to be a young lady of polished education & respectable attainments. I had formerly seen her in Washington, but it was through some of her correspondents here that I received the high & favorable impressions of her excellence & worth which I have for a long time entertained. She is not beautiful though her presence is imposing and her person, attractive. She has been accustomed to good society and exhibits in all her demeanor the manners & accomplishments of a lady.
>
> So much for exterior. To discover & define the more important attributes of her real disposition—the qualities of her heart, the depth of her understanding and the temper of her moral sensibility is another & a more difficult task. It must be allowed that with all the virtue which her friends concur in attributing to her, she has not preserved through her soc. intercourse with the world the naïveté of original & unsophisted innocence. There is a dash of the "initiated" visible in her general conduct; and a love of admiration evidently forms one of her ruling passions. But these foibles are perhaps inseparable from those very accomplishments which are so much valued in society & for the attainment of which nature must make many sacrifices to art. Besides, who is perfect?—Were we to wait until we meet with the Beau Ideal of our imaginary creations, we should at once demonstrate our folly & our despair.
>
> Miss Haskins is certainly a fine girl, but she acts like one, rather "engaged" already than desirous of being so, and exhibits much of the nonchalance, the irony, nay almost the levity, of one who has nothing more to gain or to desire.[11]

In the journal, Vinton mentioned that his brother Hammond was engaged to Pamela Brown, General Brown's daughter. "The past week has been a gay one to us, as our family have taken so much interest in the wedding of Miss

McLean, and Hammond has derived no small satisfaction from the circumstances of the occasion, so important to his & P's happiness."[12]

On 3 December 1827 the Twentieth Congress convened, and Vinton paid a visit to Capitol Hill to watch the opening ceremonies and see the new members sworn in. The spectacle increased his pride in being an American:

> Few sights are more august then to see such a body organized,—the delegation from each State separately called up to swear fidelity to the Constitution and kiss the holy book in testimony of their vow! To observe the friendly recognition of old members now meeting after their long separation, and the occasional introduction of new ones to their compatriots in the great business of Legislation! As our Country increases in power & wealth, so does our contemplation rise in sublimity when such a spectacle is presented as this,—the assembled wisdom of the Nation,—the delegated mind, of the American people.[13]

Vinton's thoughts then wandered to the "Belles" of Washington. Although he was still enamored of Martha Haskins, another young woman also caught his eye:

> Several days since, arrived in our City the rich and (as some think) beautiful Miss Silsbee. ... I have seen her twice, and saving some exceptionable traits of manner, I have been thus far altogether pleased with her. She seems to have a spice of Romance in her composition,—loves poetry,—and has sufficient of Sentiment,—that which Miss Haskins *wants*! ...
>
> Miss Haskins I should judge to be about 22 or 23 years of age, and Miss Silsbee is but 18.—Five years work on essential change in the manners as in the mind of a young lady, and this disparity of age is evident in the whole deportment of the two young ladies who now bear the belle in our City. Miss Haskins wants the soft naïveté and engaging enthusiasm of Miss Silsbee, and the latter cannot yet boast the well disciplined, and shrewd mind of our Philadelphia damsel. But must we purchase social refinement & elegant accomplishments only at the expense of natural graces?—Must all Belles whose advantages in Society have been so valuable, prove affected & sophisticated?[14]

Vinton was obviously taken with both young women, but not so much that he forgot the practical matters that needed to be considered:

> A woman bred in such scenes & imbued with such principles, can never make a good wife to a military officer. Her lot in the Army would be one of privation & endurance in comparison with her former luxury & ease, and it is easy to imagine the wretchedness which would ensue, not less to her husband than to herself, on a trial of domestic life in such circumstances.
>
> Yet the life of a mil'y man is chequered. He has often to appear in the courtly throng of elegant Society, as well as in the rude scenes of the camp or garrison, and he would desire to see the partner of his choice as alike well the accomplished lady to grace the festive hall, as the sensible matron to participate in the homely avocations of his military quarters.
>
> It would seem therefore, that an Officer's wife should be the best & most sensible of women—uniting all the elegancies of a refined education to the pure virtues of unsophisticated nature.[15]

Politics and matters of the heart aside, Vinton remained concerned about the health of General Brown. The general's recurring illness had returned, and the ministrations of a physician did more harm than good:

> For three weeks the General has been suffering from the effects of a fresh attack of his old complaint. A blister [medicated bandage] which was applied to his forehead, exuded a matter which flowed down into his eyes and produced for the time much inflammation in them. Since that time the Gen'l has recovered gradually his health in every particular but this, and now he feels more apprehension of a partial loss of sight, than of any other immediate effect likely to arise. He is still unable to read a book or commence writing hence he is shut out of more than half his usual resources and thrown back upon himself & Emmie. It is impossible for his friends to read all the time to him, nor would he desire it, hence many of his hours are insufferably tedious and even the pleasures that remain to him are all alloyed by the ever besieging reflection that this is but another warning,—not of dissolution, for that he does not dread,—but of living a lingering imbecility and dotage.[16]

General Brown's illness, partial loss of sight, and melancholy mood were having a negative effect on the relationship with those around him. For Vinton, the most troublesome duty involved having to read to the general. In analyzing the situation, Vinton revealed a medical problem of his own, a weakness in his lungs:

> The General's fears for the loss of sight, have depressed his spirits so much for the last fortnight that every hour has been to him, heavy and distressful. He conjectures that his family & Staff who are round him do not read aloud to him with willing hearts and therefore he hears them with mingled pleasure. … As to me I have not sufficient strength of lungs to read aloud more than 15 or 20 minutes, yet I am by no means exempt, on this account, from those keen animadversions which often escape the Gen'l when he imagines we are not as devoted and confiding as he w'd wish us to be.[17]

Christmas was coming, the high society parties in Washington were about to commence, and the dashing Lieutenant Vinton was sure to be in attendance. On 19 December First Lady Louisa Adams held a "Drawing Room" at the White House. Yet no matter how elegant the venue, many of the eligible young ladies of the city did not make an appearance. It simply wasn't considered fashionable to attend the first event of the season. Vinton, for his part, was not disappointed, because, "Miss Haskins however gave us the light of her fair countenance." An event the following night drew a much larger crowd:[18]

> Last evening we attended the soiree of Mrs. Taylor,[19] which as it was the first ball that has been given, was brilliantly distinguished by a full galaxy of our belles. But such a crowd!—Such squeezing and jamming—Such destruction to lace & gras de Naples, & then to pretend to dance! …
>
> The crowd however was excessive—all complained of this and many had reason to complain. Some were "wall-flowers" who hoped to be "belles" and others, ambitious at least of some attention, were perhaps entirely neglected. I never saw a greater number of disappointed faces. Too much was expected,—in the first instance, and too high a value is set upon such things generally, for true wisdom or happiness.[20]

The parties continued into the New Year, and Vinton was happy to attend them all, enjoying himself to the fullest. He was also happy to have Martha Haskins on his arm:

> On New Year's day, the President's house was, as usual on these occasions thronged with all the beauty & fashion of the metropolis,—The foreign Diplomatic functionaries in full costume, and many Members of Congress. …
>
> After the levee, some of us adjourned by appt. to Mrs. [Sophia] Ramsays[21] where we had egg nogg [*sic*] & cake. The same good fare I had at Mrs. [Sarah] Blake's[22] too and in the evening I attended a small party at Mrs. [Mary] Pleasonton's.[23] I scarcely remember to have ever passed a more happy day than the 1st of Jany. The lovely Miss Haskins was forth in all her charms, and I her proud gallant.[24]

Vinton was confiding his feelings for "the lovely Miss Haskins" into his journal, but the rules of polite society dictated that he keep them to himself until the proper moment arrived. On 5 January 1828, he felt the time had come. It's also interesting to note that in spite of his great verbosity, the words "love" and "marriage" are never mentioned:

> On Saturday, (the *memorable* 5th Jany) I found myself in that trying crisis, which all men experience perhaps once in their lives,—and surely in all the occurrences & emergences incident to social intercourse none can be more important & interesting—I had an interview with her, whose person & character had attracted my admiration & fixed my attachment. It was during a *walk*, which I managed to prolong until we reached the terrace of the *Capitol*, where I unfolded the state of my feelings and received the qualified but satisfactory answer which so nearly consummates my happiness now. I was romantic in deferring my declaration until we came to the Capitol, but when has imagination & poetry so much to do with our actions as in moods like this of mine? I would have preferred the Dome, which we intended to ascend but the day was foggy and the prospect of course shut out—So at the foot of that Magnificent Edifice, the Acropolis of America's Legislation, J.R.V. received the happy annunciation that his hopes were fairly based and his feelings reciprocated.
>
> When shall I forget the day?[25]

The love-smitten Lieutenant had little time to spend with his sweetheart. She had come to Washington to participate in the McLean wedding, and after two months it was time to return home to Philadelphia. The visit had "been the means of fixing perhaps my destiny for life, by presenting to my eyes that loveliness and worth which comprehends my beau ideal in a woman. My acquaintance with her has been short, but every act & word of her have been so uniformly correct, so ladylike, so lovely, that I cannot well be deceived in the high estimation I have formed of her, nor crossed I trust, in the halcyon hopes which I have indulged." Even General and Mrs. Brown approved.[26]

Vinton summed up his feelings on their final night together. His eventual marriage to Martha seemed certain, with only one little hurdle to clear, the approval of her mother:

> Last evening I enjoyed (at the McLean's) one of the happiest hours of my life. With that soul-felt emotion which kindred spirits feel, when they commence together, and repose in mutual confidence the sentiments of the heart. … She has felt that she ought to make no committals while absent from her mother, yet being constrained by the emergency to indicate her feelings, she has done it so delicately and in terms so qualified, in reference to her mother's will that, even these stinted favors of hers have been more highly prized by me than the utmost profusion w'd have been.[27]

On 11 January Vinton reflected on the changes that were about to take place in his life. It was also an opportunity to reflect on the giddiness of first love:

> Having found at last, one whom I know how to appreciate, and who *knows how to appreciate me*, whose taste seems to be congenial with mine, whose talents and education render her a finished lady, whose family is one of the most respectable in Philadelphia, and who without fortune, possesses those very attributes of disposition and character which perhaps fortune would have impaired, such a lady I have now found, and such do I most devotedly love. …
>
> One evening in her Society, with all the McL. family present I had unwittingly tied her handkerchief in knots while engrossed in conversation & during my delirium of good feeling, I tossed it from me towards Miss H., whose head it struck—She looked serious & reproved me, but I, with that wantonness which could only be excused on the ground of exhilerated [*sic*] spirits & boyish feelings, took up the knotted handkerchief again, and again threw it on her head. The next morning I was rec'd rather coldly by her, and on inquiring from her friend Miss Stubbs, I found that my disrespectful conduct had given

> serious offence and for twenty four hours there never was a more miserable man. My deportment and my feelings, which had previously bordered too much on *Non Chalence* [*sic*], now became respectful & guarded. I was remorseful and self condemned—My esteem & deference for Miss H. increased the more I reflected on her just rebuke and dignified frown, and my ambition was alive to regain her favour and merit her approbation. After two or three interviews, an apology & explanation on my part, restored me to her good will, and this gloomy cloud which for the time overcast my soul, was the cause of that increased admiration of her character & person which soon compelled me to unburthen my feelings and yield up my heart.[28]

Vinton concluded, "What an odd compound is the human heart! How spontaneous, involuntary and uncontrollable are some of its feelings! My mind never had less to do with my impulses than in these conjectures; never has it so shrunk from its sovereignty." As far as his friends were concerned, Vinton was "disposed of—mortgaged."[29]

Even Mother was elated. In a letter to Frank, by then a cadet at the Military Academy, she passed on the exciting news from John:

> Shall I tell you *news*, if I notify *two* new matrimonial engagements in the family. Yes, *two*. I assure you. Hammond's, you are apprised of, the other cannot be yr. Sister's, for hers, is an *old* one, nor Alexander's, nor your's, certainly for it falls on *John*, without guessing. Well, he is really & truly engaged under his own handwriting to me to Miss Martha Haskins of Philadelphia. I have his word (& Lieut. Tyler's,[30] who was also a candidate for the lady's favour) that she will suit me exactly & I shall like her exceedingly. They describe her as being sprightly, sensible, highly cultivated, & highly accomplished, graceful in person, winning in manners, fair of complexion, yet after all, not a beauty, tho Mr. Greene, who visited her with John, says she looks like yr. Sister & is handsomer, *he* thinks, than Pamela [Hammond's fiancé], whom you have seen.[31]

Neither John nor Hammond was rushing into matrimony. Their first priority was to support their mother and sister until Alex and Frank were earning a living and could take over part of the responsibility. Elizabeth wouldn't be married until July, Alex was not yet out of medical school, and Frank still had two years left at West Point. It is difficult to assess how much assistance Maine was able to provide. He was still a merchant in Providence, so his contributions may have been more personal than monetary. He also had his wife Frances and two small boys to support, and there is no indication as to how successful his business was. All in all, it looked to be a long engagement for both men.[32]

Vinton may have been consumed with his love life, but a serious decline in General Brown's health could not be ignored. On 9 February he wrote in his journal:

> Today the Genl. has encountered (or rather yielded under) another attack of his old disease, which affects his head directly,—by paralyzing his intellectual faculties, his memory & speech, and rendering him utterly unable to accomplish any business or attend to any duty. In such cases it has been always the Doctor's prescription to apply medicine, bleeding, and all manner of depleting remedies, but it is difficult to say how long the good General's constitution is to withstand such incessant racking. He certainly is becoming more exposed every day to a return of these afflictions, and consequently his life is held by a still more precarious tenure.[33]

Though still confined to his sickbed, Brown's condition seemed to improve over the next few days, though family, friends, and co-workers remained concerned for the general's long-term health. The general's partial loss of eyesight prevented him from reading handwritten documents or fine print and made him very dependent on others. A lack of improvement could force him to retire from his position as commanding general, which would have been devastating to a man so dedicated to his career. Vinton did all he could for his friend, but he must have known that Jacob Brown's time was running out.

It would be nice to have Vinton's memoir of Brown's last days, but for some reason a number of pages have been torn out of his journal at just that time. When the entries resume, we find Vinton in the middle of sharing the general's last hours on Earth. He also laments the fact that Brown's family (which will soon be part of his own family when Hammond marries Pamela Brown) will now be without an income:

> … in the office here no more, for I found his end nigh, and that night I continued to watch by the sick bed until 6 in the morning when I retired for a little repose. At 8 I was awakened by new tidings of alarm—The General was dying—His weeping family were apprised of his approaching dissolution, and

> after a last visit to his bed side, they retired never to see him more. At ½ past 12 yesterday, the 24th of Feby he breathed his last. He wore a tranquil placid countenance at the latest moment and such is the expression of it in death. He departed by all appearance in perfect confidence of mercy from his Maker, to whom during the 2 last days he seemed to address all his soul.
>
> His family bear the terrible bereavement with becoming fortitude but who can measure the extent of their afflictions? O, may God protect and preserve them! It is their Heavenly Father now to whom they are to look for comfort, for with the good General, departed all their means of support & subsistence.[34]

On 29 February 1828, Gen. Jacob Brown, age fifty-three, was laid to rest at the Congressional Cemetery in Washington. As befitted a great national hero, most all of Washington turned out to pay their respects:

> On Wednesday the funeral of the late General-in-Chief took place at noon, from the dwelling of his family, and the Corpse was borne in military procession, to the public cemetery near the Eastern Branch, and there deposited in its narrow bed. All that martial and civic pageantry could do, to honor the last obsequies of the dead, was displayed on this great occasion. Public Sentiment was highly excited in favour of the memory of the deceased. The procession was upwards of a mile in length. Most of the Members of Congress attended, the houses being adjourned for the purpose, and in spite of rainy weather the streets were filled with people to witness the sad imposing ceremony.[35]

Vinton hoped Congress would be generous in awarding a pension to the widow, but expected disappointment. A pension for life was proposed, but soon modified to allow her the remainder of the general's salary for that year. Vinton was also concerned for his own position. He was now aide-de-camp to nobody, and Congress was talking of eliminating the position of commanding general. He enjoyed being in Washington and wanted to stay there. "In this posture of affairs I find my own interests much in jeopardy and am industrious to seek out some eligible plan by which I can be retained near the Seat of Government."[36]

Vinton remained in limbo for a week before receiving special orders assigning him to work under Colonel Jones, the Adjutant General. For the moment he was satisfied, but knew it was a temporary situation. The speculation was that one of the two brigadier generals in the army, Winfield Scott or Edmund Gaines, would be elevated to major general and take up Brown's position. Because the two were so equal in their claim to the office (and bitter rivals), it was going to be a difficult decision for President Adams to make. [37]

On 22 March Vinton penned a farewell memorial to General Brown in the back of the journal he'd kept during his trip to Georgia the previous year:

> The dear friend with whom I performed this long journey,—my excellent, good patron, has left the busy scene of life in which he bore so distinguished a part, and joined the spirits of "just men made perfect." The Genl seemed to have good health on his return to Washington, but the change of his regimen, from the active life of travelling reacted upon his system and superinduced a fresh attack of his old disease in October. Of this too he partially recovered but he lost his clearness of vision,—was unable to read, and became extremely impatient with the new infirmity. He never was so well again. He was dissatisfied with himself and often thought of resigning the command of the Army. But this soon became an inferior consideration. On the 9th of Feby (Saty) he was taken with fresh symptoms,—lost his memory,—went from the office (never to return!) and after a fortnight sickness he surrendered his spirit to his Creator. On Sunday the 24th of Feby, I was still the mourning companion of his bedside and witnessed the final scene. He died as one sleeping—without a struggle or a groan. He was buried with great ceremony, on the Wednesday following, and soon I trust, a monument worthy of this hero, this Nobleman of Nature, will show where lay his mortal remains.
>
> Where shall I find his equal?—Where such a friend! Oh God! Thou hast always been my indulgent Benefactor—Thou still wilt sustain and protect me.[38]

As if Vinton's emotions hadn't suffered enough, it seems his engagement to Martha Haskins had come to an end. In a letter to Frank, Mother mentions that the passing of General Brown may have had something to do with it. "The Genl's death, gives a different complexion to all our affairs. John thinks it forbids *his* being married, & makes Ham'd marrying more necessary, for Pamela's sake, but in this, he is more guided by his benevolence, than his judgment." By 22 March the whole affair was over, and Vinton had learned a few lessons:[39]

> On the 18th I rec'd a letter from M. [Martha] which put the seal upon our further intercourse. It was what I expected, though it has been but very lately that I have been convinced how desperate were my prospects for matrimonial happiness. God's will be done! I have yet a clear conscience though there may be some who think me obnoxious to censure. Straitened circumstances,—a dependent family,—an itinerant profession, and a horror of poverty all deter me from undertaking any enterprise in which every step is irrevocable and every advance replete with peril. … I have been disappointed and the *experience* gained will be deeply impressed on my memory. Hereafter, I shall never step but with circumspection, nor judge, without light. I may not yet be aware of the danger or trouble which is to ensue from the present case. Yet again I say my conscience is clear, and my mind is undaunted.[40]

Within the space of three months, John Rogers Vinton had gone from being on top of the world to not knowing where the bottom was. With the death of General Brown, he had lost a dear friend, someone who had given stability and promise to his military career. He had also fallen in love, proposed marriage, and had seen that hope die as well. There was a future ahead, but at the moment, it all seemed rather bleak.

5

My New & Happy State of Being

For Lt. John Rogers Vinton the years 1828 to 1836 would be focused on family. During most of that time, all Mother's children would be in the Northeast, though not necessarily close at hand. All the things that make family life so important would take place: marriages, births, joyous reunions, petty squabbles, tragic losses, and the coming together in times of need. Without a doubt, these would be the happiest times of Vinton's life.

During these years, the last of the Vinton siblings would reach adulthood, and all would find their paths in life. Alex had received his medical degree but was having difficulty finding a place to set up practice. Everywhere he inquired, the prospects did not look good. With few real hospitals to offer steady employment and no insurance to guarantee payments, the medical profession was not a sure-fire road to riches. His best hope seemed to be joining the army as a surgeon, and John was doing what he could to help his brother obtain a position. As John told his mother, "The Army is the only theatre in which Alex can enter & reap any immediate profit."[1]

For the most part, the rest of the family seemed to be doing well. Mother was still at *La Plaisance*, the family farm in Pomfret, where Elizabeth was living until her marriage to Lt. George Greene. Hammond was still engaged to Pamela Brown and was stationed at Fort Independence near Boston. Frank, the youngest brother, was at the Military Academy and was doing well in his studies. So well, in fact, that even while working hard to graduate fourth in his class, he was able to study law and take the bar exam. The only one who might have been having trouble was John's older brother, Maine, who moved to Pomfret and took up farming in 1830, having closed his business in Providence for unknown reasons.[2]

After the death of General Brown, Vinton continued to work for the Adjutant General while awaiting a new assignment. The most likely outcome was a transfer back to the artillery company he was technically assigned to, from which he had been on "detached duty" while serving in Washington. Vinton was by no means opposed to the idea, as the company was stationed close to home, at Newport, Rhode Island.

In a letter to Frank, Mother praised John's self-sacrificing nature and also shed some light on the reasons for the end of the engagement to Martha Haskins:

> In order to forward Alex's prospects, he deems it prudent, to remain at Headquarters, but he prefers being at his post in Newport. You know, my dear Son, yr. brother is guided by moral duty in all his actions—this principle leads him to make *any* & *every* personal sacrifice, even to what wd. be calc'd a romantick [*sic*] extent. He has given up the idea of marrying, that Hammond may be married, & has obtained a dismissal from Miss. H. in order to be able to take the whole maintenance of the family upon himself.[3]

The letter helps explain why John would forfeit his own happiness so that Hammond could marry Pamela Brown. Mrs. Brown still had three children to support and would soon be without an income. She and her husband had been very good to Vinton during his time in Washington, and he may have felt he owed the general's family a debt of gratitude. He could repay a portion of that debt by assuming full financial responsibility for Mother, thereby freeing Hammond to marry and help support Mrs. Brown and the children.

It would hopefully be a temporary situation, until Alex got on his feet and Frank graduated from the Academy and began to earn his army pay. Alex had opened a practice in Pomfret, and Elizabeth would soon be married, so in that respect the financial burden would soon be lessened. On the other hand, Maine was about to become a temporary burden. Health problems began in October 1828, when he had a severe attack of pleurisy and acute pains in his back. Unable to work, the family moved in with Mother while he convalesced and Frances awaited the birth of their next child. As always, the family was there for one another.[4]

In July 1828 Vinton was transferred to Fort Wolcott, on Goat Island, off Newport, where he assumed command of Company "G", 3rd Artillery Regiment. Newport was about as close to home as he could get. Even then, visits to Mother would have been rare. Pomfret was about forty miles west of Providence, a six-hour trip by stage coach. Newport, on an island itself, was approximately fifty miles south of Providence by road, with a number of water crossings in between. Considering the poor state of roads at the time, it was no doubt easier to take a boat to Providence.[5]

After about a year at Newport, John was transferred to Special Duty in Boston, though what that duty entailed is not specified. While there he renewed some old family acquaintances, including a certain young lady:

> I have much to say of the Kingman's & Parker's.[6] Mrs. P. has been very polite to me indeed & so have all. Miss P's not ex-

> ceedingly beautiful though uncommonly pretty. The engagement between her & Mr. Webster[7] is said now to be entirely dissolved, a result effectuated chiefly by the influence of his friends, political & personal, among whom there were some to whose former pecuniary aid he was indebted for important benefits & now feels himself constrained in a great measure to be guided by their counsel & direction. Miss P. meanwhile, is the chief sufferer. She is an amiable girl, of excellent feelings & good mind, and it will be very questionable after all, whether Mr. W. in choosing this alternative has not put more to hazard against popular opinion than [he?] w'd have done by marrying her, as a chevalier & true knight.[8]

Miss P. was nineteen year old Lucretia Dutton Parker, daughter of Ebenezer and Sarah (Tarbell) Parker of Boston. On 9 September 1829, after about a three-month courtship, she and twenty-eight year old John Rogers Vinton were married. Unfortunately, because we have none of Vinton's letters or a journal from the time, we have no details of the courtship or his feelings, such as we had with Martha Haskins. In a 29 October letter to Mother, John tells her just how happy he is:[9]

> I need not assure you my dear Mother how full and unalloyed is the happiness of your second born. Providence has blessed me with earth's richest treasure in my dear Lucretia,—My heart outpours its flood of new affections upon her & gathers up transports of reciprocal tenderness, filling all my bosom with happiness such as, till now I never experienced—This could not be, were I not satisfied, in judgment as well as in feeling, of the intrinsic excellences of character & mind with which she is endowed—Mine is not a heart to be bestowed for mere beauty alone (though on this score I have nothing more to ask) but when I find united to it, an erect, active & sagacious mind, a warm, affectionate & devoted spirit, pleasing manners & peaceful accomplishments, I may well be allowed to descant (at least to my mother) on the felicities which flow from my new & happy state of being.[10]

John and Lucretia wasted no time in starting a family. Ten months after the wedding, their first child, Helena Lucretia, was born at Mother's home in Pomfret. Soon after her birth Vinton's special duty at Boston ended, and he, along with Lucretia and the baby, returned to Fort Wolcott. Then, about a year later, in March 1832, Vinton received orders sending him and Company "G" to

Fort Preble at Portland, Maine. Leaving wife and child with friends and relations in Boston, he went ahead to set up housekeeping. No sooner was he gone than Lucretia began writing to him:[11]

> This is almost the first leisure moment I have found since your departure to write to you and even now my pen is so bad, that I fear my writing will scarcely be legible. Dear little Helena is asleep and I seize this opportunity to write, for it is the only chance I shall have till tomorrow. How very sad I did feel when you drove from the door—I almost repented my determination to remain behind and nothing now prevents me from being discontented but the belief that it is decidedly best I should stay here, till you can arrange matters, so that I can go immediately to the Fort. All the friends in the world seem nothing to me in comparison with you and I am more disposed to remain at home all the time & take care of Helena than to go to see any of them. … But we will soon meet again & there I trust nothing will happen to separate us for a long, long time. You must write to me very often & so soon as the furniture arrives you must let me know.[12]

Now that John and Hammond had wives and families to support, Mother was depending more on the younger sons. Alex had received a "calling" and was leaving the medical profession to become a minister. Frank, now a lieutenant in the army, was also a lawyer and stationed at Boston. As if that wasn't enough, he was frequently on the road, doing engineering work for various railroad companies. West Point was the premier engineering school in the nation, and its graduates were often the only people the rapidly expanding railroads could turn to for technical expertise.[13]

The one family member rarely mentioned is Father. In a letter to Frank, Mother indicates that John had stepped in to fill the position. "Take yr. brother John as yr. model, & remember him in Character & Conduct as you do in person. He has been a father to his brothers & sister for years." The elder Vinton was not completely out of the picture, though it seems some may have wanted him forgotten. In the same letter to Frank, Mother reported some unexpected news. "Maine has lately rec'd a letter from yr. own father, dated Murfriesborough, Ten. 28th March 1832. He saw a friend & classmate of yrs. named Lea[14] … who said you told him that 'yr. father had been dead two years.' Why did you tell him so? Did you hear so?"[15]

In the meantime, Lucretia was still in Boston but eager to join her husband in Portland. The only reason she hadn't left was the weather, which was preventing the steamboat from making its rounds. Still, if she had to be stuck in Boston, at least she could eat well:

> Last evening we were invited into Mrs. Steven's—Mary Steven's younger sister had a large party of their own age & we were asked to come in also—we spent a very pleasant evening indeed. Plenty of ice cream & every thing else that was good. … I have quite feasted on lobsters since I have been back. Pa has had them almost every day for dinner & yet I am never tired of them but am always glad to get them. I hope there are plenty of lobsters in Portland. It is a luxury I could hardly give up.[16]

The weather finally cleared, and Lucretia was able to take the ship up to Portland. In a May letter to Mother, she says, "I can easily conceive it is delightful in warm summer weather; but it is winter here at least two thirds of the year. … Helena is quite well and begins to feel at home already. She soon made acquaintance with the little girl John had engaged to take care of her and is now but little more trouble to me than she used to be in Newport."[17]

In a 10 May 1832 letter to Frank, Mother related how once again, as when he had broken off the engagement to Martha Haskins, John was stepping aside to help his brother Hammond:

> You see this is my birthday … wh. makes me 59 years old. … At Ham'd's request John renounced his application & claims to a Captaincy in the Ord. [Ordnance] Corps, in his favour. A transfer to this Corps, was John's *desideration_*… affording a *permanent* residence, better adapted to his habits, wants, & wishes, it grew more indispensable, the more he tho't of it. Yet he relinquish'd it at once, at his brother's request, "in order to prove to him, his readiness to make a Sacrifice, wh. w'd be an evidence of his firm & unaltered affection for him"—These are Ham'd's expressions and he adds, "as if evidence were necessary to assure me of the fact!" Neither of them are appointed to the Ord. but John's disinterested magnanimity has won a better guard on, even a brother's love, & a knowledge of this is the best birthday present yr. mother can receive.[18]

There was happiness, but there was also tragedy. On 6 June 1832, Elizabeth's daughter Mary, not yet three years of age, died. As Mother put it, "She was with us a little space, beaming with intelligence & dignity, & better fitted perhaps by her extraordinary qualities for the society of angels." As always,

Mother turned to her religion for solace. "Our heavenly Father 'Chasteneth whom he loveth.' He wills not that any of his children sh'd perish, but that they sh'd inherit *eternal* life. He dissolves those ties, therefore, wh. bind us to earth, in order to admonish us that even the '*affections*, must be let on things above.'" Elizabeth's second child, two year old George, was also very sick. Yet life went on, and another son, Francis, was born in August.[19]

For John and Lucretia, money was a continual concern. Vinton's army pay was by no means extravagant, only about a thousand dollars a year, and he had gone thirteen years without a raise in pay grade. He was still helping support Mother by sending her a designated amount in a monthly stipend, which always seemed to be a bit in arrears. In a September letter, he mentions, "I am concerned to hear that you 'make a deficit of $60 in your accts.' This cannot have occurred in reference to my payments as they are all duly recorded except the money I pd you at Newport which I forgot to credit myself for." Emphasizing his personal economic philosophy, he declared:[20]

> But I dread poverty more than all. I have seen it, as the lurking fiend, always at hand to mar the brightest prospects, obstruct the fairest enterprises, and harass even the ordinary course of domestic comfort. "Easy circumstances" so called, is the condition of life necessary to a genuine enjoyment of our faculties & opportunities, and I think I cannot be far amiss when I so shape my affairs & my course of living as to ensure so desirable an end.[21]

As an army officer, Vinton was considered a member of privileged society and lived accordingly. Their quarters at the fort were spacious, and at times they employed three servants: a cook, a nanny for Helena, and a male servant they referred to as a "factotum." All these trappings of society cut into their limited budget, so it is surprising when he admits to a rather self-centered indulgence:

> As a commentary upon this remark let me inform you that within this four weeks I have been sitting for my *portrait* again, prompted to this extravagance a little by vanity & somewhat by a wish that my friends might have, for their own satisfaction, a faithful resemblance of my features. I think Mr. Cole[22] has succeeded pretty well yet the picture is not without its faults. It is certainly the best likeness that has ever been taken of me, though this may be but faint praise. This with some other necessary expenditures will keep me for some time not a little straitened in the fiscal department.[23]

John and Lucretia were settled in at Fort Preble and trying to talk Mother into spending the winter with them. Domestic life was agreeable to Vinton, as he told Mother in an October letter:

> It is somewhat singular that I now feel myself more contented & satisfied, in spite of disapp'd hopes as to rank & promotion, than I ever have done. Some of this satisfactory feeling is attributable to a comfortable & cheap station, but more to a disciplined understanding on the subject of ambition. … If I am not Captain, I am the tenant of ample quarters, the husband of an affectionate wife & the father of a lovely child. If I get not double rations, I save almost their amount in the milk our cow gives, the gratis vegetables our garden yields & above all the economical dispositions of my wife.[24]

He was also proud of the coal-burning central heating system he'd installed in the officer's quarters at the fort, a novel thing at the time:

> For the last few days I have been much employed in superintending the setting of grates. Both Capt. McClintock[25] & Lt. McKee[26] were disinclined to coal until I removed their prejudices, and when I undertook to prove my arguments by the test of experiment, I felt more than the ordinary responsibility of a Qr. Master in having the grates and fixtures well set & the coal well selected. Their rooms, which formerly smoked, are now tenantable, & from being cold & uncomfortable, are capable of being heated, I think, to the extent of the utmost wish. The officers are of course delighted, and, as you know I derive peculiar pleasure from experimenting in such matters, the occasion has been to me, one of great interest & satisfaction.
>
> In a climate like this, it becomes a subject of such primary interest with a housekeeper to guard against the severity of winter that the mind finds full employment for a while in the one question of how to keep warm. I have adopted the principle of the hot air chambers in each of the four grates that have been set in Officer's quarters,—and our own little rooms, I am confident will be heated thoroughly.[27]

Lucretia was also finding domestic life agreeable, which was a good thing, because another baby was on the way, as she told Mother in a post script to John's letter:

> I am more than satisfied with this station, though I have no companion on the Fort, and therefore find all my happiness *in home.* I never liked Newport, but I cannot say why. Here I see even less society than I did there, but I am abundantly more contented.
>
> My nurse has been with me for two or three days and I am now waiting, in daily expectation of needing her services. I have been particularly fortunate, I think, in procuring a good, faithful, energetic & experienced nurse and do not doubt I shall do well. I am remarkably well & comfortable and hope when next we write to announce the birth of another grandchild.[28]

John and Lucretia were able to announce the joyous arrival of Louise Clare on 15 October 1832. Throughout her life, Louise seems to have suffered from a minor identity crisis. To her father and other family members, she was always lovingly known as "LuLu," though the exact spelling took awhile to settle out. In her adolescence, Vinton sometimes addressed letters to her as Louisa Clara, but in adult life she signed her name Louise Clare.[29]

The good news from John and Lucretia was tempered by word that Elizabeth's second child, George, had passed away a week earlier, at less than two years of age. The news from Elizabeth's home did not improve as the months passed. By December, everyone was concerned for Elizabeth's health. Lucretia wrote to Mother, saying, "I am much obliged to you for giving us so minute an account of the health of our dear Sister and hope you will continue to give us your opinion of her frequently. We cannot but rejoice that there is any sign of amendment and do most earnestly hope that each account from you will inform us of her continued improvement." John added, "I need not express how great is my pleasure to hear the late favorable account of Sister's health. May Heaven grant our prayers that the dear one may [yet be?] spared to us."[30]

Their good wishes and prayers were all in vain. Elizabeth died of "rapid consumption" (tuberculosis) on 26 December. George, her husband, must have been devastated. To compound the misery, their final child, six-month-old Francis, was not doing well. Unaware of the situation, John wrote Mother, saying, "Poor little Frank—from your account of his teething must be a great sufferer & a great trouble. You speak as if his health were precarious. Heaven grant that this relic of our Beloved may at least be spared to us!" He wasn't. On the same day John wrote the letter, little Francis died.[31]

Domestic life for John and Lucretia continued at a steady pace. There were, of course, the usual childhood ailments to deal with. With Helena, it was a skin disorder:

> Her ear is entirely healed, but several large blotches came out on her face and neck, which now are nearly or quite well. One side of her back is quite thick with little sores and she has some on her legs and arms. I still continue the tar ointment which seems to arrest the progress of the humor in a great measure but as soon as I cure a sore in one place, I discover another one in another. She has been quite uncomfortable for a day or two, her back has itched so much.[32]

As for little Louise: "Our dear little baby is quite well, though she worries considerable owing probably to her teeth. She has very much improved within a week past, in the state of her bowels. She is now quite loose enough—Is it not the case generally when children are cutting their teeth that they are more loose in their bowels?" There were also problems with finding good servants:[33]

> Eliza's Mother sent for her on Monday morning and wished her to go home the same day. We sent our factotum, Weymouth, after Ruth Mitchell and she sent word that she would come the next morning, so, late in the afternoon I paid Eliza and told her she might go. Ruth came the next morning. She and Betsey get along nicely together. They get up mornings when the gun is fired and Ruth helps about so many little things that Betsey gets her work all done up quite early after breakfast and sits down to sewing.[34]

They were also planning to build a spacious house of their own, which in addition to the front rooms and bedrooms, would have a washroom, kitchen, abundant pantries and closets, two attics, and five chimneys. There was only one problem: "But I fear instead of 1,100 we cannot get such a house built for 1,500 dollars."

The Vintons' quiet domesticity was almost interrupted by sectional politics when South Carolina threatened to declare the Federal tariff laws null and void, and President Jackson appeared ready to enforce the laws by military means. Lucretia asked Mother, "What do you think of the prospect of our going South this winter? Have you not heard that Genl. Scott has requested 2,000 more troops to be stationed at Charleston? I see by the papers that five companies from Old Point have been sent there."[35]

The nullification crisis blew over, and the Vintons remained at Fort Preble. In the meantime, Frank was on a mission to deliver 150 army recruits to Prairie du Chein, in what is now southern Wisconsin. While on the trip, he ran into an old friend who mentioned meeting David Vinton. As Frank later told Mother, the friend had seen the elder Vinton, "a few miles from Nashville & rode some way with him in the Stage. When I return I will tell you all he said. Suffice it to say that he is much respected & well known in the neighborhood of Nashville & the possibility is that had I gone there as I anticipated I sh'd most probably have seen him, who has made me an orphan. He did not know that I had been at W. Point & could not associate my name but with a child." It would have been the last opportunity for any of the children to have seen their father. David Vinton died on 14 July 1833 in his room at an inn run by Shakers near the village of South Union, Kentucky, about fifteen miles southwest of Bowling Green. In a final indignity, the local Masons, unsure of his status within the organization, declined burying him with Masonic honors. The funeral dirge that was sung at nearly all Masonic funerals was not sung over the grave of the man who had written the lyrics.[36]

John and Lucretia were happy at Fort Preble, but were also aware that no posting in the army was permanent. The forces needed to be rotated on occasion to keep the men healthy and content. Vinton could no doubt remember when he had issued orders for such a rotation in 1827 while temporarily assuming the duties of Adjutant General. And while he may have liked it where he was, the idea of being transferred to a post in the West was exciting. Like many Americans, Vinton was caught up in the fantasy of easy riches to be found on the frontier:

> I doubt not think I sh'd have much reason to regret moving to the West, except that Lucretia w'd find less congenial Society there, or more difficulty accepting it than she does on the Atlantic border. This is an important consideration indeed but still not one involving remote & permanent interests. Such interests I can imagine, might be advanced by going to the West. My mind reverts frequently and cordially to scenes that I have witnessed & descriptions I have read of those splendid regions. There I could acquire immense estates by a small expenditure,—economize my resources and lay a foundation for a family name & establishment which my children to the 2 & 3[d] generation w'd bless me for. That is a country offering to every diversity of taste, a climate & soil appropriate to its desires—a country of incalculable resources and inconceivable destiny. Speculations such as these are, to be sure, in everybody's mouth now days, but they w'd prove more than mere visions of the imagination to me if I sh'd be located once in the West with my family. … O what a host of glorious images crowd upon me![37]

Vinton was excited about the possibility of moving West, but Mother was not. If John wanted to quit the army to become a farmer, she asked him, why not take over *La Plaisance*? John, having just had a visit from Frank and no doubt hearing glowing tales of the trip out West, tried to explain:

> I thank you my dear Mother for the kind suggestion you have thrown out, as a modification of my Illinois project but there is little in that suggestion that meets my views. I do not dream of leaving the Army in order to contract my sphere of action and diminish my already too attenuated income. My object in taking such a step w'd be to enlarge my prospects and give scope to my exertions, in the hope of acting a part of dignity & distinction while living, and of leaving my family in respectable circumstances at my death. The Army, unfortunately, offers no field for these exertions, and no promise of the consummation described, but Pomfret, assuredly, offers still less. To quit an income of a thousand pr annum and fix myself in a spot, cold, thankless, & recluse, with no object or employment but planting my garden & digging my potatoes, would be little short of madness.[38]

The future was in the West, and along with countless other people, Vinton had thoroughly bought into the dream of easy money in a land flowing with "milk and honey":

> If I sh'd resign with 1,200 dollars in my pocket I c'd proceed with my family to Dayton, Vincennes, Jacksonville or some other very flourishing town in the great & powerful states of Ohio, Indiana or Illinois, where I c'd at once let out my money for 10 & 12 pr cent on the best security yielding me an all sufficient income for subsistence and a considerable surplus besides. This supposes me to live in town and do nothing with my hands or my wits to increase this income. Here then I c'd have schools, churches & excellent society, and be upon the spot to look out for a plantation in the vicinity. …
>
> All this,—however plausible & romantic it seems,—is nevertheless, *practicable*. … In Illinois, the land (such as I sh'd settle on) is alluvial, and so rich & productive, that manure would *injure* it. … It is in such a sphere that I sh'd like to be acting. It is to that bright region of peace & comfort & competency, that I sh'd like to take you,—and to see following us Maine, Alex & Frank. I sh'd leave in N. England no associations, no affections

> that I c'd not easily forego, and I sh'd find in the west a field rich & copious,—inviting all my energies into exertion and giving promise of fruition equal to the utmost of all reasonable desires.[39]

In trying to convince John to remain in New England, Mother used her most potent argument, Christian morality. John wasn't swayed:

> You ask why do I so hunger & thirst for worldly possessions & things which perish? … I ought indeed to "Seek first the Kingdom of Heaven" as you enjoin, but it does not follow that competency & comfort "will be added into" me unless I adopt the *means* necessary to this end. The days of Miracles are past, and it is a weakness that I hope not to be suspected of, to suppose that excessive religiousness will be the means of living. God intended that man sh'd labour,—with his [mind?] as well as with his hands,—employing his faculties & his energies with things appertaining to this life as well as his heart & his mind, (in due measure) to the things appertaining to the life beyond.[40]

Yet John was a practical man, and as with everything else concerning the frontier, it was all speculation:

> I c'd say much more on this head, but will only add now, that the present agitation of this subject is more for the sake of speculation than of practical operation, at least for some years to come. I might, next Summer, seek for some duty at the West to get free transportation there, & if so, then to look about for a good locality to purchase,—but I sh'd not resign from the Army until I saw my way clear, and could place myself in some path of preferment or aggrandizement which the Army itself does not offer.[41]

John and Lucretia were settling in for the winter of 1833/1834 at Portland, and Lucretia was expecting another child. There had been problems with the domestic help, primarily because they were young, unsettled girls. The solution was found by hiring older, more stable women. Both Helena and little Louise were doing fine. Lucretia wrote that Helena was, "a lovely little creature indeed and has improved very much in her looks since Summer, but what is of more importance, she has also improved in her behavior & conduct generally." Louise, just over a year old, "seems to me that she is the loveliest, most amiable little creature I ever knew, and I hope time will prove that I have not mistaken her character. She seems too to be remarkably bright & intelligent, though not precocious. She certainly is a beautiful child."[42]

John had not given up on the idea of moving west, and in January 1834 he wrote to his mother, discussing other options:

> I have recorded my name at Wash'n for a disbursing agency in the removal of the Pottawatomie Indians, and if I get an appt. to that service, shall be employed for the whole season, in Indiana & Illinois,—the region of country which I am most anxious to visit. In the event of my going, it is our plan that Lu & the children sh'd reside meanwhile at La P.—while I am gathering information on the great subject of our own emigration to that glorious land. It is, however, more than probable that I shall fail in my application, the competitors are so numerous.[43]

Vinton was dreaming of a new home in the West, but his attention was riveted to the one he occupied in Maine. His and Lucretia's third child, a boy they named Parker, was born on 24 February 1834, but he was not a healthy baby. Two weeks later Vinton wrote a letter to his mother, informing her of tragic news:

> Our little Son, whom God lent us for the short season of fifteen days, has been reclaimed and is gone to the bosom of his Maker. He breathed his last yesterday,—and this afternoon I have seen his earthly remains deposited in the grave. Never was there a more beautiful infant. His countenance was intelligent & expressive far beyond his age, and his whole frame seemed the perfect model of infantine loveliness. We have had a struggle between hope & apprehension ever since he was born. There always seemed to be a difficulty in his breathing, and an irregularity in his pulse. At four days old he was attacked by serious spasms accompanied by syncope, or suspended animation, and these continued for twelve hours with interruptions,—after which he got better and our hopes were again flattered until the 14th day, when the same disorder manifested itself by similar spasms & fainting, only with more violence. This last attack we plainly saw, w'd be fatal except by an almost miraculous interposition of Providence. His constitution, which was evidently strong in other respects, sustained him beyond all our calculations, but at length yielded, and for the last few hours he slept tranquilly until the Spirit departed. …

> O the anguish of beholding our offspring struck by the marble hand of Death! How I condemn myself, dearest Mother! for speaking so slightly of the subject when you were with us, a sufferer from a similar but much aggravated tribulation! Why did I not rather encourage your tears to flow,—lead on the conversation which to you was only grateful when the lovely departed was the theme? Forgive me, Mother, if I erred by my flippancy. I shall know better, in future, how to sympathize with the torn heart, which bleeds for afflictions like this. Mysterious tie of parental affection; so totally indescribable, so utterly unappreciated but by him who has experienced its disruption![44]

The loss was somewhat offset by a long-awaited promotion. In 1834 Vinton was elevated to Brevet Captain for having gone ten years without a promotion, made retroactive to 30 September 1829, ten years after he'd been made a First Lieutenant. The lack of advancement in all that time had little to do with his capabilities as an officer. Because the army had no pension system or policy of forced retirement, senior officers often kept their lucrative positions until they died. With no openings at the top, there was no way for an officer to advance until someone higher up either died or resigned. To help ease frustration among the junior officers, Congress instituted the policy of awarding brevet promotions to officers who had either performed some conspicuous act of valor or had held the same rank for ten years. The problem with brevet rank was that while the officer enjoyed most of the privileges of the higher rank, he didn't receive a corresponding increase in pay. Vinton was playing the role of a captain, but he was still living on a lieutenant's salary.[45]

In the meantime, Mother decided John should leave the army and take up a civilian career. Her son was not inclined to agree:

> I am somewhat surprised, my dear Mother, to find you still advising me to resign my mily. commission and enter some civil pursuit—*some* civil pursuit!—but what? That is the question. I have not half property enough to support my family out of the Army—and in what line of life could I earn a sum equal or comparable to that I sh'd relinquish by resigning? In either of the learned professions, there requires more sedentary employment than w'd consist with my health. In trade I sh'd find nothing so congenial to my tastes as the Army.—In manufacturers the business is already overdone,—and in agriculture I sh'd find satisfaction only by pursuing it on a large & liberal scale. … I am occupying now the Station of a gentleman & to

> descend from it voluntarily w'd scarcely be the part of wisdom or good taste. The Army, after all is not so despisable [*sic*], especially with my rank. Promotion has held off long to be sure but in the meanwhile my Station & circumstances have been pleasant & agreeable. Illinois alone w'd offer me a rational substitute for my commission, & even that [wouldn't?] be preferable until I sh'd find the Army more unpleasant than I have yet.[46]

Mother would not let the subject rest. In September, when he reported a rumor that he might be transferred to Mobile, Alabama, she was quick to once again suggest he leave the army. Vinton was sympathetic, telling her, "I rec'd yesterday your excellent letter of the 22^d inst. [instant: this month] in which I perceive how heartily your feelings are opposed to the idea of our going to Mobile,—and I might add, *anywhere*,—inferring from the reasons & arguments you address, your repugnance to any change from our present Station." After assuring her that the rumor was probably false, he reminded her that the matter was out of his control. He then began a spirited defense of his chosen occupation:[47]

> Your denunciation of the Army as a professional occupation, is scarcely warranted by the reality. Its "moral atmosphere" is not "discharged with the spirit of slavery," but in no vocation is there prevalent a more free and independent and noble range of thought,—and I may add of action too. Our "locomotive powers" are *regulated* indeed, but in what employment known among the social officers of life, are they not *more* shackled & circumscribed? What "*regulation*" of our "intellectual powers" exists, I have yet to learn,—But compared with the employments of the Lawyer, the Merchant, the Civil Officer, the Secretary or Cashier or Machinest [*sic*] or Agent, our calling is the very broad ocean of independence, free alike from magisterial control, popular apprehension or political proscription.[48]

He was also annoyed by comments that must have alluded to a supposed obsession within the army concerning rank. Hadn't Mother done everything in her power to retain the family's social standing after Father had left? Vinton couldn't see the difference:

> And "this ideal thing called Rank—what is it?"—"A Shadow," I will grant you, if we view the subject philosophically. … I might however in reply be tempted to ask you my dear Mother, why is the longing hope, the fond desire, the eternal reaching

for caste, for social distinction, for a jealous defence of our rights to the place in the visiting circles of society to which we lay claim or aspire so egregiously entertained in our hearts & minds, that we are content to suffer almost any physical pain or privation rather than compromise our "rank?" *You* have fought *your* fight, nobly, my dear Mother, and kept your position, with what jealous care, & by what prodigious efforts, it is subject of profound admiration for me to know. But let it be admitted also, that military rank is not less substantial,—to say the least, than social. …

There are indeed professions in which I might experience a more active exercise of mind,—a more exacting development of my talents such as they are,—but there are also many of the contrary character,—in which I might labor in vain,—scramble along through a laborious, confined, slavish course of life, depending upon other's good opinions, for favor & profit, & perhaps doomed after all to see my children crying to their parents for bread!!! No. While I can hold fast to a respectable competency, I will not even subject myself to the *hazard* of a predicament like this. … I do not mean that this Army is a situation in which I sh'd be most satisfied to live, if I had the means to choose my lot. But while I lack those means, I will not throw away the pearl which ensures me the support & the rank of a gentleman.[49]

No transfers, either wanted or unwanted, were ordered, and the Vintons remained at Fort Preble for another winter and into the next summer. On the first day of June 1835, John wrote to his mother with exciting news. "This morning at 6 minutes before 5, I was presented with a fine little boy. Both mother & child are doing well." They would name the child Francis (Frank) Laurens.[50]

Once again there was talk of Mother coming to visit for the winter, but there seemed to be a problem. It appears she looked unfavorably upon certain entertainments that John and Lucretia took part in. John was unapologetic. "A game of whist or a glass of wine are gratifications that we may occasionally wish to indulge in, because I never yet heard a sufficient reason for their discontinuance,—but we will not importune you to partake of them nor incommode you with dissertations to prove their innocence."[51]

Another winter came and went at Fort Preble. The past seven years of domesticity had been wonderful for John Rogers Vinton, but as the summer of 1836 approached, a war was raging in the South, and the Vinton family was about to become caught up in its fury.[52]

6

You Cannot Write Too Often

In late 1835, not long after John and Lucretia had celebrated their sixth anniversary, war broke out in Florida. The conflict was the result of the government's Indian Removal policy, mandated by a law President Andrew Jackson had pushed through Congress in 1830. In short, the law required all Native American nations living east of the Mississippi to give up their ancestral homelands in exchange for new lands in the West. Nearly all the tribes resisted the effort to some extent, but none met with any real success. Only the Seminole of Florida were able to put up a prolonged armed resistance, tenaciously fighting the United States for almost seven years. The Second Seminole War, as it came to be known, would become the longest, costliest, and one of the most deadly wars the United States would wage against Native Americans.[1] The war affected tens of thousands of people, among them Capt. John Rogers Vinton. He would be stationed in the war zone, away from his beloved family, for nearly all of those seven years.

This was not the first war between the Seminole and the Americans. In 1818 General Jackson had invaded what was then a Spanish colony, destroying Indian villages and capturing Spanish towns. In 1821 Spain ceded the territory to the United States, and two years later a treaty was negotiated that placed the Seminole on a large reservation in central Florida. It was, at best, a temporary fix to a problem that would not go away: The Indians occupied some of the best land in Florida, and whites wanted it for their own farms and plantations. The Seminole, whose right to the land had not been contested either by the Spaniards or the British, saw no good reason to give it up. Another major point of contention was the hundreds of runaway slaves and their descendants who lived among the Indians. To the whites, they were property. To the Seminole, they were friends and in some cases, family members. Neither side was in a mood to compromise.

Ever-present tensions escalated after 1832, when the government coerced the Seminole into signing a treaty in which they gave up their Florida reservation in exchange for land in what is now Oklahoma. The Seminole, a relatively small, disunited tribe, refused to acknowledge the treaty and demanded to be left alone. As the 1 January 1836 deadline for emigration drew near, the Seminole began to prepare for war. In late December, when a column of soldiers passed through their reservation, the Seminole decided it was time to take action.

In the middle of the Florida wilderness, the Seminole ambushed the column of 108 men led by Maj. Francis L. Dade.[2] By the end of the day, only three of the soldiers remained alive. Only two survived to make it back to Fort Brooke at Tampa Bay, sixty-five miles from the sight of the battle. The "Dade Massacre," as it became known, was a violent, shocking commencement to the war, and much like the attacks on Pearl Harbor or the World Trade Center, it stunned Americans, leading to cries for revenge from throughout the nation.

For the miniscule United States Army, it was a devastating loss. The entire army possessed a strength of just over 7,000 men, of which only a few hundred were officers. Of the seven officers killed in the Dade Battle, most had been acquaintances of John, Hammond, or Frank Vinton, either at West Point, as part of the 3rd Artillery, or from John's days as Jacob Brown's aide-de-camp. The news must have filled all their homes with sadness and anger.

The war soon became a major embarrassment for the army. On New Year's Eve, a few days after the Dade Battle, the Seminole repulsed a force of 750 army regulars and Florida Volunteers who had crossed the Withlacoochee River on Florida's West Coast with the intent of attacking the nearby Seminole villages. Weeks later, Maj. Gen. Edmund Gaines, hearing of the news while in New Orleans, brought 1,100 men to Florida and ended up being held under siege near the banks of the Withlacoochee for over a week before being rescued.

President Jackson, vowing to put a quick end to the uprising, dispatched Maj. Gen. Winfield Scott with nearly 5,000 men, mostly volunteers from neighboring states. Scott's elaborate campaign proved a dismal failure when the Seminole disappeared into the familiar swamps and heavily-wooded hammocks, a land virtually unexplored by the whites. In the space of four months, a tribe that counted less than 1,500 warriors scattered throughout a vast, uncharted peninsula had shocked America and its military establishment. Americans began to realize they were in for a long, bloody war.

By summer 1836 nearly the entire army was holding its breath, wondering who would be sent to the inhospitable Florida Territory to fight the implacable foe. The reality was that until late fall, no real fighting would take place. The subtropical Florida climate, with its daily thunderstorms, flooded terrain, and hordes of disease-carrying insects, made it impossible to wage war. Until the air cooled and the skies dried, the army would abandon the interior of the peninsula and retreat to healthy posts along the coast or in the Northern states. The Vinton brothers probably felt secure in their positions until sometime late summer.

What they didn't count on were the Creek Indians of Alabama. They too were facing forced removal, and many, perhaps inspired by their Seminole cousins in Florida, decided to put up a fight. With General Scott and a good portion of the southern part of the army in Florida, Jackson dispatched Maj. Gen. Thomas Jesup[3] to lead the war against the Creeks until Scott could wrap up his failed Florida campaign. To accomplish the task, Jesup was going to need a large number of troops, and in a hurry. Orders began to flow from the War Department, and subsequent movements were reported in the *Army and Navy Chronicle*:

> Maj. Lomax's company of the 3rd Regiment U.S. Artillery … embarked [from Newport] on Sunday last, in the Steamboat *Massachusetts*, for New York, and left that city on Tuesday, for Charleston, on their way to Fort Mitchell, Alabama. … Major Lomax received his orders on Saturday, and on Sunday afternoon the company were on their way to New York. …
>
> We learn that ten companies of U.S. troops, stationed along the sea-board, are ordered by the War Department, to repair to Fort Mitchell without delay. …
>
> The whole military force stationed at Fort Independence [Boston] is ordered to Fort Mitchell, in Alabama, and will leave here this morning in the railroad cars for Providence. … Orders have been received at Fort Preble, Portland, to proceed with all possible dispatch to Fort Columbus, and from thence to Fort Mitchell. Major McClintock and Capt. Vinton are of this command.[4]

On 26 May 1836 Vinton and the soldiers at Fort Preble received their orders. Hammond and Frank at Virginia and New Hampshire respectively, also received orders. Vinton wrote to his mother, telling her:

> These are stirring times. Hammond's Warning Orders are by this time become orders for actual movement,—and now even we have today rec'd orders for movement without the previous grace of warning. The Creeks are in motion they say. The people say.—The Editors say.—And this you know is *vox populi,*—an influence which no Administration in this country can resist. So off we must go to the Creeks. Hope something better will come of it than the Seminole concern—Better country to operate in,—and above all, a better head to the Expedition. Genl. Jesup is appointed to the command and I do believe he is one of the best among the "big bugs" we have. What an Electric Shock to all of our little community at Fort Preble! Never was such a time. Look out for wives, children, pigs & chickens! … Quite a sensation indeed! The order came today,

> Wednesday—and day after tomorrow is the time set for departure—Maybe not till Monday however. …
>
> Two days are small warning for our household. Still Lucretia designs to get ready & go off with us, staying one day in Boston and then proceeding to Prov'd & Pomfret. If we go on Friday, she will be in Prov. Monday to take the Tuesday Coach to Pomf. If we delay till Monday she will stay over Tuesday in Bost. take the RR Wednesday & Pomfr. Coach Thursday.[5]

Vinton's orders may have seemed clear, but he was hoping for a reprieve. He was a brevet captain and serving in that capacity, yet his orders showed him as a lieutenant serving under some other captain. Vinton also had reason to believe he'd been promoted to a full captaincy, but believed his immediate superior had not been advised of the fact by the War Department. A letter was sent to Washington seeking clarification, and Vinton hoped that when the War Department responded, he would no longer be a lieutenant and would receive different orders. As it turned out Vinton was correct, and his promotion had an effective date of 28 December 1835, the day of Dade's Battle. One of the men slain that day was Capt. Upton Fraser,[6] commander of Company "B" 3rd Artillery Regiment, and Vinton had been appointed his direct replacement. It was a sad fact that in order for Vinton to get ahead, someone else had to perish.[7]

Vinton was also correct in his prediction of receiving a reprieve from the orders. A letter from Mother to Frank dated 21 June mentions John going back to Fort Preble, but Lucretia and the children were to remain at Pomfret. Everyone knew it was only a matter of time until he received new orders and headed south, as his brothers already had. Hammond was on his way to Alabama to serve as an Assistant Quartermaster under General Jesup, and Frank was on his way to Wilmington, North Carolina for recruiting duty, but had no intention of staying there long. He had already decided to leave the army and enter the seminary, with classes beginning in September. Mother urged Frank to quit the army early and come home for the summer. In the same letter to Frank, Mother also thanked him for a barrel of salted fish he was about to send:[8]

> … indeed, such a provision w'd be particularly acceptable, just now, when my family is increased & we are literally without "fish, flesh or fowl" in the house, or any butcher's meat except a piece of veal once a month, when our neighbors kill a calf.[9]

The army's reason for keeping Vinton in the north was a very practical one: Company "B" had been totally destroyed at Dade's Battle, and Vinton needed to recruit the men for the replacement company. It was common practice at the time for officers to recruit their own men, especially if an entire company needed to be raised. For some reason, the army selected Worcester, in the center of Massachusetts, as the place where the recruiting would take place. At least it was convenient, being only about thirty-five miles north of Pomfret.

On 2 September 1836 Vinton received word that he and the company would eventually be stationed at Fort Pickens, a newly constructed fort outside Pensacola, Florida. Vinton was pleased with the news, as he stated in a letter to Mother and Lucretia:[10]

> Now this is rather better luck than I had a right to expect. Pensacola is perfectly healthy, preferable to Ft. Jackson [Louisiana] with the certainty of perpetual com'd [command]. Preferable to Key West in everything except health and the chance of making money. This latter consideration brings us to the subject some since discussed by Lou & I as to the expediency of seeking Key West for this purpose. I sh'd like it. She w'd have to sacrifice much of Society, but she was willing to do that for the chance of mending our fortunes. Now revolve this question in your minds and say whether I had better propose an exchange with Childs[11] at once or leave the event to chance or remain at Pensacola. It is a great comfort to know where we are all destined at least. The Creek War seems to be entirely over. The Tenn. Volunteers are all going into Florida and I sh'd not wonder if that campaign be speedily terminated,—so that after all we may soon see ourselves established again in quarters. I confess I like the move. ... A new and beautiful fort, in the largest Naval Harbour S. of the Potomac & near one of the pleasantest towns in all the Southern Country.[12]

The more he thought about it, the more excited Vinton became. All of a sudden there appeared to be a number of roads to advancement, depending on who among his fellow officers did what:

> Lomax now stands at the head of the list of Captains & Fenwick has not yet resigned. If Childs resigns also, I rise two,—escape Fort Jackson and am sure of a post. Gates[13] may possibly be restored, however, which w'd retard Lomax,—Perhaps Churchill[14] will resign rather than go to St. Augustine. Finally there is no Captain of my rank in all the Artill'y who stands so good a chance of an independent command.
>
> Now comes the consideration how to get our furniture South. What to carry &c &c—Enough to cogitate upon until I

> come to Pomfret which I trust will be next week,—Tuesday or Thursday—and not Wednesday as I before said.
>
> Maine talks of passing his winter in N. Orleans. Who knows but we might be near neighbors to each other?[15]

Vinton must have spent the night fantasizing about their new home in the South, for the very next day he wrote a long letter to Lucretia outlining all his dreams. He also saw it as an opportunity for the whole family to move south. All of sudden, Florida had replaced Illinois as the Promised Land:

> Whenever a post is on the salt water it has been proved healthy. The 2d Regt. have been since 1827 at the Stations now allotted to the 3d and I know not of a single case of death or disease among the Officers on account of the climate. I shall go to the South therefore with more confidence of retaining good health than I sh'd have in remaining here. I dread the rheumatism, and believe I sh'd have it, or the consumption if I remained at the North another winter. … There is no other possible arrangement of Stations that could give me half so good a chance (or any chance at all) of an independent command,—and I had been previously preparing to invest some interests at the South, in this very neighborhood as the best field of enterprise I could find, so that the dispensation *seems* to be almost a special index [sign] of Providence. Coupled with this, is the remarkable coincidence that Maine was to pass his Winter in N. Orleans for his health, and Alex had rec'd a call to minister in the same field,—which I certainly hope he will accept—and Hammond's Station being also nearer to us than ever it has been before,—altogether, I say, the coincidence is remarkable,—and I see no better plan than that Mother should pull up stakes with us and migrate to the land of promise.[16]

It all seemed perfect, and due to the South's "peculiar institution," the move would also solve a domestic labor problem he and Lucretia had been experiencing. There was but one minor problem, and that didn't seem to worry him:

> Were it not for the Seminole War, now, nothing could be easier managed. We might go the present Autumn, bag & baggage—take a ship to carry us directly there,—and pass our Winter as pleasantly as possible. … Frank too, after his probation at the Seminary, will probably accept the call at Columbus!

> That "prettiest town he has ever seen"—and so we shall all become Southerners in a trice. No fasting about Servants there. Buy a nice little yellow girl! Make her what you please![17]

So confident was Vinton of his comfortable posting at Pensacola that he went so far as to purchase property in Columbus, Georgia, a town Frank had fallen in love with and where he had made an offer to purchase some land. Frank, of course, had left the army to take up the priesthood and no longer had use for any Southern lands, nor had he the money to invest. In mid-September 1836, John began negotiations for the purchase of several lots, including the ones Frank had made an offer on, for the price of $5,380, with 25 per cent down, and the rest paid over the next eighteen months at six-month intervals.[18]

It might strike us as odd that someone who was constantly concerned about a lack of funds was investing heavily in real estate. What we come to realize from looking at Vinton's correspondence is that he was always short of cash because any excess money he had was invested in some way. Financially conservative and with a growing family to support, Vinton was putting his money to work in the best way he knew how. Although it is hard to tell from the sketchy figures that occasionally appear in his letter books, Vinton's income from investments often rivaled his army pay.

As November 1836 rolled around, Vinton was still in Massachusetts trying to raise recruits for Company "B," but wasn't having much success. Some of the recruits had already deserted, and others were getting into trouble with the local inhabitants. Frustrated, he asked the Adjutant General if he might move up to his old home of Portland, Maine, where he felt he might have better luck.[19]

Finally, on 16 November, Vinton received orders to take what men he had and report to Fort Hamilton, at Brooklyn, New York, where he arrived on 1 December. The company was to make final preparations to head south, and there were countless details to take care of. The men's haversacks, a necessary item for holding their miscellaneous belongings, had been left out of the clothing allowance, and the regimental surgeon put in an urgent request for medications he felt would be needed in Florida. Vinton also requested copies of the Infantry and Artillery Tactics manuals and Army Regulations for his non-commissioned officers. On top of all that, he was the only officer present at Fort Hamilton, even if his posting was only temporary. That presented a problem, because there were several invalids and dependents at the post who were in need of rations, but when he left, there would be nobody there to requisition or issue those provisions. Because the army was sending so much of its strength to Florida, everyone was caught short.[20]

As always, there were financial matters to deal with, both personal and professional. The purchase of some of the lots in Columbus was proving difficult, but at least he was collecting rents on the ones he did own. More frustrating was the army's refusal to pay him as much for lodging while he was in Massachusetts as he thought they ought to, along with the denial of payment for kettles he'd purchased for the men's mess. Financial dealings with the army were always difficult, especially if it had to do with reimbursements.[21]

About this time Vinton became involved in an interesting court case that had to do with the matter of brevet pay. Normally, when an officer received a brevet promotion, he enjoyed the privileges of the higher rank, but did not receive the corresponding pay increase. One of the exceptions was if the officer was actually performing the duties of that higher rank, for which he was then entitled to the higher pay. Vinton had received his brevet promotion to captain in 1834, but it was made retroactive to 1829. During those five years he had at times performed the duties of a captain and had applied for and received the extra pay. The Treasury Department took issue, saying the brevet pay only applied to the period after he received the appointment in 1834, irrespective of the backdating, and they wanted $204 back. Vinton stood his ground. In effect, he said, "You want your money back? Sue me."

At first it seems a trifling matter. Yet we should remember that this was a time when a workman would be happy to earn a dollar a day. A lowly private in the army was only paid six dollars a month, and $204 was about two months' pay for Vinton. In addition, nearly every experienced officer in the army had held brevet rank at one time or another, and many no doubt had similar claims. The outcome of Vinton's case could have far-reaching (and expensive) consequences for the government if he won. In May 1836 the case was argued before the District Court in Maine. In early December Vinton received word of the court's decision. The justices, unimpressed with the government's argument, ruled that "retroactive" meant precisely what everyone thought it meant. Vinton could keep the $204.[22]

Although New York wasn't that far from Pomfret, Vinton was too busy with his duties to visit Lucretia, Mother, and the family. Lucretia asked him, "Do you not think you can steal a few days to run here and see us?" In the meantime, she could do little but fill him in on the news from home:

> *Your* letters are such a delight to *me*, that it makes me realize more how grateful letters from home must be to you. … I sent for Dr. Holt[23] a few days since to draw one of Helena's teeth. I found that one of her second teeth was coming so large as to occupy the space of two of her former teeth & that it would be necessary to have one of them out. She bore it like a good girl, & has been writing letters to Father almost every day since giving him an account of it. …

> Frank Laurens grows quite a tall boy—he begins to articulate a few words. The first he said was in imitation of Helena when she said Bible, he repeated it after her—he now asks for a book when he wants it—calls the cat pu, pu. … Loulou improves very much in her spelling and Helena also. They both sew pretty well and are now hemming some coarse unbleached towels for Father when he comes home.
>
> I sincerely hope that this is the last winter that we shall be separated. It seems to me now that any station would be pleasant if it were our home & you were with us. … I hope the Florida War will be brought to an end this winter. … You cannot write too often. I would rather go without a good many things and pay it in postage for yr. letters. My mind & heart are with you wherever you go.[24]

Vinton no doubt wanted a final visit with his family, but time did not permit. On 11 December he received word from the Adjutant General's office notifying him "to be in readiness to proceed to Florida at the shortest notice." Acknowledging the order's receipt, he responded, "I shall always be ready for the march with less than six hours notice." Hours stretched into days, and still he continued to wait. Finally, during the last week of December, orders arrived and the company boarded ship, headed for Charleston, South Carolina, where they would await the arrival of other troops before heading for the war zone. Many of the recruits, recent immigrants or men who found it impossible to find a better job, were unhappy to discover where they were going. In a letter to the Adjutant General, Vinton reported, "In spite of all my efforts, the list of Desertions is an uncommonly large one,—and will probably be increased. The Recruits are enlisted with no reference to their probable destination to the Florida frontier … and when they find themselves actually on the way to a Service which is anything but attractive to them, they feel no remorse in releasing themselves from it as soon as possible."[25]

The anxiety of not knowing when the company would depart for Florida was equally frustrating for Lucretia. By the time she received word of her husband's departure date, he would be long gone:

> I wonder where you are this evening—perhaps on the water. How minutely have I read and reread our late *American*, in the hope that among the list of passengers, I might find your departure from the city or among the news & items of the day learn that Capt. Vinton with his company had sailed for Charleston. But all in vain! I have not even the comfort of knowing where you sailed or even if you have sailed, though I

> infer *that*, from not hearing from you again. … I have everything about me to make me grateful & happy, yet it is not like my own dear home, where you were ever present. … How my heart dies within me, when I think of the many long, dreary, months I must spend, before we meet again. It will ever be my constant prayer that we may never, never, be separated again. … I wish you a Happy New Year, my very dear Husband and hope that we may yet enjoy it or a part of it together. All send love to you. May God preserve you & keep you in safety,—prays your very devoted affectionate wife.[26]

By the last week of January 1837, Vinton and Company "B" were in Florida, making their way up the St. Johns River. It had been nine months since he'd first heard he might be going to Florida, and things had certainly not worked out as he thought they would. The luxurious posting at Pensacola had not materialized, and he'd been forced to leave his beloved wife and children behind. It was hard to know what to expect, but little did he imagine that within two week's time he would be engaged in bloody combat with a desperate foe intent on taking his life.[27]

7

The Whistling of Hostile Bullets

By the time Vinton arrived in Florida it appeared as if the war might actually be ending. In the fall of 1836 Florida Territorial Governor Richard K. Call[1] had led yet another unsuccessful campaign against the Seminole. President Jackson, frustrated with the lack of progress, put Maj. Gen. Thomas Jesup in command of the war. The general had acted swiftly against the Creeks in Georgia and Alabama and had thus earned Jackson's confidence. Jesup understood that the Seminole were not going to be defeated in one glorious campaign, as earlier commanders had envisioned. Florida was largely unexplored by whites, and with the exception of Key West, the few major towns were all in the northern portion of the Territory. The majority of the peninsula was the haunt of the Seminole, who knew every path, lake, stream, and hiding place within it. Jesup realized the only way to defeat the Seminole was to wear them down, a process that was going to take a lot of time, men, and material.

Figure 6: Maj. Gen. Thomas Sidney Jesup

When Jesup assumed command in December 1836, he immediately began the construction of forts within the area most heavily populated by the Indians. These forts were generally a day's march apart, very well supplied, and garrisoned by mounted troops that constantly scoured the surrounding area, searching for Seminole villages and farms. Jesup meant to convince his enemy that the government was not going to give up until the Indians surrendered and headed west. He certainly possessed the necessities to get the job done, if such a thing were possible. About half of the regular army was in Florida, along with thousands of volunteers from the neighboring states. Even the navy and marines had sizeable contingents taking part in the war. For the moment, Congress and the administration were willing to spend the money, and Jesup was taking full advantage of the situation.

Jesup's efforts were concentrated in the area between Tampa Bay and present-day Gainesville, primarily in the watery district known as the "Cove" of the Withlacoochee River and the nearby Ocklawaha. This was the area where most of the Seminole lived, and where their best hideouts were. By the end of January 1837, the constant pressure on the natives appeared to be working, and the primary Seminole leader, Micanopy,[2] began to put out peace feelers. On 31 January Jesup met with several of the Seminole leaders and commenced discussions for a cease fire. On 3 February a truce was called.

Vinton, at this early stage, seemed to be enjoying the war. As he told Mother, "Really, thus far, my Southern campaign has been one undeviating course of enjoyment." And why not? He was cruising down the wide, peaceful St. Johns River in a modern steamboat, surrounded by luxuriant foliage and exotic wildlife. It was late January and the weather was perfect, especially when compared to a New England winter. While encamped on 22 January at the outpost of Volusia, he wrote home with the following report:[3]

Figure 7: Seminole Leader Micanopy

> We are now preparing transportation for ascending the St. Johns some 40 to 50 miles farther—say to the upper end of Lake Monroe, to establish there a Depot of provisions for the Army under Gen. Jesup. The Gen. has recently been operating between the Withlacoochee and the Oclawaha [*sic*], pursuing the scattered indians and endeavoring to discover their haunts,—and will probably strike the St. Johns at Lake Monroe in a week or two. … Mellon's[4] Compy. (C. 2d Arty) joined our camp yesterday and will be joined with mine under the command of Col. Fanning[5] for the expedition up the River.
>
> I like the idea of going into the virgin country, hitherto almost unexplored,—certainly unsurveyed,—though Florida is a

region possessing few striking features of landscape and but little diversity. Flat, flat, and swampy, generally wooded with pine or sand barrens but frequently with live oak, walnut, ash, magnolia, & palmetto,—indicative of rich soil, but low & wet. The climate is delicious. I breathe the air as a perfect luxury, especially when reflecting that it is now in the middle of January and all your hills are covered with relentless snows.

The future is as yet unpromising of any special "*Success*" without which I fear there will be no "*Surcease*." For the winter is fast wearing away and as yet nothing accomplished to bring this harassing war to a close. Oseola[6] [*sic*] has everywhere succeeded in all his measures and but for some lucky chance we have no means of bringing him to a general action. By dividing his forces & thus protracting the war he may keep us the pursuing but the discomfited party for an indefinite period of time. We range the few great highways, and drive our Steamboats through the principal rivers of the territory, but the dark dense hammocks & swamps, we cannot traverse, and there the indians can live & establish themselves as in impregnable fortresses, lacking little for supplies and that little furnished almost entirely by the hand of Nature herself.

Should we find Summer upon us and yet no termination to hostilities, the plan will probably be to retire again upon certain healthy positions such as St. Augustine, Fort King and Tampa Bay, and keep them garrisoned strongly to hold the enemy in check until the advent of another winter. And then again another fruitless campaign you will say! But what else can we do but tire out the enemy? Perseverance is all that will do for us, and unless we can exhaust his resources of ammunition &c, I fear Oseola may indeed protract the war to any period he chooses. But still there are hopes. Hopes in the diligence and activity of Gen. Jesup. He has large means now at his disposal, and may possibly hit upon some plan of reaching the women & children of the hostiles, to capture whom will be equivalent to a termination of the war; for even Oseola would not command sufficient influence with the tribes to keep them in arms when their wives & children were captive.[7]

Mail could take anywhere from two weeks to a month to make the trip between Florida and Connecticut, so letters were constantly crossing. An indefinite separation was something new for Lucretia, and she was finding it difficult:

> The mail of today [January 24] has brought me your delightful letter, of Jan'y 5th, 7th & 8th. How happy has it made me! Nothing delights me so much as a letter from you. O! how much I think of you, and how I long, yes *long* to embrace you again. My *last* thoughts at night, my first, in the morning, are of you; and I sometimes find myself trembling with fear, lest this separation should be our final one. But I strive against *all* such fears and do not allow them to interrupt or sadden the calm, even tenor of my way; at any rate, I suppress them before others, and reserve them for my *private* hours.[8]

For the most part Lucretia and Mother were on their own, especially when it came to making decisions in regards to the farm and handling the budget. John could give general or long-term advice, but could do nothing for the day-to-day problems that were bound to occur. Vinton's army salary was adequate, but the family was by no means wealthy. Lucretia was managing, but just barely, and assured him she always had "an eye to economy and at the same time to comfort":

> As well as I can calculate it will cost us 40 dollars a month for mere living, if not more. Whether it will amount to so much in the Summer months I cannot judge. Mother thinks that it has always cost her over 350$ a year to live here, and of course with my family added it will be much more. ... I am much puzzled what to do for a boy or man this Summer & shall not make any definite arrangement till I hear your wishes on the subject. There certainly seems no probability of getting a boy and Mother says we cannot live here without a *male*. ... With regard to large amounts, however, such as buying a horse, or giving 10, 12 or 14 dolls a month to a man, she would not expend them, without my consent. Mother says that *all* the fences are down about the lot and must be put up this Summer. What is it your intention to do in this respect? Shall I have new fences made and other repairs that may be necessary? I wish your sanction for all I do and am ready & willing to do whatever you think is best.[9]

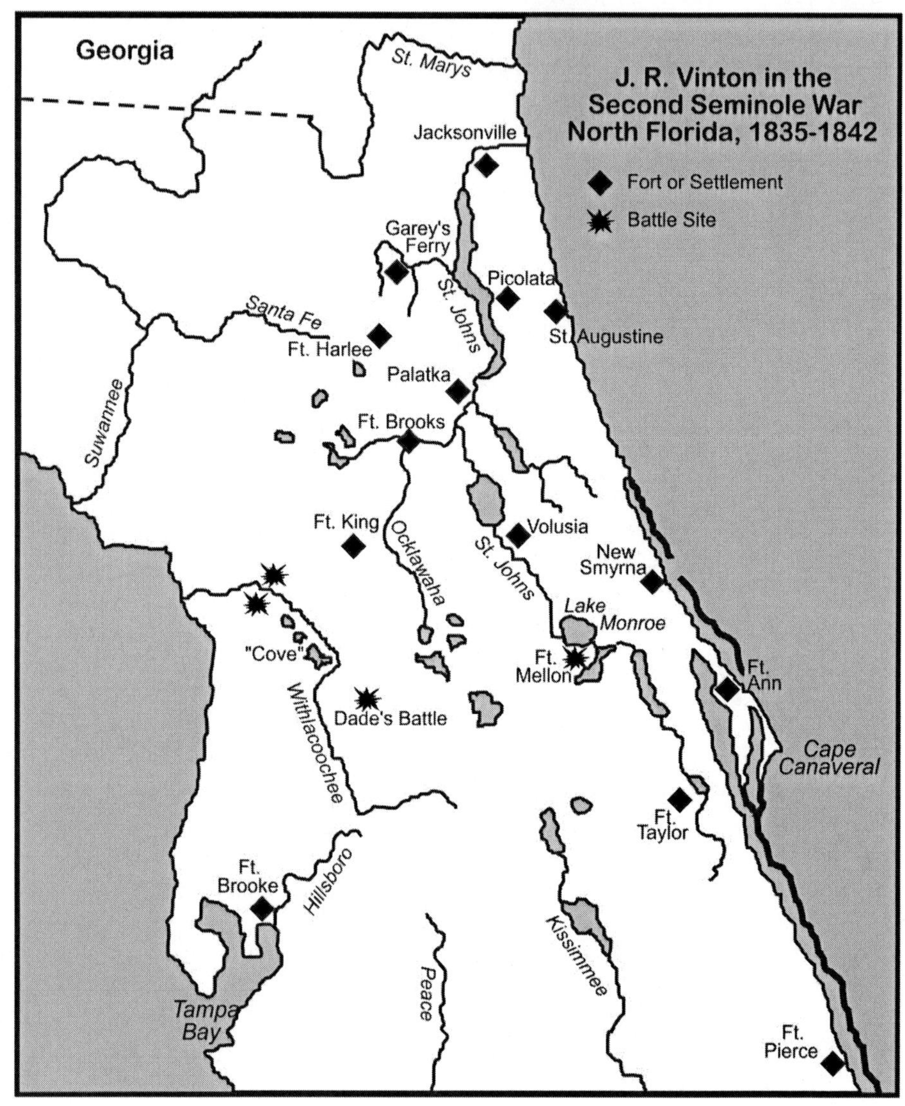

In a letter to Frank, Mother went deeper into some of their financial problems. "Lucretia says, that John utterly refused to hire a man, & if you cannot find us a boy willing to work for his food & raiment, the only alternative will be to dispose of our animals, buy milk & butter, & go on foot." Yet even getting rid of the animals was proving difficult. The old family horse was blind, useless, and eating more hay and oats than she was worth. "I offer'd to sell her for 10 dolls," she added, "but c'd not even *give* her away, except to Mr. Haskill, on condition that she sh'd be knock'd in head, for wh. he said he w'd charge nothing." As for the dog, "She has had a litter of eight puppies, 4 of wh. were dispatched, & 4 given away, after much effort, in the meantime, I had to buy & beg meat for her, as Lucretia & I have no dinner. Shall I give her away, if I can? I have offer'd to *lend* her, several times, to no purpose—nobody as yet, wants her on *any* terms."[10]

Whatever the problems were at home, they were nothing compared to what Captain Vinton and his men were about to go through. General Jesup and the main Seminole leaders may have declared a truce, but the news had yet to reach everyone in the theater of war. Vinton's company, along with several others, had been sent to erect a supply depot on the southern shore of Lake Monroe, one of the larger lakes that formed the St. Johns River system. Upon arrival, Vinton immediately had his men set up a protective breastwork, a low wall made up of horizontal logs. Considering that patrols had seen numerous signs of Indians in the area, it was a prudent precaution.

Building the defenses was a wise move, for in the pre-dawn hours of 8 February 1837, a large force of Seminole attacked the camp, and Vinton, after twenty years in the army, faced his first hostile action. The following day he took time to write an excited letter home to his wife and mother:

> We have at last had a battle with the Indians. I have heard, for the first time in my life, the whistling of hostile bullets. The sensation which I have so long wished to feel of being in a brisk engagement with the enemy Indians all around me, the effects & operations of it, has been experienced. The trial of my nerves during the perilous season, when the very welkin [air] was hissing with the deadly missives shot from the indian rifle—a trial which I have long been anxious to make has been accomplished—and I come out from the ordeal a firmer and a prouder man than I ever felt myself to be before. I have found myself cool and collected in danger and firmly composed for the execution of my duties though on my right hand & on my left my men were falling around me. So much at least I have gained by the battle of Camp Monroe.
>
> It was yesterday morning, just before the peak of dawn that we were aroused by the yells of the Savages and the discharge of fire arms. My men seemed alert and composed, and I felt an increasing confidence in their firmness, as I witnessed how orderly they repaired to their posts and returned the enemy's fire. The four companies of Dragoons were ranged round

the right & front of our camp and the 2 Comp. of Arty. round the left, all defended by a slight barricade of pine logs. The indians wd. not approach us within 150 yards and generally remained beyond a distance of 200. They were able to conceal themselves behind trees and under a low thick growth of palmetto scrub, so that our fire was aimed chiefly at the spots from which we saw issue their smoke. They had the advantage of concentrating their fire on us as to a focus, while ours was necessarily diverging throughout the whole circuit of a semicircle. There was no lack of spirit on either side and for at least the period of three hours the fire continued unceasingly. On board the Steamboat which lay moored opposite our camp some 300 yds. from the shore, was a six pounder which was plied with some effects towards such parts of the woods as seemed to be occupied by the enemy and at every discharge they wd. give a general yell,—whither of defiance or dismay I know not, but most probably of the former.

The number of indians must have been considerable for they occupied a large space of ground and threw into camp a great quantity of lead—probably their number might range from two to four hundred. We made no sally for we knew we cd. do more execution with our shot from our bulwarks than when ranging through the harsh thicket that covered the field in front, besides avoiding the risk of losing the scalps of our wounded. At length the firing ceased on the part of the indians as he fled from all quarters of the field, carrying off their killed & wounded, as our Creek allies afterward discovered they had done by many a bloody token. Our own loss was one killed and eleven wounded—2 or 3 seriously, the rest slightly. The one killed was Capt. Mellon who was shot at the head of his Compy. by a ball which entered his heart. He expired immediately without a struggle. He now occupies the honorable grave of a Soldier near the place where he fell. The most seriously wounded was Lieut. McLaughlin[11] of the Navy, a volunteer upon this service, a gentleman every inch. No other officer was touched. Of my own Company four privates were wounded. ... Another of my men fell close at my side besprinkling my dress with his blood. A ball had struck his head passing through his forage cap and grooving out a channel round his temple without entering his skull. My other men were wounded near me so the danger cd. have been nowhere more rife,—as no company on the ground had so many wounded as mine.

Thus, have I participated in fighting the battles of my country and by breasting the fire of her enemies have repaid the debt I owe her. My first resort, after the action, was to my tent there to pour forth my gratitude to God,—my Refuge & my Strength,—for my preservation amidst so many perils. Join me dear Mother and dear Lucretia in rendering due acknowledgements to our Heavenly Protector for his blessed care and protection.

Figure 8: N.W. view of Fort Mellon, Lake Monroe, E.F., 1837. Sketch by John Rogers Vinton.

The death of Mellon casts a gloom over the Camp. He was a great favorite with all, and leaves, besides other mourners, a wife and 4 children. McLaughlin's case is doubtful. We cannot tell how it will be likely to end until the eighth day. All the rest of the wounded of whom there are ten are doing well and will soon recover. … As I write the St. Boat Jno. [Jonathan] Stoney has arrived from Volusia bringing rare news. A letter from Genl. Jesup, who says he has engaged the Enemy and induced Jumper & Alligator to listen to terms. A grand talk is to be had at Fort Dade on the 18th of this month when the Inds. will be offered pardon & protection if they will abide by the treaty and emigrate. In the meantime a truce is ordered, and we are directed to break up our Camp here and fall back to Volusia. … If the Chiefs Alligator[12] & Jumper[13] are earnest—which many doubt,—they may not succeed in bending the intractable spirit of such as Oseola . …

> Feby. 11th: We shall move back upon Volusia tomorrow and there await the result of the Council of the 18th inst. If the Inds. agree to emigrate we shall have peace at once. If not the war will be continued. Strong hopes are entertained for the best. How glad I shall be that I came to Florida if such be the termination of our campaign. It will take some time to effect the removal of the tribes and the Army will not leave here until all is accomplished. No letter from home yet. Love to all & kisses for the children.[14]

Vinton may have been putting his life on the line for his country, but the government still wasn't willing to part with the $204 retroactive brevet pay the Circuit Court said he was entitled to. Not inclined to give up the effort, the Treasury Department announced they were planning an appeal to the United States Supreme Court. Somewhat vexed at the decision, Vinton wrote directly to the Secretary of War to complain. Part of his argument was that while on duty in Florida, he had no way to defend himself in court:

> I am placed at great disadvantage also, in being so engaged in an active campaign against the enemies of my country as to be unable to attend personally or by council, on the trial of the case, unless the Department shall think proper to order me to Washington for that purpose. As the object of Government cannot be to oppress or weary its officers into submission but only to ascertain what may be a just & legal interpretation of the Statute on which this question rests, I respectfully solicit either that I be promptly so rendered to Washington to answer to the suit when it comes up, or else that the U.S. Attorney may be directed to act as my council and defend my case free of expense to myself.[15]

There is no record of the Supreme Court ever hearing the case, so in all probability the justices were of the same opinion as to the meaning of "retroactive" as the Circuit Court had been, and declined to consider the question.

As Vinton had told Mother and Lucretia, news of the truce reached them the day after the battle. The dispatch also ordered them to abandon the post on Lake Monroe and fall back to the depot at Volusia. For the moment there was nothing for the soldiers to do but wait for news of the talks, which were to take place on 18 February. The Indians, however, were having trouble getting organized, and the negotiations were put off for a month, feeding rumors that nothing would come of the discussions. In a 2 March letter to Mother, Vinton gave his views on the upcoming negotiations:

> We are all waiting very anxiously for news from Fort Dade the place where Gen. Jesup is holding a parley with the Seminoles. Rumours have reached us that no faith is placed in their professions but that the war may soon be renewed. I am more inclined to this opinion than otherwise knowing that the indians have it really in their power to prolong the war indefinitely if *they choose.* Perseverance however is said to be a virtue not distinguished in their character, and it is only by some want of constancy on their part, or other feebleness of character, that they will fail to pursue their cause and their independence. The country is an endless system of defences for them, full of strong holds, almost impregnable. I sh'd soon get tired of the Army if we were compelled to remain long on this kind of business.[16]

The idea of spending several years fighting a hopeless war against the Seminole was not an appealing one to Vinton and many other army officers. Faced with the prospect of being sent to Florida, a record number of officers were resigning their commissions. Many were also lured away by employment as engineers. The Industrial Revolution was gathering steam, and public projects were being undertaken all over the nation. New railroad companies were continually forming, and thousands of miles of track were being laid. Vinton's former brother-in-law George Greene had taken on such a career and quickly became prominent in the field. In his long career, Greene would hold lead positions in the construction of Central Park, the New York City subway and elevated train system, and various major waterworks projects throughout the Northeast. He would also be one of the Union heroes of Gettysburg.[17]

Yet Vinton seemed hesitant about becoming an engineer. It had been twenty years since he'd graduated from West Point, and he may not have felt confident in his technical skills. He was willing to admit it was the one civilian career he was best suited for, but shied away from the idea of taking responsibility for projects that involved large sums of money and were of great public interest. In a letter to Mother he explained:

> I prefer a more limited range of action,—a more moderate sphere of thought, of responsibility and of rewards. I have little covetousness of fame,—little love for worldly associations or honors. … Perhaps while in this Southern Country I may see

> some opening that may induce me to enter on Civil pursuits, even at the expense of a Commission that I have been 20 years in attaining, and which, after all, is the charter of a handsome competency & a great many substantial privileges.[18]

Although Vinton was telling his wife and mother that he was better off in the army, he was also actively pursuing alternative employment in Georgia. On 4 March he sent a follow-up letter to someone he'd talked to in Boston:

> Although I feel myself entirely competent to undertake the principal charge of any Survey of Railroad or Canals, I might from my limited experience of late years, not be, at first, as acceptable to Directors, as would be an Engineer more known to the public. I sh'd not be disinclined therefore to accept a second place, for a limited period, with a salary not less however than about $3000.[19]

Faraway at home, Lucretia was worried for the safety of her husband. Yes, there had only been one fatality at the Battle of Lake Monroe, but it had been Captain Mellon, Vinton's counterpart in a company from the 2nd Artillery. The only man seriously wounded was Lieutenant McLaughlin, a naval officer who had volunteered to fight in Florida. Clearly the Seminole understood the concept of killing a snake by removing its head and were aiming for the officers. Responding to Vinton's report of the battle, Lucretia wrote:

> Oh! I am sick at heart for since the receipt of your last letter describing the battle of Camp Monroe, my fears for you are more alive than ever. It would be impossible, my best beloved Husband, to describe my feelings as I perused that letter. Never before had I realized the danger you might incur and it seemed to burst upon me all at once. You call upon me to unite with you in thanks to the Author of all Good, for His signal preservation of you. Most sincerely, most heartily, do I answer to your wish and praise God for his great mercy to us. Oh! why was Capt. Mellon taken and you left? Was there more reason to expect his fall in the battle than yours? and yet, you are preserved to your family whilst his is left without a head, a protector and father. I tremble whilst I think of it and shall know little rest till I have you once more safe among us. Oh when, when will this terrible warfare be over and we be once more united?[20]

In all her letters Lucretia would eventually return to the one subject she knew her husband was most interested in: the children. Helena was now six and a half, Louise (LuLu) was a few months past her fourth birthday, and Frank Laurens was only nineteen months:

> Our dear little children go on improving. They talk a great deal about Father, particularly Louisa, though I do not know that she *thinks* more about him than Helena. She *shows* her feelings more. They ask often when dear Father will come home, and count the months over and over till autumn. You will find them all grown very much when you return and much more mature. Laurens is getting to be a fine boy—sometimes inclined to be willful but never succeeds in carrying out his will in opposition to mine.[21]

About two weeks later she wrote again. To remind her husband of the joys of home and family, she drew him into the activities:

> Would you like to look in upon us? Well, seat yourself in the parlor, not on the sofa for the children are there, but in the corner there by the stove, then you will be next to Mother, for *there* she sits with her spectacles on, hemming some coarse unbleached towels like those you use. And on the opposite side of the stove sits dear Brother Frank talking with Mother about matters and things at the Seminary. On the sofa are all three of our dear children. Helena and Loulou with their work boxes trying to sew, and little Frank Laurens doing all he can to prevent them. "Mother," says Loulou "look at Laullens, he is stepping on daughter's box." "Laurens get off," says Mother. Off goes Laurens, and as he goes gives Loulou's box a knock and pushes down the cover, "Mother," cries Loulou, "Laully's plaguing me." "Laurens, if you do so again you must come away." So then we have peace for a few minutes, but it is not long before there comes another complaint about "*Laullens.*" But here he comes to my side, rising upon his toes and down again, as he always does when he wishes to be taken up, and saying "up Mamma, up Mamma," so I must take him up and there is an end to my writing for the present—now he is down again, after his sisters, and so it is all day long. … Heigh, ho! What's this noise? Oh Laurens chasing Loulou and trying to get dolly away from her—there "give it to him Loulou" now all is quiet and Laurens has got dolly.[22]

* * *

Back in Florida, Vinton had been ordered to leave Volusia and re-occupy the abandoned depot on the southern shore of Lake Monroe, the site of the battle of 8 February. The temporary log breastwork was replaced by a proper fort and given the name Fort Mellon, in honor of the officer who had been slain in the battle. With the truce in place the Indians took time for a friendly visit to the fort, no doubt observing the strength of the structures, the force of men, and the amount of supplies on hand. The visits also gave Vinton an opportunity to report back to the Adjutant General with additional details on the battle. In a 25 March letter he wrote:

> Two Seminole warriors, bearers of dispatches from General Jesup, have recently visited our camp, and given us information concerning our battle of the 8th Feby. which affords the first authentic account of the Enemy's numbers & loss, that we have received. Their names are Mad Tiger and Black Dirt.—The latter, a nephew of the old friendly chief of that name, was probably, himself engaged in the battle.
>
> In Col. Fanning's Official Report the assumed number of the indians opposed to us, is from three to four hundred. I was happy to say that in this instance at least the official account has not *exaggerated* the enemy's force. It is acknowledged by the Seminoles that *upwards* of 400 were actually engaged,—that Philip[23] had raised all the warriors he could assemble in the eight days preparatory to the fight,—among whom were many of the Micasukies[24];—that a reinforcement of 300 more, were expected, and did actually arrive some 10 or 12 hours after the battle, and that but for the arrival also, of the runner, bearing to them the news of the truce and the treaty, we should have been again attacked with a force exceeding seven hundred. Had this happened, the discomfiture of the enemy would have been not less signal the second time than the first,—as our defences were perfected and our men more than ever anxious for the encounter. From this it appears that Philip had poised all on one great effort to attack & overwhelm us. For once then the indians have been deluded & entrapped. They had early reconnoitered our position, but were not aware of our having subsequently raised breastworks round our camp. This may account for their assurance in coming up so presumptuously to the attack. The morning was foggy,—and long after day had dawned, they did not discover how greatly we had increased

our means of defence. In spite therefore of their own shelter of pines & palmettos, their game of *fusillade* was a losing one. The result is that they lost *fifteen* killed on the field,—and a "great many" wounded. This is the statement given by these Seminoles and not likely to be *over*charged. Another account from the indians in Gen. Jesup's camp, coming to us through Tom Carr[25] is that "We killed and wounded more at the battle of Lake Monroe than they lost in all the previous engagements with the whites since the war."

It is supposed that the general effect of the action in its influence upon existing relations with the Seminoles has been of the happiest character. We have severely punished Philip, the most inveterate & mischievous chief of them all,—and taught to the whole nation a lesson of our power and persevering resolution, to carry the war into the most secret recesses of their country.

I have taken the liberty to offer this as the first approach to what I consider an authentic account of the enemy's force and loss on the field of Camp Monroe. Being in command of the Battalion of Artillery, and the left flank of our line, I was eagerly observing the Enemy with the hope of treating him with the bayonet, (a service that had been promised me by Col. Fanning in the event of its being deemed expedient,) and from the appearance of the enemy in that quarter, my estimate of his numbers has always exceeded that contained in the Official Report. The Colonel's great anxiety, undoubtedly was, to avoid all appearance of exaggeration or vainglory. I trust I may be pardoned therefore in submitting a statement which will acquit him at last of this reputation.[26]

Vinton, as with most soldiers and Seminole warriors in the Territory, was enjoying the truce. For the moment, Florida was a nice place to be, as he related to Mother in early April:

I am on a pleasure excursion,—Steamboating up & down this beautiful river the St. John's. At this favored season of the year in this latitude, it is a perfect luxury to travel through Florida, especially in the comfortable way in which I am indulging. If I were paying thousands for my privilege, I c'd not more enjoy the pleasure of traveling than I do here. Nature, in her forest scenery, has now put on all her pomp of verdure, in colours more splendid than I have ever seen elsewhere,—and the air is so bland & soft yet so invigorating, that even the invalid would rejoice to breathe it. The news from the Army is all good,—Pacific in every feature,—So that our minds are left free to dwell on the poetic & the beautiful without allay.[27]

Figure 9: The *Marion*, Silver Springs, docked. Sketch by John Rogers Vinton.

Vinton was pleased with himself but was a bit miffed by Mother and Lucretia's responses to his report of the battle. Instead of praising him for his heroic actions in the fight, they were begging him to get out of the army. After reading their letter, he protested that:

> I confess I looked in vain for some congratulatory,—some pleasant greetings on the occasion of my having come before the public eye an actor in an engagement which demands much of the public consideration. But your first impulse is [to] discourage me from the calling in which my distinction has been gained. … Did I not declare, on that evening when I paced the room, describing our brother Alex's rising reputation, Hammond's fair fame, and Frank's hopeful perspective of it,—did I not declare that I, too, would strike for a token, and show you that my profession offered a field for renown as well as theirs? … But forgive me. I do not mean to upbraid. … The military is not, I freely allow, altogether germain [*sic*] to my tastes and

> wishes, but really it is as much so as any other vocation or employment I know if. I am continually asking myself the question in what line of life could I be bettered, but I have *not yet* been able to discover a preferable alternative. I love my ease, leisure, respectability, command, and many of my present associations,—For these I sacrifice a house & domicile of my own, town life, fashion, and civil employments. But the sacrifice is not severely felt.[28]

Making a point, he reminded them of the comfortable quarters he and Lucretia had enjoyed in Portland and how both women had grown impatient with his inactivity, imagining it would result in "imbecility." Now their wishes were realized, and they were still unhappy with his station. He then changed the subject and humorously commented on a family friend's suggested plan of subduing the Seminole by giving them no place to hide. "Does he mean to propose to cut down all the forests in Florida?" Vinton asked. "It would require 20,000 men and 20 years at 5 Dolls. a day to accomplish the Doctor's plan. If he had recommended the deposit of a barrel of whiskey on every acre in the territory it w'd prove a more effective and summary process." Vinton knew that "hard fighting" was the only way to win the war. "Every new march increases our information about the country and every new post established furnishes a new Depot of supplies. By gradually encroaching upon the indian settlements, constantly drumming up their quarters, & harrassing their wives and children we have wearied them into submission."[29]

On 18 March 1837 the Seminole leader Micanopy and several other prominent chiefs put their marks to a "capitulation" at Fort Dade on the Withlacoochee River. In theory, the war was over. The Indians had agreed to give up their claims to Florida and gather at Tampa Bay for transport to the West. It sounded too good to be true, and many people believed it wasn't. Few whites had any faith in the sincerity of the Indians, no doubt aware of the fact that the Indians had little faith in the sincerity of the white man. Still, the Seminole began to trickle into the embarkation camp near Fort Brooke at Tampa Bay, raising everyone's hopes that peace had indeed returned. At the same time, people noticed that some of the more intransigent leaders, such as Osceola and the powerful medicine man Abiaki (Sam Jones), [30] were in no hurry to turn themselves in. Doubting their sincerity, Lucretia noted, "When the Indians all come in and the Army is engaged in their actual removal, *then* and not till then, do I intend to indulge myself with the hope that all is at an end. I have been so bewildered lately with my hopes and fears, that I hardly know what to believe. One paper would contain news to encourage me, and the next would overthrow all my hopes and fill me with fears for your safety." She was, without a doubt, missing him terribly:[31]

> I have such a *lonely* feeling without you, as if all my support were taken from me. I hope *never* to be separated from you again. Do not think I am unhappy or murmur at your absence, no, I only feel that I love you above all earthly beings, and desire nothing so much as to be with you. Nothing gives me half the interest it would if you were here to share it with me—there is something wanting in all my enjoyments, a vacancy, that your presence alone can fill. Oh! Say that you will join us soon and that nothing, not even war, shall divide us again.[32]

The thrill of the battle at Lake Monroe was still fresh in Vinton's mind, and on 7 April he penned the following report, giving additional details about the battle:

> Memorandum of a Statement made by Mad Tiger and Black Dirt, 2 Seminole Warriors when they visited our camp while in conversation with Paddy Carr who related it to me.
>
> Philip, the chief of the Tohopekaliga band of Seminoles commanded in person on the morning of the 8th Feby at the attack on Col. Fanning's camp. His residence had never been approached so near by the whites and he exerted himself in assembling all the indians round about for a resolute assault,—hoping to kill half of us by rifle and then to rush in and put us all to death with the knife. With this view he collected upwards of 400 men, chiefly of his own and the Micasuky tribe, under Sam Jones their noted chief.
>
> On the evening of the 7th with these 400 men all was prepared, but many of the principal chiefs advised to wait for a reinforcement of 300 more expected to arrive the next day. The young men however were impatient of delay and the attack was ordered for the following morning. The force was divided into three parties, Philip heading that on our right flank, Sam Jones in front, and a third (name forgotten) on our left. Half an hour before daybreak the signal was given, and yells of encouragement & conventional signals were constantly uttered from one party to the other. It being dark & foggy they came up at first very near to our camp,—the sentinel discovered them, hailed & fired.—The guard were roused and all retired together to the body of the camp. They made great efforts to kill some of our sentinels hoping at least to secure their scalps, but all their shots failed of effect. Not a man was touched. The indians still advanced and continued to pour in a most spirited fire all

round our camp till one crawling on the ground approached so near as to discover our breastworks, cried out "Tohopeka, Tohopeka" (a fort—a fort) this being the first intimation they had had of our having erected breastworks. Their reconnoitering parties had ascertained our position and apparent strength several days previously, but before our breastworks had been raised—so in this matter they were completely taken in. They had also observed tracks of a large scouting party detached from our command and thinking they were still out, hoped to make an easy prey of the reduced numbers who might remain in camp.

But our fire was returned upon them so promptly, from every quarter of our camp, and in such unremitting vollies [*sic*] that they were soon undeceived, and when they became aware of our barricades they immediately withdrew to a greater distance. They kept up their fire at long shot for a considerable time to enable their men to carry off the killed and wounded, until at length a general retreat was ordered. One of the two chiefs was severely wounded (believed to be Philip) and while his men were assisting him to leave the field one of them were killed on the spot. Others were called for to carry off the dead man and in this way the attacking party were much encumbered & delayed. (*The battle lasted three hours.*) Fifteen at least were killed on the field and a *great many* were wounded,—the exact number not recollected.

Not many hours after the battle the expected reinforcement of 300 men arrived and with a force thus increased to more than 700 warriors they designed another attack, on the following night, but the messenger from Micanopy's people announcing a cessation of hostilities arrived about the same time,—and although some of the young men were eager to renew the fight, the chiefs compelled them to respect the mandate from Micanopy and all were ordered to disperse for their homes. They deposited their dead "where the wolves could not get them," discharged 2 or 3 rifles in the air and set out on their respective paths towards every point of the compass. Nothing grieved them more than not to have gained a single scalp. The sentinels at least they hoped to kill, but they all ran in escaping wonderfully the hundred rifle balls that were fired at them.

Thus for these indians. Other accounts from indians in the Camp of Gen. Jesup, especially from Abram[33], state that in this

> battle at Lake Monroe they lost more in killed and wounded than in all the other actions since the breaking out of the war. Had they renewed the attack on the second night they would have suffered still more severely. We had reinforced our breastworks & were otherwise better prepared to meet 800, than 400 on the night preceding.[34]

Like everyone else in Florida, Vinton was looking forward to the official end of the war. In a postscript to a letter accompanying his monthly and quarterly reports to the Adjutant General, he asked, "When are we to move and in what direction? What facilities will be rendered us for bringing our effects and those of the Company from the North? Are there any resignations to be expected among the Captains of the 3d?" At the same time, he and others had their doubts that the war was really over. Observing the attitude of one Indian who came to the fort to sell beef, Vinton remarked to a fellow officer, "The tall old indian who seemed to be a considerable man in his way, impressed us with no favorable ideas of his friendly feelings or those of his tribe, which we suppose to be Philip's! The tenor of his conversation was boastful and caustic, and in short I concluded that if there remained many such men among the Seminoles whose adherence was not secured, we might yet have difficulty in bringing about the issue so much desired."[35]

Lucretia was thankful that her husband had been spared, but was also reflective, and took strength from her faith. She knew all too well that it could just as well have been her husband who'd been slain in the battle, instead of Captain Mellon:

> I have placed myself in Mrs. Mellon's situation, and tried to realize my state under such circumstances. What would have become of me and my little ones if you had been taken away? … The reality of your danger at the battle, my dearest Husband, has proved to me the necessity of being prepared to die, for truly in the midst of life, we are in death. May we both be prepared for it when it comes upon us.[36]

Lucretia then made mention of troubling news from the financial world. "I do not know whether you ever see our papers; if you do, you will have learned what terrible things there are now, in many affairs. Large failures in all our cities, and among them Mr. Crawford Allen[37] of Providence, Sullivan Dorr[38] and Zachariah Allen[39] and it is feared that Philip Allen[40] will fail also. I have not heard of the names of any in New York or Boston and hope that my Father is not among them."[41]

These were not isolated misfortunes. For many years, the American economy had been fueled by foreign investment and rampant speculation in land. Vinton himself was caught up in it with his property in Georgia. The sale of land had become so profitable that for the only time in its history, the United States Government (which was selling much of that land) had managed to pay off the entire national debt. So much money was being made that banks began to issue paper banknotes backed by mortgaged land, not precious metals. People began to get nervous about the situation, including President Jackson, who issued what was known as the "Specie Circular." The policy stated that the government would henceforth accept only specie (gold or silver) for payments due, which helped trigger a run on gold and silver as people began to call in their debts. The "Panic of 1837" ensued, in which hundreds of banks failed and the speculative bubble burst. Much like in the financial collapse of 2008, nearly everyone suffered to some extent. A good many people, including the well-off, lost everything. Lucretia wrote, "Father speaks of the terrible times in New York, and hopes he shall escape without utter ruin though. We expect to suffer greatly." Even Vinton, with his guaranteed army pay, would not be immune.[42]

On the brighter side, it still appeared as if the war might be ending. On 26 April Vinton wrote to Mother, telling her the latest news:

> When I wrote to Lucretia, a few days since, I said we had received as yet no cattle from the indians, nor other very tangible proofs of their determination to abide by the terms of the capitulation,—But since that time a herd of thirty-two have been driven in, and we have more reason to believe from other tokens,—such as the coming in of several women & children, &c,—that peace is surely and definitely concluded on. Yet we must, after all, wait upon the motions of the indians, who are proverbially the slowest of the animated creation,—and cannot thus expect to make good that provision of the treaty which fixes a time for their assembling at Tampa Bay & their departure thence. Gen. Jesup knows that he has no power of coercion and unless he allows the Seminoles all the time they ask, they will in all likelihood, become refractory and break away from their engagements. It is therefore best for us to content ourselves with the lesser evil and endure the detention rather than cause a renewal of hostilities.[43]

As agreed to in the treaty, the Seminole began to come in to Fort Mellon to sell their cattle to the government prior to deportation. There were, nevertheless, a few problems. One had to do with the hundreds of runaway slaves living among the Indians. The capitulation had called for the Indians to turn all the fugitive blacks over to the authorities, but the blacks, with good reason, were doing all they could to avoid being returned to slavery. There was also the problem of location. The Seminole were supposed to be gathering at Tampa Bay, not at the St. Johns. As Vinton informed Mother:

> Indians are flocking in for provisions in great numbers.—We have in one pen already 150 cattle and more coming in every day. The Chiefs Coa Haijo [Coa Hadjo][44] and Tuskehenehaw have had a talk with our Col. and the son of King Philip [Coacoochee, or Wildcat][45] is a resident near our lines—inhabiting one of our tents. So we are confident mutually of peace & harmony. With these manifestations I can no longer doubt of a pacific issue to all these troubles, though it will necessarily be delayed beyond the time first appointed. Any thing for peace however! The getting in the Negroes will be a difficult & dangerous job for the indians but they are determined to deliver them up according to the treaty. We hear from Tampa that Genl. Jesup is disapp'd at the delays of the indians. The vessels that have been engaged to transport them have been there for some time & their daily charge for demurrage amounts to more than 4,000 dollars. The Genl. has calc'd the cost per day of the present means employed in this war and finds it to be near 25,000$. He will propose to the chiefs I hope, 2 or 3 days stipend at this rate, as a gratuity if they will hasten on their people 5 or 6—& so save large sums by the bounty.[46]

In the meantime, Vinton continued to gather reports about the Battle of Lake Monroe. In his letter book for 27 April he made the following memo:

> Coa Haijo, a Seminole Chief, avowed to Paddy Carr today that he was present at the battle here (8th Feby) and that the number of indians engaged was <u>560</u>! He is a Superior Chief to Philip and, if present, must himself have commanded on that occasion. He relates other details of the battle,—mostly coincident with former accounts. Acknowledged the number killed to be at least as much as we have been told and intimated that it was still larger. Coa Haijo adds that many of our balls struck the indians without entering beyond the skin,—that many were not driven out of the cartridge paper which enveloped them, but were taken up by the indians with the paper still tied round. A

> proof this that our men only half loaded their muskets,—spilling their powder in their haste to charge.[47]

With his duties at Fort Mellon about to end, Vinton was notified of a new assignment. Brig. Gen. Walker Armistead[48] had been appointed second-in-command to General Jesup and given control of the northern and eastern portions of the war zone. Vinton, in turn, had been appointed Armistead's Inspector General, but wasn't sure if he was pleased with the assignment or not. "This appt. is one of honor merely, though involving some hard service—especially in writing, which I do not much like. Still I shall see more of the country than by remaining here, and somewhat more of men." To some degree, it didn't matter. It was now the end of April 1837, the war appeared to be over, and the future might take him anywhere, whether he decided to stay in the army or not.[49]

8

The War is Finished ... The War is Not Over Yet

As the spring of 1837 progressed, Captain John Rogers Vinton could be forgiven if he felt as though his life were in limbo. Due to transportation problems, he was stuck at Fort Mellon and unable to take up his new duties as an Inspector General. At least he had time to take care of some personal business, part of which included finalizing the purchase of a number of lots in Columbus, Georgia, a transaction had been dragging on for about two years. His original intention had been to buy a block of lots, but there had been some difficulty securing proper title to a portion of them. The problem had been resolved, and the economic depression had forced the seller to drop his price, so Vinton was moving forward with the deal. Still, he would have preferred to sell what he already owned, as he informed the lawyer in Columbus, "This is farther than I intended to go, as property in Columb. will decline with the fall of cotton &c—but being once in the scrape I know of no better way of getting out of it than buying off a bad partner."[1]

The Seminole had signed an agreement to give up the fight and emigrate to the West, but it was going to take time for them to dispose of their cattle and gather at the embarkation camp near Fort Brooke at Tampa Bay. In the meantime, all Vinton and the other soldiers could do was sit and wait.

Vinton was ready to get out of Florida, but he was going nowhere until the Indians departed. Still, things looked promising. On 3 May he noted in his letter book, "Coi Harjo [Coa Hadjo], Tuskehenehaw, Wildcat (Philip's son) and Powell [Osceola], came in the P.M. from the Council. Pleasant talk from them. Many indians collected & cattle,—but some remain to be sought out which will require time. Perhaps a week more thinks Coi Harjo. Powell's appearance is favorable,—his professions all pacific."[2]

With no one really sure if the war was truly over, General Jesup thought it might be a good time to have the men do some topographical work. If something should go wrong and the war resume, at least the army would have better maps of the unexplored territory. Vinton was eager to take on the task and also saw an opportunity to make a trip north. Writing to the general's aide, he said:

> I have for sometime past entertained a project for the exploration of the sources of the St. John's & laying down its principal features by Astronomical determinations, but had allotted no time earlier than next winter for entering upon the task. ... I

> have a portable azimuth and altitude circle of my own in Boston, which w'd be admirably adapted to this purpose,—and could procure a chronometer probably from Washington or N. York—if the General should see fit to order me to the North for these purposes.[3]

Vinton then took the opportunity to report on the progress of the Indians in turning themselves in. As far as he could determine, things were going as well as could be expected.

> We have been visited today by Coi Harjo, Powell, Tuskeenehaw and Wild Cat [Coacoochee], with other chiefs and a great many indians of both sexes. Powell treated us with a fine ball play by his young men and his Chiefs have just returned from a Council, held not many miles from this, and express themselves confident of bringing in all the indians who are now much scattered, if they are allowed time to do so. … Their people were spread over an immense extent of territory and became more wildly scattered by sinister reports which no one could have anticipated or provided for. … In the meanwhile the success of the Chiefs in gathering their people in one grand communion here, is remarkable. Their cattle too are collected in great numbers, now appropriated by them for their daily subsistence but ready to be driven in here when they set out for Tampa. …

He then pointed out that although the Indians appeared willing to emigrate, they by no means considered themselves beaten. "In view of all these considerations it is to be recollected that they are in one sense an unsubdued people,—impelled by no positive military coercion, nor otherwise influenced but by the calculations of expediency." He continued with the letter, saying:

> If I am deceived in the earnest anxiety of Coa Harjo to fulfill his promises to you,—in the frank, confiding abandoning spirit manifested by Powell,—the bold & unequivocal concurrence of young Coa-Coochy,—the ready compliance & vigorous cooperation of John Hicks,—and withal the unlimited confidence they place in us by suffering their women & children to come in and lie about our camp at will,—If with all these tokens, added to that uniform expression of honesty which sits upon the countenance of every chief without exception, we still can be deceived,—then is this the most stupendous piece of dup-

> ery that the world has ever seen I am willing to take the cast of the die. The war is finished. The Seminole Nation will emigrate, though a hundred little accidents might yet occur to hinder and delay them.

He then offered his observations of Osceola, the most charismatic of the Seminole leaders and the man most whites considered the primary instigator of the war. He also helped clarify Osceola's position within the Seminole tribe. Most uninformed whites considered him the chief, while his fellow Indians and whites who were familiar with the Seminole regarded him merely as a gifted orator and powerful war leader:

Figure 10: Osceola, right-profile. From a sketch by John Rogers Vinton.

Figure 11: Osceola at Lake Monroe, 1837. Sketch by John Rogers Vinton.

Powell or Uscin-Yahola as the chiefs pronounce his name, is certainly a man of high consideration. Whatever may be said of his subordinate grade in the list of Seminole Chiefs, his power & influence is obviously acknowledged by them. He is unre-

> mitting in his attention to the wants & interests of his men and in return receives from them an unqualified personal devotion. I doubt if the commands of Micco Nopy or his Council could invalidate his authority over the tribe of which he is the leader. His adhesion is therefore his own individual act,—and I believe is determinately fixed by the dictates of his own good sense & mature judgment.[4]

A few days later Vinton wrote another letter to Jesup, expanding on his observations and perhaps trying to allay fears they both might have had:

> Being on the eve of my departure for Genl. Armistead's Head Qrs. and feeling persuaded that even my own humble views of the existing state of our affairs with the indians may in some sort tend to relieve your mind from anxiety, I make bold to address you directly and with a freedom which I beg may be attributed to the peculiarity of the conjecture,—and pardoned.
>
> The assemblage of so large a number of indians in this vicinity may have been surprising to you as it certainly was to us, as our vigilance has never been relaxed, we have been curious even to suspiciousness of every circumstance that might bear a sinister aspect. We have wondered that cattle were not driven in in greater numbers,—that nothing definitive was heard of the negroes—& in short that the Seminoles sh'd loiter in this neighborhood at all when Tampa Bay was the only constituted Point of Rendezvous. We have considered that if their plan were really to beguile us and protract the campaign into the Summer months they could not adopt a more skillful course of policy than exactly the one they are now pursuing. But after a full & repeated conference with the Chiefs & much fair association with them and their chief warriors, we have been compelled to dismiss all doubt of their sincerity & believe that they are determined to carry out the provisions of the Treaty & a faithful consummation. …
>
> They have delayed already much beyond your expectations and still ask for more time,—and we are now to consider the reasons they urge for it. When a period was fixed for their rendezvous at Tampa, it was calculated on the supposition that the Chiefs could readily notify their people and secure their obedience. … It is obvious too that the delivery of the negroes will be a difficult task for them to accomplish perhaps impossible

> at the full extent and on all accounts we must make up our minds for still a protracted sojourn still in Florida.[5]

Vinton then added a postscript, expressing unexpected concerns for the fort's safety. "P.S. The indians are assembled in our vicinity in large numbers,—perhaps larger than at any other point, or time heretofore. Our own force on the other hand, was never so small. Should not a company or two be added to the garrison?"[6]

By 20 May 1837 Vinton had at last left Fort Mellon and assumed his position as Inspector General for General Armistead, a position he had neither sought nor particularly looked forward to. The army in Florida had gotten so large that it had become necessary to divide it into two divisions, and Armistead had been placed in charge of the northern division. With greater size came greater opportunity for inefficiency and outright fraud. It was the Inspector General's task to visit the various commands, note any irregularities, and report them to his superiors. For commanders who were lax in performing their duties or merchants who were attempting to defraud the government, a visit from the Inspector General was the last thing they wanted.

Vinton's station now moved to Garey's Ferry, a major depot on Black Creek, a tributary of the St. Johns River southwest of Jacksonville. It was a place where boats bringing supplies from the north would offload their cargoes, and where those supplies would be stored before being distributed to the various posts throughout Florida. It was also the obvious place for an Inspector General to look for inferior quality products, spoiled food, and shortages in the amount delivered.

One of the first things Vinton did after settling in was to send out several letters exploring the possibility of employment in the civilian sector. He had begun to find army life tedious, and having fought the Battle of Lake Monroe, felt his debt to the nation had been paid. One of the letters went to an old friend from his early days in the army, William McNeill. His stated reason for seeking civilian employment seems to have come from rumors that he might be transferred to the Texas frontier:

> If you have heard of the intention of Govt. to order the Arty Regts to the Sabine frontier, you will not be surprised to hear also of my determination to quit a Service which can be rendered thus disagreeable to me. I was more than half minded before I heard this news to leave the mily for civil employments and even now fairly weaned from a vocation to which from habit more than from affection I have been so long at-

> tached. In looking about among the various pursuits of civil life, I find none so congenial to my tastes and talents as Civil Engineering. This you know as well as I do,—and more than this, you have it in your power to promote my views so far as to enable me to embrace it as my future profession on terms both favorable to my interests and compatible with my dignity. . . . [7]

The following day, 21 May, found Vinton in St. Augustine, destined for Charleston, where he arrived two days later. One of his duties as Inspector General was to handle the mustering out of the state Volunteer and Militia forces that were no longer needed. Unfortunately, the Paymaster didn't have any money, so he and Vinton took passage on a steamboat to the nearest city where they could procure the necessary funds. While there he took the opportunity to conclude the purchase of the lots in Columbus and to make further contacts concerning possible employment, even going as far as writing to Georgia Governor William Schley.[8]

Vinton may have longed to leave the army and pursue a civilian career, but as he spoke to people in Savannah and Charleston, he began to realize just how insulated he'd become from the realities of the economic downturn. From the perspective of a soldier in Florida, not much had changed since the market collapse. Florida was still a wilderness far removed from the national economy, and expensive supplies still kept pouring into the war zone. The visit to the Southern cities opened his eyes to what was actually happening. As he wrote to Mother:

> In the meanwhile however, such is the terrible condition of the money market, that half of the RRds in the country are suspended and Engineers in abundance are out of employment, diminishing my chance of course. …
>
> With regard to Civil Engineering I have still my doubts whether I w'd do well to abandon my commission for it. The uncertainty of all situations is great compared with that of a Cap'y [Captaincy] in the Army which remains a steady & respectable post when almost every other in the range of civil pursuits is shaken or ruined. … The all prevailing distress, now everywhere seen is truly melancholy. Even in the humblest avocations of Civil life men are complaining bitterly of the times—and no one knows how much he is worth or whether on the morrow he may be worth anything. The economy being unsettled the value of all property is altogether hypothetical,—and they who like us have a fixed income will now find by the

> increased value of money that they at least are benefited by the present state of the times. ...[9]

Due to the long transit time for the mail, Lucretia had no idea Vinton was beginning to question his decision to possibly leave the army. To her, his impending resignation was the best news possible:

> Never have your letters given us more pleasure—Can you guess why? Because you speak of your desire and intention of leaving the Army. You know I have always liked our Army life, and have never favored any thoughts of a speedy resignation, but the case is now altered in many respects. ...
>
> The Army was pleasant, whilst we were together, but if we must be separated, it is far otherwise. Another winter without you! No, I cannot, cannot consent to it. The Army is no place for you truly, if such are to be its sacrifices.[10]

By 16 June, his 36th birthday, Vinton had other things to worry about besides finances and a future career. The peace agreement with the Seminole had fallen apart, and the war was on again. The Indians had been gathering at Tampa Bay for embarkation to the West, but on the night of 2 June they abandoned the camp and fled back to the wilds. The reasons were numerous, and often nothing more than conjecture. The Seminole later said it was because disease had broken out in the camp. They had also been complaining of the constant harassment from slave catchers trying to make off with the Black Seminole among them. Whites, on the other hand, immediately decided the Indians had never intended to emigrate and had only been buying time, using the truce to recuperate, gather supplies, and move into new hideouts. There was no doubt some degree of truth in all of it.

Vinton had seen it coming. In a letter to his mother dated 1 June, he said, "The Indians do not intend to come in; they have planted corn & intend to eat it. I sh'd not wonder if hostilities sh'd break out again next fall, or even before. The war is not over yet—much as I sh'd like to get rid of the Army, you see we sh'd starve, but for my pay—all civil pursuits are dead except farming."[11]

Perhaps the person who was most upset by the turn of events was General Jesup. All his hopes for ending the war had been built upon the Seminole keeping their part of the bargain. He now felt betrayed and offered to resign his command. The Secretary of War turned down the proposal, knowing there was simply no one better suited to continue the war. If nothing else, the whole affair served to harden Jesup's attitude toward the Indians. From this point forward, he would no longer negotiate with the Seminole. He issued orders that if any of them came in under a flag of truce it would be to surrender, not to talk, and they would be immediately taken prisoner. In a letter to Mother, Vinton explained the situation:

> Things have lately assumed an aspect by no means favorable to a speedy termination of our campaigning, though fresh hostilities have not yet occurred. The Indians decline removing *until fall* they say,—and thus have proved themselves faithless to their engagement and unworthy of our future confidence. By placing themselves thus *in the wrong*, they give new strength to our cause,—and if we open upon them again next winter I think we shall not halt until we compel them to unconditional submission.[12]

Vinton was still hoping to make a trip home, but realized his chances had diminished. Assuming peace was at hand, the army had allowed many officers to take furloughs for the summer, leaving precious few experienced leaders in Florida and making it unlikely Vinton would be granted leave. There was still the possibility Jesup would send him north to retrieve his astronomical instruments, but with hostilities resumed, the topographical work was not a priority. Without such orders, Vinton would have to pay for the trip himself, which was an expense he could ill afford at the moment. Still, he would do what he could. "Money cannot purchase a more valuable gratification than a fresh sight of my dearest & best beloved Mother, wife & children,—and so I shall not cease in my efforts to go North this summer if it be only for a month."[13]

For the moment, the only sort of leisure he could expect was a short stay in St. Augustine. Describing his first impressions of the Ancient City in a letter home, his observations might not have been that different from a present-day tourist's:

> This is my first visit to St. Augustine. It is a place of considerable reputation and I presume when I become acquainted with the Society—I shall see something to fill out the idea I had formed of it,—but thus far I am disappointed. Although recently from the woods and my mind favorably disposed for pleasant contrasts, I cannot say that St. Augustine has justified the impressions I had entertained of it. There is no street in the place wider than the meanest lane in Boston,—and the buildings, though generally of incombustible materials (a kind of shell rock) have all the look of dilapidation & decay. Historic recollections, which are the principle attributes of its celebrity, give to St. Augustine a romantic interest to the stranger who

> sees in the ancient fort,—the Catholic Cathedral,—and the repudiated Nunnery,—now turned into Barracks,—evidence of foreign origin and Roman ecclesiastical dominion. Then, for one so long shut up in the pine woods of this interior as I have been, the salt sea & the ocean breeze are luxuries of even greater present interest than the romantic sentiments that hang about the ruined metropolis of Florida.[14]

The visit to St. Augustine gave Vinton time to reflect on his career, and he began to come to the realization that he might not be cut out for civilian life, as he wrote in a letter to Mother:

> After all I cannot conceive of a profession I sh'd like so well as the Mily if I c'd be restored to a union with my family. Even campaigning has its pleasures,—incompatible, to be sure, with domestic enjoyments, but only so during the term of absence necessarily incident to it. In the present prospects before us this may be, of long duration or not as the case may be,—still I know of nothing better just now, that I can exchange for it. One of these days I may be rich enough to take a farm near some pleasant town and live independently, but as things are now I must content myself with the lot in which Providence has placed me.[15]

For the present, the war seemed to be on hold. Although the Seminole had fled the embarkation camp, the army made little effort to pursue them. It was summer and the climate simply wouldn't allow a sustained military campaign. The news from home was mixed. Vinton's older brother Maine had returned from New Orleans, only to arrive in Boston suffering from typhoid fever. Lucretia and Maine's wife Frances immediately traveled to Boston and brought him home to Providence to convalesce.[16] The other Vinton men were doing well. Hammond was on Quartermaster duty at Tallahassee, the Territorial capital. Alex was well established in his ministry in , and Frank was about to finish his theological training at the seminary in New York. All their career paths seemed fairly well settled.

Except for John. When he had been stationed in his native New England with his wife and family close at hand, the army seemed the perfect career. The war in Florida had changed all that, and he was now ready to leave the military. Unfortunately, the Panic of 1837 and the resulting economic depression made such a move impossible. The engineering positions he was best suited to had disappeared and nothing else looked promising. Then another possibility presented itself, inspired by the earlier letter from Lucretia. On 16 July, Vinton wrote Mother from St. Augustine, telling her that while he still hoped to make a trip home, if that fell through he had an alternative option:

> This is nothing less than a plan to resign my commissis'n in Oct'r and enter the Theol'l Seminary. I have pondered over this subject for some months. While in the depths of the Florida forests I have communicated with my Maker in a spirit more solemn and exalted than usual.—I have asked for His divine counsel ... and I have been truly led providentially into a train of thought, ending in conviction, that the Army is indeed no place for me, and therefore ought not remain any longer in it than may be necessary to secure our affairs from wreck in case I sh'd abandon my commission. Other considerations, however, presented themselves as obstacles to such a serious measure as this. ... In this dilemma I saw no prospect of a favorable change to civil pursuits until I rec'd a letter lately from Lucr. suggesting the very thing that most accords with all my feelings. "Why not" she says "follow in the footsteps of Alex & Frank? I will most cheerfully live through the probationary years at La Plaisance or anywhere else,—and under every privation, to ensure so desirable a result!"—This determined me. In this I saw the finger of God. The remarkable coincidence of her own conversion and my own final, fixed determination to give myself up to God, convinced me that the fullness of time had come or was at hand.—And now for the first time in my life do I feel that there is a profession which I could resort to with perfect satisfaction,—where my mind would have ample scope for its exercise and enlargement, and where my heart might warm and glow with the congenial spirit in which I sh'd employ my faculties,—doing the will of my Heavenly Father in promoting the great cause of Religion & Morality among men. ...[17]

Vinton sounded firm in his decision, but the more he wrote, the less positive he appeared to be. The letter also revealed that he was no longer serving as an Inspector General, but had been placed in command of one of the numerous Florida forts:

> ... but I am not yet decided that this program, so delightful in vision, can ever be soon consummated in reality. I know that I have intellectual powers that ought to be turned to better purpose than any which calls for their exercise in the Army,—I

> can write & speak with fluency & my friends say, with power,—Unite these attributes with my metaphysical & religious turn of mind,—my perfect contempt for the world's pleasures, my love for my species & my desire to become a Servant of the Cross and the story is well nigh told. There only remains the doubt of my physical ability. … I might add the doubt of my being able at this late day to learn Greek & Hebrew, but I can labor for that & shall not despair of acquiring those languages at last. What think you Dear Mother am I too old?
>
> As to my resigning immediately that is not expedient as I have debts to my Compy. & to Gov't. which I can only pay by longer service. I am just now in Com'd of Fort Harlee, 25 miles from Black Creek & draw double rat's [rations] which it is desirable I sh'd hold as long as I can. Still by the last of the month I hope to set out for the North. … How to reconcile this with entering the Seminary in Oct. I know not—can one enter at any time subsequent to Oct.? If not I may find it best to delay a year,—pass the winter in Florida and next summer at Pomfret. But this will throw me back a year in my studies—I can get through in three years however, and in the meantime might be learning Greek & Hebrew. These are the doubts that perplex me. I shall be governed by circumstances as indications of the Divine Will.[18]

The final line quoted above is an example of a character trait that shows up throughout Vinton's life. Whenever faced with a difficult decision, he generally waited for events to play out, thereby providing a "sign from God" that justified whatever course of action he took.

July and August came and went, and still Vinton waited for orders to proceed north to retrieve his astronomical equipment. When September arrived he became even more anxious to begin the trip. Active campaigning could resume as soon as October, and once that started, leaving the war zone would be almost impossible. He had sent several letters to Jesup reminding him of the promise to send him north, but nothing had come of it.

The uncertainly of his plans for going north and the slowness of the mail delayed some important and tragic news from home. On 21 September Lucretia wrote:

> Your letter of the 1st of September was received yesterday, and is now before me and I take the earliest opportunity to reply to it. Frank wrote to you not long since and I sent a long letter to you not many days after, both of which I hope you have re-

ceived before this time. They informed you, my dearest Husband, that the sickness of our dear Brother Maine terminated fatally. … Poor Sister Frances was in very great affliction and refused to be comforted for a long while. She is more like herself now and has recovered her cheerfulness in a measure. Their farm is advertised for sale and it is Frances's intention to remove to Providence about the 1st of December. …

I cannot bear to think of being separated from you another winter, yet not my will, but thine O Lord, be done, I am ready to submit if it be so ordered. As it respects the ministry, my dear Husband, do not give up the thoughts of it yet. Have you not the requisites to make a good minister? You believe that your heart has been changed by the influence of the Holy Spirit. This is the most important requisite surely—You have talents also, and I see no reason why you should be discouraged.[19]

Whatever dreams or wishes Vinton and Lucretia shared, they were all subject to the realities of having to earn a living and support the family. For the foreseeable future, the army was the only viable employment available, and with the winter campaign drawing near, all other matters would have to be put aside.

9

It Is My Intention to Resign My Commission

October 1837 slipped into November and Vinton gave up any hope of going home for a visit with the family. In a letter to Frank, Lucretia said, "He has given at last the death stroke to my long cherished hope of seeing him this winter. He gives his reasons for thinking it best to remain in Florida this winter and certainly they are very urgent ones. He thinks his time is spent as profitably to himself there, as far as preparing for the ministry is concerned, as it would be here, and as he cannot enter the Seminary till next October he seems to think he had better not resign till the Spring."[1]

Vinton may have decided to leave the army come spring, but he was still a man dedicated to doing his duty while he retained his commission. Men and supplies were pouring into Florida for the upcoming campaign against the Seminole. Half of the entire regular army, about 3,500 soldiers, would be in Florida. State volunteers and militia units from as far away as Missouri would swell the total force to approximately 9,000 men. The navy was buying and building a small fleet to patrol the coastline and penetrate the rivers. This time the government was holding nothing back.

The army was preparing for an all-out campaign against the defiant Seminole, but Jesup seems to have been having second thoughts. It was going to be an expensive operation, both in terms of men and material, and perhaps it wasn't necessary. The army had captured some of the most important Seminole leaders and may have felt the time was right to make a deal with those who remained at large. Safely imprisoned in Fort Marion, the old Spanish fortress at St. Augustine, were Micanopy and King Philip, two of the foremost leaders of the nation. In the cells with them were Philip's son Coacoochee, Coa Hadjo, the Black Seminole leader John Cavallo, and the most notorious Indian of them all, Osceola.

Jesup may also have wanted to salvage his own reputation. With the exception of Philip, all these men had been taken prisoner while negotiating under a flag of truce. Many Americans were appalled at the practice and were vilifying Jesup for instituting it. The general could argue that since the Seminole had broken their promise to emigrate earlier in the year they had forfeited their right to any further negotiations, but many people weren't accepting such an explanation. As far as they were concerned, the honor of the nation had been compromised. Jesup possibly felt that if he could bring the war to a swift conclusion without a major campaign, people might decide that his decision had been a good one.

Negotiating an end to the war was a change in strategy Jesup appears to have been hesitant to suggest, knowing it was going to be a tough sell in Washington. The Seminole people were no less defiant than when the war had begun, despite many of their primary leaders having been taken out of action. The government, on the other hand, was no less adamant when it came to giving in to the wishes of any Native American tribe, especially one that had proven so embarrassing to the army and the administration. Jesup believed that if the Indians were to confine themselves to the uninhabitable southern portion of the peninsula, peace might be achieved. It was certainly worth suggesting to the War Department. Yet it would take more than a letter to convince the President and Secretary of War of the wisdom of such a move. It was going to take personal pleading. With preparations for the campaign underway, Jesup could not leave the theater of war. He would have to send someone he trusted, someone who knew the workings of the War Department and was well respected by the people in power. The obvious choice was Captain Vinton, a seasoned officer who had once served as aide to the commanding general.

All of a sudden Vinton was on his way north. It was no doubt a confidential mission, much like his earlier trip to Georgia in 1827. For the most part, he made no mention of the mission to anyone but Jesup. He appears to have left Florida around 11 November 1837 and arrived at Washington on 20 November, where he went immediately to the War Department.

Secretary of War Joel Poinsett read Jesup's letter and listened to Vinton's arguments, but remained unconvinced. Afterwards, Vinton worked on a letter to Jesup, the draft of which is in his letter book. Much of it is crossed out, and one can easily imagine him going through several sheets of paper before getting it right. Precisely what he sent is not recorded, but it must have been something similar, informing the general that the trip had been a wasted effort. Vinton walked away from the meeting with the realization that the government was still intent on driving every last Seminole from Florida. As Vinton put it, "emigration is still the *Sine Quo Non* [without which, nothing] with the Govt." In other words, without total removal, the war would not end. Vinton went on to explain Poinsett's position and his own personal view of the situation:

> In short in this as in all their points alluded to in the course of our long conversation, I found the Secy strongly disposed to accord to you every faculty and all possible freedom in the exercise of your judgment in conducting the campaign. He desired me to say to you personally that you possessed his entire confidence & good wishes.

> Much however as the Govt. desires peace with the Seminoles, I see no indication of the slightest change of policy. In the course of my argument I think I brot [brought] the Secy to a serious doubt as to the propriety of pursuing it,—for he was reduced to this sole reply, "I am not my own master in this business—we are compelled to go on."
>
> Thus, my dear Genl, there seems to be a fatality in this business, urging us forward even in spite of justice and our better reason. All eyes are upon you therefore,—and everybody hopes that the Army will achieve miracles.[2]

His mission finished, Vinton then made the much-delayed journey home to wife and family. Mother was surprised and thrilled by the visit, as she related in a letter to Frank:

> I trust you are deeply impressed, as I am, with the continual goodness of God, & now with this new manifestation of it in the return of our dearly beloved John. … My fears have been very, very great that I sh'd never see him. The perils to wh. he was exp. [exposed], war, pestilence, fire & flood … affected me deeply & I was daily exercised for the state of preparation to the will of God if it sh'd be his holy pleasure to chastise me, ever again. But adored be His goodness! My Son is not only given to me in bodily health, but I receive him, born again, in Christ, of the Holy Spirit! …
>
> I shall see very little of John. He left me, with Lucretia, last Monday, for Boston via Providence. I expect them home tomorrow after wh. he intends to remain here but one day more.[3]

By the first of January 1838 Vinton was in Savannah, headed back to Florida. As he later told Jesup, "I have hurried my return to Florida (having remained with my family but three days) and expected to have joined you a month ago, but have been detained by various impediments, among which were two storms at sea (by each of which we were driven off into the gulf stream) and necessary delays at Charleston & Savannah waiting for Steam boats."[4]

By the time he got to Florida, the fighting was nearly over. Jesup had commenced operations in December, dividing his force into seven columns that would scour the peninsula from top to bottom and relentlessly drive the Seminole toward the inhospitable Everglades. As the army moved south, many Indians were captured or forced to surrender. The campaign seemed to be having the desired effect.

On Christmas Day 1837 the Seminole made a stand along the north shore of Lake Okeechobee. About 350 warriors took up position in a dense, wooded hammock that was fronted by a wide sawgrass swamp. Among them were the leaders Coacoochee and John Cavallo, recently escaped from the prison at St. Augustine. Coming at them was a force of about 850 soldiers led by Col. Zachary Taylor. By the end of the day the army had forced the Seminole to retreat, but not before the Indians had inflicted severe casualties on the American forces, effectively putting about half of them out of action for several weeks. It was the fiercest battle of the war, and it had ended in a draw.

Several weeks later two more battles were fought near Jupiter Inlet on the East Coast. One was a clear victory by the Seminole over a combined force of sailors and soldiers under Lt. Levin Powell of the navy, whose patrol had stumbled upon a large Indian camp. The other was an indecisive battle along the Loxahatchee River with the same group of Seminole, this time fought by General Jesup and a large part of his army. The battles turned out to be the last major actions of the war.

In February General Jesup, at the urging of his senior officers, again tried to convince the War Department that it was time to end the war. Most of the Seminole had surrendered or been captured, and the remnants had fled into the Everglades. This time he dispatched his aide, Lt. Thomas Linnard,[5] to carry the message, but the answer from Secretary Poinsett was the same: The war would be continued until every last Seminole was removed from Florida.

While all this was happening, Captain Vinton was far removed from the action. Having gotten his survey instruments from home, he commenced calculating accurate positions of the posts along the St. Johns River. He was also not feeling well. Hoping for a temporary reassignment, he told Jesup, "Since my return to Florida I have been attacked by a bowel complaint which has left me quite debilitated and I think unfit to take the field for the present. On this account, coupled with another consideration, I venture to ask that some other duty may be assigned me in which I may hope to serve the public interests more usefully & effectively than in the field."[6]

In a separate letter marked "Private and Confidential," Vinton freely explained to Jesup that his religious awakening was another reason he was requesting duty that would keep him out of direct fighting. As a committed man of God, he could no longer justify the possibility of taking another life, even that of the enemy:

> My Dear General
>
> In my letter covering this, I have alluded to another consideration which added to that of ill health, induces me to solicit for the present other service than that of the field. This consideration I was unwilling to introduce into an official letter

and would now only address it to you as a friend & a Christian. I may not doubt that you will appreciate my motives when I declare frankly to you that in the present controversy with the Seminoles governed as I am by religious feelings of new peculiar force, I sh'd prefer to avoid any occasion that might place me before these savages in an attitude of personal hostility.

The question very naturally presents itself here, why remain in the Mily Service if it calls upon me for any compromise of conscience or of principle? The question is cogent and I admit its force and its propriety. My reply is simply that I am ready to avouch my consistency by abandoning my commission. I would do so now were I not persuaded that my services are required during the present campaign, and I now state to you confidentially but decidedly my settled determination to do so in the Spring in any event.

This I am aware is a delicate subject, and for you to act officially in reference to it may not be an easy or agreeable task. Act therefore, I beg of you General, independently of it, entirely,—if you so prefer. And believe me that as in my present feelings so I hope in all my future sentiments & acts respecting you, I shall only manifest what I certainly entertain, a grateful & affectionate regard for yr. person and an exalted estimate of yr. public character. That you may soon be reunited to your family with a heart relieved from all care, refreshed with the approving tokens of the Nation's gratitude, and above all warmed by the Redeemer's love,—is the fervent prayers of

Your friend & Servant
J. R. V.[7]

Vinton seemed determined to go through with his plans to leave the army and take up the ministry. Back at home the family was making plans for his return. To conserve funds, John, Lucretia, Mother, and the children were going to move in with Alex and his wife Eleanor at Providence. In a letter dated 26 January, Lucretia tried to pin John down on the details:

> He [Alex] wished to know of us decidedly if we still held to the proposed plan of living together as, of course, it would make a great difference in design of the house he should attain, and the quantity of furniture he should buy. I told him we certainly wished to abide by the proposition. ... He left here to day, therefore, with the understanding that he was to hire a house large enough for both families and that we were all to pull up

> stakes here early in the Spring. Whatever house he decides upon must be taken from the first of April. He wishes therefore to have our furniture brought from Portland at or before that time, that he may begin to put this house in order, and he would like to go in with the families, I suppose by the middle of April or first of May. … Will you be at home as soon as that? Mother says she cannot move unless you are here, and Alexander wishes you to be at home as early as possible. …
>
> Now do let me say one word about your resigning. You will have passed the winter in Florida and given proof that you do not shrink from your duty, why prolong your time of service? Why not resign the first of April or even in March? Let not *ways and means* deter you. God will take care of us, I know, and I feel confident if you give up your income from a sense of duty, to do God's service, that He will not leave you or your family to suffer. Try Him, my dearest Husband, give Him an opportunity to prove that He will never desert those who put their trust in Him. Let your faith in Him be such as shall be counted unto you for righteousness. Will you limit the power of the Almighty? *Can* He not prosper you? And if you leave *all* and follow Him, *will* he not?[8]

It was late January and most of the heavy fighting was over. While the army was recuperating and waiting on supplies, Vinton took time to report to Jesup some of his observations about his meeting with the Secretary of War in November. In the letter he mentions a "Cherokee Mediation," an attempt by a delegation of Cherokee leaders to convince the Seminole to emigrate, all of which came to naught:

> Being disappoin'd in my hope of conferring with you in person I embrace this occasion to revert to some of the circumstances attending my late visit to Washington. The main result of my interview with the Secy of War, was an unqualified conviction on my part that nothing but a thorough accomplishment of the great object of the war (the emigration of the Seminoles) would satisfy the Government. However pained & embarrassed the Executive might feel in respect to this protracted controversy, still no alternative to the principle of absolute coercion was to be admitted. I stated my own views to the Secy as to future probabilities, and I found that Maj. Cross[9] had also, on occasions presented similar ones, of which you have not been unaware,—but with no visible effect. The Cherokee Me-

> diation is now passed away among things defunct,—having produced what you anticipated, more harm probably than good. The eagerness with which such a "straw" was grasped at by the Depart't shows the feverish state of mind prevalent there. Still the idea of compromise is stubbornly rejected as the last of all possible expedients. Great interest & kindness was expressed for you General, both by the Pres't. & the Secy and by the latter, in the course of his conversation ejaculated a hope that by yr. own good efforts & the "Blessing of Heaven" we might at length get through these difficulties. Of your own tenacious efforts I told the Secy the Govt might be well secured, but of the blessing I feared we had too much reason to despair.[10]

Vinton's station had been moved again, and he was now at Fort Taylor near the headwaters of the St. Johns River. With little happening of a military nature, Vinton began to finalize his plans to leave the army. Having served faithfully for over twenty years, he felt entitled to a considerable amount of time off with pay. In late February, he wrote to the Adjutant General:

> It is my intention to resign my commission in the Spring, having already put off this design until the present campaign sh'd be finished,—from a sense of duty and fair appearance. Whether this war be terminated then or not is a question which depends not on me to settle, but having performed my share in it, I feel that I may not only claim exemption from further service but also the privilege of a *leave of absence* accords to the usage wh. [I] obtained before the occurrence of hostilities. I have been in Commission 21 years and have never I believe in that long period had more than a month's leave of absence. The object of my now addressing you is to ask if such an indulgence can now be obtained. I sh'd like a leave for a year, but if such cannot be had, please ascertain the longest that will be accorded to me by the Dept. and obliged.[11]

While Vinton waited for word on whether or not he would be granted leave, he continued to be plagued by medical problems. If nothing else, he appeared eager to get out of Florida and back to some sort of civilization. On 6 March he sent separate letters to General Jesup's aide and to General Abraham Eustis, who was temporarily in command during Jesup's absence:

> Sir [Lt. J. A. Chambers][12]
>
> I have rec'd yr. communication of Feby 4th by wh. I am permitted, in case my health be such as to render me unable to perform duty in the field, to take post at the Genl hospital at St. Augustine. My health continues to be altogether too feeble for service in the field and I shall though reluctantly, be obliged to avail myself of the alternative. I am very anxious however to join my company and if it be soon to move northwardly I sh'd like to put myself in the most eligible position to meet it. Can you inform me in what direction it will move when it leaves Fort Jupiter.[13]

In his letter to General Eustis, Vinton also took the opportunity to voice his opinion on the futility of the war effort:

> You have doubtless been informed that owing to my feeble state of health I have been hitherto prevented from joining the active duties of the campaign. There has been no time since my return into part of the territory where I could have performed a march with my Regiment and nearly every week I have been obliged to resort to medicine. I think my constitution was much weakened by my residence in this torrid climate throughout the last Summer. To reinstate my health I shall require to breathe a Northern atmosphere as soon as may be. I desire exceedingly to join my Company for a short time and then to get a leave of absence. Can you inform me how & when I can meet the Compy,—whether it will move up towards St. Augustine by water or land or if to remain any length of time at Ft. Jupiter.
>
> I trust the Govt will concur in the wisdom of yr. counsels and settle upon a peace with these Indians on terms which if I understand those that have been offered, are highly advantageous to us. The point of honor is a bagatelle in the present posture of affairs,—because we cannot retrieve it by continuing the controversy. By & bye, when we have a full knowledge of the topog'y of the country & still continue to covet a soil which really none but Ind's or the fearful alternative of a negro banditti, can ever inhabit, then we can go into the enterprise with ample preparation & a more reasonable prospect of success. To proceed now is absurd.[14]

Whatever the Vinton family plans were, they were not proceeding the way everyone expected. John still hadn't heard about a leave of absence, and back at home something had happened to derail the idea of John and Alex's families moving in together. In a letter to Frank, Mother said the plans had "been overruled by a higher power" but didn't explain what it was.[15]

Meanwhile, Vinton was once again in limbo. By 22 March he was in St. Augustine and still requesting a leave of absence from General Jesup:

> I arrived here today on my way to join my company, but meeting the Order No. 70 which details me as a member of a Ct. of Inquiry I remain of course for the execution of that duty.
>
> Although my health is improved of late, I feel that my constitution is radically impaired by the influences of this climate. A resort to a Northern Atmosphere I believe to be absolutely essential to my complete restoration, and therefore respectfully submit this as my request to the Maj. Gen. Comg. for a leave of absence for 4 months, not to commence however until the adjournment of the Court of which I am a member.[16]

It was now April and as far as Vinton's requests for leave were concerned, the army seemed to be turning a deaf ear. Obviously fed-up and frustrated, he once again appealed to General Jesup. He also took the opportunity to give the general his views on the recently completed campaign:

> The Steam Boat has just arriv'd from Ind. [Indian] River bringing the news of your passage to Tampa Bay,—by which I shall be disappointed in my earnest expectation of seeing you here. I had many things to say in person & hoped for one opp'y at least before I sh'd quit the Mily Service forever of communing with you freely & fully. The time has nearly arrived which I had fixed on for resigning. My health demands that I breathe the air of another climate, and this campaign being concluded I think I can with honor leave the Service at any hour. Our Court of which I am a member will conclude its proceedings perhaps by the first week in May,—when I shall need only to rejoin my company for a day to settle some accounts with my men, to be quite ready to retire to private life. I sh'd like the indulgence of a few months leave, after a Service of 20 years but fear that even this small boon may not be granted me by the Department. …

> Permit me to congratulate you my dear Genl. on the present aspect of the war. To those who expected miracles to be brought & the war finished with this campaign, these congratulations would appear ironical, but viewing the subject as I did, much more has been done in the capturing of prisoners and breaking down the presumptuous confidence of the Seminoles than I expected. I can not now see how anything could have been done better,—what wiser measures could have been adopted, or how a greater share of success could have been secured in this campaign. There are two orders of men in this country who will take delight in blaming you. On the one hand, you will be censured for seizing the indians in your power, & on the other you w'd have been execrated had you not done so. Whatever measures you might have adopted, you would see them condemned certainly by one party or the other.[17]

Much of Vinton's time appears to have been taken up in matters of faith. He began to keep a journal, and many of the pages are filled with religious questions, presumably in preparation for his ministerial training. One very long passage considered the matter of "doubt." For Vinton, Satan was a reality, and the Devil's most potent weapons were one's own doubts:

> They come like unwelcome guests, intruding upon our peace—*whence* we know not, or why,—but generally at *times* when from a too free indulgence of appetite, for a too flippant intercourse in worldly society, we have had our conversation less in Heaven than usual. The lurking enemy is always ready to pounce upon us at such moments. *We* may sleep but *he* is ever watchful. We may relax but he is indefatigable.[18]

On another day, he wrote about an experience he'd had while searching for the source of the St. Johns River. It was as if he were exploring the Nile:

> We journied [*sic*] far into the interior until we had penetrated to that remote region of Florida whence arise the sources of the great River St. Johns. All was one vast, wild solitude! The scenery partook much of a tropical character, and reminded us more of the Egyptian than any we could think of. The palm tree gave an Oriental feature to the landscape while the far reaching prairie,—at some seasons all overflowed by the river or the rains, resembled, we thought nothing so much as the Delta of the Nile. In the midst of this rich sea of herbage rose

a clump of palmetto trees, forming an isolated group & contrasting singularly with the open flats of prairie land which stretched off for miles in every direction. The tall straight trunks of the palmettos seemed almost as well turned and symmetrical as so many Doric Columns,—while the dense architrave of foliage above formed a canopy through which even the ardent beams of a Florida sun could scarcely penetrate.[19]

Figure 12: St. Johns River. Sketch by John Rogers Vinton.

On 22 April, Vinton wrote a letter to Mother indicating that while his religious fervor hadn't waned, his determination to leave the army wasn't as strong as it had been earlier. He was being transferred north, and there was the possibility of being assigned to the Adjutant General's office, a position he would have been happy to occupy. His devotion to his mother clearly shows in the opening paragraph:

It is with feelings of peculiar interest that I seat myself this morning to commune awhile with the beloved parent of my days to whom I owe so much of the best that life can bestow, those rudiments of moral principle, self denial of lofty piety which being planted in early life have never ceased to grow & flourish in my heart. … Thy grey hairs are unto thee a Crown of Glory. Receive the homage of thy children's grateful affection, and may God in his heavenly Kingdom reward you with the Salutation & the Crown, prepared for the righteous, through Jesus X't. [Christ] our Lord![20]

After apologizing for taking time out from his Sunday devotions to write the letter, Vinton tells her about his plans for the coming weeks:

> Since I wrote last to Lucretia, (some 7 or 8 days since) we have received orders which "send" us all (the Artillery, &c) from Florida to the Cherokee country—the highlands of upper Georgia & East Tennessee. It has been thought best to prevent hostilities among the Cherokees if possible by these precautionary movements, and as the state of the Seminole controversy is such as to permit the withdrawal of a portion of our troops, this change will be found I think quite beneficial to the health & spirits of officers & men.[21]

He was also beginning to have doubts as to his suitability for the ministry. His primary concern had to do with his health. He had been sick for the past few months and still wasn't feeling well. Would he have the strength to pursue a course of rigorous study? There was also the matter of the possible appointment to the Adjutant General's office. If he received such a position, he might consider it, "as the positive demonstrations of God's will (that I remain in the Army) and feel myself bound to obey the instruction they might seem to convey!"

After folding the letter and sealing it, he set it aside to await an opportunity to mail it. Sometime later he wrote the following on the outside of the letter: "I have just rec'd dear Lucretia's letter of Mar. 31. I feel quite concerned at her sickness. But trust in God that she is now better."[22]

Vinton feared that receiving an appointment to the Adjutant General's office would be a sign that God didn't want him to pursue a career in the church, but the fear didn't prevent him from applying for the job. On 27 April, he wrote to the Secretary of War, formally putting his name on the list of applicants. He also acknowledged the fact that most appointments to government positions resulted from personal connections, rather than a person's qualifications for the job:

> The Bill for the reorganization of the Army now before Congress proposes among other things to create several new offices in the Adj. Genl's Dept. for one of which my friends have advised me to apply. During the twenty-one years of my mily experience, exclusive of my West Point course, I have served occasionally in every department of the Army and would therefore rest my claims to preferment rather on my own mily history, than resort to the ordinary aids of political or friendly influence.
>
> It is amply in my power to secure such aids, if you sh'd deem it necessary for me to do so, but I should value the ap-

> pointment of Adjt. Genl much more if conferred with a sole reference to personal merit and the good of the Service.[23]

While Vinton no doubt wanted to get the job based on his qualifications, he was not above asking the help of friends. As it turned out, he did not submit his application until after he had heard from one of those influential friends. Although he didn't give the name in his letter book, it is most probably Gen. Roger Jones, the Adjutant General, whom he had served with while aide to General Brown a decade earlier:

> My dear Genl
>
> I need not attempt to express the pleasure I had in receiving your letter of the 11th. Suffice it to say, *I thank you*, with all my heart.
>
> The considerations which you suggest & your advice, have induced me to withhold my resignation until I can see the turn of events. I have accordingly written to the S. of W. as you proposed. There is no Dept. of the Army in wh. I could serve with more congenial feelings than in the Adjt. Genl Dept—and of course by no better appt. than Adj. Genl. could I be so readily tempted to forego my purpose of entering private life. My Mily experience, since I was graduated at W. P. 21 years ago, has been in every department of the Mily service and I feel conscious that to remain longer in my present situation is, I am painfully aware, neither doing justice to myself nor to others.
>
> I have always entertained a decided repugnance to the seeking of office by the force of political influence, and w'd rather not receive preferment unless it can be conferred on the grounds of personal merit. Yet as it is but usual course in such cases for candidates however deserving to reinforce their claims by all the additional interest they can bring to bear, I ought not to refuse, perhaps, to avail myself of similar means. Still, my dear Genl, my hopes of success will rest mainly if not entirely on your own energetic efforts in my behalf…[24]

Vinton was at a crossroads in his life and unsure of which way to go. On 30 April he entered his thoughts into his journal, seeming to weigh one side against the other, but found no clear direction. On one hand, the army had denied his request for leave. Frustrated, he remarked, "So it seems an Officer cannot be permitted to resign when he pleases and I find myself constrained to remain awhile longer with epauletted shoulders, though eager to cast off the tinsel trappings." Conversely, he added, "From other quarters I receive tokens the most flattering to induce me to remain accompanied by considerations of great weight and importance."[25]

He began to wonder if his lungs were up to a career in the ministry, where long-winded sermons were the norm. "Then again my breast begins to pain me more than ever and warns me to consider well whether I am *physically* able to undertake any professional calling which is likely to tax the lungs so severely as must that to which my thoughts have been directed." He also had to consider the hard financial times the nation was going through. "Added to all these are the extreme embarrassments in the commercial world by which I am cut off from much of my private income." [26]

Mulling over his options, he ultimately deferred the outcome to God. "How shall I discern the will of God, which I would have to be my only guidance amidst this conflict of opposing influences? Blessed Father, enlighten me,—strengthen me,—direct me,—so that I may act wisely & well."[27]

Whatever his dreams, doubts, or frustrations were, Vinton was still in the army and subject to orders. On 2 May 1838 he made the following entry into his journal:

> All things are now preparing for a movement to the Cherokee Nation where the Artillery, with one Regt. of Infy, are ordered. My health requires renovating & this expedition seems well calculated for it. At all events I do not find myself prepared or able to quit the Army forthwith and the readings of Providence are therefore more definitely drawn for my guidance.[28]

Vinton was willing to place his future in the hands of God, but he also knew that it was just as much in the hands of the War Department.

10

I Am Bound for the Cherokee Country

John Rogers Vinton was looking forward to leaving Florida. His company was being sent to New Orleans as escorts for a group of Seminole being transported west, but at the time of their departure Vinton wasn't with them. He was in St. Augustine, serving on a Court of Inquiry, and couldn't leave until the case was decided. On 8 May he made the following entry in his journal, noting that he would now be able to personally attend to business in Columbus while on the way to meet with his company. As far as he could tell, the route and timing of his trip were all part of God's plan:

> An Order to join my Company will therefore take one directly to N. Orleans from hence, by a journey through the country and by Columbus, just as I would have it. What more fortunate train of incidents could have happened? And why do I say *fortunate*? Vile remnant of Pagan folly & Superstition! There is no such thing as fortune, chance, & such like. It is God who orders all these things,—God who is the directing power, willing & effecting all his purposes, for ends & uses of His own.[1]

While in St. Augustine, Vinton took every opportunity to enjoy the social life. Being a pious, married man, most of the society he partook of consisted of dinners with like-minded friends. His journal reveals a man of high artistic and intellectual capabilities, though at times rather narrow-minded. He considers those of other faiths (or of little faith) as either unimaginative or bound to a philosophy they cannot question. It never seems to occur to Vinton that much the same could be said of him. On one occasion he noted:

> Sat late at dinner today being engaged in a pleasant argument with Mr. Hackett one of the Rom. Cath. Priests of this place who boards at our house. I am averse to entering upon polemical discussions of the kind, generally— & especially so with persons of the Romish Church. They are bound by severe injunctions to keep their faith and do not hold themselves, or I do not consider them as being held open to reason or argument upon any point of doctrine,—so far as to admit the possibility of their being converted by such argument. They may

> permit themselves to discuss theological questions but always under the saving grace of Church authority.[2]

On another occasion, having engaged a religious skeptic in a drawn-out debate during a dinner party, Vinton failed to see that the other man's philosophy was as valid as his own:

> Dined yesterday at Dr. Anderson's,[3] where I have lately become well acquainted. A very pleasant family; refined & intelligent. At table, the subject of Animal Magnetism [hypnosis] was introduced. … We slid along the links of connexion [*sic*] until we arrived at Religion, its evidences, properties & demands. … I found Mr. Northnip, the newly married son-in-law, somewhat inclined to skepticism. … Mr. N. was one of that large number of young men, of cultivated & intelligent minds, who have laid out more pains in the cultivation of the reasoning faculties than in searching into the Spiritual relations of the Soul. He was hemmed in by that fence which binds the minds & hearts of so many a persuasion that nothing is to be believed but what can be demonstrated. … He c'd not see the propriety of being required to believe, before the evidences were sufficient to compel belief.[4]

On the following day he dined at a different house but with many of the same people. The conversation eventually turned to the previous night's discussion, and Vinton was thrilled when one of his companions made a comment that meshed perfectly with his dreams:

> Party last evening at Mrs. Judge Smith's. I declined dancing of course, but when asked to play the piano forte & to sing, which is often the case, I generally consent. Sitting with Mrs. Northnip during the evening she alluded to the conversation at her father's table the day before in which Mr. N. & myself indulged in a discussion of some religious points. …
>
> "Have you never thought of embracing the Ministry?" said Mrs. N. to me, during our conversation last evening. I was surprised and startled by the interrogatory,—for I have divulged no such intention to any friend here, however intimate,— & wondered how she could conjecture such a thing. She was pleased to say, in explanation of her question that the thought suggested itself to her because she believed me to be peculiarly adapted to the office,—and in connexion with the

> successful manner in which I conducted the religious argument at her father's table, she c'd not but think that I was, in my present line of life, decidedly out of position. … I consider such incidents as tokens of God's Providence.[5]

Vinton's intestinal problems appear to have cleared up, but he was still troubled by a shortness of breath. Beyond that, he was concerned about Lucretia. She had been ill for some time, and Vinton was anxious for news from home. After receiving a letter from Mother, he wrote back:

> It is with inexpressible pleasure, my dear, my beloved Mother that I have just now rec'd & read your letter of the 23d April. How glad am I that you sent it although you had so much reason to suppose I had left Florida! But I opened it with feelings of dread, lest bad tidings of dear Lucretia sh'd be conveyed by it. I have trembled for her, ever since I rec'd Frank's last letter,—and w'd have hurried home on this serious account if my liberty had been left me. But how strangely am I transmuted! Even with a proposition on my lips to resign, I am not permitted to go as far as Wash'n to hand in my resignation. I cannot resign *forthwith* because I must first go to Columbus to receive my funds there and must meet the men of my Company once more in order to pay them what they deposited with me.[6]

After describing his proposed overland route to New Orleans, he speculated that the company would travel by steamboat up the Mississippi, Ohio, and Tennessee Rivers to the Cherokee country in the mountains of Tennessee. "If I find the mountain air agrees with me," he remarked, "I shall be tempted to breathe it a few weeks—for I consider the state of my breast so equivocal that I am frequently troubled with misgivings whether God will ever permit me to serve Him in that vineyard where it is my greatest desire to labor."[7]

Vinton continued to struggle with his decision to leave the army and take up the ministry. To make matters more difficult, friends within the service were enticing him with career possibilities that would be hard to ignore. In a letter to his mother, he explained the dilemma:

> Meanwhile let me disclose to you what I prefer sh'd not be mentioned to any one but Lucretia. Gen. Jones, my steady friend in Wash'n has written me to say I must not resign until after the present Army Bill is through Cong.—For it is his purpose to apply for the office of Adjt. Genl. for me urging it with all his strength,—an office which confers the rank of Ma-

> jor,—emoluments nearly 2500 per annum,—and a line of duty all together intellectual, and removed from any probability of personal conflicts with an indian foe. Is this a temptation of the Devil, or an interposition of God's righteous Providence, my dear Mother? Who can tell?[8]

The letter also dealt with Mother's concerns about selling *La Plaisance*. They had received an offer of $2600, and he urged her to consider it. "Viewing all the circumstances," he argued, "& the age of the house & the expense that will be req'd for repairs, I think it very providential that you have so good an offer." Mother was now sixty-five, and the children were scattered. John's family would reside in Providence after he left the army, and it was time for Mother to give up the farm and return to the city.[9]

Vinton's dream of becoming a minister may have been delayed, but was certainly not cast aside. A few days later, the dream was given a boost when he was asked to substitute for one of the clergymen in St. Augustine. He was nervous at first and not sure if his lungs were up to it, but all that gave way to the thrill of delivering his first sermon:

> Surely the place, the occasion, the object & the service are momentous circumstances! To me they have been the more impressive that I am so totally unused to any exercise of public speaking. Our auditory was very small, but large enough to make me feel a tremor through my veins & nerves, not less agitating [. . . .] than if the assembly had been more numerous. But the general sensation at my heart was one of grateful delight that I was permitted thus to speak the word of God, and, according to the opinion of my friends afterwards expressed, not unacceptably.[10]

It was now 15 May and Vinton's last day in St. Augustine. The Court of Inquiry was concluded, and several boats were in the harbor preparing to leave for Charleston. Before leaving, a friend asked him to perform a rather disagreeable favor:

> Yesterday I was much engaged in packing for my journey—and among other matters of import more than usually exciting was the chastisement of a negro boy who has been waiting on Mrs. Th. but become quite negligent and fractious. She besought me as a special favor to flog the boy and knowing her present lone & dependent situation I c'd not say nay to her request, though the work was by no means an agreeable one.

> It is the first time I believe that ever I have had occasion to strike a black person. I convinced myself of course that the punishment was merited, before I undertook it, & was persuaded that I was to execute an office of justice and necessity.[11]

Vinton arrived in Columbus on 23 May. The last time he had been there was during the Creek crisis of 1827, when it was nothing more than a ferry crossing. Now it was a thriving town where he might someday settle, if time and circumstances permitted. It was also where much of his financial wealth was tied up. He and his business partner Peter Freeman of Boston had purchased about half a dozen lots in the city, some of them improved, some not. Like many Americans of the period, he was partaking in the great scheme of land speculation. For Vinton, this was not a get-rich-quick endeavor, where someone bought a piece of wilderness for next to nothing and sold it a few years later at an immense profit. That sort of speculation was dangerous and had been the chief cause of the economic collapse a year earlier.

Vinton's speculation was more of an investment. He had paid a fair price for property in an established town, one he believed would prosper in years to come. For the long term, it was a reasonably safe bet. The cotton industry in Georgia and Alabama was growing, and Columbus's location on the Chattahoochee made it a perfect place for much of that cotton to begin its journey to the mills in Britain or New England. Columbus was bound to grow, and Vinton's property was sure to increase in value. When the time came, he could sell it and enjoy a comfortable retirement on the proceeds. It was, in a way, Vinton's Individual Retirement Account.

In the short term the land was probably worth less than what he had paid for it. The Panic of 1837 had seen to that. Still, all was not a loss. There were buildings on some of those lots and rents to be collected. Two of the lots appear to have been large commercial properties with a number of stores and shops. A couple more held warehouses. Also, if he and Freeman wanted to invest a bit more, they could build on the unimproved lots and collect more rents. The problem was that they were absentee landlords, which meant they had to deal with locals to manage the properties, some of whom they were partners with. It was all very complicated, and many of the entries in Vinton's letter books and journals are short notes about sending money to one party or another, or contain columns of computations showing what was collected and how it was disbursed. While in Columbus he wrote to Freeman, giving his partner a firsthand account of their investments:

> My long cherished design of visiting Columbus is at length realized,—and I find things very much as I expected—a very pretty city,—well built & occupying a commanding position,

> but just now in a state of near depression as is common, I believe, with almost every Merc. town in the U.S. Hearing of this embarrassed state of the people I had prepared myself for large deductions from our own expected receipts on the score of bad debts,—but to my great satisfaction I found our Mr. Wells[12] had succeeded in collecting about all that was due from the tenants. If you could see the miserable little shanties wh. we let for stores, & know the character of the tenants,—mere hucksters,—you w'd give him great credit for his *perseverance* & *industry*. From many of the tenants he is obliged to collect the rent monthly or he w'd never get it at all. No one but himself or one similarly interested could transact the business. I find him to be a very thorough, sensible, energetic man & of excellent character here for integrity & genl moral worth. I have therefore, with the consent of Mr. Robertson[13] made Mr. Wells our sole agent. The 5 pr. ct. we pay him is cheap enough for the service he renders.[14]

During the previous year he and Freeman had profited a little less than $2000. Not bad, considering his base army pay was about half that. For the most part he was happy with their investments, but saw room for improvements. "As to our other 3 lots," he advised Freeman, "they are all vacant and yield nothing—nor could we sell them now at any tolerable price." On the other hand, the large commercial lots seemed to have been a good choice. "The Bridge comes in at the foot of Crawford Street which gives to [lots] 69 & 70 a permanent value." The lots had about a dozen buildings on them, which were expected to yield around $3000 per year in rents. Ultimately, Vinton felt confident in Columbus's future and decided to increase his investment:[15]

> On conferring with friends I have concluded to improve our Lot No. 247 by putting on it a house, kitchen & fence, &c, all to cost $1000 on condition that Mr. Wells's brother—who makes the suggestion & wishes to be the tenant,—will give 250 D per ann. & will superintend the workmanship that it be faithfully done, and will advance the 1st year's rent towards paying for the house. This will give us a good tenant immediately—and cost us 750 D—only a little more than the rents coming to us next Oct. … This impr. will give us 25 pr cent on the outlay and improve the value of the lot 25 pr cent more. Labor is now compar'y low and exchange very high. This is the time therefore to use our money here.[16]

Four days after his arrival Vinton left Columbus, headed for New Orleans, where he hoped to meet up with his company. In his journal he noted, "I am bound for the Cherokee Country,—and with not a very pleasing reflection that my ostensible purpose is to drive them from their soil & dispossess them of their homes." Like the Seminole, the Cherokee had resisted deportation to the Indian Territory in what is now Oklahoma. Unlike the Seminole, they were surrounded by white settlement and had limited areas to take refuge in. Many of the Cherokee leaders were acculturated to white society and instead of taking up arms, they chose to fight for their homes in the court system. Unfortunately, as it would with nearly all other Indian nations, the system let them down.[17]

Vinton travelled overland from Columbus to Montgomery, Alabama, then by steamer to Mobile. There were two competing steamboats to choose from, and the straight-laced Vinton chose the one he did because the other carried "a pleasure party of ladies & gentlemen from Selma." In the early days of steamboat travel, if two vessels were making the same run a race was expected, and the passengers that day were not disappointed. Vinton thought little of the practice. "These two boats were rivals in speed,—and more steam was carried, I fear, than usual with them, on account of this spirit of controversy. Our boat was victorious,—much to the satisfaction of many of our passengers, but not to my own. I prefer safety to victory."[18]

On 2 June Vinton arrived in New Orleans. It is interesting to note that at the time, the Crescent City considered itself as being in competition with New York. Vinton commented, "The new Exchange Hotel is a model of sumptuous architecture. Several churches are very beautiful. The Commercial Exchange and other public edifices are quite magnificent. It is evident that the people of N. Orleans are not disposed to let this city be outdone by its rival New York." He also mentioned:

> The first peculiarity that strikes the attention of a stranger at N. Orleans is to see the water running *from* the river instead of towards it. The land is several feet lower than the surface of the Mississippi in its present stage, and but for the levee, the narrow embankment which borders all the shore, the giant river would overwhelm city & country far and wide. No serious accident of this kind, however, can well take place, as in case of a breach by the levee, sufficient force is always at hand to repair it.[19]

Having Sunday free, Vinton decided to take a stroll around town. He soon came upon a group of slaves hard at work splitting wood for a brickyard. He asked one of the slaves if he always worked on Sunday, and the man told him he did, but that they were allowed the afternoon off to work in their own gardens.

This bothered Vinton's Christian sensibilities. "Here thought I, is a grudging boon of half a day in the week and even then there is no rest—no chance for domestic repose, recreation or religious worship." He also asked if they were allowed to attend church on Sundays. The slave answered, "We never hear the word so much as named—We scarcely dared to sing much less to talk about meetings. See that man there, Sir, with the long lash wound over his shoulders? He take good care we no talk about such things." Vinton looked over at the slave driver, a black man with a whip over his shoulder. To Vinton's eye, the whip was like the epaulettes on his own shoulders, "the badge of his office & the instrument of his power" that was not to be disobeyed.[20]

Vinton had travelled widely throughout the South, and he recognized this as slavery at its worst. Yet from what he had seen in other parts of the nation, slaves generally lived in no worse conditions than the poor and immigrant classes in the free states. He conveniently ignored the fact that free people could at least strive for a better future, if only for their descendants. Perpetual bondage, for themselves and their heirs, was all a slave could look forward to. Like most Americans, Vinton was at a loss for an easy remedy to the situation, and therefore distanced himself from the subject. For him, the only hope was in religion, and he saw the work of radical abolitionists as counter-productive and dangerous:

> Here undoubtedly the negroes are the best off as they are,—and however deplorable may be the institution of slavery in the abstract, I can see neither wisdom nor practical humanity in the efforts of the abolitionists. To impress upon the minds of Southern countries the paramount truths & obligations of religion, and thence induce them to a conscientious exercise of humanity & justice towards their slaves, would be doing more for the essential welfare of the blacks than all the abolitionists can ever accomplish by agitation. It is difficult to say how far or how long the abolitionists of the North may carry their designs but the practical tendency of their operations is already obvious & inevitable. They are alienating every feeling of fraternity & good will that should subsist between the North & the South,—all striving to kindle a spirit of discord,—They are creating a temper of extreme exacerbation in both parties—and all without a possible prospect of advantage to anyone. … What issue on the other hand more disastrous, than to widen the breach which already threatens to sever the bonds of Union and plunge this glorious fabric of political & social prosperity into the abyss of anarchy & ruin! … The negro is better as he is.[21]

It wasn't that Vinton was an insensitive or amoral person. Indeed, he was just the opposite. The problem of slavery was something he felt powerless to solve, so he simply reasoned it away. He felt the abolitionists were doing more harm than good by driving a wedge between North and South, thus killing any chance of reasoned debate and compromise. It was a valid argument, shared by most Americans of the time, even many of those opposed to slavery. The sad fact may be that the only way slavery in America was going to end was by means of a bloody civil war. Vinton saw the eventuality, and rightfully feared it. For him, preserving the Union was more important than immediately ending slavery, and for good reason: If the Union split, either peacefully or by a Southern victory in war, slavery would not end. Only by preserving the Union was there any chance, slim though it might seem, of ending the institution. We may find it disturbing that he chose preserving the Union over freeing the slaves, but Abraham Lincoln made a similar choice at the beginning of the Civil War.

The moral dilemma of driving the Indians from their homes was also not lost on Vinton. Once again, the problem was much more than one man could hope to solve, so he reasoned it away. He was a soldier, and it was his duty to carry out his orders. Yet he was also a Christian, and it troubled him to make war upon his fellow man. It was one of the reasons he wanted out of the army. As with most whites of the time, especially those who were involved in Indian removal, Vinton convinced himself that it was all in the Indian's best interest, even if he knew it wasn't.

Like many other soldiers, Vinton saw Indian removal as a sad tragedy he was forced by fate to participate in. The American nation was expanding at a phenomenal rate, and no one could (and few wanted to) stop it. Conflict between the natives and the newcomers was inevitable, and nearly always brought on by the acts of unscrupulous or uncaring whites. The best a soldier could hope to do was somehow control the violence. If keeping the peace meant removing the Indians, than it was his duty to do so. He didn't have to like the job, and it certainly didn't require him to hate his enemy. As one entry in his journal shows, he had respect and even affection for the Seminole, and understood their plight:

> Day before yesterday upwards of 250 Seminole indians left these barracks for their new home beyond Arkansas. Among them, as they passed out through the gate, I discovered old Turteney, my friend of Fort Mellon,—the tall warrior & runner of Coa Haijo. He greeted me with unusual emotion not unlikened to tenderness. A shake of the hand w'd not do, but seeing him motioning to embrace me, I opened my arms to him and we hugged each other like brothers. And yet, thought I, of more balls than one from this indian's rifle did I hear

whizzing by my head at the battle of Lake Monroe. But we forget all those things when hostilities are over. And now at our last parting I commended him to heaven with a secret prayer for his future welfare. I pointed my finger to the sky above us, in token of my meaning and waved him an affectionate farewell. Whether he understood me or not I shall never perhaps find out. After their party was gone my thoughts flowed out in the following verses:

The Seminole's Farewell to Florida

We go! It is our doom,—here all our ties we sever—Our doom we know.
Tis past,—the die is cast,—these cheerful scenes we quit forever.
Ye glades, ye forest shades, O how can we be parted.
How leave these sun bright skies & fields? O how but broken hearted.

Farewell! O never tell, how the warrior's eyes were weeping
When he turned & sadly mourned o'er the grave where his sires were sleeping.
Remember not, O glen & grot! How the chieftain's look had altered,
O never let the paleface know how the Redman's footstep faltered.

Go on! We must be gone,—for we know the fate compelling.
Tis done! The setting sun marks our only place of dwelling.
Tell us not, of any spot, where our feet may soon be rested.
Where have we ever yet abode by white man unmolested?

We fought as well we ought—Honest pens will write our story.
Our brow, tho' saddened now, may one day wear the wreath of glory.
Then come;—We'll find a home, where the spirit's fire is lighted.
For here our Sun is sunk for aye and all our life is blighted.[22]

As it is today, New Orleans was a vibrant, multicultural city with a relatively relaxed morality. Stepping out to see the sights of the city, Vinton stopped by the Ball Room of the City Exchange[23] and received quite a shock to his moral sensibilities. After commenting on the grand but gaudy architecture, he turned his attention to the ceiling:

In every alternate panel is painted a group of two or more figures, generally a male & female, in a state of almost perfect nudity,—These groups are intended as displays of classic voluptuousness,—allowable perhaps in the Italian school of taste but

> such as would call forth the indignation even of the [. . . .] mob, should such scenes be ever hazarded in N. York or Boston. At least no parent, brother or husband could ever wish their sisters or daughters or wives to visit such a hall. The paintings are of sufficient merit to be attractive as works of art, and yet the eye of delicacy could not survey them without revolting. Such a scene overarching the gay throng, half intoxicated in the midnight dance & revel, is just calculated … to debauch the heart and deprave the mind.[24]

With the arrival of the remainder of his company in New Orleans, Vinton was ready to make his way to Cherokee country. Boarding a steamboat, the soldiers traveled up the Mississippi, the Ohio, and then the Tennessee Rivers until they reached Ross's Landing (near today's Chattanooga) on 26 June. Yet dealing with the Cherokee was not the foremost thing on his mind. He had received a letter informing him Lucretia was very sick and that he needed to come home as soon as possible. Vinton quickly sent a letter to his new commanding officer, Gen. Winfield Scott:

> In a few days I hope to have reunited the two parts of my company so long unhappily separated, and prepare it for such service as may be required. For myself, however, having heard of the extreme illness of my wife, I must earnestly request of you the indulgence of a two month's leave of absence. After nearly two year's constant service in Florida I may with very fair reason claim this favor independently of domestic considerations so impervious, but in all the circumstances, I feel that nothing ought to deter me from asking this privilege at your hands, without any delay. … If you have any occasions for the services of a messenger as far as Washington I sh'd be much obliged by an order to cover my transportation that far.[25]

The response Vinton received was not what he had expected. Though sympathetic of Vinton's situation, Scott chastised him for taking an indirect route to Tennessee and questioned rumors of his not wanting to serve in the Cherokee removal:

> I regret the domestic affliction you mention, but cannot, under the circumstances, grant the leave of absence requested.
>
> I am dissatisfied with you for having gone from St. Augustine to Columbus, Georgia, to meet your company there, after you had, probably, good reason to believe it would take a dif-

ferent route to this country. You ought to have come directly here where your presence would have been highly useful before the arrival of the company.

I have also heard that, whilst in Florida, you had avowed a determination to avoid if possible serving in the expected campaign against the Cherokee Indians—on grounds, I suppose, of a more enlightened conscience, or a higher sense of justice than belongs to officers who have expressed no such scruples. If you have arrogated to yourself any such superiority, I need scarce tell you that it will be admitted by no officer of this army.

For the foregoing reasons & in the hope that the indisposition in your family is not very serious, I decline granting the leave of absence.[26]

Figure 13: Maj. Gen. Winfield Scott. Engraving by Thomas B. Welch.

Vinton was obviously shocked, hurt, and angry. He also felt that some envious officer had been talking behind his back. Already planning on leaving the army, Vinton saw little reason to hold anything back and fired off a lengthy, heated, but thoroughly respectful response to Scott:

I thank you for yr. prompt reply to my communication of the 26th June, and for your expression of regret for my domestic affliction. I wish I could say that the remaining parts of your letter gave me equal satisfaction. It is evident that you wrote it under impressions not congenial with the friendly spirit which dictated mine;—and as those impressions are clearly founded on a misapprehension of facts & principles you will, I am sure, permit me to use all freedom in endeavoring to remove them.

You are dissatisfied,—you remark, with the route I took to meet my company after I left St. Augustine. I am sorry that my

> course in this respect sh'd not have met yr. approbation, but when I assure you that my orders were peremptorily & simply, *to join my company*,—that I had positive advices that it had been ordered to N. Orleans as a Garrison guard of indians, and afterwards that a separated portion of it might march by way of Columbus—that I had no option indeed, if I followed the plainest precept of military obedience,—If these facts be fairly considered, you will, I am persuaded, acquit me here of all blame.

He then went on to address the paragraph wherein Scott had accused him of attempting to shirk his duty in removing the Cherokee for reasons "of a more enlightened conscience":

> I confess, General, it was with much surprise and no less pain that I read this parg. fr. your pen. It was evidently dictated by a sharp spirit of animadversion for wh. I was not prepared. You seem to have condemned me in yr. own mind without waiting for that "alterum partem [other side]" which they who seek for truth in matters of human concernments will always be mindful to *hear* before they venture to *decide*. To your own ample experience of the ways of men I may safely appeal to prove how rife, in the world, is the spirit of detraction, and how lamentable are its issues. Let me then assure you that the whole of this charge is groundless. Let me assure you that if I had wished to avoid coming to the Cherokee Nation nothing could have been easier than for me to do so:—That I never professed to be governed by a more enlightened conscience or a higher sense of justice than belongs to many—very many of the officers of this Army;—that I never arrogated to myself any such superiority as you infer;—nor was I ever, that I recollect,—so unwise as to bring my conscientious principles at all in comparison with those of other officers in reference to the matter in question. I might rather say, as was once remarked to me by a gentleman who had himself felt the pangs of injured innocence,—"where I have had one moment of *arrogance*, I have had two of *humility*." *
>
> After this, my explicit disavowal, your own sense of justice General and your veneration for Truth, will prompt you to a very different conclusion, I am sure, from that manifested in your letter,—and perhaps, also to a frank disposition to make such reparation as may seem to be due to wounded feelings

and injured character. After a long service in the Army, I have been accustomed to indulge a complacent pride, (more gratifying to me perhaps than any other connected with it) that I had not one enemy amongst all my brethren officers who have ever known me;—for, I judged of them by the feelings of my own heart. But my error is obvious. "An enemy hath done *this*." You have certainly had around you, General, some who could not have been kindly disposed towards me or you would never have heard such a story as has now reached your ear. Justice to myself demands that I sh'd thus hasten to disabuse you of the error,—and I as freely disclose also, that with the same alacrity I am willing to forgive the detractor.

In the foregoing remarks I w'd not be understood to refer to my private sentiments as to the moral right or wrong of our indian policy. Every citizen, I presume,—Officers or otherwise, can entertain such as may seem fitting to himself, without being called in question for them. I have made it my inflexible rule, however, as I think every Officer should do, to avoid any publication of such sentiments, especially when adverse to the measures of the Government,—or to suffer them in any respect to impair his usefulness as a faithful and efficient public agent while he consents to remain in the public service. This rule as a general one I presume we all would subscribe to.

I come now, very reluctantly, to the closing paragraph of your letter which says as follows—"For the foregoing reasons and in the hope that the indisposition in your family is not very serious I decline granting the leave of absence."

I said "reluctantly," because I am compelled in reply to step beyond the mild precincts of passive self vindication and adopt the language of remonstrance. If I understand the paragraph right, it conveys nothing less than a *punishment* for my imputed transgressions. I am denied a leave of absence for reasons derived from conjectural sources, or based on grounds of Ex-parte statement. In short, I am visited with a certain penalty for faults alleged,—without trial and without recourse. I now appeal to yourself, General, whether any Officer of our Army ought not to protest firmly against the introduction of a principle so injurious to military pride and so hostile to the essential attributes of equal justice. The military service of our Country has in it many things to depress the honest zeal of its votaries,—and to cause its sanguine advocates to mourn for its decline. But should such a principle as this prevail, what more would be wanting to consummate its downfall? I will not, however, believe that you intended this. I know your high martial spirit and your pure patriotism too well. But I nevertheless lament that I am in a situation to be subjected to an ordeal that I so much disapprove,—and have therefore determined to release myself from it as soon as possible. I respectfully resign into your hands, my Commission as Captain of the 3[d] Reg't of Artillery, and request you to forward it accordingly. I should prefer this resignation to take effect at the end of July provided you will grant me leave for the intermediate time. If this small boon is denied, I then request that my resignation be immediately accepted. I cannot serve another day with satisfaction,—and ought to lose no time in repairing to the bosom of my family, where my presence is so much required.

In thus taking leave of the service and of you, General, I beg leave to add one word expressive of the very high esteem and respect for your person & character which I have ever entertained during my long service in the Army. I hope I may be able to carry the same with me, unimpaired, into the circles of private life.

Hoping to hear from you soon, I remain General

Mo. [Most] Respectfully
J.R.V.

*This was a remark of Gen. S. himself, to me when dining with him alone in Wash'n—in the year 1828. I was much struck with it, at the time, and have never forgotten it. It is a curious question now in my mind whether his memory has been sufficiently tenacious to inform him who the author of my quotation is.[27]

Vinton then wrote to his old friend in Washington, Roger Jones, the Adjutant General, explaining the situation:

I feel as if I could not take a step so serious as that of resigning my Commission without communing with you on the subject, as with an early & much valued friend. … For the first time in my life I found myself the powerless subject of an unlawful chastisement;—a member of a profession once I thought honorable & noble, but proving to be a condition so servile that punishment might be wantonly inflicted at the option of ca-

> price and the subject deprived of redress or appeal. I release myself from a bondage so intolerable.[28]

In the meantime, Scott was replying to Vinton's heated response. For Vinton, it was both a complete surprise and a vindication. In his response, Scott claims he was baiting Vinton in order to get the man's response to rumors he'd heard. It's difficult to tell if Scott was being honest or simply back-pedaling:

> I have this moment received your letter of the 3rd instant, & am as much pleased with its love of manhood, as with the courteous terms in which it is expressed.
>
> My note to which you reply was certainly written in a spirit of much dissatisfaction, & in order to give you an opportunity of explanation or vindication. Indeed, if I had had the power, I should, on the strength of the reports which had reached me have ordered a court of inquiry for their investigation the moment after hearing of your arrival at Ross' Landing. Not having such power, I felt it to be as much my duty, as it was my right, to place, in strong language, those reports before you. The course I adopted, needs in my opinion, no vindication, & it has been attended with, to me, this pleasing result:—an explanation entirely satisfactory.
>
> I shall not forward the tender you have made of your commission. Show this letter to your immediate commander, & if he shall sanction your application for a leave of absence, as I hope he may, let the fact be communicated to me, & the leave be considered as commencing forthwith. In that case, you need not wait a moment for my order. It shall be immediately forwarded to your address—given you an indulgence to the extent of sixty days.
>
> Repeating my sincere wishes that Mrs. Vinton's indisposition may not be found to be serious.[29]

Vinton was no doubt very relieved and perhaps elated. Winfield Scott was one the most powerful officers in the army, and Vinton had stood up to him and come out the victor. After sending a quick letter to Adjutant General Jones explaining the current situation and telling him not to accept the resignation, Vinton penned a thank you letter to Scott:

> I had the pleasure yesterday to receive your letter of the 5th inst. and now thank you for the very gratifying terms in which you expressed your entire satisfaction with my explanation.

Had I even dreamed that such rumors as you refer to had been in circulation to prejudice me in your esteem I should have gladly sought an investigation by Ct. of Inquiry or any other tribunal before which I might have repelled the accusations and exposed the Calumniator. My fair form has hitherto been without spot or blemish. I trust I shall be able to preserve it so to the end of my life.

Col. Gates has approved my application for leave of absence in a note which I have the honor herewith to enclose. There is no alarming scarcity of Officers here for any service that we have in prospect. Lieut. Bragg of my company is I presume only temporarily absent from it and some of the companies here have, I believe, even more than two officers present.

I shall take my departure forthwith as you have kindly suggested. My address will be at Pomfret in Con. where I shall be happy to receive your orders.

Permit me to renew, General, the assurances of my high respect.[30]

The entire incident serves to shine a light on several problems that were simmering below the surface of army life. The first was the lack of advancement available to junior officers. Vinton was not a wildly ambitious man and had learned to accept the slow rate of promotion. Many fellow officers were of a different temperament and were not above a little back-stabbing to increase their chances of climbing the ladder of rank. Had a rival captain or an underling conspired against him, or was it nothing more than common rumor that had caused Scott's irritation with Vinton? Without a Court of Inquiry, the truth would remain hidden.

Another problem hinted at in the exchange is Vinton's disapproval of Andrew Jackson's Indian Removal policy. In this respect, Vinton was not alone in his feelings. Many of the officers who had fought in Florida or escorted other removed tribes to the Indian Territory were not pleased with the task they had been assigned to perform. Most officers were West Point trained or from privileged society and prided themselves in possessing a deep sense of personal honor. To men like this the whole removal process, laced with fraud and conducted with little or no regard for the rights or welfare of the Indians, was dishonorable and immoral. They may have actually agreed with the principle of removal and may have even disliked the Indians, but they saw evil in the way removal was being carried out, and it bothered them.

Added to the moral qualms many officers faced with Indian removal was a growing frustration with conflicting orders from Washington. They were instructed to protect the Indians on their journey, but when frontier whites (Jackson's most vocal constituency) harassed or committed crimes against the Indians, the army was often discouraged from interfering. Officers who served as escorts for the Indians were charged with seeing them properly fed and cared for while on the trip, but when politically-connected contractors failed to provide proper rations or suitable shelter, the officers were often powerless to do anything about it.

Vinton's response to Scott shows the path he and other conscientious officers chose to take when performing duties they did not always agree with. He would speak his mind privately, but not publicly. As a commissioned officer who had taken a solemn oath, he would obey his orders to the best of his ability, no matter how distasteful they might be. It was, of course, a moral compromise and a bit of self-deception. In this instance Vinton could speak his mind because he had already decided to leave the army. Most other officers did not have that luxury. Taking the moral high ground is always laudable, but personal honor does not put food on the table.[31]

Vinton had been travelling for nearly two months, but he could not yet unpack his bags. It was early July 1838, he was in the remote mountains of Tennessee, and he desperately needed to be by Lucretia's side.

Plate 1: John Rogers Vinton, possibly by Joseph Greenleaf Cole.

Plate 2: Lucretia Dutton Parker Vinton. Artist unknown.

Plate 3: David Hammond Vinton, by John Rogers Vinton.

Plate 4: Rev. Francis Vinton.

Plate 5: Rev. Alexander Hamilton Vinton. Plate 6: Elizabeth Vinton Greene.

Plate 7:
Francis Laurens Vinton.

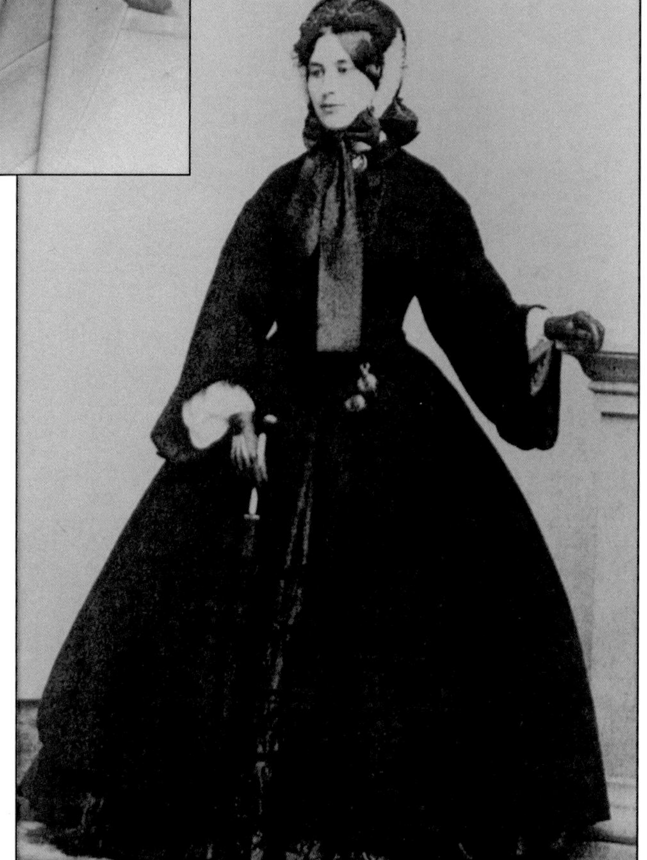

Plate 8:
Louise Clare
(LuLu) Vinton.

Plate 9: "West Point Cadet"
Watercolor by John Rogers Vinton, circa 1821.
Slightly larger than actual size of 3.875" x 4.625".

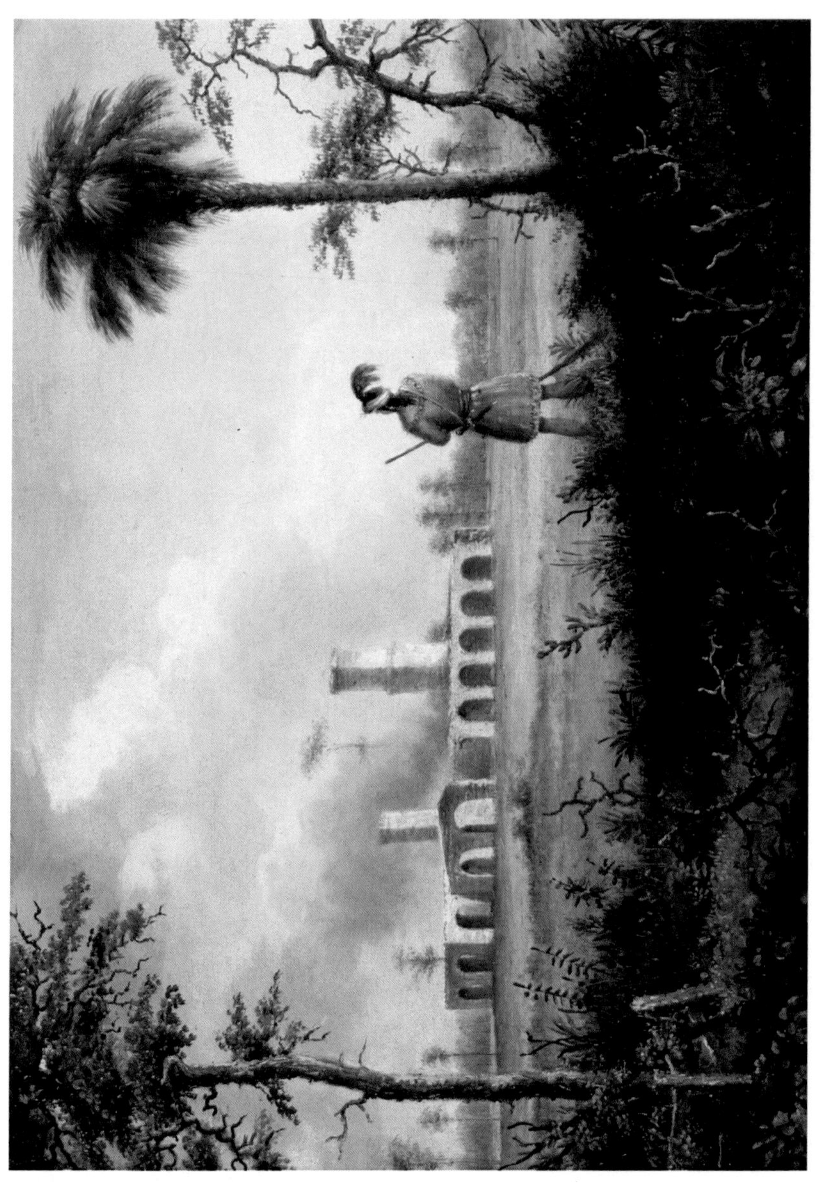

Plate 10: “The Ruins of the Sugar Mill”
Oil on canvas by John Rogers Vinton, circa 1843.

Plate 11: "Oseola [*sic*] Sitting On the Banks of a Lake"
Oil painting by John Rogers Vinton.

Plate 12: Tomb of John Rogers Vinton, surrounded by cement cannon. Lucretia's grave is to the left, Frank Laurens' is to the right.

Plate 13: Christ Church, Pomfret, Conn., dedicated to Rev. Alex Vinton. John Rogers Vinton's grandson Howard Hoppin was the architect. Each stained glass window is dedicated to a family member.

Plate 14: Tiffany stained-glass window of St. George, dedicated to John Rogers Vinton. Banner at top reads: "Hoc Ardua Vincere Docet" (This teaches us to overcome difficulties.) Lower section reads: In Memory of Major John Rogers Vinton, killed at the siege of Vera Cruz, April 1846 [*sic* - March 1847]. Faithful Unto Death."

11

Lucretia Says She Is Not Ready to Die

By mid-July 1838 Vinton was at home in Pomfret, taking care of Lucretia. Her precise illness is not specified in any of the correspondence, but some type of lung ailment was first mentioned in March. Tuberculosis was very common at the time, but it might have been some other disease that could linger for months. In any case, the decision seems to have been made to move Lucretia from Pomfret to Providence. There were doctors in the city, in addition to more family members nearby. Frank and Alex and their families were there to help, along with Maine's widow Frances. A home was found in Providence, and on 27 July John and Lucretia began a slow journey to the city. It was a trip that normally took only a day, but the couple stretched it out to two because of Lucretia's weakened condition. On the 29th John wrote to Mother to let her know they had arrived safely:

> After we left you on Friday we rode on very pleasantly until we arrived at Webster's:—there took rest & refreshments, and proceeded to Chepatchet where we arrived at ½ past 5,—& found good accommodations for the night.—Regaled on a fine supper and the next morning enjoyed a breakfast with equal gusto. Lucretia's strength & spirits sustaining her the mean-while admirably. Set out next morning at ¼ past 7.—Rested half an hour at the 8 mile house, proceeded & arrived at Frances's in Prov'd. at 11 o'clk exactly, where Lu reclined until dinner, (saltfish) which we relished well. Aunt Betsy & I set about cleaning up our house. With the help of Daniel & Isaac we got most of the furniture unpacked,—the kitchen affairs all in order & I laid in groceries &c for a few day's supply and then brought Lucr. over from Frances' 5 P.M. and instated her at her new home. Today, though the warmest day we have had this year in Prov'd.—She feels quite smart, considering her journey,—So I have good hopes. …[1]

The couple then set out for Boston by rail, the purpose of the journey being unspecified. After their return, John contacted a lung specialist and arranged for him to see Lucretia. During the first week of August, John wrote to his mother informing her of their return and asking that she send their daughter Helena to

Providence. The letter also contained news that the doctor's visit had the unintended consequence of dealing a blow to John's hopes of becoming a minister:

> We have just returned from Boston and reestablished ourselves in our own domicile. Lucretia bore the journey hence, quite well, but was more fatigued in returning. … On Wednesday morning we set out in the early cars, (having been disappointed of the P.M. cars of the day previous by a faithless hackman)—and sent out a letter, the same day, to Dr. Jackson, who resides at Waltham. He replied the next morning (Thursday) & set an hour on Friday (today) when he w'd call and examine the patient.—He came at the hour appointed and had a very thorough scrutiny of her case. The conclusion is not so favorable as we have been led to hope. Her lungs are decidedly affected and a course is prescribed for her by the Dr. which we shall be enabled to follow here quite fully. Our journey has been thus far satisfactory that we have all doubts removed as to her actual condition. I shall now bestow all my care & attention towards alleviating as far as possible her trials. …
>
> I had Dr. Jackson to examine my chest also,—not on account of any *present* disease, but of my liability to it, in the event of adopting any professional calling that might require sedentary labor &c. He was full & explicit in discouraging any such change as I contemplated. Had no doubt that I sh'd be broken down in a short time if I undertook it, and advised me to such a course of life only as w'd give me plenty of exercise & great freedom of action in the open air.[2]

Vinton was now faced with a dilemma. It was probable that Lucretia's disease would be fatal, but she might linger for months. Unfortunately, his leave was due to expire on the 7th of September. On 8 August he wrote to the Adjutant General requesting an extension of his leave:

> The leave of absence which I rec'd from Genl. Scott will expire on the 7th prox'o [proximo: next month] and I find it necessary to solicit an extension of it. The extreme illness of my wife, the only cause which induces me to make this request, has not abated but on the contrary is pronounced by our physician to be absolutely alarming and probably her last. My presence is declared to be indispensible to her comfort in affording her such slight exercise as she can yet take by occasional riding out &c.—so that it w'd be scarcely less than cruel for me now to

> withdraw it. Under these trying circumstances, I trust the General will not refuse me an additional leave of four months. Should the sickness of Mrs. V. in the meantime take a favorable turn, or which is more probable, be terminated fatally, I shall have no hesitation in giving up any unexpired portion of the leave, and report for duty. I send the Physician's statement supposing some other than my own might be required by the rules of the Department.[3]

The time had also come to sell *La Plaisance*, but it seems Mother was having second thoughts. Perhaps some of the neighbors told her she hadn't gotten a good enough price. As far as John was concerned, it was water under the bridge. On 15 August Vinton wrote her a two-page letter. One side of the paper dealt with the sale of the property, the other with personal matters:

> Today I have seen Mr. Linnard and concluded our business. Nothing can be more unwise than to get up any regrets about the sale now that it is all over, especially as they can only be founded on speculative reasons. I am fully persuaded that we c'd have got no *higher offer* than Mr. L. gave us, whatever people may pretend to say the prop'y might fetch. I think we have got every cent it is worth & more than any other man c'd be found to give.
>
> Above are some directions in Lucretia's own handwriting, which you will oblige us by carrying into effect. I had no idea she could write as well but so far as I can discover she seems as well as when she first came to town. I cannot yet renounce all hope of her recovery. Frequently she is in as good spirits & converses nearly as well as ever she did. The Doctor (who has just left us) says he perceives nothing worse,—though Frank judges that she has failed somewhat during the time of his absence in Pomfret. It is certain that we have had the weather here very favorable and the air of Providence is remarkably pleasant to Lucr's lungs, compared with that of Pomfret.[4]

Vinton had requested an extension to his leave of absence, but the reply was different from what he expected. Instead of being allowed to stay at home, he was ordered to New York to sit on a Court of Inquiry. This may actually have been a favor, allowing him to resume duty but not taking him too far from Lucretia. New York was relatively close to home, and it was much better than being sent back to his regiment in Florida, Tennessee, or wherever else it might be stationed.[5]

As if Vinton didn't have enough to worry about, a letter from Mother brought distressing news about three year old Frank Laurens:

> Sunday, Sept. 2nd: Poor little Laurens is very ill of this dysentery—I treated him with rhubarb syrup, my old, efficacious remedy for one day, but finding it failed & that he grew worse, I informed Alex who advised me to send for a physician without delay—accordingly I sent for Dr. Wheaton[6] yesterday P.M. who pronounced it a very Serious case—he has been here again today, & finding his medicine did not take hold of the disease by altering the nature or frequency of the discharges has ordered something more powerful, wh. I hope will save the dear child—the Dr. will come again this even'g & tomorrow mor'g before Alex departs for Providence. The latter will then be able to say if it is best for you to be here—I w'd not be willing to have you made anxious, or alarmed, without cause but that tender mercy w'd be cruelty wh. w'd. conceal from a parent the danger of his child—that such danger exists *now*, you may judge, when it has been necessary to give powerful medicines every 2 hours, night & day. Joanna & I have taken turns in watching last night, the turn was hers & she has been reposing today instead of going to church. My anxiety keeps me wide awake, so that contrary to my want, when my mind is quiet I am not sleepy. I shall not close my letter, or write more till I see the Dr. hoping to tell you that a favorable change has taken place in our precious little invalid.
>
> Monday 11 o'clock A.M.: Dr. Wheaton is just gone my dear Son & I am happy to tell you that he finds the medicine given, during the past night, has arrested the *frequency* of the discharge. He will, after it is ended up (if present appearances continue) give something to alter the *character* of the discharges, wh. have been as bad as can well be conceived of & they were also incessant. It is wonderful [amazing] how soon he has become emaciated. The Dr. said he sh'd call again before Alex took his departure & w'd then inform me more precisely of the case, so that you may be able to decide on the necessity of being here.[7]

The boy's condition worsened, and on 7 September Vinton received word that he needed to make the trip to Pomfret to attend to his son. One can only imagine the agony he felt in having to make the decision of whether to stay with his dying wife or be with his failing son.

Vinton made the trip to Pomfret, but early on the morning of 10 September Frank wrote to him in a letter marked, "Please send *this letter up immediately* by a *Special Messenger*":[8]

> Dr. Brother
>
> I was called up at half past one by Aunt Betsy & found Lucretia in a painful state through shortness of breath. I called the Doctor who administered a composing draught which relieved her. She is now under its influence. But she may depart hence before morning. Frances is here. Mrs. Rathbone, Mrs. Dyer are in readiness at hand. The Doctor expresses but little encouragement for us to hope that dear Lucretia will live many hours.
>
> I wish you to come down immediately. I will keep this open till the Stage starts. I returned from N.Y. on Saturday morning. Love to Dear dear Mother.
>
> Yr. Aff. Br.
>
> F.V.
>
> Lucretia says she is not *ready* to die but feels resigned. We have prayed. O may Jesus be with her in the hour of her distress & receive her to himself.

At the bottom of the letter was a note from the doctor attending Lucretia:

> Dear Sir: I found Mrs. V. this morning at ½ past 1 quite exhausted with oppressed breathing—pulse very irregular, & weak—cool hands & feet. Should not have been surprised at her dissolution at any moment.
>
> In about 45 minutes ascension commenced breathing better and heat restored to extremities.
>
> She is now under the influence of medicine, when this subsides I fear she may relapse.
>
> L. L. Miller[9]

In a letter written to Alex the same day, Frank gives additional details of Lucretia's failing condition. He tells him, "I was called up last night & found Lucretia gasping for breath—pulse quiet & low—extremities cold & face expressing extreme alarm. Went for the Doctor (Miller) at ½ past one. He administered morphine which revived Lucretia." Frank, in his capacity as a minister, then administered the last rites to his dying sister-in-law. He told Alex, "I prayed with Lucretia last night & told her to prepare for death. I asked if she was ready. She said no not ready but resigned."[10]

On 12 September 1838 Lucretia Dutton Vinton, age twenty-eight, succumbed to her illness. Whether John made it back to Providence in time is not known. The timing would have been tight. The earliest he could have received the letter was the evening of the 10th. If there were a stage going to Providence the next day, he could have been there on the evening of the 11th. The next letter we have is from John to Mother, dated the 18th from Providence, and opens with, "We arrived safely last evening." The letter doesn't specify where he arrived from, and contains no details of Lucretia's passing, only matters concerning the care of the children and funeral arrangements. Obviously, news of Lucretia's death had already been sent to Pomfret. Perhaps Frank Laurens had been too sick for Vinton to have left him. The painful decision he had faced a few days earlier had been reversed: Could he leave his ailing child to be by the side of his dying wife? It was the type of dilemma that would tear anyone's heart to pieces.[11]

Frank Laurens recovered, but Lucretia was gone. Vinton was no doubt consumed with grief, but decisions needed to be made, whether he cared to or not. Foremost on Vinton's mind was the care of the children. Like it or not, he was going to have to remain in the army, and he could not take them with him. Frank Laurens would stay with his grandmother for the foreseeable future, at least until he fully recovered from his illness. LuLu, now six years old, and Helena, eight, would have to go to a boarding school. Of more immediate concern were matters pertaining to the funeral, including a possible dispute with Lucretia's father as to the place of burial. Vinton's letter of the 18th touches on some of these matters:

> I got a letter fr. Mr. Parker & one from Cousin Mary—all well. Mary gave good reasons why she c'd not receive the girls in her own family but proposed with much earnestness that I sh'd place them with a Miss Brown who is the teacher of young children and will do every justice to ours. There they can be boarded & Mary herself will often see them & have a general supervision over them. …
>
> Mr. Parker[12] [Lucretia's father] gives good reasons for not being here at the funeral but regrets it exceedingly. As I anticipated, he designs to have the coffin removed to the family vault in Boston.[13]

If there was a dispute with Lucretia's father, no further mention is made of it, and today Lucretia rests next to her husband at the Swan Point Cemetery in Providence.

Meanwhile, Mother was at *La Plaisance* making arrangements for the future. John had found a boarding school for the girls, but no firm decision had been made regarding Frank Laurens. On 21 September she wrote to John at Providence with possible options:

> I sent you by Alex, a note from Mrs. Wheaton written in reply to the information I asked of her respecting Miss Winsor's school. … I am much pleased with all wh. Amelia tells me of her,—She has the ground work of all true excellence & ability for education, genuine piety—Amelia speaks of her peculiar management of very young children, & pointed to Laurens as a pupil whom we c'd not place in better hands. … Yet I sh'd even wish to retain a general interest & supervision of him, if not for the girls, while their dear father is far away—They have now no Mother, yet while it shall please God to spare my life, or rather I sh'd say, my mental intelligence, I trust he will keep me disposed to be to them the next best female parent, a good grandmother. …
>
> I think Laurens is decidedly convalescent—The Doctor has not seen him for two days, & I suppose therefore, he thinks so too, yet the poor little boy is very feeble & piteous—He is now dressed in the morning & sits at the breakfast table with some support after wh. I lead him about but his joints are very weak still & he is very soon tired—He certainly gains strength, however, every day & I think, if nothing untoward happens, will be pretty sound in a fortnight. …
>
> I hope you will be able to arrange yr. affairs to yr. mind, & be with me as much as you can, during the preparation for moving, but if you are called away before the 10th Oct., either Alex or Frank *must* be here. The responsibility rests on Alex perhaps—but I hope to see you next week, & will leave all till then.[14]

Life was resuming its routine, and for Vinton that meant returning to his duties with the army. Though he still had dreams of taking up the ministry, they would have to be placed on hold. For the present he needed the stability and steady income that the army would give him. Exactly what the army had in store for him wasn't clear. The hoped-for position in the Adjutant General's office never materialized, and it may have been for the best. The quiet and solitude of the wilderness might well have been the best place for him, and that was where he was headed. Whether it was against the Seminole or the Cherokee he didn't know, but Captain Vinton was once again on his way south.

12

The Indians are Still Resolute and Obstinate

What John Rogers Vinton did in the weeks after Lucretia's passing isn't recorded, and he left no written record as to how he felt. If nothing else, there was the funeral to take care of and arrangements to be made for the care of the children. There was also Frank's wedding to attend, no doubt a bittersweet affair, considering the circumstances. On top of that, there was the task of moving Mother from Pomfret to Providence and setting her up in the new home, along with the inevitable social visits with friends and relations who had come to pay their respects. By the time mid-October rolled around, Vinton may well have been ready for the peace and quiet of camp life.

Vinton left the North around 26 October 1838, arriving in Charleston on 2 November. There he wrote to Mother, telling her of his safe arrival and giving her some details of the voyage:

> I landed here this morning after a pleasant passage of 7 days from N. York. ... Already I find myself in a Summer climate. I sit with my windows open inhaling the "buxom air" and can scarcely realize that November is upon us. ... Our Regt. is still in the Cherokee country, where I shall proceed to join it,—but I hope our destination will be Florida when winter sets in. ...
>
> In Newport I found myself entertained most hospitably in that dear family of Col. Totten's.[1] ... In my present forlorn and melancholy state of mind, the friendship of Mrs. Totten and her daughters seemed a very balm to my feelings. The world had appeared to me as a bleak and arid waste—but in that sweet domicile I was recalled to a sense of something like sympathy,—and I felt a sort of surprise, that, (out of my own dear family too) there were yet some who could feel with me,—and strive to heal the achings of my wounded spirit. ... I can scarcely fancy a happier man than Col. Totten ought to be—and no doubt is—in having gathered round him a circle of children so delightful. I shall spare no pain nor expense to make my girls what they should be—pious Christians, accomplished ladies and sensible women. As to my boy I need not say how much I am indebted to you my ever venerated be-

loved Mother for your care & watchfulness over him in sickness & in health. …

I feel myself a desolate wanderer,—going I scarcely know where and to do I scarcely know what. But for the blessed conviction that I have a steadfast friend and Director in the Benign Power who overrules us all, I should well nigh despair.[2]

Vinton may have thought he was going to Cherokee country, but the army had different plans. The war against the Florida Indians was about to resume after the usual summer hiatus, but the coming campaign looked to be very different from the previous ones. General Jesup had given up command and was replaced by Brig. Gen. Zachary Taylor, who would be operating with a much smaller force. The government had tired of paying for an expensive, endless war, and was no longer willing to commit the vast resources it had in the past. In truth, there was little need to. Most of the Seminole had fled to the Everglades, and the majority of them were doing their best to avoid the whites. For the remainder of the conflict, the Seminole would fight a guerilla-style action, making small hit-and-run raids on isolated settlements and small groups of soldiers or travelers.

Lacking both the means and the will to mount a large, aggressive campaign, General Taylor decided the best approach was to protect the settlements from marauding bands of Seminole and build forts to keep an eye on the places where he thought the enemy might be hiding. It was going to be a frustrating, depressing campaign, and few soldiers were looking forward to it. Vinton was one of the exceptions. By the end of November he and the company were back at Garey's Ferry on Black Creek, awaiting orders. Informing Mother of his new location, he detailed how the regiment was to be dispersed and the outlook for the upcoming campaign:

Four Companies are to be detached under Maj. McClintock for Tampa Bay and the region round about,—while the five remaining will ascend the St. Johns and establish a post in Palatka, thence penetrate the country across to Fort King. This last is the district of country in which I shall be engaged for one or two months perhaps,—an allotment which is as pleasant as I could expect. My course of life will be somewhat more active than formerly, which with the serenity & mildness of the climate will prove very salutary to my lungs & general health.

Florida, for campaigning operations, in winter is certainly the most delightful country in our dominions, and to compare our condition with those Regiments who are operating on the Canada frontier or even in the bleak mountains of the Chero-

> kee Nation, we have every reason to felicitate ourselves on our superior lot. At all events my mind is steadily fixed on the great truth that God is the Governor & Arbiter of all, and that he will assuredly direct every thing for good to those that love him.
>
> The Camp life to which I have returned, is productive of much that interests & pleases me and I believe that in no situation could my health be better served than here. This you know is now my principal concern. Only tell me that the darling children, for whose welfare now it is my chief purpose to desire length of days, are progressing as they should do in all moral & intellectual improvement, and I see no reason to prefer any other situation to this in which Providence has placed me,—for a time at least.
>
> As to the Indian War, I can say nothing that differs from the sentiments I have always heretofore expressed. There is no prospect of its speedy termination. So long as the Seminoles prefer their Native Country to that which has been assigned them by the Govt.—and are content to persevere in their resistance—we have no means of compelling them to submit to our terms.[3]

As 1838 drew to a close Vinton found himself in command of Fort Brooks on the Ocklawaha River (not to be confused with Fort Brooke at Tampa Bay). While there he received a letter from Mother containing news of a possible offer of employment as a professor at Jefferson College in the State of Mississippi. It was an enticing offer, and he took time to consider it:[4]

> After deliberating a day & a night on the matter I have concluded that the situation is one as well suited to my tastes & abilities as any other that could be offered me. If I leave the Army at all, this is the place best suited to my health, ambition & powers of usefulness, in any department of Civil life, and I ought not therefore to reject it. The *locale* is indeed Mississippi,—as remote, nearly, as it could be from my native State,—but my health demands a Southern climate and I sh'd be obliged in any event to select a different latitude from that of R.I. were I to enter civil life in any other walk.[5]

His major objection was the distance he would be from Mother and the children, but if he obtained the position he would simply move them to Mississippi. He was flattered by the offer, but doubted he would get the job, if for no other reason than the position would probably be filled before letters could make their way to and from the Florida wilderness. The loss of Lucretia was also forcing him to reevaluate his military career. Earlier in the year he had been ready to leave the army. Now he wasn't so sure:

> I have much remaining fondness for Mil'y life. … The Army offers me so much congenial ease & freedom that I sh'd be loathe to quit it except from a high sense of duty. The highest of all w'd be to serve my God and the cause of his holy Religion. …
>
> I have just come in from an excursion, cutting roads &c through a perfectly new country 8 or 9 miles hence, & feel fatigued with the march, but as you see not too much so to sit down to my writing desk. A walk of 15 or 20 miles a day is getting to be an affair of frequent occurrence with me—and this it is which I believe will prove so beneficial to my health coupled with the admirable qualities of this sweet climate.[6]

Fort Brooks may have been a delightful place, but it was also remote, and letters from home were few and far between. In a letter dated 18 January 1839 Vinton lamented:

> But one letter have I received from home since my departure! A long interval of estrangement, certainly;—But I ought to reflect that you cannot write as often as formerly, and that I have not now a diligent & devoted wife whose chief pleasure it was to commune with her loving husband. O when shall I cease to feel the weight of this desolating bereavement? There are seasons, when from the exuberance of my natural spirits, or the play of jocund health through my veins, that I enjoy the usual temper of cheerfulness which was my former want,—the beauties of Nature, here, so wild & luxuriant, give me equal pleasure,—my intercourse with friends, has an equal zest,—the delights of Sacred reading & holy contemplations, an equal glow of devotional rapture,—but when I open other books than the Bible, my mind soon wanders,—when I ruminate upon other things than divine, my thoughts grow melancholy,—and my whole disposition seems so weaned and alienated from the world that I experience a sort of disgust for any species of worldly pursuit. … Whether this ebbing of the ambitious spirit be the result of a subsidence of youthful enthusiasm, or the desert-like condition in which my mind was left by the departure

> of my darling one, I may not presume to decide,—but the future is to me now, a most cheerless blank,—not fanciful to regard, for I see no vision of dread, but rapid, flat & uninteresting.[7]

Vinton was in mourning, but that didn't mean he couldn't enjoy his surroundings and the beauty of nature. He was also beginning to appreciate some of life's simple luxuries:

> The River here is some 30 yds. wide, of lively flow, clear & wholesome water & abounding in fine fish. My rods & lines are of course in frequent requisition. We have deer, wild turkies [*sic*], quails, pigeons &c. in any quantity, and today I dined on veal, from a calf captured yesterday, with some beeves, by one of our scouts. The other companies have all left for various duties & I am here with mine, in sole command. I like the place so well that I sh'd be content to remain here for some time. Indeed I am becoming quite attached to Florida. With only one thing, good society, and I should prefer to live here beyond any country I have seen. But the indians are still resolute and obstinate. No one can possibly foretell the day when they will be expelled. …[8]

His thoughts then turned to his children, especially his son. He knew the burden he was placing on his mother's shoulders and was appreciative of her care:

> Frank Laurens I fear will be troublesome to you. At all events I shall think so, & regret that he is with you if he keeps you from Church, or any time at home when you w'd wish to go abroad. In such an event I desire that you will put him out to school, in the country or wherever you may judge best. He is your boy. He has no other Mother, and scarcely a father. He owes you his life, as I shall ever think, by your kind & indefatigable attentions to him when so sick at Pomfret.[9]

Vinton would have been perfectly happy to remain at Fort Brooks for the rest of the war, but the army had use of him elsewhere. The Seminole were in the Everglades, and that was where the soldiers needed to be if they hoped to end the war. Vinton and Company "B" were being sent to reactivate the remote post of Fort Dallas, which would later grow into the city of Miami.

Vinton now began a journal of the expedition. He and his men marched out of Fort Brooks on the morning of 21 January, arrived at Palatka on the St. Johns the next day, and there boarded a steamboat to take them to Garey's Ferry. From there they boarded a larger, ocean-going steamer that would take them to Fort Dallas and another company to Fort Lauderdale. Accompanying the steamer was a sailing schooner carrying three month's worth of supplies for both companies. They were headed for the most remote outposts in Florida and needed to take as much food and equipment as possible. Even mail boats would be a rarity.[10]

The trip did not get off to an auspicious start. Knowing the schooner would be difficult to sail in the river, the decision was made to tow it behind the steamboat. This was no doubt a good idea, except that the schooner ran aground three times before reaching the mouth of the St. Johns. On the morning of the 28th both boats entered the Atlantic and headed south, the schooner going straight for South Florida, while the steamboat stopped at St. Augustine to take on firewood and water. While there, they picked up another passenger and some extra supplies, including seeds for a garden the soldiers would have to plant. The only way they were going to get fresh vegetables was to grow their own.[11]

Progress was slow, as they were now towing four large boats that were to be left at the forts for the troops to use in penetrating the Everglades. Firewood and water for the ship's boilers were being consumed faster than anticipated, and they were forced to put into the post at New Smyrna to procure more. Finding very little pre-cut wood available, Vinton dispatched parties to cut wood from the surrounding forest. The task took two days, but Vinton, as with all officers, never lifted an axe. Instead, he and the post commander spent the time fishing.[12]

The trip continued, but not without some minor mishaps. As they crossed the sandbar into rough seas one of the boats they were towing filled with water and had to be cut loose, taking with her the medical supplies they had stored on board. Before the morning was over, they had lost the other three. Undeterred, they continued on, passing what they thought was Cape Canaveral in the early afternoon. About an hour later they found themselves in shallow water and realized they were close to running aground on the *real* Cape Canaveral.[13]

After somehow missing the entrance to New River and Fort Lauderdale on the following day, they reached Key Biscayne around 5:00 P.M. Just offshore was the schooner carrying their supplies. To offload the men and supplies, the ships needed to enter Biscayne Bay. Several attempts were made, but an opening in the reef could not be found. An entrance was finally located, but then another boat approached, and it was decided to hire her captain to pilot them in.[14]

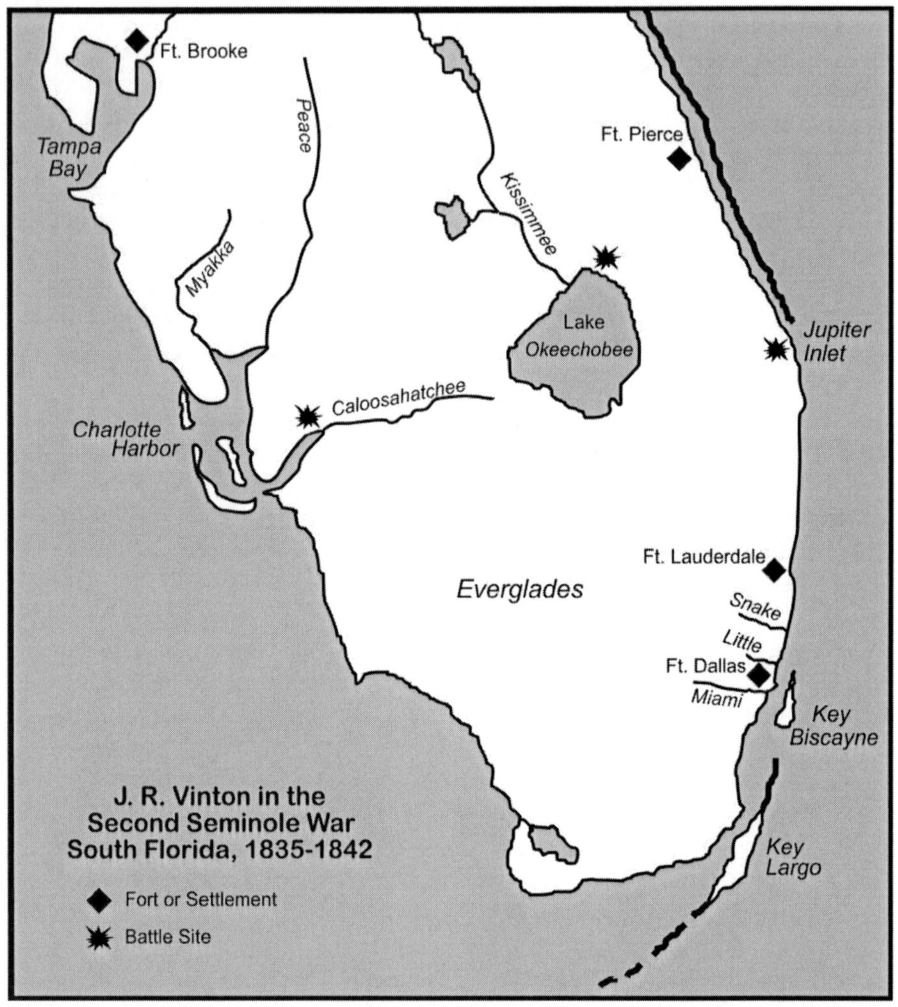

Once safely anchored behind Key Biscayne, Vinton and the other officers began to reconnoiter the area for a suitable location to erect a fort. One of the officers went up the Miami River to the site of old Fort Dallas, which had been abandoned after the previous campaign. In the meantime, Vinton documented what he found at Key Biscayne: "Luxuriant growth at these plantations and beautiful situations but the water is bad, the musquitoes [*sic*] abundant and the healthiness doubtful." He also took the opportunity to sample some of the local fruit, with varying results. "Gathered limes in plenty,—Much pleased with the cocoanut tree which grows here luxuriantly. Gathered some palma christi [castor oil] beans, one of which I was imprudent enough to taste, and in consequence was extremely sick all night. The emetic & cathartic properties of this vegetable are prodigious."[15]

The next morning, 6 February, Vinton "... took 3 boats & crews, armed, and visited the site of old Ft. Dallas, on the N. Bank of the Miami." It was a nice enough location, but the water was poor and he doubted the healthfulness of the site. The other problem was the steamer's inability to get within a mile of the place, and without the large boats they'd lost at sea, it was going to be difficult to unload their supplies. It was time to make a command decision:[16]

> Supposing it to be the object of Govt. to guard the coast as well as scout in the interior—and considering nothing more important than the health of the troops, I decided to return to the Key and there establish the new Fort Dallas. At the Key are many materials for building, such as bricks and timber—at the Miami are none. Our wagons are not arrived nor have we other means to procure timber. The superior advantages of the Key are therefore decisive in my own mind, of the question.[17]

Figure 14: Light House, Key Biscayne. Sketch by John Rogers Vinton.

The only unexposed place to store the provisions was the burned-out lighthouse across the island, which the Seminole had attacked in 1836. Having no alternative, the day was spent carrying everything from one side of the island to the other. Vinton noted that it would have been much easier on the men if the Quartermasters had included some wagons in the cargo, as they had for other posts. As an officer, he was not expected to carry crates or roll barrels, so he spent his time making astronomical measurements to determine the latitude of the lighthouse, then calculated its height.[18]

The weather was unusually warm for mid-February, and the thermometer rose to 88°F. Being it was Sunday, the troops were allowed the day off so they could relax, wash their clothes, or bathe in the ocean. Mosquito netting ("bars" as they were called), "a very essential commodity," were distributed. Vinton thought of having the men commence a garden, but wasn't sure the poor soil would yield enough produce to be worth the effort.[19]

It was a wonderful day, but as far as Vinton was concerned, one thing was missing: "We are not yet prepared for Divine Service on Sundays. I hope soon to erect the proper accommodations. If I can be in any degree instrumental in bettering the moral & religious condition of my men I shall be more happy than if I had gained a much more imposing temporal advantage."[20]

The camp began to fall into a routine. A boat came into the harbor with a large catch of Kingfish and offered some to the soldiers. "The men bought them freely, so our Camp is favored by a change in the gastronomic department ... no small matter with men confined to Bacon & bread. We have been disapp'd in the small no. of fish to be caught in this harbor.—This supply of King fish was therefore the more welcome."[21]

There was any number of things that needed to done to bring the camp to a state of military readiness. The grounds needed to be put in order and smoothed out to make suitable floors for the tents. Roofs had to be erected to protect them from the sun and rain. The well needed to be cleaned out, and the mules that had broken loose needed to be rounded up. Weapons were issued to everyone, including the doctor and musicians. At times the fact that they were in a war zone seems to have been lost on Vinton and his junior officer, Lt. George Rodney.[22] "Fished today in the bay. Better success than heretofore. Caught Grouper, Hog perch, and several other kinds of small fish, which on trial at supper proved very good. Rodney sailing in small boat,—a pastime of wh. he seems passionately fond."[23]

While the men spent the next two days putting the camp in order, Vinton continued fishing, hunting, and exploring. It wasn't just for pleasure. The fish and fowl were an important part of the men's diet, and he needed to know his surroundings in case of an attack. Although his post was called Fort Dallas, there would be no high wooden walls or protective breastwork. Their main protection was a ruined brick building where the company could take refuge if attacked.[24]

By 14 February the men were settled in, and Vinton had time to sit down and write a long letter home. Lamenting the fact that he was a long-distance parent, he began to reflect upon the care of his children and their upbringing by others. He already knew what Mother would say, and what his response would be:

> I know you will say, John, come home, and prepare a domestic hearth of your own, where, above all other places, they can best be educated. But my dear Mother, the more I reflect upon my wayward destiny the more I despair of ever realizing such a wish. Every day seems to confine me more & more in habits of recluse & single life and as the meridian of my life is perhaps gone by, I begin to settle myself in the stoical persuasion that the residue of my days must be passed much as I am passing them now, in unambitious, contented mediocrity.

He then mentioned coming across a little apron in his baggage and how elated he was, knowing that it had belonged to his son:

> I was turning over the contents of my old trunk & there found a little tattered crash apron, often worn by no less a personage than Frank Laurens Vinton. O how I seized upon the little treasure and kissed it "like mad." … I recollect, when packing my trunks, I threw in that little candidate for the "Rag Bag" thinking that the time might come when I sh'd like to set it up to bless my eyes withal. And sure enough. That same rejected little apron is now dear to me as the only tangible remembrances I have of my darling boy. …

Vinton had written the letter, but there was no way to mail it. He had no idea when the next supply boat or naval vessel might stop by, so he kept the letter open, adding to it as he saw fit. The next entry shows that while he may have decided not to enter the ministry, he hadn't given up on preaching. If nothing else, he had a captive congregation:

> 17th Sunday Evening. Today I have carried into effect my long supposed object of divine service for my Company. Even now we had no building completed to assemble in but we had boards to make seats of and I c'd not feel justified in delaying any longer. My men had the first opport'y for a great while of hearing the Scriptures read & expounded. Many might have preferred to be away about their secular employments but I tho't it best to enjoin a general attendance. I have some reason to believe that my exercises were not unacceptable to them. At

> all events I feel that I have discharged a duty & am determined to carry out my plans in future.[25]

On 18 February a steamboat arrived carrying two companies of soldiers, their officers, and Maj. Sylvester Churchill,[26] who, as senior officer, was now in command. Churchill had orders to penetrate to the sources of the New and Miami Rivers, hoping to encounter any Seminole being driven south by General Taylor's offensive to the north. They were joined the next day by a cutter from the Revenue Service (precursor of the Coast Guard) which brought a large sailboat and some row boats to replace the ones that had been lost at sea when the company first came down.[27]

On the morning of the 20th, Vinton, Captain Russell[28] of the Infantry, and their companies began to move the camp from Key Biscayne to old Fort Dallas on the Miami River. Key Biscayne was simply too far from the mainland to allow the soldiers to make frequent forays against the Indians. Soon after their arrival a party of wood-cutters noticed two Indians lurking about. Vinton and Russell immediately led scouting parties to search for any other Indians, but after two to three hours of exploring, none were found, and the troops returned to camp. The following days were spent making old Fort Dallas secure and looking for a better site up-river. That was proving difficult, as there was a shortage of the tall, straight pine trees necessary to build a fort.[29]

Vinton appears to have made a friend in Captain Russell, who was in charge of the other company at Fort Dallas. One day they made an excursion out to the nearby keys, hunting for oysters and walking the beach in search of shells. In a letter to Mother, Vinton remarked:

> I am here just now most happily associated with Capt. Russell, a gentleman whom I have known but a short time, but, whom to know, is a peculiar privilege. His company has joined mine as a garrison to this post. He is a lively Xn. [Christian] & a strong churchman. He has long been in the habit of leading Divine Service with his Company,—and now uniting with me in these efforts for the religious improv't of our men,—we find great satisfaction in our mutual cooperation. Such instances as the Capt. are rare in the Army & therefore the more to be cherished, when found."[30]

To be closer to the Indian haunts, Russell was building a second fort a few miles upriver, near where it emerged from the Everglades. He was close to the "falls" of the Miami River, a 1,200 foot long series of limestone ledges where the water dropped about five feet. This was, after all, South Florida, where ten feet above sea level was considered high ground. Beyond the falls were the vast

Everglades. Today the falls are gone, the miniscule Miami River is connected directly to Lake Okeechobee by a wide, straight canal, and the Everglades have been pushed twenty miles inland. Russell named his new post Fort Miami, but it was abandoned before he could finish clearing the land when word was received from General Taylor telling them the push from the north had been called off. Vinton and Russell were told to stay where they were and patrol the area around their post.[31]

When a steamboat paid a visit, Vinton took the opportunity to send off a batch of letters, including one to Mother. After giving her directions concerning the moral improvement of the girls, he commented on the delightfulness of his posting and remarked, "I might go on and enumerate many other pleasant attributes of my new station and crown the whole by saying that the indian war is just rife enough to lend a racy excitement to our exploring adventures."[32]

Vinton's lighthearted comment came back to haunt him two days later. After a morning excursion to the beach, he returned to Fort Dallas to find the men prepared for battle:

> 28th Feby: On inquiry I learned that Capt. Russell's boats had been fired upon in descending the river and himself *shot dead*! This was terrible information, but I had little time to meditate. Small as my garrison was, I ordered out a detachment, (26 men) and led them forth to scour the left bank of the river, cover the passage down of the boats, and cut off if possible the retreat of the enemy. But he had already gone, as usual. Traces of him in abundance were discernable. The number was supposed to be from 40 to 50. Though many rifles were fired, but one other man of ours was hit,—he is now in camp severely wounded. Lt. Woodruff[33] who com'd after the death of the Capt. says that the indians exposed themselves very much and he is confident that one or two of them at least were hit by our musketry. They displayed many of them the red flag,—a sign of a bloody determination & perhaps of rejoinder to our frequent display of the white one. ... Capt. R. was a pious, consist't Xn. [consistent Christian] & an excellent man. Just before he was struck, while the bullets were flying thick around him, he was heard to exclaim God Almighty protect me! and immediately his brain was pierced by a ball and he fell dead.[34]
>
> 1st March, 1839: The Santee [steamboat] arrived today from the Key, bringing the Maj. [Churchill] & Lt. Taylor[35] to attend the funeral of Capt. Russell. We buried him on the mound with Mil'y honors. I com'd the escort wh. was my comp'y, and his

> own followed as mourners. Maj. Churchill, Dr. Baldwin[36], Lt. Rodney, Capt. Cost, Lt. Taylor, Capt. Poinsett[37] Pallbearers. I read service, and we gave to the remains of the good Russell, all we could, the honor of military sepulture.[38]

The death of Captain Russell brought an end to the easy routine of camp life. Now, when twenty soldiers were sent out to chop firewood for the steamers, they were escorted by forty armed men. When one of the steamboats returned unexpectedly, everyone thought the worst, assuming they were bringing news that Fort Lauderdale had been attacked and overrun. In truth, the only reason for the boat's return was that it was unable to burn the mangrove wood that had been cut for use in the boiler.[39]

That in itself initiated a moral dilemma for Vinton. To get the steamer back in service the men spent all Saturday in the forest chopping wood. Major Churchill then ordered the work to continue on Sunday. Vinton noted in his journal, "On reading this I made some strong remarks in reference to my own scruples … Protesting against it as wrong in a moral and religious sense. That it was against the usages of Civil Society & in violation of the law of God,—and I believe I said I sh'd not order out my men. While the responsibility is mine, I will not. But as Lt. Rodney volunteers to do it in obedience to Maj. Churchill's order I shall wash my hands of the subject."[40]

Vinton was also not afraid to buck the system when it came to tactics. Ammunition for the men's muskets was carried in a leather cartridge box that hung from a shoulder belt on their right sides. Vinton believed that if the men were attacked, they should immediately fix bayonets and charge the enemy. He did not want them to stand around firing their muskets, making themselves good targets, and allowing the Indians to make an escape. If it came to a charge, the cartridge boxes would just be an encumbrance. Instead, he told them to carry only four extra cartridges and put them in their pockets. Neither the men nor the other officers thought much of this idea, so Vinton backed down. Even though he felt it was the correct policy, he knew that if something went wrong, he would get the blame.[41]

There happened to be a boat in the harbor headed for Baltimore, so Vinton took the opportunity to write to Mother. In it, he commented on the death of his friend Captain Russell, and then remembered the battle at Lake Monroe, where his friend Captain Mellon had been the only casualty. "This is the second time in Florida that an associate Captain has been shot, almost by my side. The Indians pick out the officers whenever they can, with keen scrutiny, and some are doubly exposed." He told of how Russell had cried out, "May God Almighty protect me!" just before being slain. Vinton remarked, "I do not pray for protection,—that is, for the preservation of my life,—because I know not that it is best that my life shall be preserved. If God chooses to reclaim what He has lent me here on earth, I ought to be ready to resign it without reserve or murmur." Vinton fully understood the irony of Russell's final prayer, but it did not shake his faith:

> Capt. Russell has left a widow and children,—who were in a great measure dependent upon his salary for support. Another instance of the great risk encountered by any lady who marries in the Army, unendowed with private resources of her own. They who look at events as illustrative of the doctrine of a particular Providence, will find it difficult to reconcile this bereavement with our notions of beneficence,—especially as the prayer for protection was so signally refuted. If the event had been contrariwise and amidst great slaughter the Capt's life had been preserved, some would have considered the result as an explicit proof of the efficacy of the petition.[42]

Biscayne Bay was turning into a busy place. Besides the steamboat and several smaller vessels belonging to the army, they were visited by Lt. John McLaughlin, commander of the naval flotilla operating in Florida waters. McLaughlin was an old friend of Vinton's from the Battle of Lake Monroe (where he had been severely wounded), but he was not at Fort Dallas for a social visit. In a combined army-navy operation, he and Vinton were going to scour the northwestern periphery of Biscayne Bay in search of the Seminole. The Indians were forcing the U.S. military to invent and learn new tactics.

The operation began the following day, 11 March 1839, with Vinton leading his men north through the woods, while the sailors scouted along the shoreline. After wading across many small streams, some waist deep, they came to Little River, about five miles north of Fort Dallas. At this point they had to be ferried across by the navy, after which they continued their march, reaching Snake Creek (Oleta River, in what is now North Miami Beach) late in the afternoon. All told, they had marched eleven to twelve miles through the dense Florida swampland. As Vinton put it, "Every body weary & dispirited."[43]

The next day was spent scouting the Snake Creek area. The navy was supposed to ferry them back at least part of the way, but when the boats didn't show up, the soldiers began the march back to Fort Dallas. Upon reaching Little River, they again waited for the navy, hoping to be ferried across. Then one of the soldiers saw some canoes approaching and reported, "Indians, Indians." Vinton, intent on avenging Russell's death, prepared an ambush. As the vessels drew closer, Vinton told his men not to fire until ordered. Then someone noticed that the presumed Indians were actually sailors. Vinton realized how close he had come to ruining his career. "Had our men fired, for wh. they were very eager, there w'd have been a calamitous issue,—and I, prob'y w'd have been the chief sufferer from it." The weary men reached Fort Dallas that evening around 5:00 P.M. Not an Indian had been seen.[44]

The routine of camp life continued, and weeks passed. Cutting wood, both for the steamboats and for construction, was the main occupation for the soldiers. A pen ("crawl") was made in the water to keep the turtles and conchs that were used as a substitute for fresh pork or beef. The soldiers didn't much care for these alternatives, but they were certainly better than army rations. During this time, only one small scout was made to look for Indians.[45]

Finally, on 26 March, it was decided to head out and make an attempt to locate the Seminole. Vinton led the expedition, and although they saw no sign of the enemy, it was no casual walk through the woods:

> Set out at early dawn with 70 men in 3 columns—Rodney com'g the right, Woodruff the left & myself the centre. Crossed the river & took a SW by S direction,—Masters & Baya our Guides, for the "Hunting ground,"—some 15 miles distant, down the coast. Country more wretched & rough than even that we lately marched over N. of the Miami. Sharp craggy rotten limestone rocks jutting up everywhere, making it difficult & painful to get along at all. We halted several times for short periods & once got entangled in a hammock but we arrived at the hour of 1 o'clk.—being about 7-1/2 hours on the way. I had tight boots wh. tortured me. Rodney wore out his & so did Woodruff. Found water only once on the route. The Steam boat was in waiting to receive us. ... We soon embarked, & returned to Key Biscayne where we left the Major & thence proceeded to Fort Dallas. Landed at twilight.[46]

No real fighting was taking place, at least not around Fort Dallas. On one quiet day, Vinton made an excursion up the Miami to accurately measure the falls. Just to be safe, a squad of soldiers scoured both banks of the river as they ascended. On Sundays, Vinton held Divine Service. Attendance was mandatory, as least for his own Company "B." For the other company, it was semi-optional:

> A majority of I. Cy. request'd to be excused fr. church. Mr. Woodruff applied for my decision in the matter. I assented, but ordered the Cy. on a 3 hours scout, as a proper alternative. Work & Mil'y service is not to be suspended on Sundays to favor idleness & consequently vice, but to furnish an opport'y—to those so disposed,—to worship God and be improved by

> moral & religious instruction. If they decline this, then the alternative is open to them. The option is plain & fair.[47]

On the last day of March a schooner arrived bearing news of a possible war with England. Since the end of the Revolution there had been disagreement over the boundary with Canada, especially in northern Maine. Even the boundary survey that Vinton had served on in 1818 had failed to end the dispute. Up until the 1830s it had been mostly an academic argument, because very few people actually lived in the contested areas. In recent years the situation had begun to change, most notably around Maine's Aroostook River, where logging operations were taking place on land claimed by both nations. Troops were gathering on both sides of the border, and war looked imminent. For Vinton and the soldiers at Fort Dallas, the possibility of war was actually good news. It looked like their ticket out of Florida. It was, "The only opening I can possibly see to a termination of the Seminole contest. Now we can patch up a peace with these ind's [Indians] without a compromise of the Nat'l honor." Yet for all the saber-rattling, neither side really wanted war, and tensions eased. The boundary dispute and other matters were officially settled in 1842.[48]

The army at Fort Dallas may not have been very aggressive toward the Seminole, but the Indians had not forgotten they were there. On 1 April the natives decided to remind the soldiers that a war was still going on:

> Alarmed by yells of Indians today within a half mile of our fort. A large body of them (say 40) were discov'd by the Guard of the wood party,—who attacked them and drove them. Lt. Rodney with a reinforcement went out & after him Lt. Woodruff. The Dr. Baldwin was accidentally on the spot & aided Sergt. Walker in directing his men. I rem'd. [remained] in garrison with a small party, thinking to be attacked on my right flank. Rodney & the Dr. returned about 2 o'clk, having pursued the Ind's. 8 miles, far into the Everglades. … Men of B. Cy. behaved gallantly but too rash.[49]

For the next week or so things remained quiet. The men continued to cut wood, and the officers kept up their fishing. Much of the time was spent in the various boats that were kept at the post, often traveling between Fort Dallas on the mainland and the depot at Key Biscayne. Because of this, Vinton held drills in boat handling and rowing. On 9 April a Revenue Service cutter stopped by on its way north, and Vinton took the opportunity to write a letter to Mother. Like millions of people who would follow, Vinton was enchanted by the South Florida climate. In addition, it appeared to be good for his health:[50]

> I continue to like this climate above all others I have ever visited. … The air I breathe is the great vital principle which must be of the purest & mildest or I feel immediately a threatening sense at my lungs of their extreme tenderness, & of my precarious hold on life. … Blowing the flute in early life so much as I did, was certainly an injury to me. Whatever may be the advantages or the delights of music to a young man, I think I w'd not consent that my Son should become a flutist. …[51]

The matter of a possible war with England was still on everyone's mind, and Vinton took time to expound upon the subject. As with religion, he could see no other viewpoint save the one he'd been brought up with. Never does it enter his mind that the British side of the argument might be as valid as the American side. Rather naïvely, he could see few downsides to taking on the world's greatest military power. To Vinton, the Seminole seemed a more unconquerable foe than the British:

> We have had quite recently, a rumor of war, which gave quite a new current to our thoughts,—A rupture with Great Britain, and a large provisional increase of the Army!—I confess the idea of such a rupture gave me no little pleasure. Not that I sh'd rejoice to see so serious an evil imposed on the Country but that it would virtually relieve us from one of even a more malignant character.—I mean the Seminole concern. But for some such excuse for withdrawing our troops from Florida, I confess I do not see how we can ever be able to do so. Once out of this scrape, and it will be long & wisely deliberated, I hope, before we get into it again.
>
> A war with Gr. Brit. would benefit this country in several ways. It would concentrate the national feeling, improve the national sentiment,—invigorate our energies,—neutralize all those sinister influences which are now at work to undermine & spoil our national fabric, such as the Abolition excitement,—the impending controversy respecting a tariff, &c &c. The Army & Navy w'd be greatly benefitted and a larger field opened for promotion. These considerations taken together are sufficient I think to counterbalance whatever expenditure of money or of life might be executed by a war—and, the cause being a just one, the defence of our nation'l honor & dignity from wanton insult & injurious aggression, I c'd not hesitate long in deciding the question.[52]

He then turned his attention to domestic matters, most notably the children. The girls were off at boarding school, but Mother and Frank Laurens were living with Alex, his wife Eleanor, and their two children. Vinton longed to be there to observe the home life:

> How I sh'd like to happen in upon you one of those evenings when you were all gathered round your parlor fireside and the little cherubs prattling about the floor! But I must clip the wings of fancy or I shall have tears in my eyes. And the daughters! Have you seen them lately and do they ever come to see you? I am extremely anxious that Helena sh'd write me. … The very quail tracks that her little hand once traced, in wanton mood, on a leaf of one of my books, are precious to my sight. And sweet little LuLu,—can she not also draw some lines to certify that she has at least taken pen in hand to render some testimonial of affection to her dear father.[53]

Vinton had also received letters from Alex and Frank imploring him to quit the army and take up the ministry. He had reluctantly given up on the matter, both for his health and for financial reasons. He felt his lungs required clean outdoor air and a vigorous lifestyle, and he needed his steady income to support his family. Besides, he might soon be needed in a war with Great Britain. "Whatever might be my future views as to leaving the Army, this is not the time for me to think of it," he explained. "This probability of a war with G. B. is of itself a suff't [sufficient] reason why I sh'd remain to serve my Country in the hour of her need. I sh'd never forgive myself for my recusancy if I sh'd be induced to resign in such a crisis. … The Army is my calling and I ought to make it good."[54]

The stalemate that had become the Second Seminole War was about to take a turn. Political changes had occurred in Congress, and there was now a willingness to reach a settlement with the Seminole. The apparently endless war had become extremely controversial and expensive, and the government was tired of paying for it. In essence, a Native American nation had forced the government to sue for peace, something that had never happened before, nor would happen again. Bowing to Congressional pressure, the administration sent Maj. Gen. Alexander Macomb (the man who had replaced Vinton's old friend General Brown as commanding general) to negotiate a peace. Although Macomb met with Indians living in the northern part of the territory, he needed to talk to representatives of the more intransigent groups, who were now dwelling in the

Everglades. To accomplish this task, he dispatched Lt. Col. William S. Harney, who arrived at Fort Dallas on 14 April 1839.[55]

Accompanying Harney were two Seminole leaders, Tomoka John and Charley Brown, along with a black interpreter, Sandy. On the 16th the trio was sent into the Everglades to try and make contact with the Seminole, but returned two days later without success. Colonel Harney, in the meantime, set up headquarters at Key Biscayne and ordered Fort Dallas abandoned and Vinton to bring his men to the key. This was not to Vinton's liking. At Fort Dallas he was commanding officer, while at Key Biscayne he would be under Harney's command. It was more than just a matter of pride. As commanding officer, he could draw double pay for rations. Once settled in at Key Biscayne, Harney designated the post Fort Russell and named Vinton commanding officer, thus smoothing the captain's ruffled feathers.[56]

On 26 April a truce was called, and it was announced that General Macomb would meet with the Indians at Fort King on 1 May. On the 29th Tomoka John and Charley Brown returned with two Seminole, and both seemed happy to hear about the truce. They were immediately sent back into the interior to contact Sam Jones (Abiaki) the most intractable of the Seminole leaders. Vinton was hopeful, but realistic. "Our hopes of a favorable issue are greatly cheered. There may be difficulties in the way of a new treaty but the entering wedge is fixed and we may soon see peace."[57]

On 20 April, a new officer, Lt. William H. Shover,[58] arrived for Vinton's company, along with thirty-two additional recruits. Two Indian runners came in to announce that Sam Jones had been contacted and was happy to hear of the truce. Sam himself would not be attending the negotiations, they said, as the old medicine man was not given to travel. In truth, long experience had taught him not to trust the whites, and he was not going to let himself be taken under a flag of truce, like Osceola and the others had been. Instead, he sent a delegation led by his war leader, Chitto Tustennuggee. Harney helped cement the deal by sending Sam a half keg of whiskey. Finally, on 9 May, all was in readiness and Harney, along with the Indians, departed by steamboat, on their way to meet with General Macomb.[59]

With the prospect of peace at hand, Vinton wrote to Mother about his hopes and concerns for the future. Like many other soldiers he had begun to understand what the Indians were fighting for. "The great object of the Indians in their pertinacious hostility & resistance of our measures, has been to secure not any particular possessions or limits of territory but only the privilege of remaining somewhere in the country in which they were born & to which they are attached more than to life."

The government was willing to let the Seminole remain in the Everglades, but Vinton saw a problem. "There will be much opposition on the part of the Floridians to any such compromise, because the whole of their territory has not been cleared of the Indians." He had also learned to respect his enemy. "They have proved themselves to be a formidable party in the fields and consequently will be a respectable one in the Council house." Still, he was mildly confident that things would work out. "But I will not suffer myself to doubt that matters may be so adjusted now as to secure to these heroic sons of the forest all that may be necessary for their future comfort & wellbeing,—and to ourselves all the jurisdiction, influence and safety to our border population which can in reason be desired."[60]

Vinton was happy that the war appeared to be ending, but he was less enthusiastic about leaving Florida. He loved the climate, even with the worrisome flies and mosquitoes. He also enjoyed the solitude, though he was reluctant to admit it. With Lucretia gone, he found he had less use for society. The only thing he really missed was the family, especially the children.

With a truce in place, Fort Russell settled into a comfortable routine of cutting wood, constructing buildings, mending boats, gardening, and fishing. Even a bakery was set up. At the request of the Adjutant General's office in Florida, Vinton sent in a report covering the status of Fort Russell and Key Biscayne:[61]

> The water at Key Biscayne is perhaps as wholesome as can be found in the neighborhood but is still far from agreeable. It is not a little impregnated with salt & like all the water in this region in the summertime, is almost tepid.
>
> The climate here is considered to be as healthy as that of any other locality in Florida and owing to the sea breezes, is undoubtedly preferable to most positions inland. But the temperature is so uniformly high as to superinduce debility in the best constitutions,—the glare of the Sun upon the sand causes night blindness and other afflictions of the eye, and the excessive prevalence of musquitoes [*sic*] & sand fleas render the place so uncomfortable that from this cause alone it w'd be almost impossible to reenlist a man with the prospect of being stationed here for any length of time. Against this latter pest (the musquitoes) the ordinary musquito bar is but a partial defence. As yet we have experienced but little of this evil compared with the aggravated extent to wh. exists in the months of August, Sept. & October. At that season it is confidently asserted by those formerly resident here, that Key Biscayne is utterly uninhabitable.[62]

In the meantime Mother was still trying to convince him to leave the army. Vinton was having none of it. He realized the time had passed for him to take up a new career:

> The supposition that I can live without my salary is altogether erroneous,—and when I look round to find a substitute for the Mily profession wh. I am asked to relinquish I see none that w'd satisfy me. The profesr'sp in Mississippi [Jefferson College] seemed just the thing for awhile, but learning that the salary was trifling & the tenure contingent, I renounced the idea at once. …
>
> I am now nearly 40 yrs. old. I have a family to support and no means sufficient for their maintenance without the aid of my salary. It w'd be suicidal to abandon this resource unless I c'd replace it by another, which other is not to be found. A few years more of frugal savings & I hope I may be able to join to agricultural life. Meanwhile I am not unhappy in the Army. I have increased means & resources every year in my increased rank & command. My children are well situated. The daughters confessedly so,—and although you think the boy sh'd be with *me* for the sake of a father's guiding hand, I am not sure I sh'd think so were I even at a Northern garrison. He is too young to be an intellectual companion for me and needs the elementary instr'n of schools wh. no garrison could furnish.[63]

Summer was coming, and Key Biscayne was becoming unlivable. It was getting hot and the rainy season had arrived. The chief complaint was the insects. "Musquitoes are becoming almost intolerable. Our nets are too coarse. The men suffer & complain much." Six days later, Vinton wrote, "Increase of musquitoes." Finally, on the last day of May 1839, Colonel Harney returned with news that the negotiations had been successful and that a treaty had been entered into. It looked like the war was over.[64]

13

As Pleasant a Situation as Can be Found

On 1 June 1839 Captain Vinton received orders to move his company to the post at New Smyrna, located at the north end of the expansive Mosquito Lagoon north of Cape Canaveral. Having received Gen Macomb's announcement of a truce, Vinton was optimistic about the war soon ending. He also hoped their new location would be more comfortable in the summer than their present quarters. He and his men departed Key Biscayne the following afternoon.[1]

Before leaving, Vinton penned a letter to Mother in which he took stock of his situation. "All my resources at the North are still locked up or dried up, and I have little else than my pay to live on. This is a bad state of things. Yet I ought to be most thankful to Divine Providence that I have been withheld from resigning a Commission which is for me so sure & unfailing a resource. … Things have so conspired that I am now linked to the Army by the bond of necessity, and necessity has no law." Stuck in the army, he was determined to make the best of it:[2]

> It is my proper course now to make my inevitable profession as agreeable and profitable as I can and indeed there are elements enough in it to justify the endeavor. … Our present exclusion from Civil Society, wh. for the time is no serious privation to me, is the chief argument against all this, and times may soon so change as to turn it to my advantage. If I c'd resign indeed upon an independent fortune & be my own master it w'd certainly be preferable to the life I am leading now,—but if the alternative be a condition of such straits & embarrassments as w'd compel me to some laborious or harassing employment for my subsistence, then I s'd be mad to renounce the Commission wh. now I hold. After 25 years of Mily life it w'd be no small hardship to bend myself to the drudgery of business in a city.[3]

Vinton and his men arrived at their new home on the morning of 4 June. His first comment was, "New Smyrna a most pleasant place."[4] Indeed it was. The settlement had been developed by Scottish doctor Andrew Turnbull in 1768, when Florida was an English colony. Turnbull had imported about 1,500 settlers from the Mediterranean, mostly Minorcans and Greeks. The colony failed, but in later years the area prospered, becoming home to several thriving sugar plantations. Sugar had been Florida's largest industry until the beginning of the war, when Seminole warriors had methodically destroyed virtually every plantation in the Territory.

The destruction caused by the war was plainly visible to Vinton and his soldiers. The fort at New Smyrna had been erected around the ruins of the stately home of the Dunham Plantation, an elegant two-story stone structure fronted by six tall columns. By the time Vinton arrived, little remained of the building's walls, the stone having been put to more practical uses in and around the fort. Only the six round columns were still standing, facing the dock that extended into Mosquito Lagoon. It was surely the grandest entrance to any fort in Florida.[5]

Figure 15: Fort New Smyrna, 1839, by Capt. Harvey Brown.

The importance of Fort New Smyrna was not its proximity to the Seminole but its location on the coast. It was one of the few places south of St. Augustine with a good inlet into the calm lagoons and rivers behind the barrier islands that ran the length of the East Florida coastline. Not only were these lagoons a place of refuge for passing boats in harsh weather, they were also vital as refueling depots for the numerous steamboats the government employed in the war effort. Steamboats were a wonderful advancement over sailing vessels, but the wood-burning engines of the day were horribly inefficient and forever in need of fuel. For this reason, wood cutting occupied most of the time for the small contingent of men at New Smyrna. There were usually no more than a few dozen men at the post, including two or three officers, a surgeon, a hospital steward, about five non-commissioned officers, two musicians, and a carpenter or mechanic.[6]

Vinton quickly settled into a routine that seemed to consist mostly of fishing, hunting, drawing, and riding. One journal entry noted, "Riding out this P.M. to Pickerel Brook saw 2 large bears. They fled when they saw me."[7] Other entries included, "Sketched Ruins. [a sugar plantation destroyed by the Seminole early in the war, now a county park] … Fishing. Thunder Showers.—Took Bass—(or redfish), catfish, trout, Blackf. Cavalley. … Fishing & Sailing A.M. Riding horseback P.M. … Fishing A.M. with Seine. Fine day. … Shot owls . … Painting Landscape. Rode with Dr. DeLeon."[8] He summed it up in a letter to his mother, saying, "It is indeed as pleasant a situation as can be found in Florida and I am much envied in being so fortunately located."[9]

Although Vinton was in the remote wilds of the Florida Territory, the divisive subject of slavery could not be avoided. Even something received in the mail could cause trouble:

> Frank sends me occasionally the Emancipator & other abolition prints, and lately I wrote a polite acknowledgement & rather advised a discontinuance of his favors. … My reason for declining to receive these prints is simply because they are interdicted by the laws & sentiment of the Southern states and are considered incendiary. As such they do, here, more harm than good, and as a Cr. [Christian] it becomes one not to do violence to the public sentiment of the community in which I happen to live. … If we of the North come among them to receive at their hands the hospitality of friends & fellow citizens, we owe it to them & to our Xn. [Christian] duty not to violate the rules of their social order. …

The army officer corps, especially those trained at West Point, had learned to be apolitical whenever possible, especially on the subject of slavery.

Vinton was feeling good, and even the war seemed a blessing. While writing about his brother Hammond, he told Mother, "He has escaped all campaigning in Florida, though his long absence from his family was sufficiently painful. But he & all of us are much the better for the Florida War. The outbreak we first thought so disastrous has been productive of much good to those who have passed through the ordeal."[10] Vinton had cause to feel optimistic. The truce with the Seminole seemed to be holding, and it appeared as if the war might indeed be over. As was their habit, the Indians were in no hurry to gather in their new reservation, but this was expected and did not seem a problem.

With little news to report from New Smyrna, Vinton commented on political matters. In a 9 July 1839 letter to Mother, he referred to a speech by John Quincy Adams, who had gone back to the House of Representatives after leaving the Presidency. Adams, like Vinton, was trying to walk a fine line on the slavery issue:

> Mr. Adams surveys a wider field than is generally visible to the eyes of our Northern Abolitionists, who hug one idea until they fall into a monomania—He looks *far*, too, as well as *wide*, & judges of remote consequences with wonderful penetration. I agree with him that bad—horrible as Slavery is,—the evils of disunion & civil war are yet more horrible still.—A choice of evils is left us, and it is our duty to choose the least. …

Vinton was still holding his Sunday Services, but wasn't getting much support from his fellow officers. At least he could count on the attendance of the enlisted men, who had little choice in the matter:

> I have two Lieuts. attached to my com'y. Rodney fr. Delaware & Shover fr. Ohio. Both young gent'm of intelligence. So is our Dr. DeLeon, fr. S. Carolina,—so that our little circle is as pleasant as can be expected from a quartette. But neither of them are religious or religiously inclined,—nor were any of our Comrades so at Key Biscayne. The Dr. is a decided infidel. So was Dr. Baldwin at K. Bis. The young Lieuts. are generally "nothing at all," in relig'n.—How seldom we find young men disposed to any serious inquiry of the kind! I have even to require my N. C. Off'rs. to make the responses in our Ch. Services, the Lieuts. not always attending and when present not inclined to enter even thus far in the active observances of religion. You may hence readily perceive how much of "up hill" work there is for any Officers in the Army who attempt to carry on relig's services for his garrison. I am not sure that I have *even one* of all my Sunday Auditory, who w'd not rather be rambling in the woods & see the church done away with.[11]

The war appeared to be winding down, and the camp at New Smyrna remained locked in its summer routine. The men cut wood for the steamboats and drank too much, while the officers worked at hunting, fishing, and paperwork. Very few Indians were seen, and none of them appeared hostile. In his journal, Vinton noted, "4 Ind's arrived—sold a bear to the men, departed again. Serg't Young drunk on guard. Luther Wardon inebriated. … 13 Ind. came in bro't venison. Women & child'n. Same family as came in before. Jack Kelly & his relations."[12]

Being interested in intellectual pursuits, Vinton was happy to pass on a "message in a bottle" that some Indians had found on the beach. The science of Oceanography was in its infancy, and gathering data was a hit-and-miss affair. The note read:

> Barque *William* of Irvine, Thomas Clark commanding, from Liverpool for N. Orleans, Jany. 19th 1839, Lat 18.54 N, Long 78.16 W. This bottle was thrown overboard for the purpose of ascertaining the direction & velocity of the ocean currents, and it is earnestly requested that those who may find it will publish the same in the Nautical Magazine or Shipping Gazette.[13]

As far as Vinton could tell, the Seminole seemed satisfied with the new arrangements they had made with General Macomb. The Indians had, after all, been granted permission to remain in Florida, the one thing they had been fighting for so desperately. Yet there were flaws in the agreement, and they soon came to the surface. For one thing, not all the diverse Seminole bands had been part of the negotiations. An outlaw group known as the Spanish Indians was not even considered part of the conflict, but could cause trouble for everyone if they became violent. More than anything, there was the simple matter of distrust. The Seminole had been lied to so often that there was little belief the agreement was everything the whites said it was. For all they knew, the whole thing was nothing more than a ploy to gather them in one place so they could be easily rounded up and sent west.

As part of the agreement, a trading post was being set up on the Caloosahatchee River in Southwest Florida, near what is now downtown Cape Coral. It was an isolated post, with only a small garrison for protection and no fort to provide refuge should the Indians decide to attack. And attack they did, early on the morning of 23 July 1839, killing about two-thirds of the approximately thirty men present. The news traveled as quickly as it could through the Florida wilderness, but it still took over a week to reach Vinton's command.[14]

Exactly why the Indians had attacked the trading post was unclear, and still is. Had the Seminole been unable to believe the white men when they were told the war was over? Was the attack the work of the renegade Spanish Indians, as a number of Seminole claimed? Was the poorly-guarded store simply too good a target to pass up? It really didn't matter. As far as the government and the majority of the American people were concerned, the Seminole had stabbed them in the back, and the war would have to be pursued to its bitter end. Vinton and the rest of the army were not leaving Florida. In a letter to Mother, Vinton gave his opinion of the matter:

> The more recent aspect of affairs in Florida is less favorable to a permanent peace than was supposed. The Seminoles have lately attacked & killed a portion of Col. Harney's party who had gone South to establish an Agency & limits for them, and now we feel that the treaty of Gen. Macomb has been violated & hostilities virtually renewed. This treacherous act on the part of the Seminoles places them altogether in the wrong: For we had granted them about all they asked for, and nothing but a savage thirst for blood could have prompted this last act of perfidy & massacre. Still this may have been only the act of a small party, unadvised by the general tribe & unapproved. But as to this no one can say.[15]

Knowing the war had recommenced, Vinton ordered the men to keep their muskets loaded and be prepared for a nighttime attack. Those same precautions had no doubt saved their lives at the Battle of Lake Monroe earlier in the war. Patrols were sent out to round up any Indians who were in the area, but none were found. A few Indians, unaware of the situation, made the mistake of coming into the fort:

> 10th Aug. This forenoon, *Six indians*, (an aged man & woman, a middle aged man & his squaw, and two children,)—came in, as they have heretofore done, to trade or beg,—and in obedience to instructions from Col. Gates we have detained them as prisoners. I have reason to suppose from their conduct that they knew nothing of the Massacre of Col. Harney's party. Relying on our good faith they have put themselves into our hands, and I am sorry that the treachery of their tribe has made it necessary to adopt on our part measures of reciprocal severity, though never I trust to the same degree.
>
> Lt. Rodney who was Offr. of the day had the two men tied, but I directed their release, trusting to the strength of our prison walls & the vigilance of our Guard. I instructed the Sergt. to treat them with all kindness consistently with their cases. Nicholson says he heard 3 signal whoops in the woods this evening near the Canal. A rescue by the friends of these indians might well [be] attempted. Doubled the guard tonight—One Sentinel being still out on the front & left flank & the other over the indian prisoners.[16]

Several days later, Vinton wrote in his journal, "Indians in some trouble last night. The warrior tried to escape,—offered his squaw to the Corp'l. (Burns) to tempt him off his guard;—then tried to hang himself. Now pretends to be sick, but will not take medicine."[17]

Hostilities may have commenced in theory, but it was still Florida in the summertime, and no one was inclined to do any serious fighting. In a 12 August letter to Mother, Vinton reminded her of how good a position he occupied:

> I believe I have spoken to you of our fine aquatic sports here. You know I am specially fond of fishing and here my opportunities for indulging in my favorite diversion are very great. Boats & men at my command & all appliances to boot. … We are surrounded with a most beautiful park of Live Oak & Magnolia,—the bay is spread out before us, which affords us fine salt water bathing,—the roads in our vicinity offer pleasant rides on horseback and we get the mail by Express once a fortnight. These are *some* of the agreeable features of New Smyrna as a station.[18]

With a minimal threat from the Indians, the fort at New Smyrna settled back into its routine of wood cutting and fishing. Considering that many posts in Florida were abandoned for the summer because of sickness, New Smyrna could be considered one of the more healthy places in the peninsula. While filling out his monthly reports at the end of August, Vinton noted that no one was on the sick list. He also had time to do a little hunting and shot an owl. He must have only wounded it because he noted, "Make a pet of him, to clear my tent of rats & mice."[19]

It was now November, 1839, the time for active campaigning to begin. The "sickly season" was supposedly over, but not everywhere. Yellow Fever was raging in St. Augustine, and a number of Vinton's fellow officers, including Lieutenant Rodney, his second in command, succumbed while visiting the city. As he told Mother, it was all part of fighting a war in Florida:

> Several of our brightest men are gone (of the 3rd Arty) of whom are Poole,[20] Rodney & Jennings.[21] They all died of the fever at St. Augustine, a place usually esteemed remarkably healthy. The pestilence joins with the savage in hostility to our Army. There does indeed [seem?] to be a Providential decree gone forth that here at least, the red man shall [maintain?] his ground. It is not in the power of any regular Army (not exorbitant in numbers) to expel the Seminoles from this peculiar & wide spread territory. The native resources for their subsist-

> ence & defense are almost exhaustless—whilst the obstacles to our success are in the same ratio numbered. It happens too that the Gov't. is now powerless for want of means,—the Treasury lean & hungry—the Congress disgusted,—the commercial world embarrassed and the Army repugnant. What then can be done?[22]

The day-to-day routine continued as autumn progressed. Hunting and fishing, while certainly enjoyable, also helped to keep the men fed. Vinton was especially happy when large schools of spawning mullet appeared. Then, as now, mullet roe was considered a great delicacy. Being surrounded by so much water, boats were of particular importance to the post, and a boatyard was constructed to keep the vessels in good repair. Vinton even went as far as to have a small sailboat built for the pleasure of the officers. He named it *Picayune*, and enjoyed taking it out in the bay and up the rivers on fishing expeditions.

One of Vinton's main problems at New Smyrna was providing accommodations for the men. There were plenty of trees to be cut for fuel for the steamboats, but most of it was short, twisted mangrove or scrub oaks. Tall, straight pine trees, the kind that made good lumber, were hard to find. For this reason, buildings were crude and small. With winter approaching, it was necessary to construct adequate quarters, and the arrival of a new surgeon who expected better accommodations only added to the problem. The Quartermaster's Department, in charge of such matters, seemed unconcerned and turned a deaf ear to requests for lumber, building supplies, and a carpenter.[23]

It was the holiday season, but there was not much opportunity to celebrate at Fort New Smyrna. Vinton and his men, like soldiers from the beginning of time, no doubt longed to be home on such special days, but duty had called them to the wilds of Florida, and they had to make the best of it. Doing his part, Vinton authorized an extra gill of whiskey for Christmas dinner, after which the men held a dance. Unfortunately, there were no women at the post to dance with.[24]

New Year's Day, 1840, wasn't much different. Vinton went on a scout and shot two cranes, while the surgeon and some companions went down to the beach and shot a porpoise. Vinton didn't record if it was part of the New Year's dinner. Once again, the soldiers held a "men only" dance to mark the day.[25]

The duty may have been pleasant, but Vinton could not forget there was a war going on, even if it was being fought in other parts of the Territory. Scouting parties were occasionally dispatched, and artillery drills held. On 24 January the men were reminded exactly why they couldn't let their guard down. As Vinton told his immediate superior:

> This morning our wood party, consisting of a Corporal & six men,—being at work about a mile from Camp,—was fired on by indians,—their number reckoned to be from 15 to 20.
>
> At the first volley, one of our men (Downing) was shot through the hand. This was the only injury they received.
>
> As soon as the alarm was given I marched to the rescue of the party with Lieut. Shover, and every disposable man from the garrison—numbering however only 10 or 11—leaving Dr. Worrell[26] with his steward, convalescents &c in charge of the fort.
>
> We scoured the woods & hammocks in the vicinity & followed the trail of the Inds. until lost in the thick hammock but c'd not succeed in overtaking them. Downing's wound is severe but not dangerous & hopes are entertained of his speedy recovery from it without permanent injury.[27]

Confined to a small outpost as the men were, it was inevitable that personality conflicts would occasionally arise, and as commanding officer it was Vinton's job to handle such matters. Unfortunately, he now began to have trouble with his new surgeon, Dr. Edward Worrell, who felt he deserved better quarters and demanded that he be assigned the cabin Lieutenant Shover was using. Vinton denied the doctor's request, pointing out that Shover had used his own labor to improve the old building. Miffed, Worrell wrote to General Taylor, complaining of bias on Vinton's part and charging him with several irregularities. He also asked for a transfer.

Vinton was happy to go along with the transfer, but in a long letter to Taylor, he vigorously disputed the charges Worrell had made. As far as Vinton was concerned, it was nothing more than childish grumbling. "As to the doctor's being 'compelled to live in a tent outside the defenses &c' he has always had the privilege of pitching his tent where he pleased. The situation of his tent is now the same as it has been for a year past when occupied by other officers, and none have ever complained of danger. I have myself always lived 'outside the defenses,' and yet sleep soundly!" The best explanation Vinton could offer for the doctor's behavior was that Vinton had denied him leave to go to St. Augustine.[28]

Vinton's chronic shortage of soldiers was finally relieved on 22 February, when a steamboat arrived carrying twenty-two new recruits, nearly doubling the men under his command. Sadly, one of them arrived with a broken leg, which the doctor was forced to amputate.[29]

As for Dr. Worrell, he was still giving Vinton trouble, and it was starting to get petty. During the monthly muster and inspection, Vinton ordered those who were sick but able to walk to fall in with the rest of the troops. Worrell ignored the order and didn't send the men out until the order was issued a second time. On the following Sunday, he refused to decide who was well enough to attend church services, saying it was Vinton's responsibility. Then the doctor demanded that one of the company corporals be brought up on charges. Vinton found the charges to be groundless and refused to have the man arrested, to which the doctor responded that he would take the matter to a higher authority. On 9 March Vinton wrote in his journal, "Another letter fr. Dr. W. Very disrespectful. But I decided not to take any notice of it. He seems to be set on making trouble, personally as well as officially. In order to put a stop to his writing I must needs refuse to receive any further comm. fr. him."[30] Matters did not improve, and an entry two days later stated:

> Artificers ordered at work on hospital. Dr. W. protested against it,—and when I went fishing stopped them fr. working. After I returned, finding no reason'l objection to them proceeding I ordered them to proceed & rebuked the Dr. for his countermanding my orders. He excused himself on the ground of his being Comg. Officer during my absence, &c. Commenced to pitch a hospital tent to please the Dr. though against my own judgment.[31]

In a letter to Mother dated 28 March 1840, Vinton discussed the matter of compulsory attendance at his Sunday Services. He had to admit that most of his fellow officers did not think it was a good idea, and that nine-tenths of his congregation were unwilling participants. One of them had even asked how he could quote the Ten Commandments, especially the one declaring "Thou shalt not kill," then send the men out the next day to shoot Seminoles. As usual, Vinton was able to reason the objection away. "I have heard many officers urge similar arguments against religious service in camp, but have always regarded their objections as superficial & trivial compared with the manifold benefits that occur from it."[32]

Another matter he wrote Mother about was the army's use of bloodhounds against the Indians. It was widely known that bloodhounds had been instrumental in ending a slave rebellion in Jamaica by being able to track the rebels to their mountain hideouts. It seemed the perfect solution to locating the hidden Seminole camps, so a number of the animals were brought from Cuba, along with their handlers. Abolitionists in the North immediately raised a howl of their own, complaining the dogs had been brought not to hunt Indians, but to catch runaway slaves. Humanitarians also worried that the dogs would tear into helpless Indian women and children. To Vinton, it was all humbug and hypocrisy:

> The pub. attention I see has lately been drawn toward Florida more by the cry of "Bloodhounds" than it could ever have been by the cries of murdered women & children. I hope the Govt. will not be deterred by this sickly sympathy on the part of our Northern dames & Spinsters from the use of these valuable auxiliaries in operating against a concealed & implacable enemy. Who objects to keeping a mastiff in our houses to defend them from the midnight robber? Who objects to those improvements in the manufacture of fire arms by which a rifle now is 5 times more efficacious (i.e. *destructive*) than it was 50 years ago? And yet when we have an emergency that requires the agency of a dog's olfactories to aid us in the pursuit of the subtle foe we hear it called cruel, inhuman, barbarous, disgraceful. Depend upon it, the most humane method of carrying on this war is that which promises to be the most prompt & effectual. I know that "ends do not justify means," but where the means are comparatively justifiable, those should be adopted which are demonstrably the best adapted to the end. Now against these stealthy Seminoles there seems to be best for us no other resource than the nose of a dog in order to follow & find them out. They have no villages,—no local habitations,— They are scattered all over the area of 45,000 sq. miles and must be hunted out like wolves & badgers, or we must abandon the territory. … Our Northern sympathizers profess great horror at the use of dogs in war, and yet tolerate, nay admire the 9 barreled Colts' rifle, or any other improvement by which the enemy can be destroyed 9 fold.—Now this is nonsense. For my part I am not more insensible than others to the claims of humanity but I wish to be consistent. War & its instruments are all bad enough & I sh'd like to see the whole swept from the face of the earth, but I cannot join in the mawkish repugnance wh. some people profess against dogs, when they tolerate the rifle, the bayonet, the sword and the blunderbuss.[33]

The whole matter wound up being a lot of talk over nothing. The Cuban bloodhounds had been bred to track runaway slaves in forests and open country, but had never been trained to follow the scent of an Indian moving through the swamp. In the end, the project was abandoned.

For the most part things remained quiet at Fort New Smyrna. The soldier who had been wounded in the hand during the skirmish was given a disability discharge. The new hospital had been completed, and a grain storehouse and bakery were under construction. Vinton was excited to hear that there was still a dispute with Great Britain concerning the Northern Boundary, which, if it came to war, would certainly cause him to be ordered out of Florida.[34]

Vinton was also getting back into his artwork. He made sketches of Osceola and Key Biscayne from memory, painted Lieutenant Shover's profile, and made a portrait of the regimental sutler, Joseph Ferriera.[35] By far the most gratifying thing was the transfer of Dr. Worrell to Fort Lauderdale on 10 May. Vinton didn't comment on the transfer, other than to make a notation in his journal a few days later that said, "Get along without a Dr. pretty well." A replacement, Dr. Charles Noyes,[36] arrived on 30 May.[37]

The summer of 1840 was approaching, and Vinton was beginning to doubt that his regiment would be transferred north. Not that he was in any great hurry to pack his bags. When he compared his present lifestyle to that of a city dweller, he saw only one downside:

> If I jump into my swift sailing little pinnace, on a bright sunny day, with my orderly to carry my fishing gear & hoist my sails,—and hie me to the sea beach or the romantic lagoons of the upper river, and so seek out the bass, the sheephead, the trout, & cavally, with which these waters abound,—or if I mount a half dozen men on horses and with my own sleek sided steed, gallop 6 or 8 miles into the pine woods & hammocks, flushing up the partridges, the wild turkies & the deer as I go,—or in a variety of other ways sh'd I indulge in my usual pastimes, I certainly feel that many a city beau, of large pretensions too, might well envy me my privilege and be not unwilling to exchange for them, his tawdry, humdrum round of courtly dissipation. … Still my dear Mother, I sh'd like of all things most to come and see you & my little children. …

There was one disadvantage to living in the wilds that he often alluded to: the lack of "society," as he called it. Most of the time, the term meant the cultural, social, and business aspects of life in the city, but once in awhile it referred to female companionship, something that was definitely lacking at Fort New Smyrna. Mother had broached the subject of her son re-marrying, but Vinton did not take the idea too seriously. He was convinced the army was no place for a married man and that an appropriate woman would be hard to find. "Perhaps there may be such a one somewhere in the world, but I sh'd have to go out of Florida to find her." As long as Vinton remained in a remote outpost on the Florida frontier, his matrimonial prospects were dim indeed, and it may have been exactly what he wanted.[38]

14

Happy No Where—Contented Any Where

The Florida War had entered its fifth year, but there was little news for Vinton to relate to the folks back home. Zachary Taylor, who had been in command of the war since 1838, was replaced in May 1840 by Gen. Walker K. Armistead. Taylor had fought a defensive war, preferring to protect the settlements rather than actively pursue the Seminole. Armistead preferred a more aggressive approach, but lacked the men and material to do much immediate campaigning, especially since the summer rains would soon be upon them. Under the circumstances, the best he could do was attempt to re-open negotiations. On 16 June 1840, Vinton's 39th birthday, orders were received to display the white flag at all posts. In the meantime, Vinton continued to send out the occasional scouting party, either on horseback or in boats.[1]

The little community at New Smyrna was growing. Besides the hospital, storehouse, and bakery, other buildings had been constructed or were in progress. Lieutenant Shover was busy building a windmill, and Vinton was making an anchor windlass for a new, larger sailboat that was being constructed. The little port was busy enough that a pilot, Captain Dummett, set up shop to guide vessels into and out of the harbor. To celebrate Independence Day, a twenty-six gun salute was fired (one for each state in the union) and a dance was held in the evening.[2]

Vinton was one of the few people at the post who had not taken time off to visit St. Augustine. He had been at New Smyrna for over a year, and except for the numerous scouting, hunting, or fishing expeditions, had not left the place. Before that he had spent more than a year at Fort Dallas, an even more remote location. Considering that most of his time was engaged in what might be considered leisure pursuits, he probably didn't need the classic military Rest & Recreation, but he did long for a little "society," so on 16 July he, Dr. Noyes, and four soldiers hopped aboard a steamboat headed for St. Augustine.[3]

For the better part of a week Vinton spent his time visiting old friends and riding about the area. On Sunday he attended church, twice. Stopping by the post office, he found a letter from one of his superiors telling him that some of the regiment would soon be headed north, and the remainder would be out of Florida by October. It sounded good, but Vinton and anyone else who had spent much time in Florida knew better than to get their hopes up.[4]

After a week in the city, Vinton noted in his journal, "Begin to be impatient to return." A few days later he was stricken with a fever, and the next notation in his journal read, "Quite sick all day." He was still sick the next day and doubted whether he would be able to make the return trip to New Smyrna. With the assistance of friends he was able to board the steamer and report on the 29th, "All returned very joyously to New Smyrna."[5]

The fever (probably malaria) lingered, though on the Post Return taken at the end of the month, he did not include himself as being on the sick list, either out of pride or because he was being nursed in his quarters and was not officially in the hospital. On 2 August he noted that the fever had broken, but on the 11th it returned. On subsequent days he wrote that he was fatigued and feeble, and too weak to conduct his normal Sunday Service. On the 17th he began to take Quinine, two grams per hour for four hours. On the 20th he was able to report that his health was improving, and on the 22nd wrote, "Recovering!" On the 26th, however, he wrote, "Rode too far & too fast today. Ill at N[ight]," and was taking Quinine the next day. He had now been sick for a month, yet in a 28 August letter to Mother, who was now residing with Frank at Newport, he makes no mention of his being ill.[6]

For most of September 1840, Vinton's health remained questionable, and by the end of September there was fear an epidemic might have broken out. One soldier had died, and seven others were in the hospital. Though no one really understood what was happening, Vinton had returned with an infectious disease, and the Florida mosquitoes were spreading it throughout the post. [7]

Perhaps the sickness led to a bout of introspection, and the need for constant care re-ignited a longing for female companionship. Whatever the case, in a long letter to Mother dated the middle of September he still does not mention being ill, but he does spend quite a bit of time examining his own priorities and habits:

> You say I am "an anomalous character,—happy no where,—contented any where."—I think so too, Mother. When I compare myself with other men, I perceive how strangely I differ from them in many particulars, and am often at a loss to decide whether I am constituted more or less happily than the average. I have a consciousness of faculties which might be usefully employed in many situations of life, but which are utterly buried in the obscurity of my actual lot. Yet I long not for labor or display on any public arena, nor covet any of the honors in the bestowal of the community. I often wish that I might be more actively employed in furtherance of some end clearly conducive to the welfare of my fellow man, but to mix with them,—to elbow them,—to struggle for preeminence,—to excite envy, or cause mortification,—I w'd rather remain in obscurity myself. …

> It is useless to disguise, however, that my prolonged detention in Florida causes me many hours of disquietude. I feel that the sacrifice is almost too much to be borne. Yet after all,—a change w'd only be a selfish gratification,—and perhaps not altogether beneficial to myself in the ultimate result & certainly not advantageous to the pecuniary interests of my children. Nowhere could I save and lay up so much for them, as I can do in Florida, where my own expenses are on the minimum scale. …
>
> But *my children*, who, after all, are the main objects of my solicitude, will soon require the egis of a *home*;—the benign & potent influence of parental supervision. As you strongly intimate,—it is time for me to take up the subject seriously, by forming a new connexion, which shall not only fulfill the important requisitions embraced on this point, but the many others on which depend so much of my future happiness. … I look around to see where my heart could rest satisfactorily in search of an object capable of answering its demands but almost in vain. My own advanced age might prove an obstacle on the one hand, and being compelled to select from corresponding age in the opposite sex, would prove no less an obstacle on the other. Where could I find a young lady willing to take a residence with his 3 children, who should herself possess intelligence, sweetness of disposition, piety, comeliness of person, respectability of conscience and a competency of this world's good? I have no doubt such candidates might be found if I had leisure & opport'y to look them up, but my time is short and my field of observation circumscribed. I do indeed know of some that would answer many of these requisitions, but not all of them; and I hardly know how I could dispense with any one.[8]

As Vinton's health improved, so did his mood. The persistent rumor that the regiment would be sent north did not prove true, and it looked like he would be spending another winter in Florida. In a letter to Mother he commented:

> Dr. Noyes tells me he has seen no Officer in Florida who bears his exile from Society so cheerfully as I do. … Officers here are generally all grumblers, of necessity. But I have many resources not usually possessed by the mass. Besides reading then I have my pencil, which (you will see by my portfolio) has

> not been idle. I have a taste for angling, which calls me forth very often to a vast field of enjoyment.—I have a mechanical turn which I can indulge here with such aids & facilities as are peculiar to a garrison. I have a garden, and I raise fowls.—Few men who can endure seclusion at all, will be more comfortable and contented than I can make myself, with the appliances I can here command. Therefore should I murmur then? I find it far more pleasant to be cheerful than to be fretful, therefore am I cheerful. …

Vinton spent the next few paragraphs justifying a new, and at first unspecified, form of recreation he knew Mother would disapprove of. He began by pointing out that a "life of sensation" was not all bad and need not interfere with intellectual and spiritual pursuits. He then went on to list the privations of life in Florida (totally ignoring the contradiction with his previous paragraph) as justification for such sensual enjoyments:

> We live upon the mere elements of existence,—the plainest food, pork & beans, the roughest shelter, the hardest bed,—sleep disturbed by constant apprehensions of the Enemy,—small scope for exercise, and a treadmill routine at that,—total privation of all society, save that of 2 or 3 individuals who may or may not be agreeable company,—few books, often read through & through,—and a mail not oftener than about once a month, the severest trial of all. …

He then dropped the bomb in the most circumspect manner, appealing to her sense of open-mindedness, mentioning all his years of self-sacrifice, all while attempting to allay any fears she might have of the consequences:

> Well, seeing what a desperate condition is ours, what objection would you have to an ingenious discovery & the adoption of a new pleasure (an innocent one of course) although it might be one of sensation? Smoking, for instance, which I have always loathed for myself, seems to be a source of rich enjoyment to those who practice it, and I have often thought I was foolishly denying myself a good thing merely because I feared to encounter the first qualms of repugnance. It has therefore become a serious question with me whether I ought not learn to smoke. … I c'd break up the habit at any time if I found it to be detrimental to my health or interests. Did I not relinquish the flute of which I was formerly so fond? Has not my life

> been all one continuity of self denial in every case where duty or expediency demanded a sacrifice? I think I sh'd never get so fond of segars [*sic*] as I am of Buckwheat cakes, yet I would give up the cakes tomorrow if I found they disagreed with me.[9]

He obviously hadn't heard of nicotine addiction, didn't consider his frail lungs, and didn't tell Mother he'd already started smoking.[10]

Vinton's health may have been improving, but not fast enough for Dr. Noyes. The doctor thought Vinton needed to get away from New Smyrna and enjoy a relaxing ocean voyage, with the opportunity to visit friends along the way. What Vinton got was two-and-a-half weeks on the steamboat *Gaston*, carrying men, mail, and supplies to posts farther down the coast. His journal recounts a few hurried stops at Forts Dallas, Lauderdale, and Pierce, with most of the time spent at sea, often while the ship fought gales. In a letter to Mother, he gave a slightly different account of the trip:[11]

> I have lately made a trip down the coast in Steam boat,—stopping at the three Mily. posts South of us and greeting many old acquaintances among the Officers. My object was to recruit my health & strength after a late slight attack of fever. The sea is a great appetizer, and whether from this, or the influence of a change simply of scene and atmosphere, I returned quite renovated, and am now as well as I ever was in my life.[12]

In the same letter, Vinton mentioned writing to the children and went on at length about the military being an excellent path to the White House. It was, after all, an election year, and an old friend, Gen. William Henry Harrison, would soon win the contest. He then gave his views on the prospects for ending the war:

> The character of the controversy is becoming every day more sanguinary and vindictive. Our prospects of ending the war by ridding Florida of the Seminoles, not at all improved,—nor is there any seer among us shrewd enough to divine by what earthly means a peace can honorably be brought about. Even the indirect measures of bribery, bonus, or gratification, (call it what you will) applied to the cupidity of the Chiefs,—will prove ineffectual,—for their control in such matters as this, extends scarcely beyond the precincts of their own family connexion, and however readily *they* might be bought to emigrate, the mass of the Nation would still hold fast to their own native

> forests,—stubborn & inflexible as they have already proved themselves to be.[13]

On Christmas Eve 1840, Fort New Smyrna had an unexpected visitor. "Capt. W. H. Freeman of the Schr. John Melburg, with his mate, came up to the fort today, reporting himself shipwrecked, and four of his crew drowned in landing, at a point on the beach 5 miles below Musq. Inlet. Sent a party to find the bodies & bury them. Unsuccessful. Probably devoured by sharks. Gave Capt. F. a pair of pants & offered him bed & board."[14]

On Christmas Day, instead of celebrating or holding services, Vinton attempted an expedition against the Indians. In a report to his superiors, he told them:

> A report having reached my ears that certain Indian signs had been discovered near the wreck of the Brig. Morris lying on the beach some twenty miles north of this post, I determined at once on an expedition to that place presuming that if the nature of the cargo had become known to the indians, I could scarcely fail to find them there. With Lieut. Shover and a detachment of my company, I have today visited the wreck and examined the shores both on the river & seaside, but we have found neither canoes nor tracks, nor any signs of indians having been in that vicinity. The Rum was in the same situation as when left by the wreckers, a short time since, pieces of sheet lead were lying exposed which no indian would have left unappropriated if he had been there.—And in all other respects, we found ample reason to believe that the report alluded to has no foundation in fact.[15]

The season for active campaigning had returned, and General Armistead began to put his troops in motion. One of the plans was for a scout along the coast. Vinton was ordered to lead an expedition south to Fort Ann, an abandoned post from an earlier campaign. There he would hopefully meet with Major Childs, who would be coming north from Fort Pierce. On New Year's Eve Vinton, Lieutenant Shover, the sutler, and twenty-eight soldiers set out in six boats, travelling up the river that ran behind the barrier islands. On the first day they made twenty miles. On New Year's Day 1841, Vinton and his men reached Fort Ann on the eastern shore of the Indian River. Finding no sign of Major Childs, the force turned around and arrived back at New Smyrna on 2 January. Later reports stated that Major Childs had killed or captured forty Indians and Blacks during his expedition.[16]

Figure 16: Indian mound near Fort Taylor, upper St. Johns. Sketch by John Rogers Vinton.

For Vinton, it was time for another visit to St. Augustine. On 3 January, he, Dr. Noyes, and Mr. Ferriera (the sutler) boarded the steamboat and arrived in the old city that evening. After stopping by the post office to pick up his mail, he wrote a letter to Mother:

> On arriving in this city a few days since, I found your letter of Dec. 5th with one from Helena also, who writes regularly once a month. It is now a half year since my last visit to St. Augustine, and I find myself again in the midst of friends and a very agreeable society of strangers from the North. The winter for the most part, is the most desirable season here, especially with reference to the company who come to visit our mild climate for health or pleasure. As an episode in the even tenor of my life, an excursion to Augustine is productive of much enjoyment. My friends seem to make a sort of jubilee of the occasion, by giving parties & dinners.—And so for a week or ten days all is gaiety & smiles. But for a permanent residence I am not sure but New Smyrna might be preferred. There I have my leisure & my field sports & aquatic diversions, which are all I prefer to a routine of those social visitations which w'd fill up my hours if in a city. But whether for better or worse, Smryna is my station and there my duty lies. This consideration with me is generally sufficient to close the argument.[17]

Although Vinton had left very strong hints that he'd decided not to leave the army, Mother wasn't listening. She still wanted John to resign his commission and come home, and she began to use his own arguments against him. Quoting a letter he had written in 1837 concerning the immorality of the Seminole War, she extended the argument to imply that the military might not be an honorable profession. Not knowing her exact situation, it would be unfair for us to speak to her motives. What we do know is that she was now in her late sixties and responsible for John's three children. Helena was now ten, LuLu eight, and Frank Laurens five. All were in boarding schools, but managing the finances, seeing to matters like clothing and school supplies, and taking care of any emergencies was her responsibility. We have no idea of her physical or mental state, or how much hardship she was under. One thing to note is that in many of his letters John asked that she give him an estimate of the expected expenses for the children, but she had yet to comply with his request.

Vinton seems to have been stung by the notion that his mother thought the military might not be an honorable profession, which was especially odd since she had worked so hard to get three of her sons into West Point. Although he usually tried to be circumspect when discussing delicate matters with Mother, this time he decided to be more direct. He had learned to accept his lot in life, and was content with his decision. His primary concern was that his children be provided for, and his steady army income seemed the surest way to do it.

He began by admitting that there were certainly questions concerning the morality of the war against the Seminole, but that the situation had changed since the Indians had broken General Macomb's agreement and attacked the trading post at the Caloosahatchee. But all that was beside the point. As far as he was concerned, the moral certainty of any single war was irrelevant to the question of his professional morality:

> It is not however from this or that particular controversy that the general question is to be decided,—whether the Mily. is a righteous profession or not. You have given it yr. sanction by choosing it for yr. sons,—and when I reflect on the whole subject and view the wide field it embraces, I see less to object to, than can be alleged against more than one half the pursuits of civil life which are called innocent or unobjectionable. If the vocation be justifiable then, it should be a matter of conscience with us to perform all the various duties of it, with alacrity & good faith. The great moral question of the rectitude of a particular cause in which the Army may be called on to engage, must be settled by the constituted authorities of the country,—whose province it is to decide them. …

> You, my dear Mother, desire of all things to have your son near you and so you condemn the Army in order that he may leave Florida. He, on the other hand, finds the Army a pleasant, an honorable, a profitable profession,—more congenial to his tastes than a laborious civil employment & necessary for his maintenance, and so he argues in favor of the military. The Seminole War is certainly a wretched & unpleasant episode in the general current of my professional experience, but it still belongs to the category and however disagreeable,—it ought not to disgust me with the Army altogether. The Country is involved in this war and desires most earnestly to have it prosecuted to a successful issue, and on whom can the Country call to execute its will so appropriately as the Army, its constituted agent for all such purposes? It would be mean and pusillanimous to back out in such an emergency, when for twenty years I have been sustained & educated & cherished by the Nation, enjoying halcyon days, & rendering easy service. No. The military is my vocation for an indefinite time to come,—on principle as well as on interest. A more respectable one I am sure cannot be found in the whole wide range of human pursuits,—a more favorable one to my health I could not conceive,—and as my rank & immunities are daily improving, I doubt if any w'd promise a more satisfactory return for service rendered.[18]

Having made his point, he changed the subject, pointing out how much he would have liked to have been with the family for Thanksgiving, and whether or not he should purchase a piano for the girls.[19]

After a pleasant two-week stay in St. Augustine, Vinton returned to the routine of camp life at New Smyrna. On 26 January a patrol was made to the north, but no sign of Indians were noted, and the only surprising thing was that six hogsheads of rum had not been taken from a ship that had been wrecked the previous year.[20] Beyond that, there wasn't much else for Vinton to report. A troop of mounted Florida Militia were operating in the area, but not finding anything of interest. At the end of January the thermometer reached 80°F, but two weeks later it was down into the mid-twenties for almost a week, and many of the nearby orange trees were destroyed, thereby removing some variety from the men's diet.

The thought of his mother considering the military a dishonorable profession was still bothering Vinton, for in his next letter home, almost the entire letter (a relatively short one) was devoted to his Christian duty as a soldier. He concluded by telling Mother, "Debatable as many of these points are I still think that the military profession is not forbidden by Christianity but is necessary to the well being of society, the preservation of order and the maintenance of National independence and dignity."[21]

Tracking Vinton's day-to-day activities now becomes more difficult. His journal ended on 28 February 1841, and if there was a subsequent one, it has not survived. We are left with only his correspondence, mostly to his mother, to fill in the remainder of his service in Florida, along with copies of some of his official correspondence from his letter book. We can assume the daily routine at Fort New Smyrna continued, especially the fishing and other aquatic pursuits, and we can also assume that the novelty had long worn off. Still, the monthly post returns show little disciplinary problems or other troublesome matters.

Doing what he could for the war effort, Vinton occasionally put his men out on patrol. Yet try as he might, there were simply no Indians in the vicinity to make war on. In a letter to his immediate superior, Colonel Gates, he detailed one of those expeditions:

> I have the honor to report, that on Monday the 15th Inst. [March] I set out with four boats and 25 men to examine the shores of the Halifax River some 35 miles up and particularly to visit Mount Oswald [now part of Tamoka State Park], a place much reconnoitered by the indians two or 3 years since. This old plantation is situated on a point of land or peninsular formed by the Halifax & Tomoka Rivers. My design was to land at night, stretch a line of men round the extreme and be prepared at day break to surprise & intercept the Enemy if he should have been there. Our bivouac for the night was made within seven miles of the place, and at 3 next morning the command was in motion. My design was well executed by the men and every part of Mt. Oswald was examined,—but without observing any sign of indians. After some further scouting in those parts, we returned to New Smyrna.
>
> We shall scout the country between this and Lake Monroe in a few days, with such force as we can mount on horses. And afterwards, an expedition to the head of Musquito Lagoon, beyond the Haulover.[22]

Vinton may have felt as if the war, and life in general, was passing him by, yet he professed it didn't bother him. If things weren't going well in this world and old age was creeping up, his faith told him there were better things ahead. As he explained to Mother, "Why then should I now find any subject of regret in the passage of years, and the approach of that Great Futurity to which the Soul was constantly reaching forward as the only Repository of true and consummate bliss? Religion alone can supply an adequate solace for the afflictions & disappointments of life."[23]

At least there was some good news to report concerning the war. General Armistead had given up trying to bribe the Indians into emigrating, and the winter offensive, limited as it was, seemed to be having some effect. In a short note dated 3 April 1841, Vinton told Mother:

> I have but a moment to write you a few lines, as a Schr. stopping here for a short time, offers a transient opportunity. We have lately been flattered with accounts of Indians coming in at Tampa for emigration to the number of 500, and more expected. Gen. Armistead is persuaded that the war is nearly at an end. We all hope, of course, that it is so,—but I shall rest in small confidence of this result until I see the indians actually shipped off. Our Mily. operations this past winter have been more active & effective than usual, to which probably more than to any other cause, is attributable the present submissive disposition of the enemy.[24]

General Armistead had been making progress in the war, but in May 1841 he was replaced by Col. William J. Worth, a much younger and more energetic officer.[25] Worth soon issued a directive rescinding a truce that had been declared by his predecessor, and ordered hostilities to be resumed. In an indication that the Florida War was winding down, the number of troops were reduced, and there would no longer be any state volunteers or militia units brought in. Even with the reduced troop strength, Worth was determined to keep the pressure on the Seminole until they surrendered. Although many of the officers and men serving in Florida couldn't always see it, the constant patrols and harassment were having the desired effect. As villages and farms were discovered and destroyed, the Indians were finding it increasingly difficult to survive. Small groups were being captured or simply giving up. Their numbers were dwindling, and if things continued as they were, sooner or later there would be too few warriors to carry on the conflict.

As the war continued inexorably on, time also passed for John Rogers Vinton. On 16 June 1841, he wrote a long, loving letter to his mother, reminding her of all that she had done for her children, and how contented he was:

> By the date of this letter, you will see that I write on my birthday,—and as my want is, I sit down to dedicate a portion of the day to you. … Forty years!! How time passes! … And yet the temper of my mind & tastes, is still youthful. I love more the simple pleasures that took my fancy most, when a boy,

> than I do the graver pursuits of merely ambition. My drawing, my mechanical tools, my fishing, sailing, or riding, belles lettres, music &c,—all these have still more charms for me than politics, or any of the stirring subjects of public life which occupy men of the world.[26]

Vinton had been at New Smyrna for almost two years and was no doubt eager to see his family and enjoy a change of scenery. At times it must have been frustrating. His children were growing, but he could not see them; there was a war going on, but not where he was; he was stationed in a wonderful location with many leisure amusements, but it was like a treadmill, and afforded him little chance of advancing his military career. He needed a change, but until the war ended, there was little likelihood of that happening. What he did not know was that things were about to change in the Florida War.

15

The War Has Been Carried On With Renewed Vigor

Congress, the administration, and the American people were getting tired of the Seminole War. The conflict had been raging for almost six years and not only was it expensive, but it had become morally questionable. Just how many men and how much treasure was the nation required to expend to drive the few hundred remaining Indians from their homes in the desolate swamplands of southern Florida?

The occasional patrols out of New Smyrna continued, but without any sign of Indians. One problem Vinton faced was that he had no junior officer to help lead the patrols. Lieutenant Shover was still there, but he had been appointed to the position of Commissary Officer, and new regulations allowed him to excuse himself from other duties. Vinton was unhappy with the situation, especially when the two other lieutenants technically listed as part of his company had been assigned to other positions in Florida. Having no junior officers to take over the company in his absence, there was little chance of him being granted the three-month's leave he was planning to request.

Summer had arrived, the heat had become oppressive, and the sick list was growing. Vinton was feeling fine, but the high temperatures were forcing him to curtail some of his beloved outdoor activities. In a letter to Mother dated 14 July 1841, he expressed surprise at her lack of reaction to a subject he had brought up some months earlier:

> I marvel that you have said nothing against smoking. Do you not recollect, that I told you, in one of my letters that I was trying hard to learn to smoke? Perhaps you think my constitutional repugnance to tobacco will be safeguard enough?— And indeed I find it uphill work. I cannot yet smoke a whole segar [*sic*] without revulsion,—But there is a little segar, in paper, called by the Spaniards "cigarito," which I can smoke with decided enjoyment, and I think without any detriment.[1]

The heat and sickness were making it hard to carry on the war effort. At one point he reported twenty to thirty men on the sick list (out of sixty) and added, "The opinion of the Surgeon, officially expressed (& my own also concurring) was that any prolonged exposure of the soldiers to the Sun's rays would almost invariably bring on fever & prostration." When another officer arrived with orders to take thirty-five of Vinton's men for a special scouting mission, only twenty-one could be found fit for service.[2]

Besides being left short-handed, Vinton was annoyed that Colonel Worth had sent someone else to lead the mission, especially since it was a scout into territory he had recently been into. Vinton felt obligated to bring the matter to Worth's attention, reminding the colonel that there was no other officer "who can command my own men & reconnoiter my own precincts with better effect that I can myself."[3]

Figure 17: Brig. Gen. William J. Worth.

That was not the only trouble Vinton was having with Worth. He had complained of the regulation that allowed Lieutenant Shover to excuse himself from company duties, and in response received a letter that said, "exception was taken to my mode of criticizing Army Regulations, my simple duty being to obey things."[4] Yet whatever his personal problems with the colonel, Vinton had to admit that the man was doing his job. Whether the result would be worth the cost was a matter of opinion, as he told Mother in a letter dated early August:

> Since Col. Worth was placed at the head of affairs in Florida the war has been carried on with renewed vigor and I hope the efforts of our troops will be crowned with some success. To carry on a Summer Campaign in such a country & in such a season as this, has always been a measure of questionable policy. Not but that the enemy might be reached & severely injured by cutting up his cornfields & other planting interests, but that the sacrifices of life & health on the part of our troops would more than counterbalance any advantage we might reap from such a course. The Colonel, however, goes for victory, at any expense.[5]

Vinton may have had a grudging respect for the way Worth was conducting the war, but he also knew a self-promoting man when he saw one:

> Col. Worth is one of our most ambitious as well as one of our most active & efficient Officers. … While, therefore, he exerts himself, with untiring assiduity, to infuse new energies & life into all the departments of his command here in Florida, he is not less careful that the newspaper editors should know it,—and that every Mily. movement, whether dignified by the name of "exploits" or not, should be presented fully to the public eye with no loss of garniture or crystallization for want of the "pen of a ready writer." And this is the way, my dear Mother, to gain popular applause in America,—and with it, the splendid rewards of popular favour. Let Col. W. go on, and have but an even chance with Dame Fortune, and it would not be surprising that he sh'd be one day President of the U. States.[6]

Back at New Smyrna, Vinton was saddened by the death of his good friend Dr. Noyes, who had been his constant companion for over a year. As he lamented to Mother, "He was an elegant & accomplished young man,—fond of music & the fine arts generally, and an agreeable companion for us all here,—but he had an organic disease of the kidneys, coupled with an attack of fever which cut him off,—suddenly, as we all thought, though not unexpectedly to himself." Noyes's replacement, Dr. Richard Weightman,[7] fared no better. Soon after his arrival he was on the sick list, and was dead by the end of October. New Smyrna was no longer a healthy place to be.[8]

Mother was still pressuring her son to come home, even to the point of urging him to get a surgeon's certificate stating he needed to leave Florida. In response to her question about his plans for the future, Vinton told her:

> Indeed it is not easy to say because so much depends on contingencies which I can neither foresee nor control. I do not regret a single day I have passed in Florida thus far and why anticipate evil? Still let me sketch out a program: By Spring I shall proby. have a post on the Seaboard—a fort on the Gulf frontier perhaps or in N. Carolina. Such a command is a good thing to build upon. Few situations in life are better. I w'd rather have it than the best farm in Ohio or Connecticut. Whether to marry or not depends on the question whether I can find the woman fitted to augment my happiness. I am very happy now. She ought to possess many graces to add still more to my stock of felicity. …

> For myself I feel less disposed than ever to quit the Military. I begin now, after a long & wearisome apprenticeship, to reap some of the advantages of a master workman. Instead of trudging in a subaltern grade, I find myself enjoying the honors & benefits of command. This is a pearl of price,—and not to be idly thrown away. … I am forty indeed but in the prime of life,—can jump as high & run as fast as ever,—graver in some things but with my accession of dignity, no increase of infirmity as yet,—nor even gray hairs.[9]

In the meantime, patrols in search of the Seminole continued, but the results were always the same: No sign of Indians. At least summer was coming to an end, and everyone at New Smyrna was beginning to feel a little more hopeful. Vinton told Mother his health was better than ever, and he credited it to his simple diet:

> Here our food is very simple & plain. Desserts and knicknacks,—sweetmeats & bons bons, we never see. Never eat between meals. Never see milk,—pies,—preserves,—and seldom puddings.—Vegetables are rare,—and even potatoes are not to be had at some seasons of the year. Thus plain meat & bread, with such little varieties as we can add in the way of fish, oysters, turtle, crabs & partridges, constitute the whole scope of our larder. These latter we get for the trouble of hunting or fishing after them,—but when we would buy potatoes we must consent to pay at least 3 dollars a bushel for them. Buckwheat cakes for breakfast, however, I can almost always have,—and this is a luxury which will compensate for a thousand privations. …[10]

He told Mother that there were once again rumors of the regiment being sent north, but he didn't sound very confident in them. General Scott was making promises, and Colonel Worth was predicting a quick end to the war, but Vinton had his doubts. "I confess I see even now but little hope of a speedy end of the war with the Seminoles." It all depended on the Seminole. As long as they held out, his future was up in the air.[11]

In family news, Vinton was happy to hear that Frank was about to re-marry, his first wife having died in childbirth. Always conscious of social standing, Vinton welcomed the news that the bride-to-be, Elizabeth Mason Perry, was the only daughter of naval hero Oliver Hazard Perry. The only problem he could see was that she was not a wealthy woman:

> I agree with you that the alliance with Miss. P. w'd be highly satisfactory to our side of the house and I cannot but prefer it much to the other name mentioned. Our family w'd then be connected by intermarriage with two of the noblest houses known to the chivalry of our country [referring to Hammond's marriage to Gen. Brown's daughter Pamela]. If Frank makes no account of wealth, or at least a portion with his wife, I can see no obstacle in the way. For an Officer of the Army, I am more than ever convinced that this consideration is, in a matter of wedlock, too important ever to be overlooked. I c'd no more be happy without "competency" in the married state, than I could without "health" or "peace,"—the three ingredients, according to Pope, which are necessary to our temporal felicity. Frank's situation is different.[12]

Perhaps inspired by Frank, Vinton had not given up on the thought of remarriage. Unfortunately, there was little he could do about it on the Florida frontier. For the moment, he was happy to let Mother do the matchmaking:

> I am glad to find that in the midst of yr. rejoicings you have not forgotten me. The names you mention struck me very agreeably,—yet among them all I hear no further mention of that fair young widow of N. York whom you formerly described so pleasantly and distinguished as your preference, over all yr. acquaintances! As a mother for my children, no one can have better early prepossessions than Sarah F. knowing them all from their birth and associations many kindly recollections with their juvenile years—a friend of their Mother and always intimate in the family. But under her wing the girls w'd not grow up with those advantages of social & intellectual eminence which w'd place them in the front walks of society.[13]

Vinton had often told Mother that he was satisfied with his military position, and that he was not an ambitious person. Yet it is hard to believe that he wasn't disappointed when he saw his old West Point classmates or younger officers being promoted ahead of him. In a draft letter addressed only to "Dear friend" (with "much modified" written across it), he vents some of his frustration:

> Your letter of Sept. 17 addressed to Capt. G.—reached us yesterday & at the same time came news of that officer's sudden death. Thus are we falling one by one in Florida not by the en-

emy rifles but by a pestilence not less deadly & alas without the solace of that poor recompense of honor which might follow the being slain in battle. …

You speak of brevets and name several officers whose claims have never struck me as being surpassingly prominent, and humble as are my own pretensions I must think that they are nearly as respectful as those of D.D.T. [Daniel D. Tompkins][14] and J.D. [Justin Dimick].[15]… My term of service has been much longer than the others you mention & scarcely less devoted. But the truth is I am hidden, forgotten, buried, in this remote wilderness & have disdained to seek the mediation of any friend to have my claims shown up at HdQrs.

Here is, perhaps, the fatal point. For the action at Ft. Mellon & for other things, Fanning & Harney were both brevetted. I com'd the Batt'n of Arty on that occasion. Davidson[16] is dead and no other Capt. than myself now serves in the Army who was present on that occasion. Now, my Dr. Sir, I do not say I deserve a Brevet for that or any other service, speaking absolutely, but if Brevets are to be conferred on such as you have named, then my relative claims take a substantive character which I think cannot justly be overlooked. Enemies have done me injury I fear. It is time that friends sh'd do me good. Yet I w'd rather cut out my tongue than ask a Brevet, as what honorable man w'd not? I sh'd hold such a distinction as of little value if grounded on favor or partiality. Yet with all my modesty I think shall be excusable in grumbling if Bvt. Maj. is given to T. & D. and some others left uncared for. …

He also noted receiving orders to leave New Smyrna. He and his company were being transferred south, closer to where the action was:

We are on the eve of our departure for the South, to operate with Maj. Childs. If under the Egis of his good fortune we can succeed in finding any indians, I hope we shall give a good account of them. Here I have been scouting all Summer in spite of my enormous sickness, but have encountered not one. Some trust for a better field to the South. The order assigning our Regt. to the Gulf posts is looked upon as almost cruel. A poor return truly for our long course of exile & hardships in Florida. I begin to despair of ever seeing a right administration of things at Wash'n and of course suffer some relaxation of my Mily. zeal.[17]

In a letter written to Mother he goes into more detail, revealing that his ultimate destination appears to be New Orleans:

> The truth is our services are required here while the enemy are still holding out, and even a sense of justice to our claims is not of power sufficient to counteract the demands of necessity, or at least of expediency. In the meanwhile they have ordered me to *Fort Lauderdale* where I am now writing (Nov. 7th) having on the 1st inst. evacuated New Smyrna altogether. The change will be greatly to our advantage on the score of health, and not less agreeable in most other particulars. …
>
> Maj. Childs commands the district and is very zealously disposed to carry on the measures of the Florida commander to end this war. He has pushed very far into the recesses of the Everglades in pursuit of the enemy's secret haunts & will not cease until Sam Jones be hunted out. A gen. order has been published at Wash'n making our stations at the forts along the Gulf,—Pensacola, Mobile, N. Orleans &c. Mine is at the latter place. A residence in N. Orleans in the winter would suit me excellently well and there is little doubt but in Summer I might generally get leave to travel North.[18]

Vinton arrived at Fort Lauderdale on 6 November 1841, and as senior captain, was in command of the post. In a letter reporting his arrival to Major Childs, he noted, "By a statement handed in by Lieut. Wise [Wyse][19] it appears that the number of serviceable canoes at this post, including those now in use by Capt. Wade,[20] is *twenty*—each capable of carrying 5 men with 20 days provisions."[21] Vinton was ready to see some action, and quickly put his men into motion:

> Some hours after we landed here yesterday the Sch. Francis, Capt. Cooper, came down from the North & reported that he saw on the beach, about 2 miles south of Hillsborough Inlet two indians who seemed by their gestures to be making signs to him. I immediately dispatched Lt. Churchill[22] and 20 men of my company for the place described. After marching some 12 or 14 miles, the Lieut. found signs on the beach which verified Capt. Cooper's statement. The moon soon rose so that the footprints could be well discerned. Fresh tracks of three persons, 2 large & one small, barefoot or with moccasins, and farther on tracks of 2 persons wearing shoes. These were followed up through various windings until they terminated on

> the point forming the south shore of Hillsboro Inlet, where there was every indication that the party had crossed over into the opposite country. Having no means of pursuing, the Lieut. returned this morning to the fort.
>
> Capt. Wade being now in that very quarter, with most of our canoes and a respectable force precludes the necessity of further movement on my part, while it is hoped that he may be able to discover & capture them.[23]

A few days later Vinton was able to report to Childs about the results of Captain Wade's expedition. Little by little, the Seminole were being taken out of action:

> I have the pleasure to inform you that Capt. Wade ret'd from his scout last evening with 49 Ind. prisoners of whom 9 were men, 15 were women and 24 were children. Destroyed 2 Indian villages, 20 of canoes, took or destroyed 13 rifles & left 8 dead on the field, who were shot [. . . .] while endeavoring to escape.
>
> The expedition seems to have been exceedingly well conducted as but 9 or 10 belonging to the seven villages were known to have escaped. He was guided to these villages by an Indian previously captured on the beach and it is believed that the same man may be made useful as a guide in future operations. One old man whose family are among the prisoners was sent out by Capt. Wade to bring in others, he is expected to return to this post in three days. In the meantime the situation of the Prisoners here is anything but comfortable, our accommodations are small & not of the safest character, I await therefore with some impatience your orders here to dispose of these Indians.[24]

Colonel Worth's aggressive policies appeared to be having the desired effect, and the good news kept coming in, as Vinton's next letter to Childs indicates:

> I have the satisfaction to report that the old indian referred to in my corres'n of the 12th inst. whom Capt. Wade sent out to bring in others, returned this morning with four men and two boys. These with himself & the 48 brought in on the 11th— swell the number of captives now at this post to fifty five. This old man, who is called *Chiachee*, has thus evinced such a dispo-

> sition to be useful to our cause and such punctuality in fulfilling his promises, as to raise him high in my estimation as a guide, but his knowledge of English is so imperfect that without an interpreter we can avail ourselves but partially of his services. Capt. Wade returned yesterday from Ft. Dallas but without the interpreter John, who is still absent with Capt. Burke.[25] Lt. Wise with 3 Lieuts., 70 men & old Chiachee will set out tomorrow morning for Lake Worth and vicinity,—provisioned for 12 days.[26]

Vinton remained in Fort Lauderdale for the rest of December and into January of 1842. The Seminole War was now entering its seventh year, and Vinton was certainly ready for it to be over. During the second week of January, he moved his men to Fort Pierce, about ninety miles north of Fort Lauderdale. He immediately put the troops in motion and issued the following orders to one of the lieutenants under his command:

> You are charged with the conduct of an expedition to scour the country about the Head Waters of the St. John's and in such other quarters as may seem to you advisable from information gathered from your guide & the incidents of your journey. It has been suggested that the murders lately committed at Mandarin[27] were by indians from the St. John's—and that even Sam Jones may have taken refuge there or on the Kissimmee instead of the Halpatioka. The trail of the nine warriors discovered on my recent scout near the eastern shore of Okeechobee, bore north westerly and of course towards the Kissimmee. These general limits will be sufficient for your guidance towards the main object of your enterprise. Circumstances must, after all, govern your movements, viewed, as I am sure they will be, with that sound judgment & earnest zeal which you have never failed to evince on similar occasions. Wishing you full success & a happy issue to your expedition![28]

The war was nearing its termination, and everyone knew it. There were only a few hostile bands of Seminole yet to be found, and the army was slowly closing in on them. Near the end of January, Vinton told Mother:

> I have lately traversed the Everglades on command of a considerable expedition, and again through the Halpatika & other regions here, but it has not yet been my good fortune to meet & capture Sam Jones,—who must be captured, I presume be-

> fore our Regt. is relieved from field duty. I can as yet form no definite expectations as to when I shall come home though, unquestionably I shall apply for leave if our Regt. be not ordered North. The order sending us to N. Orleans did not imply that we sh'd necessarily be allowed to go there immediately. Indeed we have often been amused with such orders & suffered our hopes to rise accordingly but only to see them disappointed. But after all, I like this station better than N. Orleans and if we must be at the South, shall not be unwilling to abide by it.[29]

Little did Vinton know it at the time, but for him and the men of the 3rd Regiment of Artillery, their service in the Florida War was about to end. The persistent rumors about being sent to New Orleans became definite orders, and by early February, John Rogers Vinton was making his way out of the war zone.

16

Once More Housed in Comfortable Quarters

The Seminole War had not yet concluded, but the end was in sight. Most of the truly dangerous Indian bands had been killed or captured, while the rest were doing their best to avoid the soldiers by hiding out in the Everglades. Sam Jones still eluded the army, but he was little threat to white settlers unless provoked. The most visible leader of the tribe was now Holata Micco (Billy Bowlegs),[1] who was willing to negotiate if his people could be left in peace in the desolate swamplands of South Florida. With only a few hundred Seminole remaining in the peninsula, the government seemed willing to make the concession. Colonel Worth was able to declare the "interminable" Florida war over on 14 August 1842.

In the meantime, the army wanted to get as many men out of Florida as possible. The summer sickly season would soon be approaching, and the war had already cost the army dearly. The death toll from the war would be close to 1,500 men, with about 90 per cent of them dying from disease, not Seminole bullets. That didn't include losses among the state volunteers, the navy, the marines, civilians, and, of course, the Seminole. One of the first units to receive their orders was Vinton's Company "B," which was being transferred to New Orleans. First stop on the journey was Palatka, a major depot on the St. Johns River. While there on 6 February, Vinton took time to request a much-deserved leave of absence:[2]

> Be pleased to present this as my application for leave of absence to the Colonel Commanding the Army in Florida. I desire that it may be for sixty days with liberty to apply for an extension.
>
> My long service in this territory furnishes me ample ground to hope for the indulgence while the present nature of my private affairs compels me to urge my claim with no little importunity. Still if considerations of the public service at this particular juncture should render it almost improper that my departure should be delayed awhile I shall submit cheerfully to the judgment of the Colonel Commanding.[3]

Vinton wanted to get home to see his family, but was in no hurry to leave the sunny South while it was still cold up North. He also wanted to avoid the unhealthiest time of year in New Orleans. Just to make sure things went smoothly, he wrote a letter to his old friend Roger Jones, the Adjutant General in Washington, who was usually the final authority on granting such requests. He also knew it was going to be an expensive trip, especially if he waited until he was in New Orleans, so he included a personal note asking if Jones might find some special mission that would allow the army to pick up a portion of the travel expense:

> *Private*
> Dear Genl
> Enclosed with this is my official application for leave. Maj. Childs, Capt. Wade, &c took their departure from Pilatka [*sic*] a few days since, but I preferred to accompany the column and superintend personally the establishment of my company at N. Orleans. I feel that my claims for this indulgence surpass that of any other Officer and am therefore bold to ask of you the favor of an *Order* to proceed North on some duty about the time I have named so that my transportation may be covered. A Court Martial,—a visitation at W. Point, or simply to proceed to Washington where I have unadjusted accounts to settle. This privilege has been granted by Col. Worth I believe to several (Capt. Wade for example) and my case is certainly fourfold stronger than his.
>
> Yrs. faithfully
> J.R.V.[4]

On 17 March 1842 Vinton arrived in New Orleans. He seemed happy to be out of Florida and was looking forward to the social life of the Crescent City before heading home on leave. As he wrote to Mother:

> I have now the pleasure to announce to you my arrival at this station after a pleasant passage of 3 days from Cedar Keys in Florida. Our march across from Smyrna to Pilatka and thence to Cedar Keys was laborious, but very interesting. I find here Maj. McClintock and several other officers of our Regiment, who, with Dr. Hawkins[5] form a very agreeable society. Thus has my campaigning ended for the present, and I find myself once more housed in comfortable quarters. …
>
> As to my future prospects of domestic life, all seems to be doubt & uncertainty. Many considerations present themselves in favor of marriage, and my choice may in some measure be governed by the exigencies of my situation. I see little prospect

> of my being able to quit the Army, and the lady whom I may elect must therefore be willing to partake with me all the inconveniences of this kind of life,—unless she can bring wherewithal to enable me to enter upon some civil pursuit equally germane to my tastes & preferences. Such a chance is hardly to be expected, and I must make up my mind therefore to the practical view of the case.[6]

As the time for Vinton's leave drew near, he wrote to Mother, indicating when he might be expected. He was especially eager to be with his son. The last time he had seen Frank Laurens, the boy had been only three years old and was still recovering from the bout of dysentery that had nearly killed him. Vinton wondered if his son would recognize him:

> Whether I shall come by way of Newport or Boston, I know not. If the latter, I sh'd propose to you to go down to Warren with me and witness the interview with the Darlings. Frank Laurens w'd not know me—probably—but I sh'd like to try the experiment by meeting him in the Street "improviso" and see whether there be anything in natural impulse. I could stop at the Tavern,—and you go & get him to walk out with you and so witness the reencounter. This would be an exciting interview with some little trouble to plan & carry out.—But on the other hand,—I may reach Newport first and so on through to Conn. to Boston.[7]

By the end of April Vinton was ready to depart New Orleans and wrote to Mother prior to departure:

> It seems almost a superfluous matter to write again, when so near the eve of my departure hence,—but you do not like surprises and would prefer, no doubt, to be informed of the time, as nearly as I can predict, when you may expect me in Boston. I therefore drop these few lines to apprise you of my plan of travel from which to deduce the period of my probable arrival. On the 2d or 3d of May, I shall be ready to leave here & take the first Steam boat that ascends the river for Pittsburg [*sic*]. It will take perhaps seven days to reach that city. My object in taking that route is to visit the great improvements that have been made in the interior of Pennsylvania & elsewhere during the last ten years and in order to "get my money's worth." …

> If therefore I succeed in reaching Boston by the 20th I shall have accomplished my journey with all reasonable dispatch.[8]

Vinton's estimate was accurate, for he arrived in Boston on 19 May. The reunions were no doubt joyous. Did Frank Laurens recognize his father? Helena was nearing twelve, and was probably exhibiting some of the physical changes a girl is likely to go through at that age. Even LuLu must have grown quite a bit. The rest of the family was also close at hand. Frank and Alex were both well established in the Episcopal Church. Frank was Rector (minister) of Trinity Church in Newport and expecting his first child, and Alex had just been installed as Rector of St. Paul's Church in Boston. As for Mother, she was residing with Alex when John arrived and immediately wrote to Frank, saying, "This has been a happy day to me, & to us all,—the same train of cars that brought the joyful news of the downfall of Dorr's party, brought also our dear John. 'What shall I render to the Lord, for all His benefits? I will take the cup of Salvation, & be thankful.'"[9]

Her mention of the "downfall of Dorr's party" referred to a political crisis that had a direct effect on John's stay at home. Rhode Island's Constitution, derived from its original colonial charter, gave the vote only to propertied white males. In the early years of the republic such restrictions had been the norm, but by the 1840s Jacksonian Democracy had swept the nation, and every other state had removed the property restrictions. Many Rhode Islanders, especially the growing number of immigrant factory workers who did not own property, demanded the right to vote. Led by Thomas Dorr, they drafted a new constitution and held a referendum in which the new constitution was approved by a large majority.[10]

Conservative Rhode Islanders (among them the Vintons) were generally opposed to the new constitution and denied the legitimacy of the referendum. Among those speaking out against the Dorrites was the Rev. Francis Vinton, who sermonized, "The real issue in the late controversy in our State was the question of government or anarchy, law or the mere will of a numerical majority, informally and irregularly expressed."[11] Frank pointed to the Biblical verse "render unto Caesar the things that are Caesar's, and to God the things that are God's," to make his case that pious Christians owed obedience to the duly constituted authorities. "The Bible utters but one voice on the subject. … It is not an uncertain sound."[12] When opponents argued that the Founding Fathers had rebelled against the duly constituted authority of the English monarch, Frank responded that the present grievances were simply not serious enough to warrant the civil unrest that was unfolding.[13]

Both groups held elections, resulting in two men, Thomas Dorr and Samuel King, claiming to be the new Governor of Rhode Island. When King took office and showed no sign of accepting the new constitution, Dorr and his followers resorted to violence. On 17 May, two days before John arrived in Boston, they attempted to seize the state arsenal at Providence but were repulsed, and Dorr fled the state.[14]

Vinton stayed with his family for several weeks, but was in Washington by late June. On the 28th he was in New York, where he wrote a short note to Mother, who was still in Boston. Dorr was returning to Rhode Island, and his followers were threatening to take the government by force:

> I have arrived from Wash'n where I staid [*sic*] only one day, hearing the critical news from R.I. and determined to proceed directly for Providence & offer my services to Gov. King. I saw the Pres't, Sec. of War, Maj. Gen. &c and explained my wish to act in R.I.—The answer was—I may proceed only on my own responsibility. This I am willing to do, let the issue be what it may. I only fear I may be too late to render my services in the best time.[15]

Unable to stand up to the conservatives, Dorr's Rebellion collapsed, and Vinton was able to avoid taking any further part in the crisis. Hoping to diffuse the issue, the conservative legislature adopted a more liberal constitution in 1843, dropping the property requirements for most citizens, with the exception of immigrants.[16]

By mid-July Vinton and a friend were preparing to visit the White Hills in Maine for a twelve- to twenty-day fishing trip. After that he intended to spend time with Mother and the children and also visit Frank. Things did not go as planned, as he told Frank:[17]

> When I wrote you last I was on the eve of my departure for the White Hills,—but the very day I set out, I was visited by a return of my old Florida intermittent. I stopped at Andover 3 days shaking & burning & then returned here where the arch-fiend has continued to afflict me ever since. I hope soon to be well enough to come & breath yr. Newport air.[18]

By August Vinton was fully recovered and in Newport, where he seems to have become a public speaker. On the 23rd he wrote Mother:

> I now write you from my chamber at McLellan's, having just returned from Westminster Hall. The audience was large,—highly respectable,—and very attentive. A more favouring & friendly auditory, no speaker ever had, but I was scarcely half satisfied with myself. If the public were pleased it is more than

> I dare flatter myself with. I had a preamble written out which I delivered by a frequent & awkward reference to my paper,—but I have no doubt if I had trusted to an extemporaneous effusion of words, my speech would have been better. The audience applauded however exactly in the right places, and all went off swimmingly. When I entered the room too, the applause was very flattering and so when I finished my lecture. Still I would rather drill than lecture.[19]

Dorr's Rebellion had given the people of Rhode Island a scare, especially when they found their militia totally unprepared to handle the threat of violence. In response, the authorities turned to Vinton and asked that he train the militia in basic military maneuvers. This he gladly did, happy to support the conservatives against the more liberal elements who were demanding reform. Yet he was in no hurry to use force against the opposition, and he told Mother, "We resort to the military only as a necessary evil and are ready to put it by the moment we find that our institutions & our firesides are no longer in danger."[20]

Vinton's actions in connection to the Dorr Rebellion shed some light on his personal politics. Like most army officers, he was cautious not to get involved in national politics. The crisis in Rhode Island was something different; it was local and personal. As later letters from Mexico would show, he was very proud of his Anglo-Saxon Protestant heritage. Most of Dorr's supporters were Irish Catholics. Vinton could accept people of Irish descent, provided they were educated and well-mannered. Indeed, many of his fellow officers were of Irish or Scots-Irish background. He was less accepting of recent immigrants, and very intolerant of Catholics. As a member of the privileged, propertied elite, Vinton was prepared to do what he must to protect that status.

With the crisis passed, life returned to normal. If nothing else, there were numerous social events for Vinton to attend: "The dinner at Gen. Greene's,—The party at Miss Hoppin's this evening. On Wednesday, Commencement Dinner at the College & wined at Moses Ives'[21] & soiréed at Dr. Waylands[22]—all very pleasant & instructive. Thursday Dinner party at Moses Ives'—Evening party at Mr. Duncan's.—Ball (military) at the Lockwotton's." It was definitely not the Florida frontier.[23]

Vinton's time on leave was winding down. He seems to have made the most of his remaining time at home, visiting with family as often as possible. In mid-September he was in Providence, on 1 October he was in Newport, and back in Providence a week later. A week after that he was in Boston, and a week later in Warren, Rhode Island, where the children were in school. He was getting ready to return to his military duties, but he was not going back to New Orleans. Instead, he was returning to Florida.

17

St. Augustine is Healthy and Delightful

The war against the Seminole had officially ended, but that didn't mean a perfect peace had settled over the Florida Territory. It would take time for all the scattered bands to move onto the reservation in Southwest Florida, and for those who had agreed to emigrate, there was the characteristic slowness in gathering at the embarkation point. There was also the problem that anytime a nervous settler saw an Indian, real or imagined, the military would have to investigate. It would be some time before all troops were moved out of Florida.

Yet things had certainly changed. There were no patrols to hunt the natives down, and nearly all of the forts in the peninsula were abandoned. On the west coast Fort Brooke, a major installation on Tampa Bay, guarded one of the best harbors in Florida and was kept active. The city of Tampa would grow up around it. On the east coast, St. Augustine was the natural place for the troops to be stationed. There was the spacious St. Francis Barracks (still in use today as the Headquarters of the Florida National Guard), and the imposing Fort Marion (now the Castillo de San Marcos National Monument). Exactly why the War Department had decided to move Vinton's company from New Orleans to St. Augustine is unknown, but there was probably no complaint from Captain Vinton.

On 11 November 1842, the day after his arrival in St. Augustine, Vinton wrote to his children, telling them of his travels after he had left Rhode Island:

> My dear Daughters
>
> You are entitled to the earliest intelligence of your father's arrival at his station after so long a journey, so I shall proceed to inform you how I travelled after I left you, and where I went. You know I proceeded first to Newport and on my way met the Governor and his Military Retinue, escorted by the Bristol and Warren Artillery.—They very kindly pressed me to return and dine with them at the great dinner given by the Warren Company, but I had marked out the line of my own movements and thought it best to adhere to it, however tempted to deviate. So I proceeded on to Newport where I met your dear Uncle Frank and Aunt Elizabeth about 2 P.M. I staid [*sic*] with them over Sunday, and Monday afternoon embarked in the Steamer *Iolas* for Providence,—waited there awhile for the

train of cars from Boston then crossed over to the Depot of the Stonington Railroad,—took the cars there without delay and arrived at Norington by 9 in the evening,—There the Steamer R. *Island* was waiting for us. We embarked immediately & got underway for New York where we arrived next morning. …

In New York I was detained till Saturday, when I embarked on board the Brig. *Saratoga* bound for Savannah. On Sunday, Monday & Tuesday the wind blew fair and brought us opposite Savannah light house by Wednesday morning. Was not this a quick passage? On board we had only four passengers other than myself, so we were not much incommoded for want of room. Arrived in Savannah we found no Steam boat for Florida, so we had to wait till Monday, the 6th Nov. before we left that city. … On the 9th I arrived at Picolata in Florida, a place situated on the banks of the St. John's River. Slept there all night and in the forenoon of the next day, the 10th, rode over to St. Augustine 18 miles and so here I am comfortably situated in my new quarters. …

St. Augustine is healthy and delightful. Today I am sitting with the windows open, enjoying the mild air but at evening we keep fires. Our society here is not large,—not so many families to visit as we should have in Warren, but still there are some very agreeable ones among them.[1]

Two days later, in a letter to Frank, Vinton took time to describe his fellow officers, one of whom would later find fame in the Civil War:

I said I was pleased with my new post. Always the most important consideration would be with me the character of the Officers with whom I was placed in juxta position or obliged to associate. You should know then something about my companions. First of my own company there is Lt. Shover my first Lieut. A young man of good appearance though not graceful in his carriage. Very intelligent, strictly moral & upright in his character & habits,—devoted to his duty, accurate, judicious & energetic in the performance of it, yet very moving at Reveille, & indefatigable in all his pursuits but apt to languish after the attainment of his object. His social qualities are less attractive than is customary among young officers,—still he is not without agreeable points.

Lt. Hammond[2] has just joined me. He comes in the place of Lt. Churchill who has gone to the Light Com'y at Baltimore. Lt. H. is rather small of stature but well formed and of very agreeable presence. He too is intelligent, upright & gentlemanly but more fond of conviviality than Shover. On duty he appears elegant & well informed & I trust will wear well. But getting up at Reveille is a thing he w'd not be apt to practice as long as he can help it. I fancy he will be a favorite among the ladies if he is disposed to devote himself to them.

Of the other comp'y Lt. [Braxton] Bragg[3] is now the only Officer, but *such* an Officer that two ordinary ones could hardly make up his equal. Tall in figure though not graceful, a plain but strikingly intelligent countenance,—calm in deportment but of a character infinitely firm & energetic,—devoted to his duty but apt to grumble at his lot,—gentlemanly in all his feelings,—high minded and virtuous in all his principles,—cordial, faithful, and self denying in his friendships,—but critical and exacting & caustic in his estimation of the bulk of mankind,—moral & exact in all proper observances even to the point of going to church though not religious. …[4]

St. Augustine was a comfortable posting, but the threat of disease was ever-present. In late November, Vinton was forced to decide whether it was more important to protect the health of the city or keep the military out of civil affairs. Smallpox had broken out in Palatka, and the Mayor of St. Augustine asked Vinton for a number of soldiers to take up position on the road coming from Palatka, hoping to prevent carriers of the disease from entering St. Augustine. Vinton, concerned about possible altercations between soldiers and civilians, declined the request.[5]

Vinton had made many friends during his time in Florida and was well regarded as an artist. One of those friends, John Lee Williams, was writing a book about the Florida Territory and asked Vinton to contribute some illustrations. In response, Vinton told him:[6]

You requested me when I last saw you to furnish you with such sketches of scenery in Florida for your forthcoming work, as I may have made during my various excursions, and as might be interesting to your readers. Likewise to give you such notes touching any important incidents of the war against the Seminoles, as might tend to clarify the history of our campaigns. My time has hitherto only allowed me to comply partially with your wishes. I send accordingly two sketches—one of the Lighthouse at Key Biscayne, which is connected with one of the most thrilling events of the war. I mean the attack by the Indians made on the Lighthouse Keeper who with one negro took refuge on the top & there remained roasting by the fire which was burning like a furnace within, and shot at by a horde of Savages from without. The other sketch shows the face of the country about Lake Winder and presents a remarkable indian mound, from which I saw dug out many ancient Memorials of the indian race. Both these are exact views of the actual landscape, but for want of bolder features cannot much interest the lover of the picturesque.[7]

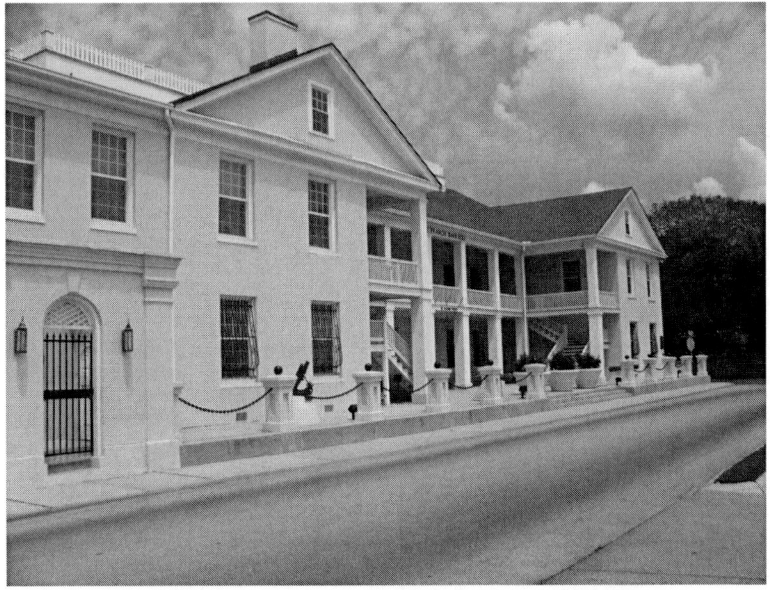

Figure 18: St. Francis Barracks, St. Augustine, Florida.

Near the end of December, Vinton made a report to the regimental Inspector General concerning the status of his command:

1. I took command of the post on the 10th of November 1842, relieving Lt. Bragg 3d Arty.
2. The "*condition of the command*" at the time was highly respectable. The troops being recently from campaign did not appear in that highly finished state either of equipment or instruction which is looked for in garrison long estab-

lished—but the course of discipline entered on and the zeal & energy of the Officers directing it, gave earnest that a little time only was necessary to perfect the troops on these points.

The Barracks, furnish ample & wholesome accommodations for two companies, but they are in a dilapidated condition and require very extensive repairs. The Qr. Master is about entering on his duty. A new roof will be put on, and other improvements made in the building so as to meet the wants of the garrison.

Fort Marion, which is about 3 quarters of a mile North of the Barracks, and commands the town & harbor of St. Augustine, is now dismantled and undergoing repairs by the Engineer Department. Vessels of moderate draft, say of nine feet can enter the harbor over the bar & find good anchorage. The fort is in no danger from attack by water. On the land side, by regular approaches from the North, it could be the most easily assailed, but being well & scientifically built considering its age, it would hold out for a long time against an ordinary siege. Within the fort there are at present no *quarters*, *furnaces*, *store houses*, or other conveniences proper for a garrison. While these are being prepared and the walls in some places rebuilt, the troops are all ably situated in the barracks they now occupy. The "*store houses*" near the barracks are ample & in good order, though some alteration in their arrangements are very properly contemplated.

"*The Officers*" present at the post, (namely 1st Lieut. Bragg & 1st Lieut. Shover, & 2d Lieut. Hammond & 2d Lieut. Reynolds)[8] are "active, attentive, sober, and well instructed in their duties." Exemplary in all respects and an honor to the service.

"*The Sergants & Corporals*" are generally good & efficient though not without exception. The love of drink is often the besetting evil among the best. Men who otherwise might acquit themselves with great credit are here weak & faulty. At least one half of them are "*foreigners*." Some objections are occasionally raised by the soldiers who are native Americans against this appt. of so large a portion of foreigners, but these objections commonly proceed I imagine from interested motives or a captious spirit, and, practically considered, are not entitled to much regard. The best of our men, that is the most steady, and temperate & obedient, are not generally Americans,—It is ex-

> tremely difficult with the widest range for selection amongst our enlisted men to find good materials for N. C. Officers. But to restrict the choice to within the narrower pale of native candidates would greatly increase the difficulty. Theoretically considered, it may seem inconsistent & objectionable that the American Army, maintained to support American interests and illustrate American honor, should be so largely composed of aliens by birth, and especially in the non commiss'd grades,—but for the actual service as we know it to exist,—where the duties are chiefly those of a peace establishment,—where the exigency involving the national honor is scarcely ever known to arise,—but where the qualities of temperance, industry, obedience & martial aptitude are in daily request,—then foreigners of respectable character may be even preferred to the American.[9]

Vinton's assistance to the Rhode Island authorities during Dorr's Rebellion was appreciated by the political establishment in the state, especially his work organizing and training the militia. In gratitude they sent him a handsome gift, which he described to Mother on 13 January 1843:

> I received here, yesterday the Silver pitcher & pair of Goblets presented by the Mily. Companies of Providence. They are very beautiful & the inscription on each admirably engraved. You will like to know what they are. On the pitcher is—"To John R. Vinton, Captain in the U.S. Army—From his fellow citizens of the Chartered & Volunteer Companies of the City Regiments of Providence, Rhode Island—In acknowledgment of his Valuable Military Instructions and of their appreciation of his private worth. Sept. 1842." On each goblet is "To John R. Vinton, Captain in the U.S. Army from his fellow citizens of the Chartered & Volunteer Comp's of the City of Prov., R.I. Sept. 1842."—The letter was very complimentary & signed by the Representatives of 14 Companies.—You will probably see the correspondence published,—and if so tell me what you think of it.[10]

For much of January 1843 Vinton was engaged in a Court of Inquiry at the small town of Palatka on the St. Johns River. While there, he had the opportunity to reunite with a pair of old friends and note the changes time had wrought. When he returned to St. Augustine he wrote to Mother, telling her:

Since I rec'd yours of the 10th Jany, I have been engaged on a Court of Inquiry … a duty which has absorbed most of my time. At that court I met two old friends, after a long interval since last I saw them, viz, Genl. Eustis & Lt. Col. Hitchcock.[11] Of the General you have heard me often speak, as one of those who were linked with my early fortunes, & in some points he was instrumental in *advancing* them. My first & best ideas of Mil'y. service were *imbued* while under his command, and it was chiefly by his recommendation that I rec'd the high distinction of being raised to the Genl Staff. Twenty years have gone by since that period of my life, yet all the incidents of it are as fresh as ever to my memory. I met the Genl. now after a lapse of some 6 or 8 years, I believe, and of course the interview was extremely interesting to me. But how altered he was! In appearance I mean. The head bald,—his frame bent forward, and his legs tottering with infirmity. But his mind seems to be still vigorous & all his observations as *pungent* and sarcastic as ever. He is good company for one who wants the mind stimulated, but for gentleness or urbanity of manners few would wish to imitate Genl. Eustis.

Hitchcock, an old classmate of mine, & a very dear friend, was altered too,—so far as age could alter—a bald head!—How is it that mine is still so richly adorned with a full crop of black hair while nearly all my companions are gray or bald! But my time is at hand no doubt. Hitchcock is a profound thinker. Even while a Cadet, metaphysics was his favorite study and Hume his favorite author. Infidelity of course was the consequence and I doubt if twenty-five years of additional reading & observation has brought him one step nearer Christianity. I am sorry for this. Such is the very high character of Hitchcock for moral excellence and intellectual acumen, that the influence of his example is calculated to do no service to the cause of Religion. I talked with him somewhat about it, and besought him that whatever he might do or say on other points to beware of an assault upon the holy course of Christianity. He might enjoy his own belief or disbelief as he would, but let nothing induce him to attempt to shake or unsettle the faith of those who found in it a consolation & a hope for suppressing every earthly consideration,—compared to which all intellectual triumphs were as empty pageants.—He promised to observe my admonition, saying also that he had generally forborne all discussion of religious subjects whenever there was a chance of its doing the harm I deprecated. …

St. Augustine continues to be pleasant—the people kind & courteous. We have built a handsome bowling alley,—and are favored occasionally with the company of the ladies to join in the games.—This furnishes us an opportunity to return some of the many civilities we are constantly receiving from them—For we generally wind off with a supper. No Officer here is married, and therefore female parties we cannot have except in this bachelorlike mode. When I see the fine little boys running about here I cannot but wish that Frank Laurens were with me. He w'd be a great deal of company,—though perhaps some trouble. To be brought up with Northern Constitutions is, after all, a great advantage for him & for his sisters, though I hope it may not be many years before I can have them all under my own roof.[12]

The army had lost a many good men in the Second Seminole War, and they were not forgotten by their comrades. At the end of the war Colonel Worth had ordered the remains of all the officers who had died in Florida and the enlisted men who had been killed in battle to be brought to St. Augustine and buried beneath three stone pyramids in the little cemetery adjacent to St. Francis Barracks. A monument to Dade's Command, which had been annihilated at the beginning of the war, would later be erected at West Point. In both instances, officers and men were asked to contribute toward the memorials. Considering that Vinton commanded a company that had replaced one of those wiped out at Dade's Battle, he and his men were happy to make a contribution. In a note to Lieutenant Bragg, who was collecting the funds, he said:

I hand you herewith the sum of Forty Dolls. subscribed by the Officers, & soldiers of B Company 3d Arty as their contribution towards raising a Monument to the Memory of the Officers & soldiers who fell at Dade's Massacre. In offering this, our stipend for an object so laudable, we might be justified in expressing our preferences as to the place where the Monument should be raised, (which would probably be West Point) but such is our admiration of the very prompt & munificent spirit manifested on this subject by the Officers & soldiers of the 4th Infantry, that we would rather defer entirely to their wishes on the subject,—and shall be satisfied with any location of the Monument which may be selected by the members of that generous minded Regiment.[13]

Now that Vinton was in a city with proper churches, one might have thought he would dispense with holding his own services. Unfortunately for the conscripted parishioners of Company "B," such was not the case, as Vinton told Mother on 6 March:

> I have just returned to my quarters after attending a meeting in the Barracks where, as usual on Sunday evening we have divine service for the Enlisted men, so I have on Sundays three opportunities of public worship. This meeting of the men is conducted alternately by our Episcopalian Minister Mr. Rutledge, and our Presbyterian Mr. McClure. The latter gentleman is very acceptable and shows much tact in addressing himself the plain understandings of our soldiery. I make all my company attend. The other compy. which is now commanded by Lt. Bragg, is not compelled to join though some few of them do so, voluntarily. As usual I have no coadjutor among the Officers, though I meet with no opposition,—save that spirit of indifference which shows itself by their never attending the meetings.[14]

Vinton was comfortable in St. Augustine, but the situation wasn't going to last. By the end of March 1843 orders were received, and Company "B" was once again on the move.

18

My Home Here is Very Pleasant

Vinton's new posting was at the Federal Arsenal in Augusta, Georgia, and he arrived there on 30 March 1843. His arrival, however, raised an immediate problem. He and his men were part of the Artillery Corps, and their purpose was to guard and maintain the facility. The Arsenal itself was part of the Ordnance Department, which was a different branch of the army. The post's previous commander, Lt. George Talcott[1] of the Ordnance Department, was remaining but was not inclined to relinquish full command. To Talcott's way of thinking, Vinton was in charge of the men, while he would be in charge of the buildings. To Vinton, it was an impossible situation. Some of the buildings were there to house and care for the men, and part of the men's duties was to service the buildings. How could you separate the two? The impasse forced Vinton to write to headquarters requesting clarification as to who was in charge of what.[2]

The problem was complicated because Talcott's father was in charge of the Ordnance Department in Washington, and had objected to Vinton's company being sent to Augusta because there were supposedly insufficient quarters for the troops. Unmentioned was the fact that the junior Talcott stood to lose prestige and a considerable amount of extra wages were he to be removed from command. Vinton responded that there was plenty of room, and that compared to the posts where his men had been stationed for the past six years, "these quarters are comfortable almost to luxury," and were certainly better than any other place they were likely to be stationed. Vinton and his men remained at Augusta, sleeping in rented quarters, with the matter unresolved.[3]

Annoyed, Vinton wouldn't let the matter rest, and the subject became a bone of contention within the War Department, with commanding general Winfield Scott taking Vinton's side, and Colonel Talcott and the Secretary of War taking the side of the younger Talcott. For their parts, both Scott and Vinton were determined to see the issue through, but after nine months with no resolution to the situation, rumors began to circulate that Vinton and his men would be moved elsewhere.

By mid-January of 1844 the matter of who was in charge at Augusta seemed to have been decided in Lieutenant Talcott's favor, and Vinton received orders to leave the arsenal and take part of his company elsewhere. Yet in what may have been an indication that matters were not completely settled between General

Scott and the War Department, Vinton was not given specific orders as to where to report, but seems to have been given his choice of postings. Friends urged him to choose Charleston, but he sensed some personality conflicts there and instead chose Fort Macon, a newly-constructed fort outside Beaufort, North Carolina. Upon arrival, he seemed pleased with his choice:[4]

> Fort Macon is a work of some importance, of modern construction, occupying a site which commands the entrance to the harbor of Beaufort & furnishes a good place of refuge to our ships of small draft, in time of war. It is just at the mouth of the Inlet, near Cape Lookout,—a low sandy shore, as all the coast of N. Carolina is,—and but little garnished with trees or shrubbery of any kind. Still we can have a garden here and the fishing privileges are unsurpassed. No place can be more healthy. The "open sea" is all on one side of us and across the harbor on the other side to Beaufort is nearly 2 miles. … I am occupying a small house outside the fort where I have "two rooms & a kitchen," conformable to Regulations. I find our mess table quite respectably furnished, and so far as creature comforts are concerned, I see no reason to complain.[5]

Figure 19: Aerial view of Fort Macon (1965)

After giving Mother an account of the other officers at the fort, he said, "With these, & my books and pencils & my gun & rod, with good health & letters from home occasionally you may well suppose that I shall not fail to be quite happy." He was also ready to resume his duties as a father, and told Mother, "Situated as I am here, I have no doubt as to the expediency of bringing out Frank Laurens with me when I return from the North next Summer. I can here attend to his lessons very well and keep him effectually out of harm's way." If nothing else, the boy probably needed the strong hand of a father to help mold his character. A letter from a relation had left Vinton with the impression that Frank Laurens was getting out of control. A later letter from his daughters' teacher eased his mind, and actually made him a bit proud. As Vinton told Mother, "The upshot of the whole matter is then, that the poor little fellow has been detected in 3 fibs. Bravo, Frank Laurens! I thought from Cousin Mary's alarm clarion, that he had committed arson or theft,—set fire to somebody's corn rick or robbed their hen roost,—in short grown to be an arch little reprobate. But I have yet to learn that the boy is worse than other boys."[6]

As for the girls, they would remain in boarding school at Warren, Rhode Island, which would probably have been the case were he stationed near home or even if their mother had still been alive. That was how most middle and upper class children were educated at the time. Although Vinton could not be there to watch over their education, he did as much as he could from a distance. It was important to him that his daughters receive a well-rounded education, which included Latin and the classics. If he couldn't be with them to guide their studies, he could comment on their letters, as one response to LuLu illustrates:

> I observed several words misspelt [*sic*] in your letter. This requires attention. There are for example—"yestoday"—"discribe"—"automatom"—"nurseing,"—"coloquy,"—"chatechize"—"confermation"—"Trogans" & one or two more. This indicates carelessness rather than ignorance, for I have known you to spell some of the same words correctly, heretofore.[7]

While a good education for his girls was extremely important to Vinton, he was also a man of his times, knew the limitations faced by nineteenth-century women, and fully concurred with those restrictions. Ultimately, he felt the most important thing was for the girls to find a good husband, be a subservient wife, and have a happy home. When Helena showed signs of being interested in "moral science," he worried she might become too philosophical for her own good. As he told Mother:

> I hope, however, this predilection will not lead her to a sphere of mental abstraction, incompatible with the graceful cultivation of those feminine attributes which form the most attractive qualities of the sex. The aversion men feel for female pedants & blue stockings, does not proceed so much from a *fear* of them (as some allege) as from the general persuasion that such characters are unfitted for domestic life and its principal requirements. A husband wants not, in his wife, a literary disputant, but a sweet solace for his over wearied thoughts,—a recreating balm in the cheerful, playful, graceful attentions of his other, though opposite, self. While, therefore, I would wish my daughters to grow up intelligent, strong minded women, I should still regard their education as very defective if they were not endowed also with sweetness of temper, grace of manner, and a taste & talent for the light accomplishments which adorn the character of a polished lady.[8]

In the meantime, Mother was keeping an eye out for a suitable replacement for Lucretia. Vinton was too, but he was setting his standards very high. When Mother mentioned someone she thought might fill the bill, Vinton was quick to reject the suggestion and listed his reasons. His rationale may seem callous and self-centered to the modern reader, but Vinton had always been a practical man, a trait that time and experience only served to reinforce:

> She has no property, and to marry a *poor* girl is only increasing my cares & involving myself in new responsibility. She has no advantage of high family connexions,—& therefore I sh'd gain nothing towards raising or reinforcing myself in the social scale. She has no beauty therefore I should have nothing to admire of her as an object of loveliness & good taste. She has no musical endowments therefore one large resource of domestic enjoyment calculated on in forming a matrimonial connexion would be shut out. … Well it is hard to be suited,—and considering that I am growing old & am a widower with 3 children, I may also find it hard to suit others. … Nothing is more plenty in market than good poor girls.[9]

Vinton had been planning to take leave in late May or early June and return home to visit the family and pick up Frank Laurens. As it happened, in early May he was unexpectedly called to Washington and was able to apply for leave while there, thus avoiding paperwork delays and part of the expense of travelling north.[10] After spending several weeks in New England, father and son headed south, arriving at Fort Macon on 14 July 1844.[11]

Single parenting is always difficult, especially at an isolated army outpost. With no schools in the area, the boy's education was Vinton's responsibility. There was also the problem of keeping a nine year old amused. Writing to his sisters, Frank Laurens explained how he stayed occupied:

> I study Latin, Grammar, Read in the No. V. and spell as we did at Boston, and have a writing lesson. This is all I study. I study the lessons 2 hours in the morning, and 2 in the afternoon. We have the most delightful place for bathing here, and there is an old stump of a tree which has been cut down, and the roots which are sticking out in all directions afford a very nice place to hang our clothes upon. All we have to do in the morning is to run down to the shore, take off our clothes, and jump in, have a nice bath, jump out again, dress, and run home; much cooled & refreshed, but I have told you so much about batheing [*sic*] that I shall not have paper enough to tell you half. We have 12 geese, 15 ducks, 0 ducklings, 12 hens, 0 chickens, and a duck pond before the house & with all these we have quite a little farm. You know all the playthings I have, so it would be of no use to tell you.[12]

Vinton loved music and considered it an indispensible part of his children's education. To that end he made a considerable investment in not one, but two pianos. One was delivered to the girls, while the other was sent all the way to Fort Macon for his own pleasure. He told Mother, "I find great comfort in the presence of my piano & do not value the money it cost, when weighed with the pleasure it yields."[13]

As might be expected, he was finding it a challenge to raise a boy who had known little male discipline. Bad habits had formed, and it would take time to undo them. He was also missing his daughters, and told LuLu, "Your likeness & Sister Helena's, that I painted, hang up in our bedroom so we can be reminded of you at least every morning & night,—and as much oftener as you may readily guess."[14]

If Vinton thought that by going to Fort Macon he would be getting away from disputes with junior officers, he was mistaken. Lieutenant Christopher Tompkins, who Vinton considered a good friend, had for some reason become critical. It is difficult to say what the problem was, but it ended up costing Tompkins his house. Because Tompkins was the only married officer at the post, Vinton had allowed him and his young wife to occupy the large four-room house that was normally set aside for the commanding officer, while Vinton occupied a two-room cottage. As he explained to Mother, "But on drill he found fault with my manner of command,—in conversation he was captious [found fault] and objurgatory [highly critical],—and at the mess table he was disputatious & unpleasantly critical, so that I found it best to quit the mess & keep house." Exercising his right as commanding officer, Vinton took over the larger house and forced Tompkins into the cottage. It didn't take long for Vinton to put the extra space to good use:[15]

> I now can entertain company as befits my circumstances. I have given two parties already since I occupied my new quarters, much to the satisfaction of our Newbern gentry, who are summering at Beaufort. My piano makes music for dancing, so the young ladies are pleased as well as the lovers of music. My parlor is adorned with pictures (no less than eleven) beside the noble bust of Brother Alex,—& a piano, sofa, clock, center table, sideboard & chairs.[16]

At times it was a lonely existence for father and son. The isolation no doubt made Vinton long for some female companionship. "My avocations being now more domestic than formerly," he wrote Mother, "I feel the more need of a wife to fill out the program of a pleasant home. You will oblige me by casting about for me once more & try to find someone who while she can be content with a garrison, shall yet have qualities that would adorn the best society of a luxurious city."[17]

Winter was approaching, and more time was spent indoors to ward off the cold air coming in from the Atlantic. Letters continued to flow back and forth between New England and North Carolina, between mother and son, father and daughters, and brother and sisters. As a sort of game, Frank Laurens and Helena would often send each other Latin phrases to translate. To LuLu he wrote, "Father is playing on his piano while I am writing. We live in the only house there is here, the others are merely little cottages. We have two servants, one has a screeching infant and gives us music enough without the piano."[18]

Vinton was enjoying his time at Fort Macon, but his leisurely seaside posting was about to end. The matter of who should be in charge at the Augusta Arsenal had finally been settled, and General Scott had come out the victor. On 13 November 1844, Vinton received orders to take his men and return to the arsenal.

Although the orders from the War Department were quite clear as to who was in command, Lieutenant Talcott was not ready to accept the inevitable. As Vinton told Mother:

> The order for our returning here was gall & wormwood to Lt. Talcott and he has thrown every obstacle in my way, he possibly could do, in my efforts to establish myself in the command. The quarters he occupies are those always occup'd by the Comg. Officer, as I had no sympathies of friendly feeling to induce me to postpone my own right of selection, but every reason of an official character to prompt me to a full assertion of my place & dignity, I have determined to "turn him out" as the delicate phrase is among his clique of friends in Augusta.[19]

Figure 20: Commandant's House, Augusta Arsenal. Now the Admissions Office, Augusta State University, Augusta, Georgia.

Vinton soon realized he was going to have much less time to devote to his son's education and considered enrolling him in school. He was also thinking of buying the boy a pony so they could go riding together. If nothing else, he felt the opportunity to take Frank Laurens out into polite society would do the lad a world of good.[20]

The position of commanding officer at the arsenal was considered an important one in the community, and Vinton was happy to occupy it. On Christmas Eve he wrote to Mother, telling her, "I wish you c'd see our parlor here, decorated as it is by my own taste & my Lieuts. My pictures hang upon the walls,—Alex's noble bust fills an appropriate niche on its pedestal,—my piano, chairs, sofa &c all in their places & a pretty new carpet on the floor. We expect soon to give a party at which the ladies of our acquaintance will doubtless be present. This climate in the winter is admirable. Christmas is a jocund season at the South. We have divers invitations to dine out, & everywhere, merry making is the order of the day."[21]

Figure 21: Parlor, Commandant's House, Augusta Arsenal.

The frivolities of the holiday season soon passed, and as 1845 began Frank Laurens was enrolled in school. Writing to his grandmother, he told her about one of the idiosyncrasies of the Southern dialect. "I have formed some pleasant friends here and I have noticed a peculiar custom here even among the most genteel of the boys of putting (done) before the verb as (I've done written my letter.) but I do not think this custom is very superfine."[22]

Unfortunately, Frank Laurens' schooling was soon interrupted by the death of the schoolmaster, Mr. Copp.[23] Back in Rhode Island, Helena's education was also running into problems. It was intended that she would move to a new school in the summer, but plans were put off for another year when the chosen school suddenly shut down. Vinton tried to tell her it was part of God's plan and all for the best, but was then forced to explain why it was also for the best that a close relative had just died:[24]

> You have heard doubtless of the death of your Aunt Pamela. What a stroke of affliction to Uncle Hammond, and what a terrible bereavement to the children. It is difficult you will think to apply the rule above stated to a case like this, but even here, I am ready to bow in perfect acquiescence to the Almighty behest, believing that even this great adversity may be sanctified as a blessing both to father & to children.[25]

With summer approaching, Vinton was once again thinking of taking leave and returning north to visit the family. Helena had been dropping hints that she would like to return with him, but Vinton discouraged the idea, preferring her to pursue a higher education. He even planned to leave Frank Laurens in Augusta, confident his lieutenants and the new schoolmaster would take good care of the boy during his absence. Vinton told his mother what the schoolmaster thought of Frank Laurens, and added some comments of his own:[26]

> He says of F. L. that he has excellent parts and dispositions, but has also many faults,—the principal of which is an overweening conceit of himself. Praise does him more harm than good,—leading him to self satisfaction and idleness rather than stimulating him to higher efforts. F. L. is assuredly no negative character. He is active, perspicacious, inventive & original. When within doors, he always succeeds in finding amusements on very small resources. His pencil is nowadays his chief resource,—with which he draws pictures & figures with no little skill, considering the very little instruction & encouragement he gets from me. His keen relish for the ridiculous makes him seize on all the grotesque & outré properties of a subject, in preference, and out comes a caricature. His comrades at school admire his genius in this line, & encourage him greatly, no doubt, by their praises,—while they dread above all things to be themselves the subject of one of his graphic lampoons.[27]

It seems odd that Vinton, a lover of both art and music, was unwilling to encourage these pursuits in his son. Although there was a piano in the house, he never mentions giving the boy lessons or of hiring a music instructor, though later reports indicate Frank Laurens was a talented musician as an adult. Vinton clearly noticed the boy's innate skill as an artist, but again, gave his son no lessons, even though he was an accomplished artist himself. His reasons, related to LuLu more than a year later, seem odd to us today, but, as always, it was done out of love for his children:

> As to drawing, my dear daughter, this is a branch which I have purposely omitted in your program of studies. Too much application to it injures the health, and besides this, I have always reserved this as the branch I wished to teach you myself, when you shall come home to your father's roof. It is a diversion that one can engage in at almost any period of life, while in the days of juvenescence other and more important pursuits should occupy all the time proper to devote to sedentary studies. Frank Laurens had a strong love for drawing and it was always a source of discomfort to me to see him leaning over a table with paper & pencil, bending in his chest & injuring his constitution. You see my darling child, I refuse you this only for the strongest reasons.[28]

The matter of whether he or Lieutenant Talcott was in command at Augusta had been settled, and Talcott had left the post on a special assignment. Vinton reported the man as being in Pensacola, but seemed rather miffed because he had received no official information as to what Talcott was doing, who had issued the orders, or how long he would be gone.[29] But if he thought the disputes with junior officers were over, he was again disappointed. This time the trouble came from his own First Lieutenant:

> We have had here another squabble about quarters,—that inexhaustible theme of controversy in garrison. My 1st Lieut., whose name is Wyse, a conceited, captious, shallow blockhead, is very fond of making a figure in society & covets the finest house & establishment of course. When I came here fr. Fort Macon I was silly enough to concur in his proposition of "living together," not only in one mess but to occupy jointly the same parlor, so that he really became ensconced with all the dignity & style of Comg. Officer. This lasted a season very well, for he was exceedingly polite & gentlemanly & deferential, until about a month since, when he began to be disagreea-

> ble to me. Things came soon to that crisis which made it expedient that we should separate,—and when I claimed the exclusive possession of my rooms, he had the assurance to say that one of these was his by right, and this he has been contending for with no little virulence until now that his appeal to higher authority has been rejected & he placed in the wrong, he sits down to digest his spleen as he may.[30]

The troubles with Wyse continued to mount. On 17 May Vinton wrote in his journal, "Lt. W. being Off'r. of the day, applied to go to town *on Qr. Mr. business* a plea that he has often urged in similar cases.—Stayed till 3 P.M. In the even'g he left the post without my permiss'n though he got Ripley[31] to stay in his place." Vinton obviously felt Wyse was conducting other than Quartermaster's business. Asserting his authority, Vinton officially informed Wyse that the officer of the day must remain at the post unless permitted to leave by the commanding officer. He also issued an order that no horses were to be used except by permission of the commanding officer.[32]

Things seemed to remain quiet between the two men for the next week, but trouble soon flared up again. On the 26th Vinton reported that various differences between him and Wyse had caused the breakup of the officer's mess.[33] On the following day, relations completely fell apart:

> Dr. Steiner[34] breaking up his household. Having a large office table in his quarters & no further use for it, I applied for it, being pub. property. He said he had promised a table to Lt. Wyse but as he had already let him have one he presumed this might go to me. I had it forthwith carried to my office.—At 2 P.M. I went in the room & found the table gone, & learned that Lt. Wyse had it moved upstairs to his quarters. ... I sent for Mr. W. who began to give his reasons for removing the table. I told him it was a gross invasion of my quarters—& before I c'd hear a word of expl'n the table must be returned—& I ordered him to return it. He replied "*I will not.*" I *arrested him.*[35]

While this small conflict was going on at the Augusta Arsenal, much larger troubles were brewing out West. James K. Polk, an ardent expansionist, had won the presidential election of 1844 and had taken office in March 1845. One of the first policies he pursued was the annexation of Texas, which Mexico still considered its territory, even though the Texans had won their independence. If the United States went through with the annexation, there was a good chance war would break out. In addition, there was the ongoing disagreement between Britain and the United States over who owned the Oregon Territory. There had been a joint occupation of the thinly-settled area for a number of years, but with American settlers pouring in and expansionists in control at Washington, war with England was a distinct possibility. Vinton found out just how serious matters were when he applied for a summer leave of absence. "Gen. Wool has answered my application for Leave of Absence by saying that the services of all Officers will be required at their posts this Summer unless in cases of very peculiar emergency."[36]

On 20 June, a Court Martial was convened to hear the case against Lieutenant Wyse. It was no minor affair, having a number of senior officers present and lasting ten days. Vinton himself testified for four days. In the meantime he attended a public funeral for the death of Andrew Jackson and a Fourth of July parade, in which he was Grand Marshall. The absent Lieutenant Talcott returned, and Vinton noted that he and the man reconciled whatever differences there were between them. When the court announced its verdict in the case of Lieutenant Wyse, Vinton must have felt vindicated. He told Mother: [37]

> He was found guilty of all the charges preferred against him and sentenced to forfeit his pay proper for 1 year, to be suspended from rank & confined to the post for the same period and to be reprimanded in orders by the Com'g. General. Here he is now a prisoner,—and it would amuse you to see what *sympathy* has been [. . . .] here among the ladies for "poor dear Mr. Wyse." … Wyse is a pestilent, insubordinate, worthless officer, an arch mischief maker, and well understood to be such by all who know him in the Army. But being a man of insinuating manners and polite address, the ladies imagine that he must be a dear young gentleman and to be thus shut up in disgrace is an outrage. They send him grapes & figs & sympathy therefore, in profusion. A few of the more zealous have even visited him! Never mind. In this, as in every other controversy, I shall come out the conqueror at last. Talcott is ousted: Wyse in limbo,—and J. R. V. is the undisputed lord of Augusta Arsenal.[38]

On the 27th of August, Vinton welcomed a new Lieutenant as a replacement for Wyse. It was an officer he had known in Florida, and he must have been happy to see the man, because he underlined the officer's name when he made his journal entry, something he rarely did. "*Lt. W. T. Sherman*[39] reported for duty with my Comp'y."[40]

In his memoirs, Sherman gave his own perspective on the conflict, saying, "During the autumn of 1844 [1845], a difficulty arose among the officers of Company B, Third Artillery (John R. Vinton's), garrisoning Augusta Arsenal, and I was sent up from Fort Moultrie as a sort of peace-maker. After staying there some months, certain transfers of officers were made, which reconciled the difficulty, and I returned to my post, Fort Moultrie."[41]

The threat of war with Mexico was rising. After the company muster at the end of August, Vinton noted, "Comp. in good order & ripe for Texas." Orders continually crossed his desk concerning movements of other units and changes of station for fellow officers. It seemed only a matter of time until he and his men would move out. Knowing he might soon be sent to the Texas frontier, Vinton began to make plans for his children. He was looking for a school in New England for Frank Laurens, but also considered taking the boy with him on the Mexican campaign.[42]

Like many Americans, Vinton held the average Mexican in low esteem and foresaw a quick and easy victory if it came to war. He was also a firm believer in Manifest Destiny, a general notion that it was God's will for the United States to expand its territory over all of North America, as a letter to Mother indicated:

> I entertain no apprehensions of anything unpleasant even should there be an outbreak. Without asserting that I should like to see a war with Mexico, I may freely say that if it be ordained that our Nation be forced to contend for its rights & its honor, I shall be most eager to engage in the strife. It is my *profession* (that of Arms,)—and if my Country calls for action, I desire to perform at least my *devoir* [duty], and for the sake of reputation, *a little more.* … It appears to be the fiat of Divine Providence that from our Anglo Saxon race, as from a nucleus, shall proceed the diffusing streams of political justice, moral light, and human freedom. Such is the onward & irresistible progress of things.[43]

There was, of course, the problem of what to do with Frank Laurens if war broke out. Writing to fifteen year old Helena, Vinton remarked, "He is very desirous of going with me but I fear he would be an incumbrance [*sic*] and in a situation besides not calculated for his moral or intellectual improvements. If I leave him here I shall have much anxiety about his health & morals,—and to send him North would be difficult."[44]

As for ten year old Frank Laurens, most of his time was still devoted to his studies, including French and Latin, but there was always plenty of time for play, even at school. In a letter to his grandmother, he told her of one of the popular games he participated in, something that sounds very similar to the ball game played by the Creek Indians who used to inhabit the area:

> Many games are carried on by the boys at school; in the summer, marbles and the top, in the winter a game called skinny, a very good exercise for winter. It is made up by forty or fifty boys each with a skinny stick or a stick corresponding to the size of the boy, with a kind of bend or crook at the end to seize the ball or to knock it further. The field is a plain about fifty feet long and just as many broad. Then the boys form sides, and two-buck the ball as it is called, a very funny verb; but it is done in this manner. The one that is to buck, holds the ball in one hand and his stick in the other then he says to the boy bucking with him ("High buck, or low doe") and if he says high buck the ball is thrown up into the air and they both try to strike it with their sticks to knock it on its course to their side. But when the boy says "low doe" the ball falls and down come the skinny sticks after it; After the game has fairly begun it is a glorious scene, running, knocking, jumping, breaking shins; here and there a boy lying without the use of his legs, smashing toes, knocking heads against trees, knocked over by the ball. Sometimes a boy running at full speed is tripped down by a skinny stick thrown out before his legs; sometimes the ball comes to a stand between the sticks of two champions and then the dust flies away when by a successful blow the ball is sent buzzing along the sand or lifted by enormous blows and sent over trees forty feet in height till at last the ball has reached the bounds of the victorious party, and then a long deafening shout of victory is sent up to the sky and the combatants covered with sweat and dust sit down to rest, and to sigh forth their wishes to have a good cool lake to bathe in.[45]

Living in the South, Vinton was constantly faced with the institution of slavery, and may even have hired slaves as household servants. Over the years, his attitude toward slavery hadn't changed. Like many Americans he was not comfortable with the institution and found ways to either ignore or reason away the more troubling aspects of slavery. He also knew that trying to force the South to abandon the practice only made them hold on to it more tenaciously. Discussing the subject with Mother, he wrote:

> Opposed as every thinking man & Christian is, (or ought to be) to Slavery in the abstract, I have never been able to justify in my own mind the obtrusive course of the abolitionists in this country or in England towards our Southern States. … I have often heard of an *Eleventh* Commandment, which is, "To mind

> our own business and let other people's alone,"—and I do believe that about as much evil results from its infraction as from the violation of many of the other ten. Slavery in its social aspect appears to me, here, in no unfavorable light, for all the servants are as well treated here as at the North, and appear to be even more happy. But the blighting effects of Slavery on the general condition of the country at large are obvious enough,—and there is not one intelligent Southerner in ten, I think, who would not rejoice to see Slavery abolished and his state rise, in consequence to a parallel scale of prosperity & strength with the co-states of the North. But no man has yet proposed any plan by which a general manumission of slaves can be brought about, without conditions which are impracticable or inadmissible. At least I have heard of none. The evil is *entailed* on the Southern States, and *curse* as it is, so it must remain until means, not yet apparent, are devised for its abatement or removal.[46]

By November 1845, relations with Mexico seemed to be at a stalemate, as both sides attempted to avert war while maintain national dignity. For the moment, the bigger problem appeared to be the Oregon question, as Vinton told Mother.

> The difficulties with Mexico seem to be in a fair way of being adjusted, but the lowering clouds on the Eastern horizon are more portentous. England is probably determined to insist on her claims to Oregon. America is not less zealous in the assertion of her own rights,—and both nations are too proud to back out of the respective positions they have assumed. The discussion of the question of relative *right* however to the territory of Oregon is a matter of subordinate interest. The claims of either party rest on moonshine, viewed in a strictly moral sense of the subject. It is a question of power simply,—and we Americans think we are able to defend our position. Far higher & deeper considerations are involved in the issue—The spread of Republican institutions. The checking of England's inordinate ambition for territorial aggrandizement. The great principle that the earth belongs to the inhabitants thereof, and not to certain families & Dynasties who happen to wear crowns & coronets. We live in an age pregnant of great events and in a country where the institutions of society, for the first time since the creation of the world are sufficiently free & favoring

> to enable the minds & faculties of men to expatiate untrammeled over the whole realm of moral & physical nature.[47]

Vinton's thoughts may have been wandering to foreign adventures, but things were not completely peaceful at Augusta Arsenal. For the entire summer and into the fall, Lieutenant Wyse had been causing as much trouble as he could around the post, consulting with a lawyer, harassing some of the men and other officers, and sending letters to Washington. His efforts must have been effective, for on 12 November his sentence was remitted. He was immediately transferred to another company and left the post for his new station, yet even after he was gone, he continued to cause trouble. On 30 November, Vinton received word that Wyse had preferred charges against him. On 30 December, Vinton retaliated and applied for a Court of Inquiry into the matter.[48]

Despite these problems, the new year of 1846 opened quietly, and Vinton's letters were filled with the usual political matters and the concerns of choosing new schools for Helena and Frank Laurens, whom he had decided to send home when the time came. In the years before widespread public education, choosing a school was no small matter. For some reason it seemed the best schools were always out of town, perhaps in another state. Because these were private or church-affiliated institutions, the reputation and views of the headmaster or mistress were all-important. Vinton was certainly not above writing to the school and asking for a prospectus and clarifications on any questions he had, but above all, he depended on the advice of friends who had children who were already attending the school. The exact curriculum was important, but so were the religious leanings. Vinton had heard good things about two different schools, but was worried because the Episcopal Bishop in charge of one was too "Romish" [Catholic] in his leanings, while the other might be too Unitarian. Vinton was normally tolerant of other Protestant sects, but he was definitely anti-Catholic.[49]

On 17 February, the Court of Inquiry into the Wyse matter opened and lasted until 24 March. A little over three weeks after it adjourned, Vinton received the Court's findings and wrote to Mother informing her of the outcome:[50]

> Last evening's mail brought me the decision of the Court of Inquiry,—which is another mortifying overthrow to that poor driveller Wyse. The Court exonerated me completely of every allegation,—hazarded by W. (they say) "with a most censurable recklessness." They add, "The Court deems it solemnly due to the principle of subordination,—so vital to the good of the Service,—to express the opinion that the charges preferred by Lt. W. against Capt. V. are frivolous & vexatious, in a good

measure the mere gossiping of enlisted men; that the Service has been unjustifiably harassed;—that the course pursued by Lt. W. shows him to have been influenced rather by motives of personal feeling & vindictiveness than regard to the reputation and welfare of the Army; and that the discipline and dignity of the Service require a stern vindication at the hands of the high authorities with whom the final decision on their proceedings may rest."

Now in all my experience in the Army, I do not recollect to have seen a more entire acquittal on the one part, coupled by so sharp & scorching a rebuke on the other. Yet this poor ass will still hang on to the Service which he dishonors, & dream that he is a gentleman! He ought to be cashiered,—and the question in my mind now is,—ought I to push the matter & demand a more exemplary punish't on him,—or rest satisfied as the case now stands. What think you, dear Mother?[51]

Unsure of whether to push for a harsher punishment, Vinton adopted a middle course. "I despair of having Wyse dismissed as he ought to be (I do not say I wish it) yet I am unwilling to let Gen. Wool suppose that I am satisfied with his milk & water order." Vinton then sent a letter to General Wool stating his dissatisfaction with the lack of punishment, but not calling for any further action."[52]

On 7 May, troubling news arrived from the Mexican border. In what became known as the "Thornton Affair," a force of Mexican soldiers attacked a much smaller American force in the disputed territory between the Rio Grande and Nueces Rivers, killing sixteen American soldiers. Vinton expected a Declaration of War to be announced soon, along with orders to take his men to Texas. He immediately informed Mother, "We are now in daily expectation of Orders for the Rio Grande. You will have learned that a collision has at last taken place between our troops & the Mexicans, and it seems to be altogether probable now that war must be waged on a grand scale. I am quite pleased with the prospect of a campaign & the hope of reaping some laurels in the land of the Montezumas."[53]

Vinton's prophecy was correct, and orders were received on 13 May, the same day Congress declared war.[54] He immediately began to prepare his men to move out. Wagons were hired and baggage was packed. By the next day, the company was ready to go. Then a new order was received telling them to stay put. Besides getting the soldiers ready to depart, he also had to send Frank Laurens home. On the 14th, he sent a hurried letter to Frank in Brooklyn:[55]

> We have received provisional Orders for Texas and only await final instructions to take up the line of march.
>
> In this emergency I am obliged to send my Son to N. York without other protector than such friends as chance may throw in my way. He goes to Charleston tomorrow and is to embark on Saturday 16th May in the Ship *Charleston.* I shall ask the Captain to set him off with a guide to find your house, unless you happen to know of the arrival of the vessel so as to meet him at the wharf in N. Y. His passage will be paid in Charleston, to N. York and I have given him $4.00 for pocket or contingent fund, the balance remaining from this sum I wish you to make him account for & receive into your own keeping. This with the $70 I send in a check appended hereto, & some small balance you have of mine I believe will enable you to pay his way to Warren & Pomfret, & your own if you will accompany him, besides making an advance to Mr. Park towards his 1st quarter's board & tuition. By attending to this you will add another to the many obligations by which I am bound.
>
> As to the time F. L. may stay with you or at Warren or whether he goes to Boston, you will please exercise a sound discretion. He wishes much to see his Sisters and I should like to have him indulged.
>
> We are all on tiptoe, full of exciting expectations, & anxious for a movement.[56]

News continued to arrive from the war front, both of victories by Gen. Zachary Taylor and the deaths of fellow officers. On the 23rd Vinton again wrote to Frank, thanking him for looking after Frank Laurens and giving his views on the unfolding war:[57]

> Your favor of the 19th was rec'd yesterday. Your kind promises to receive & dispose of my little Son after his arrival in New York are just such as expected of you,—and I trust you may be able to see to him & his affairs without prejudice to your professional interests or duties. You will certainly be conferring on me a great favor. The dear boy has become the apple of the eye to me. I miss him exceedingly and would not part with, were circumstances otherwise than they are. I hope he may be pleased with Pomfret and Mr. [Roswell] Park. Pray excite his imagination a little, by presenting pleasant pictures of Mr. Park's School, so that his early impressions may be favorable. . . .

> The news from the Del Norte is glorious. There is not a page of our history so resplendent with the glory of martial exploit as that which shall tell of the early days of May 1846. The battles of the 8th & 9th were fine altogether, exhibiting our well drilled regular Army carrying all their points against immense odds, by the power of superior tactics & discipline. Everything was carried on scientifically,—orders given & obeyed in true military style,—all exact as to time & place,—and accomplished with a precision & gallantry that will resound to the permanent advantage of the Army, in the estimation of the Country—and of our country in the estimation of the Nations of Europe. Many think the Mexicans will not fight again. Perhaps not. But our Gov't. will not stop until we conquer a permanent and advantageous peace. I feel very anxious to be in the affray. It is a harvest field—which is open for us now just once in a lifetime—and it will be unlucky for me if others are to reap all the laurels while I remain perched in a seacoast garrison.[58]

While waiting for final orders, Vinton kept up the preparations. Efforts were made to recruit men to bring the company up to its full one-hundred-man strength. Rifle practice was held, and financial matters were attended to, both personal and military. On 29 May he received a letter from Mother that Frank Laurens had arrived safely at home.

Orders were finally received, and on 11 June 1846, Vinton wrote a hurried note to his mother, who was now residing in Brooklyn with Frank:

> We are on the eve of departure today for Point Isabel, in the good brig Mobile.—I have 3 Lieuts., and 86 men, well disciplined, armed & equipped,—and really could not set out under more favorable auspices. We may be some weeks on our passage, but a sea voyage just now is much to my taste & I think will be beneficial to my health.[59]

It was now almost thirty years since Vinton had graduated from West Point, and he was just shy of his forty-fifth birthday. He had seen action against the Seminole, but that had been a limited, guerilla war. Fighting against thousands of well-armed Mexicans would be another matter indeed.[60]

19

Capt. Vinton Deserves All the Credit

Much had changed since the early days of Vinton's career, when he had carried dispatches to Georgia Governor Troup in the crisis over the Creek land cession. Back then, it had taken him a week to get from Washington to Augusta, traveling in bone-jarring stage coaches over barely-passable roads. Now the War Department's orders had taken a mere two days to reach him, and his troops traveled to Charleston by railroad.[1]

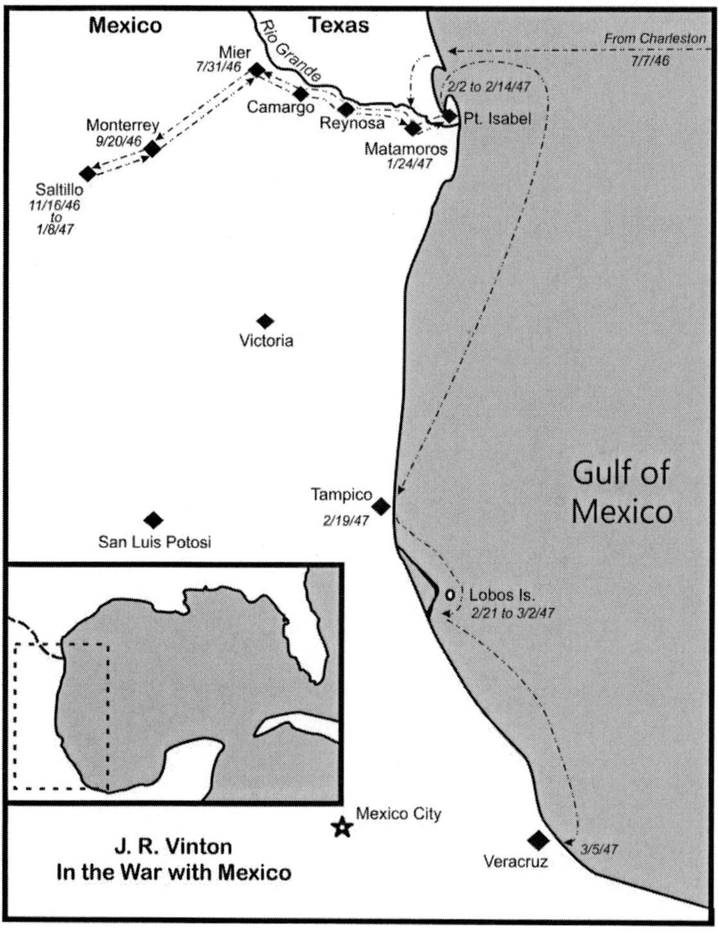

On 11 June 1846, Captain Vinton and his men began their voyage. Between sandbars, rough seas, and unfavorable winds, it took almost a month to make the trip to Port Isabel, Texas. It took another two days to get the men and material ashore.[2]

After reporting to General Taylor, Vinton received orders to march his men south and meet up with other units gathering at Matamoros, on the Mexican side of the Rio Grande. While on their way they passed the battlefields of Palo Alto and Reseca de la Palma, places where Taylor had scored decisive victories a few months earlier. Vinton took time to tour the latter of the two battlefields, commenting that he "saw vast *debris* of the battle,—carcases [*sic*] of horses, pieces of clothing,—caps,—canteens, &c."[3]

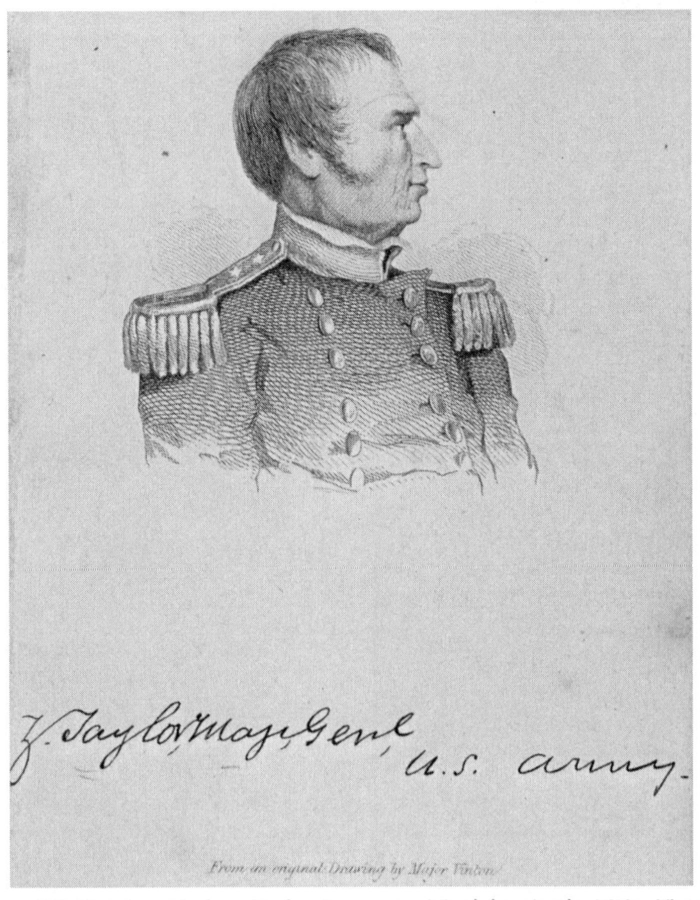

Figure 22: Maj. Gen. Zachary Taylor. From an original drawing by Major Vinton.

Vinton met again with Taylor outside Matamoros on 17 July and noted, "I … found the old gentleman occupying a single tent & certainly one of the shabbiest looking ones in all the camp. In his personal appearance he is plain to excess, but his qualities of mind, heart, and character are such as endear him to all his followers." Waiting for Vinton at Matamoros were several letters from home, including one from Frank Laurens, who was corresponding with his father almost totally in French.[4]

In a letter from Mother, she expressed her concerns about her son being in a war zone and living in unhealthy conditions. Vinton acknowledged the dangers but pointed out that this was where he wanted to be:

> The privations & perils of a campaign like this are certainly numerous,—but I am still very happy to be here, far more pleased than I was while luxuriating in sumptuous quarters at Augusta Arsenal. … Hundreds of old acquaintances among the Officers now greeting me whom I have not met for years, and many new ones not less valuable being made every day. If I gain renown in this campaign it will be very well. If I do not I shall still be delighted with the new scenes & associations which the country & the circumstances afford, and congratulate myself that I have served in Mexico. If I die or am killed in battle my exit will at least be more respectable than if I died in my chamber,—and whether sooner or later by a few years, is to me, a matter of small moment. … Believe me, my dear Mother, although I may yet have severe things to endure, I now feel as happy in the prospect before me, as ever I did in my life.[5]

Two days after arriving at Matamoros, Vinton and his men boarded a steamboat for a four-day voyage up the Rio Grande to Camargo. As if the war wasn't devastating enough on the Mexican people, Vinton reported that much of Camargo had been destroyed in a recent flood.[6] On 27 July he wrote to Mother, giving her his impressions of the town, the people, the campaign, and camp life:

> I write in my tent surrounded by Regiments & Brigades of Soldiers, and every sound & scene round about is only Military: Every person I have to speak to, an Officer or Soldier. We endure of course all the pains of privations of camp life, wet when it rains,—great heat when it shines,—and little else to put into our mouths than commissary rations for food & bad water for drink. …

Everything in this & the other towns I have seen here is different from all we are accustomed to in the U. States. The arts of civilized life have here been so little cultivated that the general impression, on viewing the people & their habitations, is that we are among a savage or aboriginal race, rather than a community calling themselves civilized. The Spanish language is indeed spoken by all, but so adulterated with provincial dialects as to be understood with difficulty by a Castilian. So at least I am told. The houses of this town are nearly all built of clay with thatched roofs, with every appurtenance thereof of the rudest possible kind. A single object presents the token of a Christian population,—a Catholic church, with a low steeple on it, surmounted with a cross. A few other buildings of stucco fronts & some architectural display in their forms & arrangements serve to relieve the town from the otherwise universal aspect of a wild indian village. The people, here as elsewhere in Mexico that I have been, are darker in color than one would have supposed. I have always heard that it was a medley race & thence expected to see much diversity of complexion, but a tolerably light colored person is rarely to be found. The climate being generally warm, few are clad entire,—the children especially being so scantily dressed that a prudish taste would be shocked at every turn. Many of the better classes, they say, have left these parts and retired to the interior on the approach of our troops, and this being so, perhaps it would be doing great injustice to Mexico to suppose these that remain to be even a tolerable specimen of the general character of the people. …

We must move altogether on our own resources, with little or no hope of drawing supplies from the country,—and of course the means to be provided both of subsistence & transportation, are very large. We are unused to carry on war in an enemy country, and everything is done disadvantageously & awkwardly, but still we are so decidedly superior to the Mexican that I anticipate nothing but success. The more I learn of the circumstances of the late battles with them the more exalted is my respect for the Anglo Saxon prowess. Both in numbers, in munitions of war & in strength of position the Mexicans had many fold the advantage of us, but the indomitable spirit of our regular troops led by highly educated Officers, more than counterbalanced the physical advantages of the adversary. Still the Mexicans are not to be despised. One Regi-

> ment, the Tampico, fought so well that out of 700 men, 72 alone remained unkilled or unhurt, and then only would they quit their position & colours.[7]

A few days later Vinton and his men were dispatched several miles west to the town of Mier. Upon arriving Vinton sent word to the Alcalde (mayor), stating that if the Americans were welcomed as friends, they would treat the inhabitants in a reciprocal manner. Probably having little choice in the matter, the Alcalde invited them in. While the officers took up residence in a house next to the church, the men appropriated a large school and made it into their barracks.[8]

In a sense, Vinton had been preparing for this war all his life. The training at West Point and nearly all other military tactics he had studied focused on a possible conflict with a European adversary. Although Mexico was a New World nation, the war would be fought in classic Napoleonic fashion, with ranks of soldiers marching toward each other or assaulting a fortified position. For men like Vinton, the honor and glory to be gained from fighting in such an exposed fashion was all-important. Still, he knew there were other dangers, even when things seemed quiet, as he told Mother:

> On the 31st July I took possession of this town with the troops under my command, who now form its garrison. It capitulated without offering resistance,—and although it contained many who would have been glad to have repulsed us, yet the majority of the inhabitants, I imagine, are not,—or soon will not be unfavorable to the presence of American troops. My determination is to maintain strict discipline among my own people and to cultivate amicable relations with the inhabitants of the town. Thus far everything has gone on well. I am assured by all that the disposition of the citizens is friendly enough, but I am careful to avoid being lulled into a false security by any such professions, and keep up a steady & jealous vigilance. Mexicans are notoriously treacherous and unscrupulous. My position now is the post of danger & therefore of honor,—But I hope not to be left behind here when the Army marches on to Monterey [*sic*]. It is only in that field & with that Army that glory is to be won. Gen. Taylor can hardly march till the 1st Sept'r.—when he will have with him perhaps 7000 men. It will be a pity if, with such a force we cannot overwhelm any that Mexico can bring into the field. The more the better, for unless the odds are at least two to one in her favor our laurels will hardly be worth the wearing.

Vinton also took time to examine the condition of the people of Mier, and sent home the following observations:

> It is curious to see the way people live here. No house has a chimney, and scarcely a fireplace. The people cook their simple meals at a fire made up on the stone or clay floor, and when ready they all sit down on the same floor and with their fingers instead of knife & fork, they proceed to discuss their food. Tables and chairs are very rarely seen, even in the best houses. Children go very thinly clad if clad at all, as full half of them are not.—In Mier there are more fine looking men & women than I have elsewhere seen. Every body, old & young, has fine teeth. In all the town I have scarcely seen one exception to this remark—and the same may be said of the generality of Mexicans,—owing I suppose to their simple diet.
>
> Slavery is said to be abolished in Mexico but the condition of the poorer classes is virtually the same as that of our Negroes. A landed proprietor *owns*, it may [be] said, all the serfs or occupants of his soil. The laws of Mexico give him the right to enforce labor in payment of debt. His tenants owe him money, and he by continued payments of small sums in money, goods, &c. easily manages to keep them in his debt and so the relation is perpetuated. Until the debt is paid, the Serf and all his family are held to bondage. Our slaves have this advantage over the Mexican: When they grow old and imbecile their Masters must take care of them, but the Mexican Master cuts himself loose from his serf when he pleases. Families cannot be involuntarily separated however, nor individuals sold to other Masters. This is in favor of the Mexican.
>
> The Catholic religion prevails here in utter exclusiveness and of course the people are benighted and bigoted, but they are good natured, and from their intelligent bright countenances I doubt not might be brought to a respectable grade of civilization could proper means be applied for their emancipation.[9]

Vinton settled in at Mier and began to scout the territory. With permission from headquarters, he hired a Mexican named Buché to act as a spy and sent him about 50 miles to the southwest to scout the defenses of Monterrey, Taylor's next objective. Buché returned with what must have been heartening news, for it seemed the Mexicans were fighting more amongst themselves than against the Americans:

> 2000 Regulars 3000 militia at that place. Fortified by 4 or 5 redoubts or batteries, &c—Paredes [Mexican Gen. Mariano Paredes] was march'g towards Monterrey with 8000 men when at San Luis Potosi he heard of a revolt at Carretta & Valladolid, & turned back to quell it. His own troops arriving at Coretta pronounced also in favor of federation, joined the revolutionists & made Paredes prisoner. Vomex Farré [Valentin Gomez Farias][10] chosen President in Mexico.[11]

On 22 August Vinton and his men joined a large column of American troops headed for Monterrey. On the 25th they arrived at Cerralvo, about half way to their destination, and waited for the rest of the army to catch up. On 9 September, Taylor and the remainder of the troops arrived. Vinton noted in his journal, "Tents to the right & left as far as eye can see."[12]

Now that the army was gathered and ready for battle, it was time to get the troops fully organized. Taylor divided his force into two Divisions, one under General David Twiggs[13] and the other under General Worth. Vinton found himself serving under Worth, the same man he had served under at the end of the Florida War. Each Division was divided into Infantry and Artillery Battalions, and because Vinton was the third highest ranking Artillery officer in his battalion, he assumed the position of Battalion Major, which must have pleased him greatly. If nothing else, the position entitled him to the use of a horse, which certainly made the march much easier.[14]

On 13 September the army began its march toward Monterrey, arriving outside the city on the 19th. Vinton wrote in his journal, "Advanced parties fired on by the Enemy's cannon which indicates a determination on their part for Battle." On the 20th Taylor sent Worth's Division, which included Vinton's battalion, to approach Monterrey from the west. It was a difficult, round-about march, and the force stopped for the night after covering only seven miles.[15]

Monterrey looked to be a formidable target. To the north, standing between Taylor's forces and the city, was the imposing citadel of Fort Independencia, called the "Black Fort" by the Americans, which could not be taken without suffering heavy casualties. To the south was the Santa Catarina River, which effectively blocked approach from that direction. To the east were several small fortifications, and this was where Taylor intended to make his main assault.

Worth's force, coming from the west, was meant more as a diversion, though the general would certainly do all he could to capture the city if the opportunity presented itself. To the west of the city were two elongated hills, both of them well-defended. The most strategically important was Independence Hill, which had a large, abandoned stone building known as the Bishop's Palace overlooking the city. To the south, Federation Hill had small bastions at either end with one cannon apiece. Worth's intention was to take both hills, set up artillery to fire on Monterrey, and, if feasible, lead his troops into the city and capture it.

On the morning of 21 September Worth and his men began to move toward the two hills, but before they could reach the road that ran to Saltillo they were attacked by a large force of Mexican cavalry. After a sharp fight in which more than a hundred of the enemy were killed, Worth's men were able to force the Mexicans to retreat. The Americans were now in control of the only road that could bring supplies or reinforcements to the besieged city.[16]

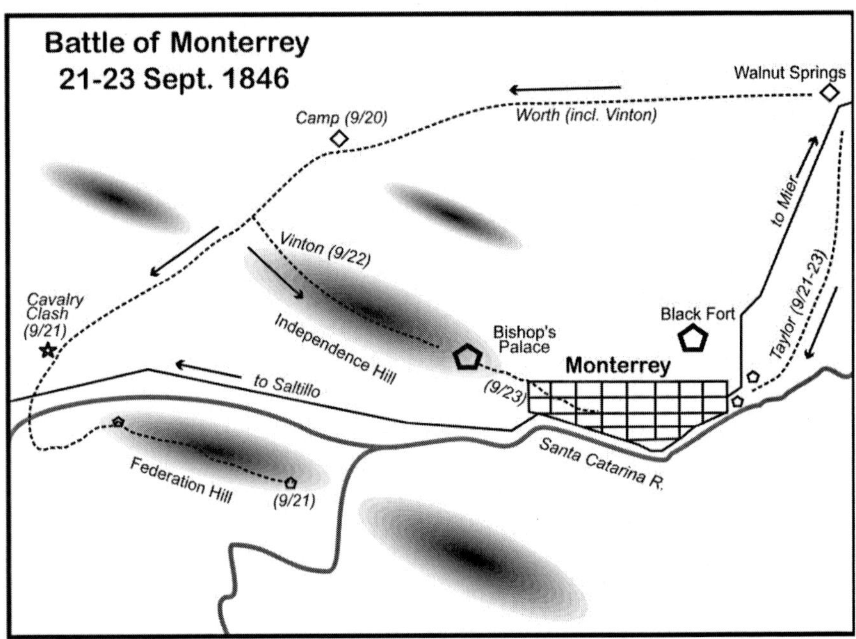

The Americans attacked the less heavily fortified Federation Hill from its west end, and were soon able to drive the outnumbered defenders from their posts at the west bastion. The fleeing Mexicans failed to disable the cannon, so the Americans turned the gun around and trained it on the small fort at the opposite end of the hill. Before long the enemy's one gun was out of action, and the Mexicans retreated. The American's now controlled Federation Hill, with a clear view of both the city and the Bishop's Palace.[17]

In the meantime, Taylor attempted to enter the city from the east. Although his forces were able to capture some of the defenses, they were forced to fall back that evening after suffering heavy losses. Monterrey was besieged, but certainly not conquered.[18]

The next day, while Taylor's half of the force rested, Worth launched his assault on Independence Hill and the Bishop's Palace. Vinton's journal entry from 22 September gave the basic facts:

> This morning at 3 o'clk set out with a comm'd under Col. Childs to take the 2d height where stands the Bishop's palace. He assigned to me 2 Comp's of Regulars & Walker's Texans to ascend part of the hill & with the rest he went up the other. We received the enemy's fire when near the top, but rushing forward we drove him from the summit, with little loss on our part,—He took refuge in the Bishop's palace, a castle like building situated halfway down the hill towards the town. Col. Childs now offered a flag of truce which I was to carry,—but no heed was given to it and I was ordered forward with Scott's comp'y & 3 others to occupy an advanced position 300 yards nearer the castle.
>
> Here I remained about 8 hours in sharp encounters of musketry & ready for an assault—receiving all the while a constant fire from the Enemy, but concealing my men as well as I could. About 2 o'clk the Cavalry charged us, and according to my previous orders, the men rose at the signal, closed on the centre, charged the Enemy down the hill & even to the bottom of it. We entered the old Castle in triumph,—Ayers took down the flag, Bradford occupied the building & I pointed the howitzer against the town, giving the flying foe several discharges.—Col. Childs soon came in with Col. Staniford[19] & the rest of the com'd on the hill.—Gen. Worth & a train of Artill'y soon after rode up and the principal part of the Division soon occupied the *Bishop's palace*, the *Key* to the whole position.[20]

In a letter to a friend, Senator Albert C. Greene[21] of Rhode Island, Vinton gave a more detailed account of the capture of the Bishop's Palace. Knowing that advancement often required political support, he was not above practicing the fine art of self-promotion:

> Permit me to ask the favor of a line from you at an early leisure moment. Remote as we are from the heart of our country, any intelligence you may see fit to communicate will be most gratefully received by me. Pray inform me, if any action may be soon expected on the Brevet nominations. It is quite probable that the number offered may be so great as to cause the Senate to demur in conferring them. If my name should be on the list

> I shall depend on you my dear Sir, to press my claims to a successful issue. I have lost rank heretofore by just such a conjunctive with no effort made to set forth any just claims.

Having made his request, Vinton then described the details of the assault on the Bishop's Palace, placing himself in the third person, perhaps in hope that the report would be anonymously circulated, thereby enhancing his reputation:

> The first height being now in our possession, General Worth lost no time in setting forward an Expedition for the capture of the *second*,—which was of chief importance, inasmuch as the Bishop's Palace occupied its north eastern declivity. That ancient edifice,—massive & huge in its proportions,—was now so strongly armed, and garrisoned & fortified, that notwithstanding its comparative state of dilapidation, it presented an imposing attitude of defense. From almost every point of view in & about Monterey, the old Castle reared its head as a conspicuous object in the landscape, and regarded in a military sense, it might very properly be considered as the Key to the whole position. The summit of the hill rose to a height considerably above the level of the top of the Castle, and was occupied by a strong body of Mexican troops. To dislodge these was now the first object of the Expedition.
>
> At 3 o'clk A.M. on the 22^d^ September, Lt. Colonel Childs was sent forward from Gen. Worth's camp on the Saltillo road, with a detachment consisting of 3 companies of the Artillery Battalion, 3 of the 8th Inf'y, and about 150 Texan Rangers, with orders to carry the height. The morning was wet and very dark and the way intricate, but with the aid of a trusty guide the Colonel found himself at the base of the hill by the dawn of day. Here he divided his force,—a first column commanded by himself, was to ascend the hill on the south side,—and a second, commanded by Capt. J. R. Vinton, after making a short detour to left, was to ascend on the northwest. So well timed and well conducted was this movement that the enemy was probably taken by surprise, as the assaulting parties were more than half way up the hill before the first gun was fired.
>
> Our troops, nothing daunted by the shower of balls that now came rattling down amongst them, nor yet by the steep rocks and thick underbrush which they had to surmount, pushed forward most gallantly. The two columns gained the Summit about the same time. The conflict was short. The Mex-

icans were driven entirely from their position and fled for refuge into the Bishop's Palace. This success was achieved not without the sacrifice of some valuable lives, but our loss was far less than might have been expected from such a service, and the relative disadvantages under which the assaulting party labored.

The Summit of the hill being carried, the next object of attack was the old Castle, from which the enemy were now pouring forth a sharp and continuous fire of musketry & artillery. Halfway down to the Castle was a notch or inequality in the ground which offered good cover for light troops. Col. Childs immediately ordered that excellent Officer, Capt. J. B. Scott,[22] with his own and several other companies to occupy that position. It proved to be a very important one, as it afforded our light troops the only opportunity they could have of annoying the enemy through the windows of the building. This advanced party was soon afterwards increased to six companies and Capt. Vinton placed in command. These companies were deployed as skirmishers, the men spreading themselves down the sides of the hill to the right & left of the ridge. The firing between the parties thus situated, was kept up with little intermission for seven or eight hours,—the Enemy, in the meantime attempting one or two sorties without effect.

It was obvious that nothing decisive could be accomplished by remaining in this situation. The Enemy must be either driven from his stronghold by Artillery,—or be induced to sally & charge upon our line,—in which latter case, we might hope, not only to repel them with the bayonet but follow them so closely in their flight as to enter the Castle with them & take it by a *Coup de Main*. This plan had been conceived, and determined on by Capt. Vinton in case circumstances should favor it,—and having now a command sufficient, as he thought, for the purpose, he made his dispositions accordingly. Orders were given to the companies extended on the declivities of the hill, to rise promptly at a given signal and join by the inner flanks, on the top of the ridge and there form in close order so as to present a firm rank of bayonets to any advancing force of the Enemy, and be ready for such further action as might be required.

At intervals during the forenoon, the companies of this advanced party had been changed by regular reliefs from the reserve stationed on the Summit of the hill. The company of

Texans under Capt. Walker[23] had been thus relieved by Capt. Blanchard's[24] Louisiana Volunteers who came forward with great spirit eager to engage the Enemy. They were directed to take up a position on the extreme left and somewhat in advance of the line where they were able to deliver their fire very effectively. The situation & names of the other companies at this time were as follows:—On the left were Company A 3d Arty. commanded by Lt. Ayers[25] & Comp'y. H 8th Inf'y. commanded by Captain Bomford[26]. On the right were Companies G & K 5th Inf'y. commanded by Captains Chapman[27] & Merrill[28] & Company G 4th Artillery commanded by Lieut. Bradford.[29]

In the meanwhile a howitzer, which Gen. Worth had ordered to be carried up the hill, was by great exertions placed in battery on the Summit, and soon began to play successfully upon the Castle,—occasionally throwing a shell inside,—to the evident discomfiture of the garrison.

Anxious to bring out the Enemy to a charge,—and observing that the critical moment had arrived, Captain Vinton now ordered Capt. Blanchard's Company to fall back on the general alignment. This movement, apparently retrograde, had the desired effect. A strong body of the Enemy, chiefly Cavalry, sallied forth, with shouts from the Castle and charged briskly up the hill, expecting doubtless to drive us all before them. The appointed signal was now given. Our skirmishers rose, and with the promptitude and accuracy of troops on drill they formed in close order, on the central ridge, and there presented to the advancing Cavalry such firm and bristling rows of bayonets as no Mexican horseman might dare to encounter. The Enemy were appalled. They had come up within 20 yards of our position when they were thus suddenly met, as by an apparition.

Capt. Vinton now ordered one volley,—then a charge,—and on rushed our soldiers, with a general hurra, driving all before them, horse and foot,—not into the Castle, but down the hill to its very bottom, quite into the town. So eager were our men in the pursuit, that they were recalled with great difficulty, from following the fugitives into the streets, where there was danger of their being cut off. The rout was complete. Not a Mexican was left on the hill, save the wounded and a few prisoners in the Castle. Orders were now given to take possession of the building,—to strike the Mexican flag from the walls and raise the banner of the Stripes & Stars,—to repair the guns which had been spiked & rolled from the platforms of the outwork and place them again in battery. This latter service was so promptly executed by Lieuts. Bradford & Farry[30] of the Artillery that a howitzer was discharged upon the fugitives before they were yet beyond the range of its fire.

The forces on the Summit of the hill, under Lt. Colonels Staniford & Childs soon joined. Duncan's[31] battery of six pounders came galloping up the hill and at the same time appeared the Commanding General of the 2d Division who was received by all with 3 hearty cheers. The Bishop's Palace was ours. Nearly half the city lying adjacent to the hill, was soon abandoned by the inhabitants, and a wide space left free for our descent, the next day, upon the town.[32]

Lest we think this was all bravado on Vinton's part, Captain Blanchard of the Louisiana Volunteers was an old friend of Frank Vinton and sent him the following account:

On the 22d of Sept., my company was ordered to go over to assist in the attack on the Bishop's Palace.—The extreme point of the hill had been stormed only in the morning by a portion of the 1st Brigade, and was in their possession when we arrived there.—Soon after, my company went forward on the left flank to relieve the Texans who had been skirmishing in the advance.—I found Capt. J. R. Vinton of R. I. in command of the advance, and he then told me that his plan was to try to draw out the enemy from their position in and near the Palace, and when they were fairly out, to rise and charge them vigorously and if possible get possession of the Palace.—The advance was covered as much as possible behind the rocks to protect them from the dreadful shower of grape & musketry which the enemy kept up from their defences.—I asked him if we should advance and fire. He told me that I might if I did not expose my men too much, and that he wished me to fall back whenever I saw the enemy coming out, until we were upon his line of ambush and then to close on him, and rush on them.—It was a well conceived plan, and the result showed that it was well executed.—The enemy was induced to come out and charge, and as they came up the hill Capt. Vinton shouted, "Now, my men, close, and drive them!"—With a wild hurra, they rose, closed to center, delivered our fire and with

> charged bayonets rushed upon the Mexicans.—They were thunderstruck, and after a few moments stand, broke and ran.—Our men were in the Palace and fort before they could all escape, and in ten minutes their own guns were turned upon them.—The main body under Col. Childs came down in solid column and we were the victors.—It was a stirring, thrilling scene, and I cannot do it justice, for it should be seen & be felt.—Capt. Vinton deserves all the credit which his position enabled him to obtain, and I shall always be of the opinion that his plan was an admirable one.—I hope he will be promoted not only for his skillful and gallant conduct on that day, but for his general meritorious conduct as an officer.[33]

On the following day, 23 September, Taylor again advanced from the east, this time taking a more cautious approach, so as to minimize casualties in the intense house-to-house fighting. Instead of exposing themselves in the open streets, the soldiers advanced by breaking through the interior walls of whatever building they were in and clearing out the Mexican defenders in the next room. To the west, Worth launched his own assault, as Vinton related in his journal:

> Gen. Taylor's divis'n. attacked the town on his side yesterday and today. At noon we descend the hill in two columns,—Col. Childs com'g. I take the left—enter the streets—push up our troops to the burial ground. Move on to the first Barricade.—Occupy houses during the night. I find myself under Gen. Smith's Orders.—Mortar plays during the night. Houses & walls pierced by sappers & gradual approaches made to the plaza.[34]

Early the next morning the Mexicans sent out a flag of truce, and the remainder of the day was spent negotiating the surrender. On 25 September, the defeated Mexican army began an orderly departure from the town. The battle for Monterrey was over.[35]

Gaining recognition in battle was one of the few ways an officer could hope to advance in the army, and Vinton wanted to make sure the reports gave him all the credit he felt was due. In his journal entry from the 26th, he showed how the process began, writing, "Col. Childs making his Report. Read a portion to me. Satisfied as to what he says of my doings on the hill, but he gives me small credit for my march with the 2d Column attacking the town." On the following day he wrote, "Interview with Col. Childs con'g [concerning] the above & a word with Gen. Worth." Vinton knew how competitive a business he was in. If a man did not stand up for himself, no one else would.[36]

It had been a fierce fight, and Vinton had seen many of his fellow soldiers die. He also knew that he could easily have been one of them. In a letter to Mr.. Roswell Park, the minister in charge of the boarding school Frank Laurens was attending, Vinton thanked the man for his attentions to his son. He also took time to speculate on the possible political outcome of the war, and in the process showed more than a little religious intolerance:

> Our Boundary must be considerably enlarged to repay us the Expenses of the War,—but this may be chiefly on the Pacific Coast, where we need good harbors & can improve & populate the country but where Mexico can have few or no interests that can benefit herself. Wherever the besotted Catholic of this country inhabits, there is darkness, indolence, vice, & stupidity. In God's Providence the Anglo Saxon Protestant seems to be the only race that can meliorate the soil, illumine the mind, and advance civilization. If this country could be covered with such a population it might be made the paradise of the Earth.

He then expressed regret that one form of duty had forced him to pass another duty on to others:

> I think intensely & unremittingly of my dear little boy and the difficult task you have to mould & reform him to salutary impressions. … In the order of Providence it has been my lot to be separated from my children for a very large share of my life,—and while I feel I have been discharging my duties to my country in full measure, I yet have sometimes cause to regret that to my children I have not been able to render all that a parent owes. To those therefore who may supply a parent's place I shall ever feel most gratified.[37]

The battle for Monterrey had been bloody and difficult, but it could have been much worse. When the Americans took time to consider what they were up against, they were surprised at how easily the city had fallen. In a 6 October letter to Mother, Vinton told her:

> We saw the Mexican Army, with [Gen. Pedro de] Ampudia[38] at their head, file past us, in numbers far exceeding our own,—all armed *cap a pie* [head to toe] and thus did they abandon to us their city, their forts, & their vast supplies of public property & munitions of war. We remain masters of one of the most commanding positions in Northern Mexico, from which three

> times our own number could not now drive us. Who can read this riddle? It astonishes every body. By our superior prowess and by our superior tactics we have gained this victory, and established once more that *prestige*, which endues us with a moral power, that does not fail to operate in our favor in all our relations with the Mexicans. Still they are an Enemy not to be despised. They sometimes fight exceedingly well. They are as expert in the use of arms, especially of Artillery, as we are,—Their ammunition is of a superior quality, and they fight on their own soil, having all the resources of the country at their command. The animal man, bodily & intellectually, is certainly inferior to us,—and wherever we meet on terms of anything like parity, we must conquer.—But we must ever be cautious how we give them the advantage.[39]

Vinton was a philosophical and ethical man, and the moral implications of the war did not escape him. Still, he was a man of his time, with all the contemporary prejudices, and caught up in the excitement of belonging to a vibrant, expanding nation. Like all those who are convinced of the righteousness of their cause, Vinton couldn't see that the traits he applied to the Mexicans could as easily be applied to the Americans:

> Such is the comparative view I take of the parties engaged in this controversy. But why the controversy you will ask—Why be warring against a people avowedly our inferior & whom we ought rather to pity than oppress? To oppress them, we have no wish. We desire peace. We tell them so constantly. We have been driven into the War and are at all times ready to come to reasonable terms. But they are proud & conceited & overbearing. They think they can whip us and they scorn our "pity" or our sympathy. They are vindictive & savages and would wreak on us a diabolical vengeance if they had the power.[40]

By mid-October many of the men were coming down with fevers, and Vinton was one of them. For the next few weeks he was confined to his bed or simply not feeling well. Orders and letters began to arrive from Washington, and Zachary Taylor was not pleased with the tone of some of them. As always happens in wartime, rumors began to fly. On 12 October Vinton wrote Mother, passing along one of those rumors:

> I hear that Gen. Scott has applied again to take command of this Army. There are many here that would be glad of such an

> arrangement,—for although Gen. T. is a brave & a lucky man they cannot accord to him the qualities necessary for a great general. Larger views,—brighter talents, sharper intellect & greater activity of body than his, are all essential. I know not how Gen. S. would prove, since he has never been tried, but he would please & coalesce better with Gen. Worth who is the redeeming spirit (in a strictly military view) of our Mexican Army. Gen. S. is, himself, getting old and might lack energy & perhaps judgment,—but Worth would stand as his right arm as well as his Mentor, and Jove and Minerva would not then clash in counsel or repel in spirit.[41]

More interesting to Vinton and his compatriots was gossip concerning the movements and strength of the Mexican Army. On 17 October Vinton wrote in his journal, "Rumors. Mexican Army has left Saltillo. St. Anna may move forw'd to defend Tampico. Late dispatches to Gen. Taylor requiring him to detach Gen. Patterson[42] to Tampico—Gen. T. will not listen to it."[43] On 3 November Vinton noted, "Gov't disapproves the truce and directs vigorous prosecution of the War. Doubtful where our next movement will be. Gen. Taylor will not move to the interior with less than 15,000 men." Three days later Taylor dispatched an officer to the Mexican army, telling them the truce was over and hostilities had been resumed.[44]

Vinton began to recover from his fever and visited a hot spring on 7 November. In the meantime he attempted to learn Spanish and was busy with financial matters, sending money to various people and placing several investments. He also wrote letters to friends and family and spent a portion of the time sketching.[45]

Finally, on 13 November, Taylor marched a small part of his army out of Monterrey, heading south for Saltillo. They occupied the city four days later, but Vinton was apprehensive. "Gen. Taylor sends forw'd a reconnoitering party on the San Luis road. Santa Anna in San Luis with 18 or 20,000 soldiers—our force scarcely exceeds 800 men. We need Reinforcements."[46]

In a letter to Mother, he tried to make light of their exposed position, but had to admit that their situation was, indeed, precarious. He also gave her his opinion of Mexican society:

> Are not we Yankees an exceedingly bold people? Here we are, masters of the Capital of Coahuila, with an Army numbering scarcely 800 men;—well appointed, it is true, but far distant from our resources, depending alone on our superior discipline and the *prestige* of our arms, for our success & security. … The famous mountain pass of the Rinconada was said to be strong-

ly fortified also,—and, in short, to capture Saltillo was thought to involve dangers & difficulties as great as those we encountered at Monterey. But not so. The Enemy concluded to abandon not only their forts at the Rinconada but the city also, and rally once more at San Luis Potosi. … There Santa Anna now is, with his army amounting to *20 odd thousand men*,—and yet he dare not attack us! … Indeed, in this very city, there are more than 3,000 men,—perhaps each with a musket in his house,—who might rise and overwhelm us,—but they dare not. We have established a moral control over their spirits which keeps them subdued. They hate us, and are mortified to see such proud strangers in their city, but they bow and scrape, and make us obeisance wherever they meet us;—But let us once experience a reverse! Let once the wheel of fortune revolve so as to put us in the descending scale,—then how would they come down upon us! Every farming Ranchero that now puts on the obsequious, would then put on the savage,—and thousands would find courage to throttle us with the lasso, or stab us with the poniard, who dare not now even attempt an enterprise for the liberation & defense of their country. …

And here is the *Republic* of Mexico! A kind of government of which the people seem to be proud,—and yet the very Banditti with which the country & the capital are infested, have better organization, better laws and better police than the nation itself. What has Mexico gained by throwing off monarchy? *Two words*, which find place in all their public dispatches, *Dios* y *Libertad*,—two words, of which, in sober verity, they have not yet learned the meaning! Their religion is mockery, idolatry, priestcraft,—their liberty, an ever changing government of venal rulers,—extending to the people no security of life or property, but oppressing them with every species of taxation.[47]

So far the war with Mexico had proven an almost enjoyable experience for Vinton. He had seen exotic places, felt the thrill of battle, and earned the much-sought-for glory that a military man yearns for. Yet the war was only half over. Northern Mexico may have been conquered, but the dangerous campaign to vanquish the heart of the nation had yet to commence. It would prove to be Vinton's final campaign.

20

He Fell Last Evening In the Trenches

Vinton and his men occupied Saltillo until 8 January 1847, when orders were received to prepare to move out. They left the town the next morning, passing through Monterrey four days later. A week after that they were at Camargo on the Rio Grande, where they boarded a steamer that took them to Matamoros. From there they marched thirty miles north and encamped at Palo Alto on the 24th.[1]

While waiting for further orders, Vinton received a bit of good news. Congress was considering an Army Bill that would create several new positions as Majors. Vinton applied for one of the promotions, and General Worth endorsed the application with, "Capt. Vinton is eminently qualified & as eminently deserving the promotion he asks,—and would acquit himself with honor in a yet higher grade."[2]

Zachary Taylor had scored some impressive victories in the north of the country, but the Mexican Government was intent on continuing the fight. President Polk and the War Department decided the only way to bring the Mexicans to the negotiating table would be to strike at the nation's heartland. Polk dispatched Gen. Winfield Scott with orders to invade Mexico from the Gulf and take Mexico City.[3]

Some people felt Taylor should have been put in charge of the campaign, and although Vinton disagreed with them, he still had high regard for the general. In a previous letter to his mother he had called Taylor "lucky" and was afraid she would take it the wrong way. Writing again, he told her, "I must acquit myself of the suspicion you entertain that by the use of this word, I intended to impair the just merits of Genl. Taylor. The old gentleman is a great favorite with all of us, but more for his stubborn honesty of character, his moral purity,—his goodness of heart, & exalted courage,—than from any remarkable brilliancy of talent or extensive attainments in the art of war."[4]

To reach Mexico City the army was going to have to land at Veracruz on the Gulf Coast and march inland. This was going to be the United States's first large-scale joint army/navy amphibious landing on a foreign shore, and there was ample opportunity for things to go wrong. About fifty civilian vessels were hired from the East and Gulf Coasts to transport the troops and their material. Specially designed flat-bottom landing craft were constructed, made in three slightly different sizes so they could be nested on the decks of the transports.[5]

On 2 February Vinton and his company boarded a steamboat and waited for General Scott to arrive aboard the steamer *Massachusetts*. Back in Rhode Island, his daughter LuLu penned a letter, the last he would ever receive:

> My dear Father
>
> It is now time for me to write to you, although I have had no answer for my last letter. I hardly hear anything about you now dear father, for we do not take any papers which relate the war affairs. But I trust, you are well, my dear father. … We have fifty six scholars this term at school. I study Arithmetic, Algebra, Geometry, History, Latin Grammar, Sallust,[6] and French. … I am just getting over the *mumps*. They came on Friday night and Saturday and Sunday pained me a great deal. … We have to write Compositions once a week at school. I love to compose dearly. I suppose one reason is, because I have written so many letters. … I have saved all the compositions I have written since Mr. Wooster took our school and I am going to show them to you when you come home. …
>
> Lillie[7] sends her love to you, she is a sweet girl. We room together and are with each other a good deal. I hope I shall hear from you soon dear father. Uncle Kinnicutt never fails to ask me, when he comes in if I have heard from you. Mr. Adams always inquires too and I guess many others. Cousin Martha sends her regards to you. I must now close and so Good bye. May God protect and keep my dear father under the shadow of his loving, prays
>
> Your affectionate daughter
> Lulu Clare[8]

On 14 February Vinton and his men boarded the *Massachusetts*, and their baggage was brought aboard the following day. The vessel got underway on the 16th, steaming south. Two days later they were anchored off Tampico, Mexico, which had already fallen to the Americans. The next two days were spent ashore, visiting with old friends and socializing with new ones. Finding the anchorage at Tampico insufficient for all the ships that were gathering, Scott decided to move the fleet a bit south to a sheltered area behind Lobos Island and the adjacent point of land known as Cabo Rojo.[9]

On 27 February, while the fleet stood at anchor, Vinton took time to write a letter home, the last he would send to his beloved mother:

> My confidence in the overruling Providence of God is unqualified so that I go to the field of action fully assured that what-

ever may befall will be for the best. I feel proud to serve my country in this her time of appeal,—and should even the worst,—death itself,—be my lot, I shall meet it cheerfully, concurring fully in the beautiful Roman Sentiment, "*Dulce et decorum est, pro patria mori.*" [It is sweet and glorious to die for one's country.]

I have hitherto lived mostly for others,—having only for nine years of my life been permitted to enjoy "Domestic bliss"—"the only happiness that has survived the fall."—But my children will reap some of the fruits of my self-denial by the means I shall leave them, of living independently & securing a good education. I commit them in full reliance to the parental care of their Heavenly Father, and I hope their trust in Him will ever be at least as firm & increasing as has been my own. That He may ever preserve & bless my dear Mother is the constant prayer of your

Affectionate Son
John[10]

For the next week the ships stood at anchor, waiting on the remaining vessels to join them. In the meantime, Vinton did paperwork, made whatever preparations he could, and enjoyed the fishing. On 26 February a fleet of twelve to fourteen vessels arrived with General Twiggs and his forces. On 1 March General Worth arrived, the last man Scott was waiting on. It was time to proceed to Veracruz.[11]

Worth also brought details about the Army Bill that had passed Congress. Vinton wrote in his journal, "Army Bill has passed, and so we have a new Maj. to each Reg't. *Query*, what are my chances?—But all will be for the best." What he did not know was that he had indeed received one of the coveted new positions. Although he would never hear the news, he was now Brevet Major John Rogers Vinton.[12]

Vinton knew he was entering upon a dangerous mission and had related some of those fears to his mother. She, in turn, relayed them to Helena:

I have rec'd many letters from yr. dear father. He gives us frequent accounts of the progress of this sad & wicked war. … My dear child! This is the most momentous & solemn transaction of yr. dear father's life! I will copy a part of his letter, that you may judge of the dangers that surround him, & of the necessity of our fervent prayers to Almighty God, our heavenly Father for deliverance & safety.

> "The movements of troops by Sea, is a delicate affair, always, & where a landing is to be made in an enemy's country, & at a boisterous season of the year it is decidedly perilous. The elements, however, are the only enemies we fear, if enemies they be, but like good soldiers, we must be prepared for all things. Very large preparations are made, for a grand descent on Vera Cruz—The point of our debarkation is not yet known to us, altho' it may be known, ere this, to Santa Ana, as the courier conveying important dispatches to Genl. Taylor, was captured by Mexicans, & the escort party, made prisoners. The fleet of transports, are ordered to rendezvous under the island of Lobos, wh. is some 40 miles south of Tampico, from wh. point a movement will be made, of sufficient force, to secure the position, on wh. we may land. Anton Lizardo, 12 miles south of Vera Cruz, is a fine harbor & presents excellent facilities for landing. Alverado, is also another good point, but is not to be taken, perhaps, without a conflict. Having secured a landing at either of these points, with 7,000 men, & a good siege train, we may attack Vera Cruz in the rear with every prospect of Success."
>
> I have given the extract from yr. dear father's letter to yr. Uncle Alexander, my dear daughter, that you may realize the peril, by Sea & by land, to wh. he is exposed. O let us "pray without ceasing," to Him, who governs all events, that He will continue His loving kindness & tender mercy towards us.[13]

The fleet got underway on the 2nd, but the wind was so light that only the steamers could proceed. A fierce "norther" blew in two days later, and by the 5th nearly all vessels were in sight of Veracruz. Not wishing to tempt the guns of the Mexican forts, Scott gathered his fleet a little south of the city, at a point of land called Anton Lizardo. While waiting for the rest of the fleet to gather, Scott and his officers made last-minute plans. At one of those meetings, Worth appointed Vinton as his acting Major.[14]

The place chosen for the landing of the nearly 12,000 men was Collada Beach, a few miles south of Veracruz. Just offshore was the island of Sacrificios. On 9 March, soldiers began to transfer from the transports to three warships that would ferry them toward the beach. On that same day, Vinton took a few minutes to write a quick note to Rev. Park, Frank Laurens's schoolmaster:

> I have just rec'd your letter of Feby. 3d while on board the Steamer Massachusetts, just on the point of landing before Vera Cruz. Of course I am in a hurry & write under disad-

vantages, but, cannot refrain from giving you an immediate & most grateful acknowledgement for all you have said about my dear son. God be thanked! It gives me fresh spirits for the encounter at hand. I wrote to the little boy also a day or two since. I should have acknowledged more particularly your former letters of October & subsequently. Your change in the price of tuition &c is quite satisfactory to me of course. I see by your account that a balance was still in my favor so I have made no recent remittance. Should any be required please call on my Brother Frank.

Tell Laurens that I have rec'd & read his nice little letter with very great pleasure. Present my best respects to Mrs. P. & believe me dear Sir yr. attached & much obliged friend

J. R. Vinton[15]

A later notation written across the face of the letter reads, "This letter is probably the last my beloved Son ever wrote."

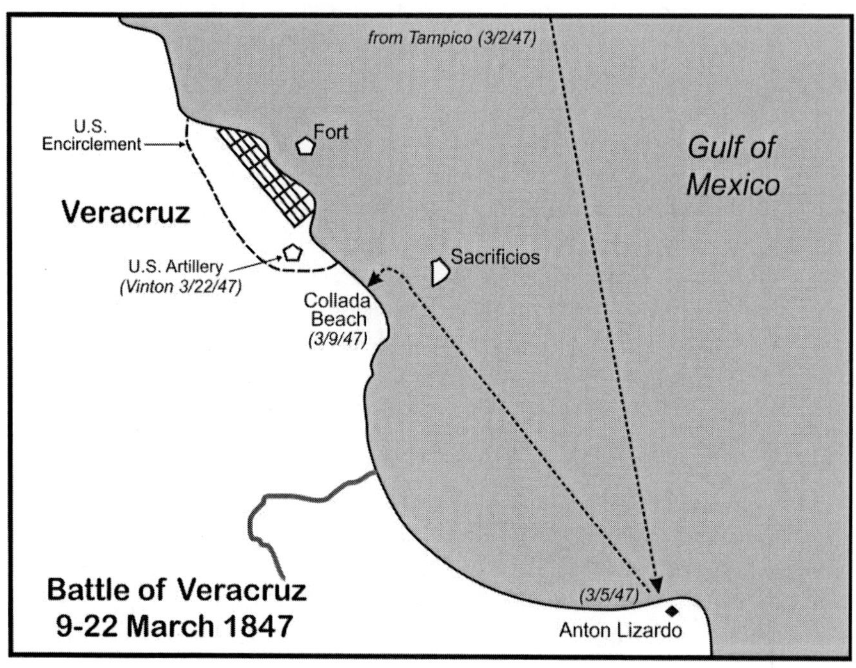

As the troops continued to board the landing craft, Vinton made the final entry in his journal. "No Norther. All fair & southerly wind. Troops shifting to the vessels of war Raritan, Albany, St. Mary's &c to go forward to the landing. Doubtful whether the Enemy have a battery near Sacrificious [*sic*]."[16]

The landing went off precisely as planned. The warships sailed between Sacrificios and the mainland and dropped anchor off Collada Beach. The troops climbed down the ladders and into the waiting flatboats. In order to land with overwhelming force, the landing craft were kept together until they were all filled. Then, as a group, the boats rowed toward shore. General Worth, with Vinton no doubt close behind, was the first man to step ashore, followed by the 5,500 soldiers of the first wave. By nightfall, the whole army was ashore.[17]

Veracruz was well fortified, and Scott had no intention of making a direct attack on the city. Instead, he proposed to lay siege and pound the city into submission with a devastating artillery barrage. Troops immediately spread north, encircling the city and cutting off all avenues of escape or relief. Getting the massive artillery into place would take longer. Trenches were dug south of the city, and preparations were made to bring the huge guns ashore. In all, it took nearly two weeks before the artillery was ready to open fire.

On the morning of 22 March 1847, Maj. Edmund Kirby[18] sent his brother-in-law Hammond Vinton an update of the campaign, in which he took time to inform him of how Hammond's older brother was doing:

> J. R. Vinton landed with the first line under Worth, & next day, was detached with two companies to occupy a Lime Kiln, on the beach in advance & quite near to the Town. A post of peril, the communication with which has been kept up only in the night. Last night he was withdrawn & sent to man the mortar battery, not far from his post. I saw him a few moments in the evening—well & in good spirits. He has all the enthusiasm & ambition of a young soldier & stands very high in the confidence of the general-in-chief, who would gladly have him in his staff.[19]

That same day, Scott issued a final call for the City of Veracruz to surrender. They officials adamantly refused, and Scott gave the order to commence the bombardment. In response, the cannon at Veracruz opened fire, sending cannonballs and explosive shells toward the American position. The shells were largely ineffective, killing or wounding few of the American artillerymen. Still, as Scott would report the next day, one of his most valuable officers had been slain:

> That officer was Capt. John R. Vinton, of the U.S. 3d Artillery, one of the most talented, accomplished, and effective members of the Army; and who highly distinguished himself in the brilliant operations at Monterey. He fell last evening in the trenches, where he was on duty as field and commanding officer, universally regretted.[20]

That evening, at 10:00 P.M., Maj. Kirby sat down to the difficult task of writing another letter to Hammond:

> I am overwhelmed with grief, your brother, my friend, the gallant, gifted accomplished Vinton, is no more. His head was struck off by a shell, about sunset this evening, in the trenches. I wrote to you this morning, that the town would be summoned this afternoon. At two o'clock Capt. J. E. Johnson [Johnston][21] went in with a flag, carrying the General's demand for the surrender of the City to a superior force, prepared to enforce the demand. The Governor, Gen. Morales, in courteous terms declined.—The batteries opened at half past 4. Seven mortars, disposed in three batteries, one of which was commanded by J. R. Vinton. The fire was returned from four times the number of our guns from both town & castle & was kept up with great animation on both sides, for some three hours.—The gun boats (five) of the squadron & the Spitfire & Vixen Steamer, taking part for an hour or two. The bombardment from our side is kept up & will be all night.
>
> Vinton who has held an important out-post, the Lime Kiln on the beach, for the last ten days, was last night ordered to the trenches, to man & command battery No. 3. It appears that he raised himself above the parapet to observe the effect of his fire, with a view to give it more efficiency, when his head was struck by a cannon shot or shell & carried away, so we have the report—it may not be critically, accurate. This sudden dispensation has spread deep gloom through the whole army. I have been, for several hours on a sand hill, in a crowd of perhaps a hundred officers who were uniting their voices in lamentation.
>
> Just now at Gen. Scott's tent, to a large circle of the Staff, the General pronounced a most eloquent & feeling eulogium upon the deceased, that went to the heart of every listener; he spoke of his rare talents & accomplishments & high soldiership, as placing him in the front rank of his profession. Before leaving Washington, the General recommended him for the

> appointment of Assistant Adjutant General with the rank of Major, with the view of making him chief of his staff, in the field. He (the Gen.) mentioned this to me when I first joined him, & no longer ago than yesterday lamented to me that the Government had paid no attention to his recommendation. He spoke of it again this evening, with highly complementary reference to virtuous, gallant & distinguished services at Monterey for which he had recommended him for a brevet.
>
> The campaign at Monterey, brought me in contact with him after 20 years separation, & we were a month together on board the Massachusetts, coming to this place. Our sympathies were much together as to men & things—the war & events passing around us—we thus cemented a close & cordial intimacy, which makes his loss fall most heavily upon me. How keenly will it be felt in his own cherished family circle. How will his venerable Mother be affected? I almost fear it will bow her revered head, in sorrow to the grave.
>
> Gen. Scott remarked this evening, that the instantaneous surrender of the City & Castle would not assuage his grief nor compensate the country for the loss of such a son.
>
> The stillness of the night is broken by the booming of the cannon, hurling destruction among the unoffending inhabitants of Vera Cruz. Every shell takes effect & in a bombardment, it is impossible to discriminate, for shot aimed at batteries & barracks are liable to fall among the dwellings of peaceful inhabitants, who are innocent sufferers of the horrors of war, in its most dread form. The destruction of life & property must be very great. I hope that the Governor will relent & for the sake of humanity, invoked by Gen. Scott, will surrender the City tomorrow. I shall endeavor to cause the effects of our friend to be forwarded to you.

The following morning, after receiving more accurate reports, Kirby continued the letter, giving details of Vinton's death:

> I have today learned from Mr. Van Vleit, of Capt. Vinton's company & who was near him when he fell, the particulars of his death, differing somewhat from the report brought in from the trenches last night. The shell (8 inch) first struck the parapet & then, being partially spent, the left side of his head fracturing his skull, without disfiguring his face—the fuse made a wound across his breast, from which his blood flowed, as well

as from his nose & mouth. He fell dead. The shell did not burst & did no further damage. He was brought to camp when the company was relieved, at 4 o'clock this morning. He looked almost life-like but was slightly changed, retaining a sedate but not harsh expression. His remains were followed to the grave at 4 o'clock this afternoon by his company & by the General-in-chief & a large body of Officers—The funeral service was read by Col. Childs. The place of burial is a sand knoll, near the shore, whence it is proposed to remove the remains to a Cemetery near the town.

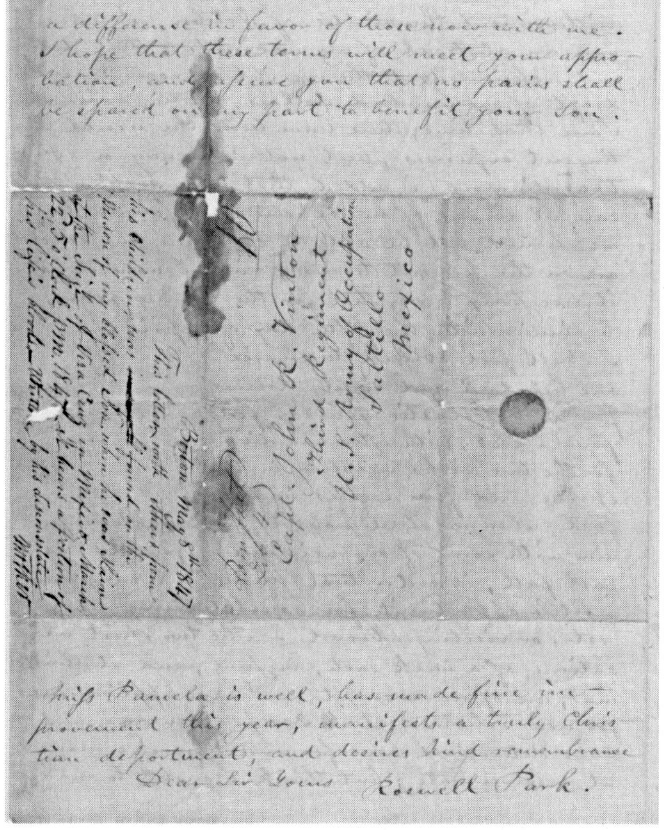

a difference in favor of those now with me. I hope that these terms will meet your approbation, and assure you that no pains shall be spared on my part to benefit your son.

Capt. John R. Vinton
Third Regiment
U.S. Army of Occupation
Saltillo
Mexico

Boston May 5th 1847

Miss Pamela is well, has made fine improvement this year, manifests a truly Christian deportment, and desires kind remembrance.
Dear Sir Yours Roswell Park.

Figure 23: Letter from Mr. Roswell Park, stained with Vinton's blood. Notation above address reads: "This letter, with others from his Children, was found on the person of my blessed Son, when he was slain at the Siege of Vera Cruz in Mexico, March 22nd, 5 o'clock P.M., 1847. It bears a portion of his life's blood. Written by his disconsolate Mother."

I assisted Lieut. Van Vleit in making such arrangements as were deemed necessary, having been so requested by my friend Vinton, when he left the ship to come on shore if the necessity should occur. His effects will be all packed up & I shall endeavor to send them by the Princeton which sails for New York. I have thought best to send everything as it is. There is neither time nor opportunity to have anything washed. There are a thousand little things of no intrinsic value, which will be invaluable as relics to his children. We buried him in the clothes in which he fell, an old frock coat &c. In his breast pocket we found several letters, apparently, without examination, from his children, which are stained with his blood from the wound in his side. I requested Mr. Van Vleit to place them in his trunk. His watch crystal & tooth brush were broken by his fall. I send his mess basket, the mess furniture was owned by him & his company officers jointly—The articles are of little value & I requested the mess to retain them. Every thing will be packed in his trunk & a large box which will be directed to you at New York—you had best inquire for them, on board the Princeton, immediately after her arrival.

By his Memorandum book, he appears to be indebted to his company fund about $160 dollars. To one of the Sergeants of his compy $50 & to another $70. To two of his privates $20 & $10 respectively. His purse contained $37.50. Mr. Van Vleit paid the two privates $20 & $10, leaving $7.50, which will be found in his purse, in the trunk. The two sergeants have the Capt's receipts for the $50 & $70 respectively, corroborating the memorandum book & will apply to you or his administrator, for payment as will also the commander of his company for the post fund. He drew his pay from me on the 28th day of February, for January & February $237 for which I gave him a check on Bank of America for $220 & $17 in money.

I hear, at this moment, that it is probable, the Princeton will sail tomorrow morning for *Philadelphia*, instead of New York. I will write a line to Tomkins, supposing him to be at Phila. requesting him to see to the forwarding of the box & trunk. I will endeavor to get them on board in the morning & will go with them out to the ship. There are a number of keys which should have been put in the box but are left out. I will make them in a package directed to you & place them in charge of some officer to be forwarded to you in Phila. I may fail to get the baggage on board, for the surf is running very high tonight & it may be very difficult to get off to the ship in the morning but I will do the best I can.[22]

The siege of Veracruz lasted three punishing days. On 25 March the Mexicans called for negotiations, and on the 27th, the city surrendered. On the following day, Maj. Kirby once again wrote to Hammond:

I have, I believe, omitted to correct an error in my first statement of the particulars of John R. Vinton's death. Instead of commanding a battery, he was acting field officer & commanding in the trenches & instead of looking over the parapet was in the trench passing from one battery to another, when an 8 inch, spherical case shot, passed through the crest of the parapet obliquely, which deadened its force, & at the distance of perhaps 12 feet, struck him on the left side of his head as before stated. I have examined the place carefully. Maj. Martin Scott[23] was a few steps from him, (being in command of the covering party). Lieut. Van Vleit, of his company, was a few steps from him on the other side. Happily, the shell did not explode or the destruction would have been dreadful, for several of the men seeing him fall rushed to him. But he fell dead. The shell contained one pound of powder & 320 musket balls. I have secured the shell & placed it in charge of Lt. Rowan[24] on board the Princeton, to be delivered to you. I shall enclose herewith, a note from Lieut. Stone[25] of the Ordnance that he extracted the fuse from the shell—took out one pound of powder, & returned to the shell, 320 musket balls & returned the fuse. Let this be kept in remembrance, lest there should be uneasiness hereafter, from apprehension that it is still charged.[26]

Figure 24: Fatal cannonball atop tomb of Major John Rogers Vinton.

After the fall of Veracruz, Scott began his long march inland, and after numerous bloody battles, captured Mexico City on 14 September. For all practical purposes, the war with Mexico was over.[27]

The end of the war was glorious news for the people of the United States, but no doubt bittersweet for the family of John Rogers Vinton. Mother, devastated by the loss, turned to her faith to ease the burden. Although nearing seventy-five, she did her best to rally her grandchildren and to keep the memory of their father alive in their minds. Helena was seventeen, almost a full-grown woman. LuLu was not yet fifteen, and Frank Laurens was twelve. All were living in boarding schools, with no close relations nearby. Since the time of Lucretia's death, their father had often referred to them as orphans, due to his long absences. Now they truly were. In a letter to Helena, Mother wrote:

> I have been alarmed & made very anxious by a letter from yr. Uncle Frank, who has received information from Mr. Park that Laurens is so much wrought on by his father's death, that it seems to affect his health. My heart is already bowed to the dust, & this intelligence is a sore weight indeed. I pray our heavenly Father, to spare this dear little representative of my precious Son! ... It is very difficult to realize, that we are never more to hold communion in this life, with him, in whom was centered all the affections of our hearts. It will be a long time before we shall cease to expect letters from him. But we must learn the sad lesson my dear daughter. We shall know him no more in the flesh. Yet, blessed be our Father in heaven "We do not sorrow as those without hope." He is "not lost, but gone before." ...
>
> I need not tell you to remember all his requirements. ... His letters to you dear Helena, & to Lulu, wh. I read over with admiration & tears, contain all a father's & all a mother's care & love. ... When you read these letters, will you realize that yr. dear father is talking to you? ... Preserve his letters, my dear daughters Helena & Lulu, as long as you live: learn them *by heart* in the true sense of the word: let them stand as a monument in yr. memory, of his love, & care & wisdom. He lives for you, in them. He speaks to you.[28]

To LuLu, she mentioned receiving the trunk from Mexico containing Vinton's possessions, then asked both girls to pay particular attention to Frank Laurens:

The opening of yr. dear father's trunk gave me a sight of some familiar objects wh. seemed to bring him before me for a moment. But the delusion changed into the heart rending certainty that I sh'd see him no more. Besides these, there were many memorials of his skill & talents, of a recent date, that showed his unremitted industry & calm courage to the last hour of his death. These give a consistency & dignity to a combination of moral elements, wh. have been rarely, if ever united in one character. O what a loss he is to his country & to his family! How shall we become reconciled to it? …

I desire you, my dear children, to write often to yr. little brother, & press him to answer yr. letters punctually. This will divert his mind from the lonely & desolate feeling, wh. the death of yr. dear father & the separation from his dear sisters, has produced. Let yr. dear father be the often topic of yr. letters, so that his reminiscences of him, while he was with him may be called up, & preserved, if he sh'd live, to bless his future days, when mature years will enable him to appreciate the noble & beautiful character of [his] Sainted Sire.[29]

In the summer after John's death Mother travelled to Pomfret, where she was able to spend time with Frank Laurens. The visit probably did them both good. For the girls, familial care was still administered through the mails, but at least Helena and LuLu were now at the same school and able to console one another. Mother wrote Helena:

I see Laurens almost daily. He grows faster & Mr. Park thinks he improves. I hope you & Lulu write to him often. … My dear Helena, you are the first born, & now having almost arrived at womanhood, you will be called to use the advantage of yr. seniority in every way, to produce good influences, on yr. sister & brother. I expect much of you my daughter. Much has devolved on you, because of our great bereavement. …

You say you "Cannot reconcile y'rself to yr. dear father's death," but I trust my child, your heavenly Father thro' Christ, will reconcile you to *Himself* & make you humbly submissive to His holy will. … I hope you will never as long as you live, cease to realize the unspeakable worth of yr. father, & yr. unspeakable loss. There never was a *human* father so good, & I fear, we shall never look upon his like again.[30]

The people of Vinton's native Rhode Island were also saddened. Mother commented to LuLu, "We are grateful while we are astonished to find how everywhere, among all ranks of people both high & low, yr father's patriotism is known & his death lamented."[31]

The state petitioned the army to have the remains returned home, and more than a year after his death Rhode Island paid Vinton their final honors with a funeral fit for a conquering general, with most of the state and city's political establishment in attendance and much of Providence closed down. John Rogers Vinton was home at last, near the family and country he loved so deeply. (The full text of the newspaper announcement, including a poem dedicated in his honor, is printed in Appendix A).

So how can we assess the life of John Rogers Vinton? Do we even have the right? True, we have read his letters and journals and have seen how others reacted to him, but none of us were there, none of us looked him in the eye or went through his experiences. We can draw conclusions, but we will never really know if we are right or wrong; our own prejudices and experiences affect our reasoning in more ways than we can imagine. The telescope of time has a very narrow field of view, and the truly important insights are often hidden from view.

If we are looking for a window into the world of an early nineteenth-century military man, Vinton provides us with much to examine. If, on the other hand, we are looking for answers to the great moral and social questions of the day, he doesn't have much to offer. Indeed, he had an all-too-human ability to sidestep difficult and troubling matters. He abhorred the idea of slavery, but was willing to accept it while in the South. He justified slavery by saying it was no worse, in some respects, than Northern factory work or Mexican peonage, but avoided confronting the evil in any of those institutions. He disapproved of the government's Indian Removal policy, but helped carry it out nonetheless, taking refuge behind the need to do his duty. Perhaps the greatest lesson we can take away from Vinton's experiences with these issues is how impossible to solve they truly were.

We are, at times, struck by Vinton's indecisiveness, and it is one of his most interesting character traits. The more time he has to think about something and the more choices there are, the more he procrastinates, waiting on a sign from God. It seems ironic that a man of such strong faith should fall prey to his own doubts. Yet he was also a man of action. Give him a situation where there was a clear objective or his personal honor was in question, and he would show little hesitation to act, even in the face of grave consequences.

We are not psychiatrists, so we won't attempt to psychoanalyze Vinton's relationship with his mother, especially since we have so few of her own words to refer to. She was obviously the strongest, longest-lasting influence in his life, imbuing him with her ideals of responsibility, self sacrifice, piety, and class consciousness. She leaves the impression (perhaps false) of being overly pedantic and morally strict, but what also comes across is the deep love she shows to and nurtures in her children and grandchildren. In many ways, Mary Vinton is the most interesting member of the family, and we would love to discover a diary where she set down her innermost thoughts.

Yet it's Vinton's relationship to the army, more than anything else, that is the focus of this book. He devoted his life to the military and never knew any other career, but until the last decade of his service, he didn't seem truly enthusiastic about being a soldier. It was only after the loss of Lucretia and his experiences in the Seminole War that we see him truly embrace the profession. It's doubtful that he actually chose to be a soldier. After all, he was only twelve years old when he entered the Military Academy. He enjoyed certain tasks and positions, such as the survey work or serving under General Brown in Washington, but those were more akin to civilian jobs than to any warlike pursuits. The years he served in Maine, when he was newlywed and his children were born, were no doubt his happiest, but they were good years because of his family, not because he was in the army.

We first notice the change in attitude at the Battle of Lake Monroe, his first real military action. He was obviously excited and proud, but the separation from family and then the crisis of Lucretia's illness soon overtook those emotions. After the passing of Lucretia, when he was left alone with his thoughts in the Florida wilderness, he began to reevaluate his position. Pressure from Mother to leave the army forced him to take a hard look at his life, and this was when he truly begins to accept that being a soldier was the life he was best suited to. Perhaps it was simply a rationalization to avoid a difficult decision, but by the time of the War with Mexico he had a true enthusiasm for camp life, campaigning, and the thrill of battle. He no longer wanted anything but to be a soldier and a father, and did not see the two as necessarily incompatible.

Vinton's life was cut short, but it had been a full life nonetheless. Perhaps what saddens us most is the lost opportunity to spend more time with his children. Had he survived the war he might well have received a permanent promotion and a comfortable posting to go with it. He may even have returned to Washington or New York as part of Winfield Scott's staff. Even if none of those things came to pass, he would most probably have been stationed at a coastal fortification where he could have brought the children to live with him. Perhaps his investments would have allowed him to retire. Any of those options would have been nice, but futures are never guaranteed.

Yet it is not the loss we should consider, but the life that was lived and the accomplishments attained. Like the vast majority of mankind, Vinton's achievements were not the sort that changed the course of history. His were of a more personal nature, and we can all take a measure of inspiration from the life he lived. Indeed, if we look at the high points of Vinton's life closely and take a rather callous point of view, his accomplishments seem of little historical consequence. Yes, he was proud to be the first Rhode Island graduate of West Point, but that was a matter of circumstance and not of his own doing. The boundary with Canada would have been surveyed without him, and someone else could have carried the dispatches between Washington and Georgia in 1827 with little difference in the outcome. In the Seminole War, his presence certainly did not lengthen or shorten the conflict or change the end result. Nor did his actions in the Mexican-American War, and even his death, have any lasting military consequence.

But if lasting consequences are all we judge a person's life by, then we are certainly missing the point. By seeing what this one man did, we can all appreciate what any one of us can do. All of us can work hard to improve our lot in life, put up with painful hardships to perform our duty, take responsibility when the need arises, and show consideration for our fellow man and love to our family. We can even, if need be, lay down our lives for what we feel to be a worthwhile cause. All of this is not something new; we instinctively know it. Yet we also tend to forget these lessons as we go through life, and we all need to be reminded of them on occasion. That is what history is for.

Vinton's children may have been orphans, but in such a close, loving family, they would certainly not be abandoned. They remained in their boarding schools, watched over by Uncles Frank and Alex and their grandmother until her death in 1854 at the age of eighty-one. Helena soon finished her schooling and appears to have moved in with Uncle Frank at his parish in Brooklyn. She remained there for several years, perhaps pursuing a higher education. As an adult, she may also have taken a more direct role in the upbringing of LuLu and Frank Laurens. In 1856 she applied for a passport so she could travel to Europe, and listed her address as being in care of Rev. Francis Vinton. Her description on the application listed the twenty-six year old woman as being five-foot five-inches tall, with blue eyes, brown hair, and an oval face. By 1860 she was back at the family's old hometown of Pomfret, living in the household of John H. Gilliat, a widowed Episcopal clergyman. She was probably working as a teacher, for there were a number of young, unrelated children also residing at the house. Two years later, at the age of thirty-two, she would marry Rev. Gilliat, and their first child would be named John Rogers Vinton Gilliat. Vinton had always stressed the importance of education to his children, and the message stuck with Helena. A year after her husband's death in 1873, Helena was living in Newport and had opened a girl's school. She advertised, "English, Mathematics, and Latin thoroughly taught. A foreign lady will reside in the family to teach French and Music. Competent teachers also employed for other branches." It was the sort of life Vinton, a firm believer in God and education, would have liked for his daughter.[32]

LuLu (Louise Clare) married Dr. Washington Hoppin on the day before her twentieth birthday, and the couple set up housekeeping in Providence. She gave birth to six children, the first (Helena Lucretia Hoppin) being named after her sister, and the last (Francis Laurens Vinton Hoppin) after her brother. In the 1870s she returned to Pomfret, where she and other members of the Hoppin family spearheaded an effort to turn the town from an old country village into a thriving summer resort for families from Providence. Her "fine character, executive ability, and faith in Pomfret's future, here found full vent and lasting appreciation." Years later her third child (and namesake), Louise Clare, would recall, "My mother was a pretty woman, gay and clever too. She had six children and she used to say that if my father had gone on living she would probably have had twelve." LuLu's devotion to home and family would have warmed her father's heart.[33]

Frank Laurens followed in his father's footsteps, attending West Point and graduating in 1856, tenth in his class. Although appointed a lieutenant in the cavalry, he immediately took a leave of absence, travelled to France, and soon resigned his commission. He spent the next four years at the Imperial School in Paris and graduated with a degree in Mining Engineering. All those hours spent practicing French with his father had paid off. Returning to America, he worked for a while as an instructor, and then travelled to Central America to conduct mineralogical studies.[34]

The Civil War called him home, and he resumed his career in the regular army as a captain, but soon became a colonel in the New York Volunteers. After fighting in at least half a dozen battles, he was severely wounded at Fredericksburg while leading a charge. Although promoted to Brigadier General, his wounds left him too disabled to continue in the military, forcing him to resign his commission in 1863. He then returned to New York and devoted himself to his chosen profession as a mining engineer. He co-founded the School of Mines at Columbia University in 1864 and was Chair of Mining Engineering from 1864 to 1877. He then retired from academia and moved to Colorado, where he worked as a Consulting Engineer. His father, who had given his life so that America could expand westward, would have been proud to see his son fight for his country, become an accomplished educator, and help the nation grow. It was the sort of legacy John Rogers Vinton hoped to leave.[35]

Appendix

The Vinton Obsequies
Providence Daily Journal
Thursday, May 11, 1848

STATE OF RHODE ISLAND AND PROVIDENCE PLANTATIONS

Headquarters, Providence,}
April 28, 1848}

The Commander-in-Chief [governor] having accepted the invitation of the Committee of Arrangements appointed by the General Assembly, to be present at the funeral ceremonies of the late MAJOR JOHN R. VINTON, which are to take place in Providence on the 11th day of May next, makes known the following orders:

1. The Officers of the General Staff, the Aides of the Commander-in-Chief, and the General and Staff Officers of the several Brigades, will report themselves fully equipped for duty to the Adjutant General at Headquarters, on the 11th day of May next, at 9 o'clock A.M.

2. The Major General will also report himself at Headquarters at the same time and place, fully equipped, with his Staff, and will take command of the companies Active Militia who may take part in the ceremonies.

3. The line will be formed on Broad street, the right resting on Durrance street, facing to the north, at 9 o'clock, A.M., upon the day designated. The Newport Artillery, Col. Perry, will be detailed for the firing party, and the Volunteer Sea Fencibles, Capt. Cameron, will be stationed on Smith's Hill, and will fire minute guns from 10 o'clock, A.M., until 12, M.

4. The Quartermaster General will furnish the ammunition for the occasion, upon requisition of the commanding officers of the companies detailed for firing parties.

By order of the Commander-in-Chief,
T. A. JENCKES, Adjutant General

The General Assembly, at the May session, 1847, passed the following resolutions:

Resolutions in honor of the late MAJOR JOHN R. VINTON, of the 3d Regiment of the United States Artillery.

Resolved, That this Assembly tender their sympathy to the family and friends of MAJOR JOHN R. VINTON, of the 3d Regiment of United States Artillery, a native of this State, in the bereavement they have been called to experience by his early and lamented fall at the siege of Vera Cruz; that they appreciate and honor his skilled and admirable conduct at the storming of Monterey, and in the dangerous but honorable position he occupied in the approaches to Vera Cruz; and bear a willing testimony to that able and conscientious discharge of duty for which, as a citizen and a soldier, he was through life eminent.

Resolved, That as a mark of respect to the deceased on the part of his native State, Gen. Thomas J. Stead, Gen. Elisha Dyer, Jr., Col. William W. Brown, Col. George W. Hallet and Col. Christopher Grant Perry be a Committee to cause his remains to be interred, with the consent of his family, in the city of Providence, with such manifestations of respect as to said Committee may seem proper.

HENRY BOWEN, Secretary

The Committee appointed by the General Assembly by the foregoing resolutions in honor of the late MAJOR JOHN R. VINTON, announce the following Programme, route of procession and general directions to be observed on that day.

MUSIC
GENERAL COMMANDING
Rhode Island Guards, Col. Murrill.
Wickford Pioneers, Col. Thomas.
Kentish Guards, Col. Bodfish.
Woonsocket Guards, Col. Tourtellott.
Providence Light Infantry, Col. Brown.
Providence Artillery, Col. Blanding.
MUSIC
Pawtuxet Artillery, Col. Tucker.
Providence Marine Artillery, Col. Simmons.
Warren Artillery, Col. Pearce
Providence Horse Guards, Col. Potter.
Rhode Island Horse Guards, Col. Palmer.

Committee of Arrangements, mounted.
Chaplain and assistants, in carriage.

BODY

The Newport Artillery as a Guard of Honor.	4 Majors as bearers	{ *On a 6-pounder gun-* } { *carriage, drawn by* } { *four horses, with a* } { *groom to each horse.* }	4 Majors as bearers	The Newport Artillery as a Guard of Honor.

Horse, fully caparisoned, led by a groom.
Family of deceased, in carriages.
HIS EXCELLENCY THE COMMANDER-IN-CHIEF
And Suite, mounted.
Officers of the Division Staff, mounted.
Brigadier General and Staff of First Brigade, mounted.
Brigadier General and Staff of Second Brigade, mounted.
Brigadier General and Staff of Third Brigade, mounted.
Brigadier General and Staff of Fourth Brigade, mounted.
Brigadier General and Staff of Fifth Brigade, mounted.
Grand Marshal and Assistants, mounted.
Officers of the Army and Navy of the United States, in carriages.
Marshal.
His Honor the Lieutenant Governor, the Secretary of State,
the General Treasurer and the Attorney General, in a carriage.
Members of the Honorable Senate, in carriages.
Speaker and Members of the House of Representatives, in carriages.
Marshal, mounted.
Mayor and Aldermen of the city of Providence, in carriages.
Members of the Common Council of the city of Providence, in carriages.
Marshal, mounted.

Fire Department of the City of Providence
The Board of Firewards.
Hydraulion Company, No. 1.
" " " 2.
Fire Engine Company, No. 1.
" " " " 2.
" " " " 3.
" " " " 4.
" " " " 5.
" " " " 6.
" " " " 7.

“ “ “ “ 8.
“ “ “ “ 9.
“ “ “ “ 10.
Forcing Stationary Engine Company, No. 1.
“ “ “ “ “ 2.
Hook and Ladder Company, No. 1.
“ “ “ “ “ 2.
Forcing Steam Engine Company, No. 1.
Marshal, mounted.
Pioneer Engine Company, not attached to the department.
Other Associations and Companies that may volunteer to join the procession.
Marshal, mounted.
Citizens and Strangers.

ROUTE OF PROCESSION.—Up Broad, through Fenner, High and Westminster streets to Market square, down South Main, through Power, Benefit and Olney streets to the East Turnpike, and thence to the Swan Point Cemetery, where the funeral service will be performed. [Ed.: About four miles]

Returning by East Turnpike and Olney streets, through North Main and Westminster, where the whole procession being in line, the ceremonies of that day will end.

1. The line will be formed on Broad street, with its right resting on Durrance street, facing north, at 9 o'clock A.M.

2. The column will move precisely at 10 o'clock, A.M.

Alfred Wright, Esq.,
Having accepted the appointment of Chief Marshal,
and

Gen. William C. Gibbs
William Simons,
Charles F. Harris,
Nathan Porter,
William P. Sheffield,
Byron Sprague,
Augustus M. Tower,
Lewis P. Child,
George A. Rhodes,
Frederick A. Sumner,
Edward C. Mauran,
Cromwell Whipple,
Samuel A. Briggs,
Moses B. Almy,
Walter B. Chapin,
William C. Beckwith,
Joseph Warren Taylor,
William H. Taylor.
Benjamin C. Gladding.

And other gentlemen, Assistant Marshals, will be respected accordingly.

[Ed.: There is no line 3 in the original.]

4. The Marshals will be mounted, and designated by a plain baton and flowing scarf of black crape on the left arm, and will meet on the Great Bridge at half past 8 o'clock, A.M.

5. Headquarters will be at the Earl House, where the officers of the General, Division and Brigade Staff will meet at 9 o'clock, A.M.

6. The carriage for the reception of the remains will be at the Depot to meet the arrival of the train from Stonington, and the General in command will detail a detachment of Horse to escort the same to their place in the line.

7. The Commander-in-Chief will be escorted from headquarters to the line by a squadron of Horse.

8. The Commanding General will detail from the line eight officers of the rank of Major to serve as pall bearers.

9. The Newport Artillery having been detailed as a guard of honor, will be the firing party at the grave.

10. Minute guns will be fired by a detachment of the Volunteer Sea Fencibles, under the command of Capt. Cameron, from 10 A.M., to 12, M.

11. The only crape worn by the officers of the line or staff, will be a knot on the sword-hilt.

12. All music brought into line will be under the direction of the Committee of Arrangements, and will be posted by and play only when ordered by them.

13. The Fire Companies will bring no Engines or other apparatus into line.

14. The Firemen will form a line at 9 o'clock, A.M., on Westminster street, with the right on Exchange street, facing north, and will be conducted to their place in line by Marshals.

15. The Lieutenant Governor, Secretary of State, General Treasurer and Attorney General, and the members of the Senate and House of Representatives, will meet at the State House at 9 o'clock, A.M., and will be conducted to the line by Chief Marshal and Assistants.

16. The Mayor, Aldermen and members of the City Council will be conducted from the City Hall by Marshals, at 9 o'clock, A.M.

17. Officers of the Army and Navy of the United States are invited to meet at Headquarters at 9 o'clock, A.M.

18. Other Companies and Associations not named in the order of procession who may wish to join in the ceremonies, will report themselves to the Committee of Arrangements previously to the 11th inst., or to the Chief Marshal before 9 o'clock, A.M., of that day, and will form on Mathewson street, right on Broad street.

19. Citizens and strangers who intend to join the procession will meet in Eddy street, between Westminster and Broad, and form with the right on Broad street.

20. The line being formed, the family of the deceased will be conducted by the Chief Marshal and Assistants to their place in line.

21. Carriages for the family of the deceased will be stationed in Greene street.

22. Carriages for the members of the General Assembly will stand on the east side of North Main street, heading south.

23. Carriages for the Mayor, Aldermen and City Council, will stand on the west side of South Main street, heading north.

24. The Chief Marshal will post his assistants at the points at which the troops from out of the city may arrive, to conduct them to their places in line.

25. The Committee request that the colors on the several flag staffs in the city, and on board the vessels in the harbor, may be hoisted at half mast during the day.

26. The Committee urge upon the City Marshal and the officers of the city police, and upon all good citizens, that they lend their aid to prevent accidents by keeping the streets through which the procession is to pass clear from carriages, and particularly that none be left to stand in the streets on the route of the procession, from 9 A.M., to 2 P.M.

Finally, the Committee recommend that places of business on the route of the procession be closed, and that all should join to render the ceremonies worthy of the State and the occasion.

THOMAS J. STEAD,)
GEORGE W. HALLET,) Committee
ELISHA DYER, JR. : of
WILLIAM W. BROWN,) Arrangements
C. GRANT PERRY,)

THE FUNERAL CEREMONIES decreed by the General Assembly in honor of Major John R. Vinton, will take place today according to the programme published on the first page of this day's paper—The pageant will doubtless be a solemn and imposing one. The committee recommend that the stores and places of business on the route of the procession be closed, and we doubt not that the good citizens generally will comply with the recommendation and that the people will unite in the demonstrations of respect which are to be paid to the memory of a gallant soldier and an accomplished gentleman. Many of our readers were attached to him by the ties of personal acquaintance, and all of them respect him for the noble and generous qualities which adorned his character.[1]

Vinton's Welcome Home

Pomfret, Ct. Nilla[2]

Soldier, rest! Thy warfare o'er
Welcome to thy native shore!
"Brothers, let the banners wave,
Gently o'er the warrior brave;
March with slow and measured tread,
Bear him to his lowly bed!

Let the city's turmoil cease;
See, the soldier sleeps in peace;
"Fathers,—lo, his fight is done;
Look upon thy valiant son!
Softly raise the coffined head,
Lay him in his narrow bed!

"Kindred, bend above his bier,
Shed for him affection's tear;
None a nobler race have run,
Husband—Father—Brother—Son!
Firm yet gentle, true and brave;
Kindred, weep beside his grave.

"Poet, wake thy harp at will
For a Brother's lyre is still
String the chords to notes of woe,
Let the dirge be sad and low;
Weep for us, but loud and free,
Strike for him a jubilee!

"Painter, seize the living brush,
While the flood of memories rush;
Let again his features glow;
Winning smile, and noble brow!
Mourn with us, a brother fled,
Chant a requiem for the dead!

"Scholar, bending o'er the page,
Gaze upon the soldier-sage!
Never—nevermore for him
Shall the lamp burn low and dim;
See, a nation mourns today,
Leave thy page, and homage pay!

"Minstrel ere the dirge is o'er
Let the chords ring out once more;
Cold the hand and closed the eye
Once could wake sweet melody!
Let the soul of music sweep
Through the chords, then turn and weep!

"Sisters pluck a garland now,
Twine a wreath to bind his brow;
Gather laurel, let the rose
Mid its leaves of green repose,
Let the hay of glory be
Intertwined with posey!

"Christian, wipe the tearful eye
Lo a Christian passeth by!
Lo a soldier of the cross!
His the crown, and ours the loss!
Come and see his lowly bed;
Welcome to the noble dead!

Love Poem

John Rogers Vinton to Martha Haskins, 1/11/1828

1

I've seen the pelting pitiless storm
Assault the tender Rose,—whose form—
Shrinking with its fears.—
Bent low before the raging blast
While every leaf was shedding fast
The melancholy tears—
But the dark cloud soon passed away
The Sun beamed forth in brighten day
And gladdened all the scene—
The Rose, with renovated glow
Shed sweeter, lovelier colours now
Than if no storm had been.

2

I've seen the Lightning's vivid flash,—
Have heard the breaking Thunder crash,
And felt the panic dread—
The mighty oak was scathed and riven
And from the frowning face of Heaven
Even Hope awhile seemed fled.
But when the tempest-cloud had passed
When Thunder's roar and Lightning's blast
No more their terrors showered
The Landscape's Smile—the Zephyrs balms,
Were sweeter in that hour of calm
Than if no clouds had lowered.

3

So with the fond, confiding heart,—
When disappointment's withering smart
Has rankled at the core;
Should eyes it doats on—*once more smile*,—
They chase each case—each pain beguile,
And sorrows ver no more.[3]

Picture Credits

Frontispiece: John Rogers Vinton, artist unknown. Courtesy of Print Collection, Miriam and Ira D. Wallach Division of Art, Prints and Photographs, The New York Public Library, Astor, Lenox and Tilden Foundations, Image ID: 5203132.

Figure 1: West Point, circa early 1820s. Painting by W. G. Wall, engraving by John Hill. Courtesy of Library of Congress, http://www.loc.gov/pictures/item/2011661799/.

Figure 2: View of the Village of French Mills, New York. Sketch by John Rogers Vinton. Courtesy of David M. Rubenstein Rare Book & Manuscript Library, Duke University. John Rogers Vinton Papers, Journal (1817-1819), Microfilm No. 293-01-2.

Figure 3: Repeating circle owned by Dr. Ferdinand R. Hassler, possibly used by John Rogers Vinton. Courtesy Division of Medicine & Science, National Museum of American History, Smithsonian Institution, Catalog No.: PH*314640.

Figure 4: "View of our Station at Chateaugay River." Sketch by John Rogers Vinton. Courtesy of David M. Rubenstein Rare Book & Manuscript Library, Duke University. John Rogers Vinton Papers, Journal (1817-1819), Microfilm No. 293-01-2.

Figure 5: Maj. Gen. Jacob Jennings Brown, by John Wesley Jarvis. Courtesy of National Portrait Gallery, Smithsonian Institution, NPG.98.2.

Figure 6: Maj. Gen. Thomas Sidney Jesup. Courtesy of State Archives of Florida, http://floridamemory.com/items/show/8283.

Figure 7: Seminole leader Micanopy. Courtesy of Ah-Tah-Thi-Ki Museum of the Seminole Tribe of Florida.

Figure 8: N.W. view of Fort Mellon, Lake Monroe, E.F., 1837. Sketch by John Rogers Vinton. Courtesy of Mark F. Boyd Collection, Special Collections, University of Miami Libraries, Coral Gables, Florida, ID: ASM0037, Box 1, Folder 13.

Figure 9: The *Marion*, Silver Springs, docked. Sketch by John Rogers Vinton. Courtesy of John Lee Williams Papers, Special & Area Studies Collections, George A. Smathers Library, University of Florida, http://ufdc.ufl.edu/AA00017224/.

Figure 10: Osceola, right-profile. Sketch by John Rogers Vinton. Courtesy of John Lee Williams Papers, Special & Area Studies Collections, George A. Smathers Library, University of Florida, http://ufdc.ufl.edu/AA00017224/.

Figure 11: Osceola at Lake Monroe, 1837. Sketch by John Rogers Vinton. Courtesy of Mark F. Boyd Collection, Digital Collections, University of Miami

Libraries, Coral Gables, Florida, http://merrick.library.miami.edu/cdm/ref/collection/asm0037/id/2

Figure 12: St. Johns River. Sketch by John Rogers Vinton. Courtesy of John Lee Williams Papers, Special & Area Studies Collections, George A. Smathers Library, University of Florida, http://ufdc.ufl.edu/AA00017224/.

Figure 13: Maj. Gen. Winfield Scott. Engraving by Thomas B. Welch. Courtesy of Library of Congress, Prints and Photographs Division, http://www.loc.gov/pictures/item/2012645266/.

Figure 14: Light House, Key Biscayne. Sketch by John Rogers Vinton. Courtesy of John Lee Williams Papers, Special & Area Studies Collections, George A. Smathers Library, University of Florida, http://ufdc.ufl.edu/AA00017224/.

Figure 15: Fort New Smyrna, 1839, by Capt. Harvey Brown. Illustration from *Six Columns and Fort New Smyrna* by Charles W. Bockelman. Daytona, FL: Halifax Historical Society, 1985.

Figure 16: Indian mound near Fort Taylor, upper St. Johns. Sketch by John Rogers Vinton. Courtesy of John Lee Williams Papers, Special & Area Studies Collections, George A. Smathers Library, University of Florida, http://ufdc.ufl.edu/AA00017224/.

Figure 17: Brig. Gen. William Jenkins Worth, by Mathew Brady, ca. 1860-1865. Courtesy of National Archives, File No: 528455.jpg.

Figure 18: St. Francis Barracks, St. Augustine, Florida. Photo by the authors.

Figure 19: Aerial view of Fort Macon (1965). Courtesy of the State Archives of North Carolina, ID No: N_72_2_62 Fort Macon, 1965.jpg.

Figure 20: Commandant's House, Augusta Arsenal. Augusta State University, Augusta, Georgia. Photo by the authors. Permission of Carol Cross, Admission Services Coordinator.

Figure 21: Parlor, Commandant's House, Augusta Arsenal. Augusta State University, Augusta, Georgia. Photo by the authors. Permission of Carol Cross, Admission Services Coordinator.

Figure 22: Maj. Gen. Zachary Taylor. From an original drawing by Major Vinton. Courtesy of Print Collection, Miriam and Ira D. Wallach Division of Art, Prints and Photographs, The New York Public Library, Astor, Lenox and Tilden Foundations, Image ID: 5111199.

Figure 23: Letter from Rev. Roswell Park, stained with Vinton's blood. Courtesy of Dr. Samuel Smith.

Figure 24: Cannonball atop tomb of Maj. John Rogers Vinton. Photo by the authors. Permission of Swan Point Cemetery, Providence, RI.

Color Plates

Plate 1: Portrait of John Rogers Vinton, n.d., Watercolor on paper, Artist unknown, Negative #RHi X17 1200. Courtesy of the Rhode Island Historical Society.

Plate 2: Portrait of Lucretia Dutton Parker Vinton, n.d., Oil on canvas, Artist unknown, Negative #RHi X17 1201. Courtesy of the Rhode Island Historical Society.

Plate 3: Portrait of David Hammond Vinton, n.d., by John Rogers Vinton, Negative
#RHi X17 1197. Courtesy of the Rhode Island Historical Society.

Plate 4: Elizabeth Vinton Greene. Artist unknown. Courtesy of Worcester Portrait Prints Collection, American Antiquarian Society.

Plate 5: Rev. Alexander Hamilton Vinton. Image from *Memorial of St. Mark's Church in-the-Bowery*. New York: Thomas Whittaker, 1899.

Plate 6: Rev. Francis Vinton. Brady-Handy Photograph Collection, circa 1855-1865. Courtesy of Library of Congress. http://hdl.loc.gov/loc.pnp/cwpbh.02882.

Plate 7: Louise Clare (LuLu) Vinton. Courtesy of private family collection.

Plate8: Francis Laurens Vinton. Courtesy of University Archives, Rare Book & Manuscript Library, Columbia University in the City of New York, Historic Photograph Collection, Box 120.

Plate 9: "West Point Cadet," watercolor by Lt. John R. Vinton, circa 1821. Courtesy of West Point Museum Collection, United States Military Academy, Accession No. 20069.

Plate 10: "The Ruins of the Sugar House," oil on canvas by John Rogers Vinton, circa 1843. Courtesy of Sam and Robbie Vickers Florida Collection.

Plate 11: "Oseola" [sic] sitting on the banks of a lake. Oil painting by Capt. John Rogers Vinton. Courtesy of Private Collection, New Orleans.

Plate 12: Tomb of John Rogers Vinton, surrounded by cement cannon. Frank Laurens' grave is to the right, Lucretia's to the left. Photo by the authors. Permission of Swan Point Cemetery, Providence, RI.

Plate 13: Christ Church, Pomfret, Conn., dedicated to Rev. Alexander H. Vinton. John Rogers Vinton's grandson Howard Hoppin was the architect. Each stained glass window is dedicated to a family member. Photo by the authors. Permission of Christ Church, Pomfret, CT.

Plate 14: Tiffany stained-glass window of St. George and the Dragon, dedicated to John Rogers Vinton. Caption: "Hoc Ardua Vincere Docet" [This teaches us to overcome difficulties.] Major John Rogers Vinton, Killed at the siege of Vera Cruz, April 1846. Faithful Unto Death." Photo by the authors. Permission of Christ Church, Pomfret, CT.

Notes

Abbreviations

AGO	Adjutant General Office
ASPIA	*American State Papers: Indian Affairs*
CHS	Connecticut Historical Society
IRCML	Indian River County Main Library
JRV	John Rogers Vinton
NA	National Archives
PPL	Providence Public Library
RG	Record Group
RIHS	Rhode Island Historical Society
RLDU	Rubenstein Library, Duke University
UDL	University of Delaware Library
USHD	*United States House Document*
USHR	*United States House Report*
USMA	United States Military Academy Library

Preface

1 John Rogers Vinton (hereafter JRV) to Helena Vinton, August 25, 1844, John Rogers Vinton Papers, box 1, Rubenstein Library, Duke University (hereafter RLDU).

2 JRV to Mary Vinton (hereafter Mother), September 31, 1839, John Rogers Vinton Letters, Notes: Correspondence, Indian River County Main Library (hereafter IRCML).

Chapter 1

1 JRV to Mother, February 27, 1847, John Rogers Vinton Papers, box 1, RLDU.

2 Littell, *Littell's Living Age,* XIII: 236.

3 JRV to Mother, April 5, 1841, John Rogers Vinton Letters, Notes: Correspondence, IRCML.

4 Westgate, comp., *Mayflower Families,* 19: 167; Drake, *History of Middlesex County,* 2: 169.

5 Westgate, comp., *Mayflower Families,* 19: 1.

[6] Ibid., 167; Arnold, *Vital Record of Rhode Island,* 6; Vinton, *Vinton Memorial,* 204; Gray and Morrison, eds., *New Perspectives on the Early Republic,* 109, 113; Cooper and Gleason, "A Different Rhode Island Block-and-Shell Story," 182.

[7] Vinton, *Vinton Memorial,* 1, 3, 109-111; Carlton, ed., *Genealogy State of Vermont,* 2: 92; *Vital Records of Medford, Massachusetts,* 315.

[8] Vinton, *Vinton Memorial,* 110-111; Drake, *History of Middlesex County,* 2: 169; *Massachusetts Soldiers and Sailors of the Revolutionary War,* 16: 341.

[9] Bayles, ed. *History of Providence County,* 2: 584; Flynt and Fales, *Heritage Foundation Collection of Silver,* 347.

[10] Greene, *Providence Plantations,* 65, 68, 128; Bishop, *History of American Manufacturers*, 2: 39.

[11] Vinton, *Vinton Memorial,* 205; *American Church Silver,* 377; Flynt and Fales, *Heritage Foundation Collection of Silver,* 231, 345, 347; for images of David Vinton's silver pieces see Fowler Museum at UCLA Photos, accessed November 10, 2016, http://www.travelphotobase.com/s/CAAWUF.HTM and The Metropolitan Museum of Art Online Collection, accessed November 10, 2016, http://www.metmuseum.org/collection; Kane and Keeton, *Fort Benning,* 89.

[12] Vinton, *Vinton Memorial,* 204; Greene, *Providence Plantations,* 150.

[13] Amos Maine Vinton, John Rogers Vinton's oldest brother, was a commercial merchant and auctioneer in Providence. During the War of 1812, at the age of 16, he joined other Providence citizens in erecting fortifications for its safety. He married Frances Jones Dyer of Providence on October 25, 1824, and they had five children: four girls and a son who died in infancy. Maine died of typhoid fever on July 12, 1837 and is buried at Swan Point Cemetery in Providence. Vinton, *Vinton Memorial,* 281-282; *Providence Directory,* 68; Stone, *Life and Recollections of John Howard,* 332-333; Arnold, *Vital Record of Rhode Island,* 469.

[14] Gen. David Hammond Vinton, Vinton's younger brother, entered the Military Academy at West Point on September 1, 1818, graduated 14th in his class on July 1, 1822, and was promoted to 2nd Lieutenant, 1st Artillery. He served on ordnance duty and recruiting service until June 10, 1823. During that time he was transferred to the 6th Infantry and served for the next two years in a garrison at Ft. Atkinson, Iowa, being promoted to 1st Lieutenant. In March 1826, he was transferred to the 3rd Artillery and spent the next two years at Fort Monroe Artillery School for Practice in Virginia. On July 25, 1829 he married Pamela Brown, daughter of commanding general Jacob Brown, and had seven children. From 1829-35, he served in garrisons at Fort Independence, Massachusetts, and Fort Monroe, Virginia. He then served as Quartermaster General in the Florida War until 1838. After leaving Florida, he served in a variety of quartermaster positions along the northern border, and in 1848, he was Chief Quartermaster on the staff of Major-General Wool in the Mexican War. On November 2, 1848 he married Eliza Aresthusa Arnold, following the death of his first wife three years earlier. They had five children. After that, he served as quartermaster at several posts throughout the nation, ending up at San Antonio, Texas, at the outbreak of the Civil War. Captured by the Confederates, he was soon paroled and returned to New York, where he resumed his quartermaster duties. He retired from the military in 1866 at the age of 62 and died on February 21, 1873 at his residence in Stamford, Connecticut. He is buried at Swan Point Cemetery in Providence. Vinton, *Vinton Memorial,* 284; Cullum, comp., *Biographical Register,* 1: 283-284; obituary in *New York Times*, February 22, 1873.

[15] Rev. Alexander Hamilton Vinton, Vinton's younger brother, was enrolled at Brown University for three years before enrolling at Yale where he studied medicine. Upon graduating in 1828, he practiced medicine in his hometown of Pomfret, Connecticut, until 1832 when he turned to the ministry and entered the Episcopal Theological Seminary in New York. He graduated and was ordained a deacon in 1835, married Eleanor Stockbridge Thompson on October 15 of the same year, and had seven children. A year later he was ordained a priest, and after a year at St. Paul's Church in Portland, Maine, he was rector successively at Grace Church, Providence (1836-42), St.

Paul's in Boston (1842-58), Holy Trinity, Philadelphia (1858-61), St. Mark's, New York (1861-70) and Emmanuel, Boston (1870-77). He received a degree of A.M. from Brown University (1836), a D.D. from the University of New York City (1843) and the same from Harvard College (1853). He died on 26 April 1881, in Philadelphia. A Boston Daily Advertiser writer described him as "the ablest sermonizer in the Episcopal church, and a man of profound logical thought." He is buried at Swan Point Cemetery in Providence. Vinton, *Vinton Memorial,* 285-286; *National Cyclopaedia of American Biography,* 9: 58; *Memorial of St. Mark's Church in-the-Bowery,* 94-97; *New England Historical and Genealogical Register,* 35: 288-289.

16 Rev. Francis Vinton, Vinton's youngest brother, received a cadetship to the Military Academy on 1 July 1826, graduated fourth in his class on 1 July 1830, and was appointed a 2nd Lieutenant in the 3rd Artillery. While assuming his military duties, he studied law in his spare time and was accepted into the Massachusetts Bar in 1836. His first station was Fort Independence, Massachusetts. During 1831 and 1832 he was on topographical and engineering duty, assisting with the construction of several railroads. He then served at Fort Constitution in New Hampshire, in the Creek Nation, and on recruiting service. On August 31, 1836, he resigned his commission, but instead of going into law, he decided to enter the ministry. He was ordained deacon in 1838, married Maria Whipple that same year, and ordained priest in 1839. He and Maria had one child, Francis, who was born on 6 June 1840. Both Mother and child died during childbirth. On November 3, 1841, he married Elizabeth Mason Perry, the daughter of War of 1812 naval hero Oliver Hazard Perry. The couple would eventually have twelve children, in addition to caring for the three orphaned children of his brother John. In 1844, the family moved to Brooklyn, New York. He was elected Bishop of Indiana in 1848, but declined the position. In 1869 he was appointed Professor of Ecclesiastical Polity and Canon Law for the Episcopal Church. Although he had left the army in 1836, the institution at West Point always remained close to his heart. He was twice appointed to the Board of Visitors, once as its president. He was also instrumental in founding the Association of Graduates of the Military Academy. In February 1862, Rev. Vinton consoled President and Mrs. Abraham Lincoln following the death of their son Willie and loaned them copies of his sermon regarding death. Francis Vinton died at Brooklyn on September 29, 1872, and is buried at Island Cemetery in Newport. Vinton, *Vinton Memorial,* 286-287; Cullum, *Biographical Register,* 1: 449-450; *National Cyclopedia of American Biography,* 9: 537-538.

17 Vinton, *Vinton Memorial,* 204-205, 282; Brown and Brown, *Directory of Printing,* 172; Flynt and Fales, *Heritage Foundation Collection of Silver,* 347.

18 Vinton, *Vinton Memorial,* 205.

19 Rugg, *History of Freemasonry in Rhode Island,* 361.

20 Cole, "Pleyel's 'Masonic Dirge,'" 29; Guthrie, "Author of Funeral Dirge," 12.

21 Vinton, *Vinton Memorial,* 206.

22 Greene, *Providence Plantations,* 70.

23 Ibid.

24 Ibid., 71.

25 Ibid., 71-72; Stone, *Recollections of John Howard,* 332-333.

26 JRV to Mother, June 16, 1841, John Rogers Vinton Letters, Notes: Correspondence, IRCML.

27 Ibid.

28 Ibid.; Schantz, *Piety In Providence,* 19.

29 JRV to Mother, June 16, 1841, Ibid.

30 Vinton, *Vinton Memorial,* 282; Joseph G. Swift, Cadet (1801), 2nd Lieutenant, Corps of Engineer (1802), 1st Lieutenant, Corps of Engineer (1805), Captain, Engineer (1806), Major, Engineer (1808), Lieutenant Colonel, Engineer (1812), Colonel and Chief Engineer (1812), Brevet Brigadier General (1814), Superintendent Military Academy (1812-1817), resigned 1818. Cullum, *Biographical Register,* 1: 51-56; Heitman, *Historical Register,* 941.

[31] Adjutant General's Office (AGO). United States Military Academy Cadet Application Papers, 1805-1866, M-688, roll #3, NA.
[32] Crackel, *West Point,* 71.
[33] Ibid.; Pappas, *To the Point,* 71-72.
[34] Ibid., 48, 74; Pappas, *To the Point,* 62-63.
[35] Pappas, *To the Point,* 72, 79.
[36] Crackel, *West Point,* 73; Pappas, *To the Point,* 67, 70-71, 77.
[37] Greene, *Providence Plantations,* 72.
[38] Ibid.
[39] Ibid., 73.
[40] JRV to Mother, June 16, 1841, John Rogers Vinton Letters, Notes: Correspondence, IRCML.
[41] Cole, "Pleyel's 'Masonic Dirge,'" 29; Guthrie, "Author of Funeral Dirge," 12.
[42] For David Vinton's words to "Pleyel's Hymn" and his biography, accessed November 10, 2016, http://www.masonicsites.org/MasonicFacts/Pleyel's%20Hymn.htm, and http://www.mpoets.org/Vinton.htm; Cole, "Pleyel's 'Masonic Dirge,'" 30; Guthrie, "Author of Funeral Dirge," 12.
[43] Guthrie, "Author of Funeral Dirge," 12-13.
[44] Ibid., 13; Cole, "Pleyel's 'Masonic Dirge,'" 30; Mary Vinton to Francis Vinton, June 21, 1836, Francis Vinton Papers, MS 68306a, Connecticut Historical Society (hereafter CHS).
[45] Pappas, *To the Point,* 88.

Chapter 2

[1] Vinton, *Vinton Memorial,* 205. The fourth graduate was Silas Casey, Cadet (1826), 2nd Lieutenant, 2d Infantry (1826), and Brevet Major (1847, 1862 and 1865); Seth Capron, John Fessenden, and Samuel Allston were born in Rhode Island but were residents of other states when they enrolled. Cullum, *Biographical Register,* 1: 272, 328, 364, 383.
[2] Dana, *Memoir: Major John R. Vinton,* 5.
[3] John Rogers Vinton Papers, M-293-01-2, roll #1: Journal (1817-1819), RLDU.
[4] Journal entry July 1817, John Rogers Vinton Papers, M-293-01-2, roll #1: Journal (1817-1819), RLDU.
[5] Bvt. Maj. John James Abert, Cadet (1808), graduated but declined appt. (1811), Brevet Major Topographical Engineer (1814), Brevet Lieutenant Colonel, Topographical Engineer (1824), Colonel Topographical Engineer (1838). Heitman, *Historical Register,* 150.
[6] Christian E. Zoeller was an instructor of drawing at the Military Academy (1808-1810) and (1812-1819). Heitman, *Historical Register,* 1069.
[7] Journal entry July 1817, John Rogers Vinton Papers, M-293-01-02, roll #1: Journal (1817-1819), RLDU.
[8] Ferdinand Rudolph Hassler was an American astronomer and professor of mathematics at the Military Academy (1807-1810). Carroll, *A Good and Wise Measure,* 72; Heitman, *Historical Register,* 510.
[9] Daniel D. Tompkins was Governor of New York (1807-1817) then Vice President (1817-1825). United States Congress. *Biographical Directory,* 1925.
[10] Journal entry, no date, John Rogers Vinton Papers, M-293-01-2, roll #1: Journal (1817-1819), RLDU.
[11] Journal entry, no date, Ibid., between April 16-25, 1818, "On the Height at the West End of Base of Verification."
[12] Journal entry, no date, Ibid., between April 16-25, 1818, "Newark, NJ."
[13] Journal entry, January 20, 1818, Ibid.
[14] Journal entry, April 16, 1818, Ibid.

[15] Maria Matilda Camman of New York, wife of Lt. William Gibbs McNeill, accessed November 10, 2016, http://americanhistory.si.edu/westpoint/graduates_print1.html.
[16] Journal entries, April 25 and 26, 1818, John Rogers Vinton Papers, M-293-01-2, roll #1: Journal (1817-1819), RLDU.
[17] Journal entry, April 30, 1818, Ibid., under "Ride to Springfield Mountain."
[18] Journal entry, May 6, 1818, Ibid.
[19] Carroll, *A Good and Wise Measure*, 35-94.
[20] John Rogers Vinton Papers, M-293-01-2, roll #1: Journal (1817-1819), RLDU.
[21] Col. John Ogilvy, British commissioner to determine the Canadian boundary with the United States. Carroll, *A Good and Wise Measure,* 96; for Ogilvy's biography, accessed November 10, 2016, http://www.biographi.ca/en/bio/ogilvy_john_5E.html.
[22] Carroll, *A Good and Wise Measure,* 74.
[23] Journal entry, January 19, 1819, John Rogers Vinton Papers, M-293-01-2, roll #1: Journal (1817-1819), RLDU.
[24] Journal entry, March 20, 1819, Ibid.
[25] Journal entry, April 28, 1819, Ibid.

Chapter 3

[1] Journal entry, March 20, 1819, John Rogers Vinton Papers, M-293-01-2, roll #1: Journal (1817-1819), RLDU; Cullum, *Biographical Register,* 1: 101, 159.
[2] Mary Vinton to JRV, September 5, 1821, Vinton Family Papers, MS 60090, CHS.
[3] Ibid.
[4] David Vinton in nineteenth-century American Masonic history and biography, accessed November 10, 2016, http://www.masonicsites.org/MasonicFacts/Pleyel's%20Hymn.htm, and http://www.mpoets.org/Vinton.htm; Whicher, "Letter to Newton," 110-115; Guthrie, "Author of Funeral Dirge," 13.
[5] Whicher, "Letter to Newton," 110-115; David Vinton's biography, accessed November 10, 2016, http://www.mpoets.org/Vinton.htm.
[6] Cullum, *Biographical Register,* 1: 159-160; AGO. Returns from U.S. Military Posts, M-517, roll #197 (Charleston Harbor, SC), NA.
[7] AGO. Returns from U.S. Military Posts, M-617, roll #97 (Bellona Arsenal, VA) and roll #792 (Fort Monroe, VA), NA; Cullum, *Biographical Register,* 1: 159-160.
[8] Cullum, *Biographical Register,* 1: 159-160.
[9] Vinton, *Vinton Memorial,* 282-238.
[10] Cullum, *Biographical Register,* 1: 283-183; *New England Historical and Genealogical Register,* 35: 288; *Passengers Who Arrived in the United States,* 226; *United States City Directories,* 68; Vinton, *Vinton Memorial,* 282; Arnold, *Vital Record of Rhode Island,* 469.
[11] JRV to Mother, July 19, 1824, Vinton Family Papers, MS 60090, CHS.
[12] Porter, "Picturesque Pomfret," 3.
[13] *United States Federal Census,* 1820.
[14] Mary Vinton to Francis Vinton, January 11, 1825, March 5 and April 16, 1832, Francis Vinton Papers, MS 68306a, CHS.
[15] Mary Vinton to Francis Vinton, January 11, 1825, Ibid.
[16] Maj. Gen. Jacob Jennings Brown, Brigadier General (1813), Major General and presented with gold medals (1814), Commander in Chief of the Army (1815-1828). Heitman, *Historical Register,* 252.
[17] Vinton, *Vinton Memorial,* 282-238.
[18] JRV to Mother, February 10, 1843, John Rogers Vinton Letters, Notes: Correspondence, IRCML; Cullum, *Biographical Register,* 1: 159-160; Morris, *Sword of the Border,* 235.
[19] Morris, *Sword of the Border,* 229-231.

[20] JRV to Mother, July 31, 1825, Vinton Family Papers, MS 60090, CHS.
[21] Ibid.
[22] JRV to Mother, November 7, 1825, Ibid.
[23] JRV to Mother, March 27, 1826, Ibid.
[24] Bonner, "Journal of a Mission to Georgia in 1827," 74-75; *American State Papers: Indian Affairs* (*ASPIA*) 2: 864-865; Remini, *John Quincy Adams*, 91-92.
[25] Governor George Michael Troup, state representative, U.S. congressman, U.S. senator, Georgia Governor (1823-27), accessed November 11, 2816, http://www.georgiaencyclopedia.org/articles/government-politics/george-troup-1780-1856.
[26] Bvt. Maj. Gen. Edmund Pendleton Gaines, 2nd Lieutenant, 4th Infantry (1801), 1st Lieutenant, 2nd Infantry after being transferred (1802), Captain (1807), Major 8th Infantry and Lieutenant Colonel 24th Infantry (1812), Colonel 25th Infantry and Colonel Adjutant General (1813-1814), Brigadier General (1814), Brevet Major General and presented with gold medal (1814). Heitman, *Historical Register,* 442.
[27] Bonner, "Journal of a Mission to Georgia in 1827," 75; Remini, *Adams,* 94-95.
[28] Secretary of War James Barbour to Lieutenant J. R. Vinton, January 30, 1827, *ASPIA,* 2: 865.
[29] Remini, *Adams,* 95-96; Troup, "Letter to Secretary Barbour," 212; *ASPIA,* 2: 865.
[30] John Rogers Vinton Papers, M-293-01-2, roll #1: Journal (1827-1828), RLDU. All quotes in this chapter not attributed to a different source are from this journal.
[31] United States Congress. *House Document No. 127* (*USHD* 127), 7.
[32] Ibid., 5.
[33] Believed to be Richard Wylly Habersham, U. S. District Attorney, resigned in 1825 to "prevent a disruption between the administration and Gov. Troup." Johnson and Brown, eds., *Twentieth Century Biographical Dictionary,* 5: 3; Hargreaves and Hopkins, eds., *Papers of Henry Clay,* 6: 242.
[34] Col. John Crowell, Agent for Indian Affairs. United States Congress. *House Report No. 98* (*USHR 98*), 133.
[35] Little Prince (Tustennuggee Hopoi), Lower Creek headman who sanctioned the execution of McIntosh and others. Ibid., 340, 620.
[36] Paddy Carr, half-breed Lower Creek interpreter. Ibid., *98*, 694.
[37] Believed to be Luther Blake, licensed trader in Creek nation on Flint River, Deputy Postmaster. Ibid., 342.
[38] Thought to be Tuskeeneehuh, Lower Creek chief. Ibid., *98*, 620.
[39] Mad Tiger, Lower Creek chief. Ibid., 620.
[40] Thought to be Tustenuggee-malo, Lower Creek chief. Ibid., *98*, 620.
[41] Remini, *Adams,* 96-100.
[42] Col. Arthur P. Hayne, 1st Lieutenant, Light Dragoons (1808), Captain (1809), Maj, 1st Light Dragoons (1813), Colonel Inspector General (1814), Colonel Adjutant General to rank from previous year (1815), reverted to Colonel Inspector General (1816), Major Paymaster (1836). Brevet for gallant conduct at New Orleans, LA (1814). Heitman, *Historical Register,* 515.
[43] Capt. John Erving, 2nd Lieutenant, Artillery (1809), 1st Lieutenant (1812), Major Assistant Adjutant General (1813-1815), retained as 1st Lieutenant, Corps. Artillery (1815), Battalion Adjutant (1817-1818), Captain (1818), transferred to 4th Artillery (1821), Brevet Major (1828), Major, 3rd Artillery (1841), transferred to 2nd Artillery (1843), Lieutenant Colonel (1846), Colonel, 1st Artillery (1857). Heitman, *Historical Register,* 407.
[44] Col. John Roger Fenwick, 2nd Lieutenant, Marines Corp. (1799), 1st. Lieutenant (1801), Captain (1809), resigned (1811), Lieutenant Colonel, Light Artillery (1811-1821), Colonel Adjutant General (1813-1815), Colonel 4th Artillery (1822). Brevets for gallant conduct on the Niagara frontier (1813) and faithful service (1823), Heitman, *Historical Register,* 417.

[45] Col. Cornelius Austin Ogden, Cadet (1814), 2nd Lieutenant, Engineers (1819), 1st Lieutenant (1824), Brevet Captain (1834), Captain (1835), Major (1838), Heitman, *Historical Register U.S. Army,* 757. Cullum, *Biographical Register,* 1: 206.
[46] Col. Duncan Lamont Clinch, 1st Lieutenant, 3rd Infantry (1808), R. Paymaster (1808-1810), Captain (1808), Light Colonel 43rd Infantry (1813), transferred to 10th Infantry (1814) and 4th Infantry (1815), Colonel 8th Infantry (1819), transferred to 6th Infantry (1821) and 4th Infantry (1821), Brevet Brigadier General (1829). Heitman, *Historical Register,* 310.
[47] Brig. Gen. Henry Atkinson, Captain, 3rd Infantry (1808), Colonel Inspector General (1813), Colonel, 45th Infantry (1814), transferred to 37th Infantry (1814) and 6th Infantry (1815), Brigadier General (1820), retained but declined Colonel Adjutant General then assigned Colonel 6th Infantry with Brevet Brigadier General (1821). Heitman, *Historical Register,* 174.
[48] Judge John McLean, Supreme Court of Ohio (1816-1822), U. S. Postmaster General (1823-1829), Justice of the U. S. Supreme Court (March 1829-April 1861), accessed November 11, 2016, www.supremecourt.ohio.gov/MJC/places/jMclean.asp.

Chapter 4

[1] Journal entry, September 20, 1827, John Rogers Vinton Private Journal V, MSS 097, Item 062, University of Delaware Library, Special Collections (hereafter UDL). Digital image, accessed November 14, 2016, http://www.lib.udel.edu/ud/spec/findaids/pdf/mss0097_0062.pdf.
[2] Journal entry, September 20, 1827, John Rogers Vinton Private Journal V, UDL.
[3] Journal entry, September 28, 1827, Ibid.
[4] Adjutant General, Col. Roger Jones, Captain, 3rd Artillery (1812), Major Assistant Adjutant General (1813-1815), Lieutenant Colonel (1814), Brevet Major (1814), Colonel Adjutant General (1818-1821, 1825), Colonel (1824), Major, 2nd Artillery (1827), Brigadier General (1832), Lieutenant Colonel, 4th Artillery (1834-1835), Major General (1848). Heitman, *Historical Register,* 582.
[5] Journal entry, October 3, 1827, John Rogers Vinton Private Journal V, UDL.
[6] Journal entry, October 16, 1827, Ibid.
[7] Journal entry, November 9, 1827, Ibid.
[8] Journal entry, November 10, 1827, Ibid.
[9] Capt. Joseph Pannel [Pannell] Taylor, 3rd Lieutenant (1813), 2nd Lieutenant (1813), 1st Lieutenant (1814), honorable discharge (1815), reinstated as 2nd Lieutenant, Corps. Artillery (1816), Brevet 1st Lieutenant (1814), 1st Lieutenant (1817), transferred to 3rd Artillery (1821), Captain (1825), transferred to 2nd Artillery (1827), Captain C. S. (1829), Major, C. S. (1838), Lieutenant Colonel, A. C. (1841), Brevet Colonel (1848), Colonel Commissary General Sub. (1861), Brigadier General Commissary General Sub. (1863); brother of Zachary Taylor. Heitman, *Historical Register,* 947-948; biography, accessed November 11, 2816, http://www.findagrave.com.
[10] Journal entry, November 12, 1827, John Rogers Vinton Private Journal V, UDL.
[11] Journal entry, November 24, 1827, Ibid.
[12] Journal entry, November 28, 1827, Ibid.
[13] Journal entry, December 3, 1827, Ibid.
[14] Ibid.
[15] Ibid.
[16] Journal entry, December 10, 1827, Ibid.
[17] Journal entries, December 10 and 14, 1827, Ibid.
[18] Journal entry, December 20, 1827, Ibid.
[19] Believed to be Mrs. Jane H. Taylor, wife of New York Representative John W. Taylor, Speaker of the House (1820-21) and (1825-27). United States Congress. *Biographical Directory,* 1901.
[20] Journal entry, December 21, 1827, John Rogers Vinton Private Journal V, UDL.
[21] Mrs. Sophia Ramsey, wife of William Ramsey, member of PA General Assembly (1825-1832) and Congressman (1833-1835), Lanman, *Biographical Annals,* 410.

[22] Mrs. Sarah Blake, wife of IN Congressman Thomas H. Blake (1827-1829), Lanman, *Biographical Annals*, 43.
[23] Mrs. Mary Pleasanton, wife of Stephen Pleasanton, Fifth Auditor in the Treasury Department (1817-1855). Lanman, *Biographical Annals,* 397.
[24] Journal entry, January 4, 1828, John Rogers Vinton Private Journal V, UDL.
[25] Journal entry, January 7, 1828, Ibid.
[26] Journal entry, January 10, 1828, Ibid.
[27] Ibid.
[28] Journal entry, January 11, 1828, Ibid.
[29] Ibid.
[30] Probably 1st Lieutenant Daniel Tyler, Cadet (1816), 2nd Lieutenant, Artillery (1819), 1st Lieutenant (1824), resigned (1834), Colonel Connecticut Volunteers (1861), Brigadier General (1861). Heitman, *Historical Register,* 977.
[31] Mary Vinton to Francis Vinton, January 27, 1828, Francis Vinton Papers, MS 68306a, CHS.
[32] Vinton, *Vinton Memorial,* 282, 285; *New England Historical and Genealogical Register,* 35: 288; Cullum, *Biographical Register,* 1: 449.
[33] Journal entry, February 9, 1828, John Rogers Vinton Private Journal V, UDL.
[34] Journal entry, February 14, 1828, Ibid.
[35] Journal entry, February 29, 1828, Ibid.
[36] Ibid.
[37] Journal entry, March 7, 1828, Ibid.
[38] Journal entry, March 22, 1828, John Rogers Vinton Papers, M-293-01-2, roll #1: Journal (1827-1828), RLDU.
[39] Mary Vinton to Francis Vinton, March 26, 1828, Francis Vinton Papers, MS 68306a, CHS.
[40] Journal entry, March 22, 1828, John Rogers Vinton Private Journal V, UDL.

Chapter 5

[1] JRV to Mother, April 1, 1828, Vinton Family Papers, MS 60090, CHS.
[2] *Rhode Island Marriages, 1724-1916; United States Federal Census,* 1830; Cullum, *Biographical Register,* 1: 283-284, 449-450.
[3] Mary Vinton to Francis Vinton, May 1, 1828, Francis Vinton Papers, MS 68306a, CHS.
[4] JRV to Mother, July 19, 1824 and Alex Vinton to JRV, January 10, 1829, Vinton Family Papers, MS 60090, CHS.
[5] Cullum, *Biographical Register,* 1: 159; AGO. Returns from U.S. Military Posts, 1800-1916, M-617, roll #1456 (Fort Wolcott, RI), NA; JRV to Mother, July 31, 1829 and JRV to Lucretia and Mother, October 2, 1831, Vinton Family Papers, MS 60090, CHS.
[6] Ebenezer and Celia Kingman Parker, father and stepmother of Lucretia Dutton Parker Vinton. Hurd, ed., *New England Library of Genealogy and Personal History,* 346-347.
[7] Possibly Senator Daniel Webster of Massachusetts, whose first wife Grace died in January 1828 and who remarried in December 1829. Webster was certainly looking for a new wife at the time and was rumored to have been engaged to a Maria Parker, though no mention of Lucretia is made in any of his papers. Remini, *Daniel Webster,* 289, 309-310.
[8] JRV to Mother, June 13, 1829, Vinton Family Papers, MS 60090, CHS.
[9] Lucretia and JRV to Mother, October 29, 1829, Vinton Family Papers, MS 60090, CHS; *Massachusetts, Town and Vital Records, 1620-1988*, 147.
[10] Lucretia and JRV to Mother, October 29, 1829, Vinton Family Papers, MS 60090, CHS.
[11] Cullum, *Biographical Register,* 1: 159-160; AGO. Returns from U.S. Military Posts, 1800-1916, M-617, roll #958 (Fort Preble, ME), NA.
[12] Lucretia to JRV, March 20, 1832, Vinton Family Papers, MS 60090, CHS.

[13] Mary Vinton to Francis Vinton, April 16, 1832, Francis Vinton Papers, MS 68306a, CHS; *New-England Historical and Genealogical Register,* 35: 228; Cullum, *Biographical Register,* 1: 449-450; *National Cyclopedia of American Biography,* 9: 58, 537.
[14] 2nd Lt. Albert Miller Lea, Cadet (1827), Brevet 2nd Lieutenant, 7th Infantry (1831), 2nd Lieutenant, 7th Infantry and 2nd Lieutenant, 1st Dragoons (1833), resigned (1836), Major Commissary Sub. and Lieutenant Colonel Engineers, C.S.A. War (1861-1865). Heitman, *Historical Register,* 621; Cullum, *Biographical Register,* 1: 472.
[15] Mary Vinton to Francis Vinton, April 16, 1832 and Francis Vinton to Mother, July 22, 1833, Francis Vinton Papers, MS 68306a, CHS.
[16] Lucretia to JRV, April 20, 1832, Vinton Family Papers, MS 60090, CHS.
[17] Lucretia to Mary Vinton, May 2, 1832, Ibid.
[18] Mary Vinton to Francis Vinton, May 10, 1832, Francis Vinton Papers, MS 68306a, CHS.
[19] Mary Vinton to Francis Vinton, June 22, 1832, Ibid.
[20] JRV and Lucretia to Mother, September 1, 1832, Vinton Family Papers, MS 60090, CHS.
[21] Ibid.
[22] Thought to be Joseph Greenleaf Cole (1806-1858), New England painter who worked in Portland (1825-26, 1832) and later moved to Boston and continued as a painter. Biography accessed November 11, 2016, www.mainememory.net/bin/Features?fn=243&fmt=list&n=1&supst=Exhibits&mr=all.
[23] JRV and Lucretia to Mother, September 1, 1832, Vinton Family Papers, MS 60090, CHS.
[24] JRV to Mother, October 2, 1832, Vinton Family Papers, MS 60090, CHS.
[25] Capt. William L. McClintock, Private and Sergeant, 3rd Artillery (1812-1813), 3rd Lieutenant, 3rd Artillery (1813), 2nd Lieutenant (1813), transferred to Corps. Artillery (1814), 1st Lieutenant (1817), transferred to 4th Artillery (1821), Captain (1823), transferred to 3rd Artillery (1827), Brevet Major (1833), Major, 2nd Artillery (1843), transferred to 3rd Artillery (1843). Heitman, *Historical Register,* 657.
[26] 2nd Lt. William Robertson McKee, Cadet (1825), 2nd Lieutenant 3rd Artillery (1829), 1st Lieutenant (1836), resigned (1836), Colonel 2nd Kentucky Cavalry (1846). Heitman, *Historical Register,* 671.
[27] JRV and Lucretia to Mother, October 10, 1832, Vinton Family Papers, MS 60090, CHS.
[28] Ibid.
[29] Vinton, *Vinton Memorial,* 284.
[30] Lucretia and JRV to Mother, December 20, 1832, Vinton Family Papers, MS 60090, CHS; Vinton, *Vinton Memorial,* 284-285.
[31] JRV to Mother, February 22, 1833, Ibid.
[32] Lucretia and JRV to Mother, April 6, 1833, Ibid.
[33] Ibid.
[34] Ibid.
[35] Lucretia and JRV to Mother, December 20, 1832, Ibid.
[36] Francis Vinton to Mother, July 23, 1833, Francis Vinton Papers, MS 68306a, CHS; Guthrie, "Author of Funeral Dirge," 13, 18.
[37] JRV to Mother, August 11, 1833, Vinton Family Papers, MS 60090, CHS.
[38] JRV to Mother, October 29, 1833, Ibid.
[39] Ibid.
[40] Ibid.
[41] Ibid.
[42] Lucretia and JRV to Mother, December 28, 1833, Ibid.
[43] Lucretia and JRV to Mother, January 19, 1834, Ibid.
[44] JRV to Mother, March 12, 1834, Ibid.
[45] Cullum, comp., *Biographical Register,* 1: 159.
[46] JRV to Mother, June 8, 1834, Vinton Family Papers, MS 60090, CHS.

[47] JRV to Mother, September 27, 1834, Ibid.
[48] Ibid.
[49] Ibid.
[50] JRV to Mother, June 1, 1835, Ibid.; Gen. Francis Laurens Vinton, John Rogers Vinton's son, was born at Fort Preble, ME on June 1, 1835. He entered West Point in 1851, graduated tenth in his class in 1856, but resigned his commission to attend the School of Mines in Paris, France. After returning home in 1860, he briefly taught at the Cooper Union in New York before conducting mineralogical studies in Central America. At the commencement of the Civil War, he returned to the United States, offered his services to the Union, and was commissioned as a captain in the regular army. After serving in the defense of Washington, Vinton was offered several higher positions with various state volunteer forces, and accepted a position as Colonel in command of the 43rd New York Infantry. Vinton's unit was assigned to the Army of the Potomac, and he participated in the siege of Yorktown, Battles of Williamsburg, Gaines's Mill, Savage Station, and Glendale, and a skirmish at Harrison's Landing. He was then placed in command of the 6th Corps of the Army of the Potomac, and fought in the Maryland and Rappahannock Campaigns. At the Battle of Fredericksburg on December 13, 1862, he was severely wounded while leading the charge, and was promoted to Brigadier General while on convalescent leave. Unable to return to the field because of his injuries, Vinton resigned his commission on May 5, 1863. He returned to mining, and soon became Professor of Mining Engineering at the School of Mines, Columbia College, New York. He rose to become head of the Engineering Department, but seemed unhappy in the academic life. As a friend later noted, "We have heard Prof. Vinton express bitterly, long before he left the chair of mining at Columbia, his dissatisfaction with the confinement of such a position. ... Highly accomplished in mathematics, drawing, music, and many other branches, he seemed to take refuge in these things. ..." Wanting to get back into the field, Vinton left Columbia in 1877 and moved to Leadville, CO, which at the time was experiencing a mining boom and was the second largest city in Colorado. Vinton died suddenly on October 6, 1879 at the age of forty-four. His friends reported, "We recognized in him a man far above the generality of his kind, a gallant soldier, a profound scholar, a true friend, and one whose place it will be difficult to fill." In a town that was better known for gunfights and lawlessness, thousands turned out for his funeral. His remains were later removed to Swan Point Cemetery in Providence, and he lies at the foot of his father's grave. Vinton, *Vinton Memorial,* 284; Cullum, *Biographical Register,* 2: 424-425; Rothwell and Rossiter, eds., "Death of Francis Laurens Vinton," 257-258, 293-294, 298, 311, 313.
[51] JRV to Mother, August 26, 1835, Vinton Family Papers, MS 60090, CHS.
[52] Vinton, *Vinton Memorial,* 285.

Chapter 6

[1] General information on the Seminole War is taken from John and Mary Lou Missall, *The Seminole Wars: America's Longest Indian Conflict* (Gainesville: University Press of Florida, 2004).
[2] Bvt. Maj. Major Francis Langhorne Dade, 3rd Lieutenant, 12th Infantry (1813), 2nd Lieutenant (1814), transferred to 4th Infantry (1815), 1st Lieutenant (1816), Captain (1818), Brevet Major (1828), Heitman, *Historical Register,* 350.
[3] Maj. Gen. Thomas Sidney Jesup, 2nd Lieutenant, 7th Infantry (1808), 1st Lieutenant (1809), Captain (1813), Major, 19th Infantry (1813), transferred to 25th Infantry (1814) then to 1st Infantry (1815), Lieutenant Colonel, 3rd Infantry (1817-1818), Colonel Adjutant General and Brigadier General Quartermaster General (1818). Breveted for distinguished and meritorious service, gallant conduct and distinguished skill in the battles of Chippewa and Niagara (1814) and Major General (1828), Heitman, *Historical Register,* 573.
[4] "Newport, (R.I.) May 28, (1836)," *Army and Navy Chronicle,* 2: 348.
[5] JRV to Mother, May 26, 1836, Vinton Family Papers, MS 60090, CHS.

[6] Capt. Upton S. Fraser, Ensign 15th Infantry (1814), 3rd Lieutenant (1814), transferred to Corps. Artillery (1815), 2nd Lieutenant (1816), 1st Lieutenant (1818), transferred to 3rd Artillery (1821), Captain (1828). Heitman, *Historical Register,* 434.
[7] JRV to Mother, May 26, 1836, Vinton Family Papers, MS 60090, CHS; Cullum, *Biographical Register,* 1: 159.
[8] Mary Vinton to Francis Vinton, June 21, 1836, Francis Vinton Papers, MS 68306a, CHS.
[9] Ibid.
[10] JRV to Mother and Lucretia, September 2, 1836, Vinton Family Papers, MS 60090, CHS.
[11] Maj. Thomas Childs, Cadet (1813), 3rd Lieutenant & 2nd Lieutenant, 1st Artillery (1814), transferred to Corps., Artillery (1814), 1st Lieutenant, Corps. Artillery (1818), 1st Lieutenant, 3rd Artillery (1821), Captain, 3rd Artillery (1826), Major, 1st Artillery (1847). Brevets for planning attack on Indians and good conduct at Fort Drane, FL (1836), gallant conduct and successes in the war with the FL Indians (1841), gallant conduct in battles of Palo Alto and Resaca-de-la-Palma in War with Mexico (1846), gallant and meritorious conduct in defense of Puebla, Mexico (1847). Heitman, *Historical Register,* 299, Cullum, *Biographical Register,* 1: 115-116.
[12] JRV to Mother and Lucretia, September 2, 1836, Vinton Family Papers, MS 60090, CHS.
[13] Maj. William Gates, Cadet (1801), 2nd Lieutenant, Regiment of Artillery (1806), 1st Lieutenant (1807), Captain (1813), transferred to Corps. Artillery (1814), Captain, 2nd Artillery (1821), Brevet Major (1823), Major, 1st Artillery (1832), Major, 2nd Artillery and Lieutenant Colonel, 3rd Artillery (1836), Colonel, 3rd Artillery (1845). Brevet Brigadier General (1865). Heitman, *Historical Register,* 449-450, Cullum, *Biographical Register,* 1: 67-68.
[14] Maj. Sylvester Churchill, 1st Lieutenant, 3rd Artillery (1812), Captain (1813), transferred to Corps. Artillery (1814), Major Adjutant Inspector General (1813-1815), retained as Captain, Corps. Artillery (1815), transferred to 1st Artillery (1821), Brevet Major (1823), Major, 3rd Artillery (1835), Colonel Inspector General (1841). Brevet for gallant and meritorious conduct in battle of Buena Vista, Mexico (1847). Heitman, *Historical Register,* 301.
[15] JRV to Mother and Lucretia, September 2, 1836, Vinton Family Papers, MS 60090, CHS.
[16] JRV to Lucretia, September 3, 1836, Ibid.
[17] Ibid.
[18] JRV to A. Sibley and to Wm. Rathbone, September 14, 1836, to Jn. Fontaine, September 19, 1836, John Rogers Vinton Letters, Notes: Letterbook (1836-1838), IRCML.
[19] JRV to Adjutant General, November 10, 1836, Ibid.
[20] JRV to Assistant Quartermaster and to Adjutant General, December 6, 1836; to Commissary General, December 18, 1836; to Dr. Mower, December 21, 1836; Ibid.
[21] JRV to P. Rathbone, December 7, 1836; to Quartermaster General, December 10, 1836; to Jno. Fontaine, December 15, 1836; to 2nd Auditor, December 22, 1836, Ibid.
[22] United States Federal Judiciary. *The Federal Cases.* Book 28: *United States v. Vinton, Case No. 16,624 (1836),* 379-382.
[23] Believed to be Dr. Hiram Holt of Pomfret, CT, where he practiced for fifty years. *New England Historical and Genealogical Register and Antiquarian Journal,* 25: 315.
[24] Lucretia to JRV, December 10, 1836, Vinton Family Papers, MS 60090, CHS.
[25] JRV to Adjutant General, December 11, 1836 and January 1, 1837, John Rogers Vinton Letters, Notes: Letterbook (1836-1838), IRCML.
[26] Lucretia to JRV, January 8, 1837, Vinton Family Papers, MS 60090, CHS.
[27] JRV to Mother, January 22, 1837, John Rogers Vinton Letters, Notes: Correspondence (1836-1842), IRCML.

Chapter 7

[1] Florida Territorial Governor Richard Keith Call, 1st Lieutenant, 44th Infantry (1814), brevetted for gallant conduct at Pensacola, FL and New Orleans, LA (1814), transferred to 1st Infantry

(1815), Captain (1818), resigned (1822), elected to 18th Congress (1823-1825), FL Territorial Governor (1835-1840, 1841-1844). Heitman, *Historical Register,* 274; United States Congress. *Biographical Directory,* 937-938.

2 Micanopy (Sint Chakkee), hereditary chief of the Alachua band of Seminoles. Mahon, *Second Seminole War,* 125-127, 383.

3 JRV to Mother, January 22, 1837, John Rogers Vinton Letters, Notes: Correspondence (1836-1842), IRCML.

4 Capt. Charles Mellon, 3rd Lieutenant, 1st Artillery (1814), 2nd Lieutenant (1814), transferred to Corps. Artillery (1814), 1st Lieutenant (1818), transferred to 2nd Artillery (1821), Brevet Captain (1828), Captain (1835). Heitman, *Historical Register,* 702.

5 Maj. Alexander C. W. Fanning, Cadet (1809), 1st Lieutenant, 3rd Artillery (1812), Captain, 3rd Artillery (1813), Captain, 2nd Artillery in reorganization of the Army (1821), Brevet Lieutenant Colonel (1824), Major, 4th Artillery (1832), Lieutenant Colonel, 4th Artillery (1838), transferred to 2nd Artillery (1841). Brevets for gallant conduct at Fort Erie (1814), gallant and meritorious conduct in battle near Withlacoochee under Gen. Clinch and in defense of Ft. Mellon (1835). Heitman, *Historical Register,* 412-413, Cullum, *Biographical Register,* 1: 107-108.

6 Osceola (Tallahassee Tustennuggee; Powell; Asi-Yaholo), son of trader William Powell and Creek mother, leader and war spirit of the Seminoles during the Second Seminole War. Mahon, *Second Seminole War,* 91, 384.

7 JRV to Mother, January 22, 1837, John Rogers Vinton, Notes, Letters: Correspondence (1836-1842), IRCML.

8 Lucretia to JRV, January 24, 1837, Vinton Family Papers, MS 60090, CHS.

9 Ibid.

10 Mary Vinton to Francis Vinton, January 30, 1837, Francis Vinton Papers, MS 68306a, CHS.

11 Lt. John T. McLaughlin, U.S. Navy, commander of the Florida squadron during the Second Seminole War, joint Army and Navy teams, equipped with canoes and flat-bottomed boats for land-sea operations against the Seminoles. Buker, *Swamp Sailors,* 100-101.

12 Alligator (Halpatter Tustennuggee) was one of the principal Seminole leaders.

13 Jumper (Ote Emathla) was a close relation to head chief Micanopy and often considered the second leader of the Alachua band.

14 JRV to Mother and Lucretia, February 9, 1837, John Rogers Vinton Letters, Notes: Correspondence (1836-1842), IRCML.

15 JRV to Secretary of War, February 9, 1837, John Rogers Vinton Letters, Notes: Letterbook (1836-1838), IRCML.

16 JRV to Mother, March 2, 1837, John Rogers Vinton Letters, Notes: Correspondence (1836-1842), IRCML.

17 Cullum, *Biographical Register,* 1: 301.

18 JRV to Mother, March 2, 1837, John Rogers Vinton Letters, Notes: Correspondence (1836-1842), IRCML.

19 JRV to Thos. Butler King, March 4, 1837, John Rogers Vinton Letters, Notes: Letterbook (1836-1838), IRCML.

20 Lucretia to JRV, March 12, 1837, Vinton Family Papers, MS 60090, CHS.

21 Ibid.

22 Lucretia to JRV, March 23, 1837, Ibid.

23 King Philip (Emathla), chief of the Mikasukis, father of Coacoochee (Wildcat). Mahon, *Second Seminole War,* 102, 127, 385.

24 The Seminole were not one tribe but made up of several groups. The two largest were the Alachua Seminole and the Mikasuki. The were also a number of Creeks from Georgia and Alabama, plus a few smaller bands.

[25] Tom Carr, Englishmen and father of Creek interpreter Paddy Carr. Woodward, *Reminiscenses of the Creek, or Muscogee Indians,* 49.

[26] JRV to Adjutant General, March 25, 1837, AGO. Letters Received, Main Series, 1822-1860, M-567, roll #152, NA.

[27] JRV to Mother, April 2, 1837, John Rogers Vinton Letters, Notes: Correspondence (1836-1842), IRCML.

[28] Ibid.

[29] Ibid.

[30] Sam Jones (Abiaki), headman of the Mikasuki and powerful spiritual leader. He was one of the primary leaders in all three Seminole Wars and is revered by present-day Seminole as the person most responsible for keeping them in Florida. West, "Abiaka, or Sam Jones," 367-368, 376-377, 387, 393, 395.

[31] Lucretia to JRV, April 4, 1837, Vinton Family Papers, MS 60090, CHS.

[32] Ibid.

[33] Abraham, Black Seminole leader and interpreter. Sprague, *Florida War,* 73.

[34] Letterbook entry, April 4, 1837, John Rogers Vinton Letters, Notes: Letterbook (1836-1838), IRCML.

[35] JRV to Adjutant General, April 8, 1837 and to Lt. J. A. Chambers, April 18, 1837, Ibid.

[36] Lucretia to JRV, April 24, 1837, Vinton Family Papers, MS 60090, CHS.

[37] Crawford Allen (1798-1872), merchant of Rhode Island, partner in Philip Allen & Sons, cotton broker under Crawford Allen & Co., and brother of renowned Providence industralist Zachariah Allen. Historical note, accessed November 10, 2016, http://www.rihs.org/mssinv/Mss1084.htm.

[38] Sullivan Dorr (1778-1858), prosperous merchant in Providence. He served as a Brown University trustee (1813-1858) and was the second president of the Providence Washington Insurance Company (1838-1858). Historical note, accessed November 10, 2016, http://www.rihs.org/mssinv/Mss390.htm.

[39] Zachariah Allen (1795-1882), Providence textile manufacturer, founded Manufacturers' Mutual in 1835, a factory insurance company to help factory owners develop methods to prevent fires and disasters in their factories. Historical note, accessed November 10, 2016, http://www.rihs.org/mssinv/Mss254.htm.

[40] Philip Allen (1785-1865), son of industralist Zachariah Allen, merchant, Governor of Rhode Island (1851-1853, U.S. Senator (1853-1859), United States Congress. *Biographical Directory,* 775.

[41] Lucretia to JRV, April 24, 1837, Vinton Family Papers, MS 60090, CHS.

[42] Ibid.

[43] JRV to Mother, April 26, 1837, John Rogers Vinton Letters, Notes: Correspondence (1836-1842), IRCML.

[44] Coa Hadjo, Seminole chief. Mahon, *Second Seminole War,* 79, 377.

[45] Coacoochee (also known as Wildcat), King Philip's son and prominent leader of the Seminoles after the death of Osceola. Mahon, *Second Seminole War,* 127, 224, 377.

[46] JRV to Mother, April 26, 1837, John Rogers Vinton Letters, Notes: Correspondence (1836-1842), IRCML.

[47] Memo, April 27, 1837, John Rogers Vinton Letters, Notes: Letterbook (1836-1838), IRCML

[48] Bvt. Brig. Gen. Walker Keith Armistead, Cadet (1801), 2nd Lieutenant, Corps. Engineers (1803), 1st Lieutenant (1805), Captain (1806), Major(1810), Lieutenant Colonel (1812), Colonel and Chief Engineer (1818), Colonel, 3rd Artillery in reorganization of the Army (1821), Brevet Brigadier General (1828). Heitman, *Historical Register,* 169; Cullum, *Biographical Register,* 156-57.

[49] JRV to Mother, April 26, 1837, John Rogers Vinton Letters, Notes: Correspondence (1836-1842), IRCML.

Chapter 8

[1] JRV to William P. Rathbone, April 28, 1837, John Rogers Vinton Letters, Notes: Correspondence (1836-1842), IRCML.
[2] Memo, May 3, 1837, Ibid.
[3] JRV to General Jesup, May 3, 1837, Ibid.
[4] Ibid.
[5] JRV to General Jesup, May 7, 1837, Ibid.
[6] Ibid.
[7] JRV to Maj. William G. McNeill, May 20, 1837, Ibid.
[8] JRV to Governor William Schley, May 23, 1837, Ibid.
[9] JRV to Mother, May 29, 1837, Ibid.
[10] Lucretia to JRV, June 10, 1837, Vinton Family Papers, MS 60090, CHS.
[11] Mary Vinton to Francis Vinton, June 17, 1837, Francis Vinton Papers, MS 68306a, CHS.
[12] JRV to Mother, June 16, 1837, John Rogers Vinton Letters, Notes: Correspondence (1836-1842), IRCML.
[13] Ibid.
[14] Ibid.
[15] Ibid.
[16] Lucretia to JRV, July 10, 1837, Vinton Family Papers, MS 60090, CHS.
[17] JRV to Mother, July 16, 1837, John Rogers Vinton Letters, Notes: Correspondence (1836-1842), IRCML.
[18] Ibid.
[19] Lucretia to JRV, September 21, 1837, Vinton Family Papers, MS 60090, CHS.

Chapter 9

[1] Lucretia to Francis Vinton, November 11, 1837, Francis Vinton Papers, MS 68306a, CHS.
[2] JRV to General Jesup, November 20, 1837, John Rogers Vinton Letters, Notes: Letterbook (1836-1838), IRCML.
[3] Mary Vinton to Francis Vinton, December 3, 1837, Francis Vinton Papers, MS 68306a, CHS.
[4] JRV to General Jesup, January 22, 1838, John Rogers Vinton Letters, Notes: Letterbook (1836-1838), IRCML.
[5] 1st Lt. Thomas Beasly Linnard, Cadet (1825), 2nd Lieutenant, 2nd Artillery and 2nd Lieutenant (1830), 1st Lieutenant (1835), 1st Lieutenant, Corps. Topographical Engineers (1838), Captain (1842). Brevets for gallant conduct, activity, and enterprise in the War against the Florida Indians (1836) and for gallant and meritorious conduct in the Battle of Buena Vista, Mexico (1847). Heitman, *Historical Register,* 634, Cullum, *Biographical Register,* 1: 452-453.
[6] JRV to General Jesup, January 22, 1838, John Rogers Vinton Letters, Notes: Letterbook (1836-1838), IRCML.
[7] Ibid.
[8] Lucretia to JRV, January 26, 1838, Vinton Family Papers, MS 60090, CHS.
[9] Maj. Trueman Cross, Ensign, 42nd Infantry and 2nd Lieutenant (1814), transferred to 1st Infantry (1815), 1st Lieutenant (1818), R. Quartermaster (1816-1818), Captain (1819), Captain Adjutant Quartermaster General (1818), Major Adjutant Inspector General (1820), retained as Captain, 1st Infantry, transferred to 7th Infantry (1821) and relinquished rank in line (1835), Major Quartermaster (1826), Colonel Adjutant Quartermaster General (1838). Heitman, *Historical Register,* 341.
[10] JRV to General Jesup, January 25, 1838, John Rogers Vinton Letters, Notes: Letterbook (1836-1838), IRCML.
[11] JRV to Adjutant General R Jones, February 27, 1838, Ibid.
[12] Lt. James A. Chambers, Cadet (1814), 2nd Lieutenant, Light Artillery and transferred to Corps. Artillery (1820), 2nd Lieutenant, 2nd Artillery in reorganization of the Army (1821), Brevet 1st Lieu-

tenant (1830), 1st Lieutenant, 2nd Artillery (1832), Assistant Quartermaster (1836-1838), Captain, Staff—Assistant Quartermaster (1838), Captain, 2nd Artillery (1838). Heitman, *Historical Register,* 294, Cullum, *Biographical Register,* 1: 250-251.

[13] JRV to [Lt. James A.] Chambers, March 6, 1838, John Rogers Vinton Letters, Notes: Letterbook (1836-1838), IRCML.

[14] JRV to General Eustis, March 6, 1838, John Rogers Vinton Letters, Notes: Letterbook (1836-1838), IRCML.

[15] Mary Vinton to Francis Vinton, March 20, 1838, Francis Vinton Papers, MS 68306a, CHS.

[16] JRV to Chambers, March 22, 1838, John Rogers Vinton Letters, Notes: Letterbook (1836-1838), IRCML.

[17] JRV to General Jesup, April 10, 1838, Ibid.

[18] Journal entry, April 18, 1838, John Rogers Vinton Letters, Notes: Journal (April 10-June 8, 1838), IRCML.

[19] Journal entry, April 21, 1838, Ibid.

[20] JRV to Mother, April 22, 1838, John Rogers Vinton Letters, Notes: Correspondence (1836-1842), IRCML.

[21] Ibid.

[22] Ibid.

[23] JRV to Secretary of War [Joel Poinsett], April 27, 1838, John Rogers Vinton Letters, Notes: Letterbook (1836-1838), IRCML.

[24] JRV to Adjutant General, April 27, 1838, John Rogers Vinton Letters, Notes: Letterbook (1836-1838), IRCML.

[25] Journal entry, April 30, 1838, John Rogers Vinton Letters, Notes: Journal (April 10-June 8, 1838), IRCML.

[26] Ibid.

[27] Ibid.

[28] Journal entry, May 2, 1838, Ibid.

Chapter 10

[1] Journal entry, May 8, 1838, John Rogers Vinton Letters, Notes: Journal (April 10-June 8, 1838), IRCML.

[2] Journal entry, May 4, 1838, Ibid.

[3] Believed to be Dr. Andrew Anderson, Sr. of New York, a physician for lung disease, who moved with his family to St. Augustine (1829), retired from medical practice and head of the temperance society (1830), chaired a meeting against statehood (1838), Justice of the Peace (1839) and died that year of yellow fever. Biography, accessed November 12, 2016, www.drbronsontours.com/bronsonandrewanderson.html.

[4] Journal entry, May 10, 1838, John Rogers Vinton Letters, Notes: Journal (April 10-June 8, 1838), IRCML.

[5] Journal entry, May 11, 1838, Ibid.

[6] JRV to Mother, May 11, 1838, John Rogers Vinton Letters, Notes: Correspondence (1836-1842), IRCML.

[7] Ibid.

[8] Ibid.

[9] Ibid.

[10] Journal Entry, May 13, 1838, John Rogers Vinton Letters, Notes: Journal (April 10-June 8, 1838), IRCML.

[11] Journal Entry, May 15, 1838, Ibid.

[12] Elbert Wells, sold lots to John Rogers Vinton in Columbus, GA, as referenced in Vinton's correspondence.

[13] Mathew Robertson, agent for properties in Columbus, GA, referenced in Vinton's correspondence.
[14] JRV to P. W. Freeman, May 25, 1838, John Rogers Vinton Letters, Notes: Letterbook (1836-1838), IRCML.
[15] Ibid.
[16] Ibid.
[17] Journal entry, May 27, 1838, John Rogers Vinton Letters, Notes: Journal (April 10-June 8, 1838), IRCML.
[18] Journal entry, May 29, 1838, Ibid.
[19] Journal entry, June 2, 1838, Ibid.
[20] Journal entry, June 4, 1838, Ibid.
[21] Ibid.
[22] Journal entry, June 5, 1838, Ibid.
[23] The City Exchange was destroyed by fire on February 11, 1840.
[24] Journal entry, June 7, 1838, John Rogers Vinton Letters, Notes: Journal (April 10-June 8, 1838), IRCML.
[25] JRV to Gen. Winfield Scott, June 26, 1838, John Rogers Vinton Letters, Notes: Letterbook (1836-1838), IRCML.
[26] Gen. Winfield Scott to JRV, June 29, 1838, John Rogers Vinton Letters, Notes: Correspondence (1836-1842), IRCML.
[27] JRV to Gen. Winfield Scott, July 3, 1838, Ibid.
[28] JRV to Adjutant General Rogers Jones, July 3, 1838, John Rogers Vinton Letters, Notes: Letterbook (1836-1838), IRCML.
[29] Gen. Winfield Scott to JRV, July 5, 1838, John Rogers Vinton Letters, Notes: Correspondence (1836-1842), IRCML.
[30] JRV to Gen. Winfield Scott, July 7, 1838, John Rogers Vinton Letters, Notes: Letterbook (1836-1838), IRCML.
[31] For an excellent review of this subject, see Samuel J. Watson, *Peacekeepers and Conquerors: The Army Officer Corps on the American Frontier, 1821-1846* (Lawrence, Kansas: University Press of Kansas, 2013).

Chapter 11

[1] JRV to Mother, July 29, 1838, Vinton Family Papers, MS 60090, CHS.
[2] JRV to Mother, August 4, 1838, Ibid.
[3] JRV to Adjutant General [R. Jones], August 8, 1838, John Rogers Vinton Letters, Notes: Letterbook (1836-1838), IRCML.
[4] JRV to Mother, August 15, 1838, Vinton Family Papers (1803-1868), MS 60090, CHS.
[5] JRV to Mother, August 28, 1838, Ibid.
[6] Dr. Levi Wheaton (1761-1851) of Providence, entered Military Hospital in Providence (1778), received his degree (1779), awarded honorary M.D. degree (1812) and appointed professor of theory and practice of medicine (1815) from Brown University; member of the Board of Trustees of Brown University and Rhode Island Medical Society. Smith, ed., *Boston Medical and Surgical Journal,* XLV: 213-216; biography: accessed November 12, 2016, http:www.brown.edu/Administration/News_Bureau/Databases/Encyclopedia/search.php?serial=W0200; *Transactions of the Rhode Island Medical Society,* 3: 530.
[7] Mary Vinton to JRV, September 2, 1838, Vinton Family Papers, MS 60090, CHS.
[8] Francis Vinton to Alexander Vinton and to JRV, September 10, 1838, Francis Vinton Papers, MS 68306a, CHS.
[9] Francis Vinton to JRV, September 10, 1838, Ibid.; thought to be Dr. Lewis L. Miller, an accomplished surgeon of Providence. *Biographical Cyclopedia,* 362, 539.

[10] Francis Vinton to Alexander Vinton, September 10, 1838, Vinton Family Papers, MS 60090, CHS.
[11] JRV to Mother, September 18, 1838, Ibid.
[12] Ebenezer Parker, Lucretia Vinton's father, was a prominent Boston merchant during the early to mid-nineteenth century. He was the second occupant at Central Wharf in Boston where he was in business for 40 years until his death in 1857. He was one of several merchants and lawyers responsible for building Colonnade Row, a block of twenty-five brick buildings on Tremont Street, and was a founder of Park Street Church. Hurd, ed., *New England Library of Genealogy and Personal History,* 346-347.
[13] JRV to Mother, September 18, 1838, Vinton Family Papers, MS 60090, CHS.
[14] Mary Vinton to JRV, September 20, 1838, Ibid.

Chapter 12

[1] Col. Joseph Gilbert Totten, Cadet (1802), Lt. Col. for gallant conduct at the battle of Plattsburg, NY (1813), Colonel for ten years faithful service in one grade (1824), Col. Chief Engineer (1838), Brigadier General Chief of Engineers (1863), Brig. Gen. for gallant and meritorious conduct at the siege of Vera Cruz, Mexico (1847), Major General for long, faithful and eminent service (1864). Heitman, *Historical Register,* 966; Cullum, *Biographical Register,* 1: 63-67.
[2] JRV to Mother, November 2, 1838, John Rogers Vinton Letters, Notes: Correspondence (1836-1842), IRCML.
[3] JRV to Mother, November 28, 1838, Ibid.
[4] Jefferson College is located in Washington, Mississippi. It was chartered in 1802, opened its doors on January 11, 1811, and held its last classes in 1964. The college is listed on the National Register of Historic Places. Early history, accessed November 12, 2016, http://www.mdah.ms.gov/new/visit/historic-jefferson-college/.
[5] JRV to Mother, December 29, 1838, John Rogers Vinton Letters, Notes: Correspondence (1836-1842), IRCML.
[6] Ibid.
[7] JRV to Mother, January 18, 1839, Ibid.
[8] Ibid.
[9] Ibid.
[10] Journal entries, January 20 and 26, 1839, John Rogers Vinton Diaries: Journal I (1839-1841), Miscellaneous Manuscripts. Providence Public Library, Special Collections (hereafter PPL). Digital images, accessed November 12, 2016, http://hub.provlib.org/special-collections/.
[11] Journal entries, January 28 and 29, 1839, Ibid.
[12] Journal entries, January 30-February 2, 1839, Ibid.
[13] Journal entry, February 3, 1839, Ibid.
[14] Journal entry, February 4 & 5, 1839, Ibid.
[15] Journal entry, February 5, 1839, Ibid.
[16] Journal entry, February 6, 1839, Ibid.
[17] Ibid.
[18] Journal entry, February 9, 1839, Ibid.
[19] Journal entry, February 10, 1839, Ibid.
[20] Ibid.
[21] Journal entry, February 11. 1839, Ibid.
[22] 1st Lt. George Clayton Rodney, Cadet (1833), 2nd Lieutenant, 3rd Artillery (1837), 1st Lieutenant (1838), died of yellow fever at St. Augustine (1839). Heitman, *Historical Register,* 842; Cullum, *Biographical Register,* 1: 683.
[23] Journal entry, February 12, 1839, John Rogers Vinton Diaries: Journal I (1839-1841), PPL.
[24] Journal entries, February 13-14, 1839, Ibid.

[25] JRV to Mother, February 14, 1839, John Rogers Vinton Letters, Notes: Correspondence (1836-1841), IRCML.
[26] Maj. Sylvester Churchill, 1st Lieutenant, 3rd Artillery (1812), Captain (1813), transferred to Corps Artillery (1814), Major Assistant Inspector General (1813-1815), retained as Captain Corps Artillery (1815), transferred to 1st Artillery (1821), Brevet Major for 10 years faithful service in one grade (1823), Major, 3rd Artillery (1835), Colonel Inspector General (1841), brevet Brigadier General for gallant and meritorious conduct in the Battle of Buena Vista, Mexico (1847). Heitman, *Historical Register,* 301.
[27] Journal entries, February 18-19, 1839, John Rogers Vinton Diaries: Journal I (1839-1841), PPL.
[28] Capt. Samuel L. Russell, 2nd Lieutenant, 2nd Infantry (1819), 1st Lieutenant (1827), Captain (1836), killed in action with Seminole Indians near Key Biscayne, FL (1839). Heitman, *Historical Register,* 854.
[29] Journal entries, February 20-23, 1839, John Rogers Vinton Diaries: Journal I (1839-1841), PPL.
[30] Journal entries, February 23-24, 1839, Ibid.
[31] Journal entries, February 24-25, 1839, Ibid.
[32] JRV to Mother, February 26, 1839, John Rogers Vinton Letters, Notes: Correspondence (1836-1842), IRCML.
[33] Lt. Charles E. Woodruff, 2nd Lieutenant, 2nd Infantry (1837), 1st Lieutenant (1839). Heitman, *Historical Register,* 1057.
[34] Journal entry, February 28, 1839, John Rogers Vinton Diaries: Journal I (1839-1841), PPL.
[35] Lt. George Taylor, Cadet (1833), 2nd Lieutenant, 3rd Artillery (1837), 1st Lieutenant (1838), Captain (1847). Brevets for gallant and meritorious service in the war against the Florida Indians (1842) and in the Battle of Huamantla, Mexico (1847). Heitman, *Historical Register,* 946; Cullum, *Biographical Register,* 1: 679-680.
[36] Dr, Isaac Hite Baldwin, Assistant Surgeon (1836), resigned (1841). Heitman, *Historical Register,* 186.
[37] Capt. Josiah Poinsett, captain of the privately owned steamboat *Santee* which was under charter to the military during the Second Seminole War. Mueller, "Steamboat Activity in Florida," 420.
[38] Journal entry, March 1, 1839, John Rogers Vinton Diaries: Journal I (1839-1841), PPL.
[39] Ibid.
[40] Journal entry, March 2, 1839, Ibid.
[41] Journal entry, March 3, 1839, Ibid.
[42] JRV to Mother, March 10, 1839, Vinton Family Papers, MS 60090, CHS.
[43] Journal entry, March 11, 1839, John Rogers Vinton Diaries: Journal I (1839-1841), PPL.
[44] Journal entry, March 12, 1839, Ibid.
[45] Journal entries, March 13-25, 1839, Ibid.
[46] Journal entry, March 26, 1839, Ibid.
[47] Journal entry, March 31, 1839, Ibid.
[48] Ibid.
[49] Journal entry, April 1, 1839, Ibid.
[50] Journal entries, April 2-9, 1839, Ibid.
[51] JRV to Mother, April 9, 1839, John Rogers Vinton Letters, Notes: Correspondence (1836-1842), IRCML.
[52] Ibid.
[53] Ibid.
[54] Ibid.
[55] Journal entry, April 14, 1839, John Rogers Vinton Diaries: Journal I (1839-1841), PPL.
[56] Journal entries, April 16-27, 1839, Ibid.
[57] Journal entries, April 26-29, 1839, Ibid.

[58] Lt. William H. Shover, Cadet (1834), 2nd Lieutenant, 3rd Artillery (1838), 1st Lieutenant (1839), Captain (1847), Capt., Staff—Assistant Quarter Master (1847). Brevets for gallant conduct at Monterey, Mexico (1846) and for gallant and meritorious conduct in the Battle of Buena Vista, Mexico (1847), Instructor of Artillery and Cavalry at the Military Academy (1848-1850), Heitman, *Historical Register,* 884; Cullum, *Biographical Register,* 1: 703.
[59] Journal entries, April 20-May 9, 1839, John Rogers Vinton Diaries: Journal I (1839-1841), PPL.
[60] JRV to Mother, May 8, 1839, John Rogers Vinton Letters, Notes: Correspondence (1836-1842), IRCML.
[61] Journal entries, May 10-17, 1839, John Rogers Vinton Diaries: Journal I (1839-1841), PPL.
[62] JRV to Capt. E. Scriver, Assistant Adjutant General, May 17, May 1839, John Rogers Vinton Letters, Notes: Letterbook (1839-1841), IRCML.
[63] JRV to Mother, May 20, May 1839, John Rogers Vinton Letters, Notes: Correspondence (1836-1842), IRCML.
[64] Journal entries, May 21-31, 1839, John Rogers Vinton Diaries: Journal I (1839-1841), PPL.

Chapter 13

[1] JRV Journal entry, June 4, 1839, John Rogers Vinton Diaries: Journal I (1839-1841), PPL.
[2] JRV to Mother, June 9, 1839, John Rogers Vinton Letters, Notes: Correspondence (1836-1842), IRCML.
[3] Ibid.
[4] Journal entry, June 5, 1839, John Rogers Vinton Diaries: Journal 1 (1839-1841), PPL.
[5] Bockelman, *Six Columns and Fort New Smyrna,* 36.
[6] AGO. Returns from U.S. Military Posts, 1800-1916, M-617, roll #851, (New Smyrna, FL), NA.
[7] Journal entry, June 14, 1839, John Rogers Vinton Diaries: Journal I (1839-1841), PPL.
[8] Dr. David Camden DeLeon, Assistant Surgeon (1838), Major Surgeon (1856), Surgeon C. S. A. war (1861-1865). Heitman, *Historical Register,* 366.
[9] Journal entries, June 15, 17-19, 21, 26, 1839, John Rogers Vinton Diaries: Journal I (1839-1841), PPL.
[10] JRV to Mother, June 29, 1839, John Rogers Vinton Letters, Notes: Correspondence (1836-1842), IRCML. Cullum, *Biographical Register,* 1: 284.
[11] JRV to Mother, July 9, 1839, John Rogers Vinton Letters, Notes: Correspondence (1836-1842), IRCML.
[12] Journal entries, July 18-19, 1839, John Rogers Vinton Diaries: Journal I (1839-1841), PPL.
[13] JRV to *National Intelligencer,* July 20, 1839, John Rogers Vinton Letters, Notes: Letterbook (1839-1841), IRCML.
[14] Journal entry, August 1, 1839, John Rogers Vinton Diaries: Journal I (1839-1841), PPL.
[15] JRV to Mother, August 12, 1839, John Rogers Vinton Letters, Notes: Correspondence (1836-1842), IRCML.
[16] Journal entry, August 10, 1839, John Rogers Vinton Diaries: Journal I (1839-1841), PPL.
[17] Journal entry, August 18, 1839, Ibid.
[18] JRV to Mother, August 12, 1839, John Rogers Vinton Letters, Notes: Correspondence (1836-1842), IRCML.
[19] Journal entry, August 31 1839, John Rogers Vinton Diaries: Journal I (1839-1841), PPL.
[20] Lt. Benjamin Poole, Cadet (1826), 2nd Lieutenant, 3rd Artillery (1830), 1st Lieutenant (1836). Heitman, *Historical Register,* 797; Cullum, *Biographical Register,* 1: 453.
[21] Lt. Rowley S. Jennings, Cadet (1833), 2nd Lieutenant, 3rd Artillery (1838). Heitman, *Historical Register,* 572; Cullum, *Biographical Register,* 1:717.
[22] JRV to Mother, November 17, 1839, John Rogers Vinton Letters, Notes: Correspondence (1836-1841), IRCML.

[23] JRV to Asheton, December 17, 1839, John Rogers Vinton Letters, Notes: Letterbook (1839-1841), IRCML.
[24] Journal entry, December 25, 1839, John Rogers Vinton Diaries: Journal I (1839-1841), PPL.
[25] Journal entries, January 1 and 20, 1840, Ibid.
[26] Dr. Edward Worrell, Assistant Surgeon (1832), honorable discharge (1842). Heitman, *Historical Register,* 1060.
[27] JRV to Lt. Col. William Gates, January 24, 1840, John Rogers Vinton Letters, Notes: Letterbook (1839-1841), IRCML.
[28] JRV to [Maj.] L. [Lorenzo] Thomas, Assistant Adjutant General, February 12, 1840, Ibid.
[29] Journal entry, February 22, 1840, John Rogers Vinton Diaries: Journal I (1839-1841), PPL.
[30] Journal entry, March 9, 1840, Ibid.
[31] Journal entry, March 11, 1840, Ibid.
[32] JRV to Mother, March 28, 1840, John Rogers Vinton Letters, Notes: Correspondence (1836-1842), IRCML.
[33] Ibid.
[34] Journal entries, March 30 and April 3, 4, 23, 1840, John Rogers Vinton Diaries: Journal I (1839-1841), PPL.
[35] Journal entries, April 10 and May 4, 7, 12, 1840, Ibid.
[36] Dr. Charles Noyes, Assistant Surgeon (1838), died (1841). Heitman, *Historical Register,* 753.
[37] Journal entries, May 10, 15, 30, 1840, John Rogers Vinton Diaries: Journal I (1838-1841), PPL.
[38] JRV to Mother, May 17, 1840, John Rogers Vinton Letters, Notes: Correspondence (1836-1842), IRCML.

Chapter 14

[1] Journal entries, June 15 and 16, 1840, John Rogers Vinton Diaries: Journal I (1838-1841), PPL.
[2] Journal entry, July 4, 1840, Ibid.
[3] Journal entry, July 16, 1840, Ibid.
[4] Journal entries, July 17-24, 1840, Ibid.
[5] Journal entries, July 23-29, 1840, Ibid.
[6] AGO. Returns from U.S. Military Posts, 1800-1916, M-617, roll #851, (New Smyrna, FL), NA; Journal entries, August 4-27, 1840, John Rogers Vinton Diaries: Journal I (1838-1841), PPL; JRV to Mother, August 28, 1840, John Rogers Vinton Letters, Notes: Correspondence (1836-1842), IRCML.
[7] Journal entries, September 1-8, 29, 1840, John Rogers Vinton Diaries: Journal I (1838-1841), PPL; AGO. Returns from U.S. Military Posts, 1800-1916, M-617, roll #851, (New Smyrna, FL), NA.
[8] JRV to Mother, September 14, 1840, John Rogers Vinton Letters, Notes: Correspondence (1836-1842), IRCML.
[9] JRV to Mother, October 15, 1840, Ibid.
[10] Journal entry, October 11, 1840, John Rogers Vinton Diaries: Journal I (1838-1841), PPL.
[11] Journal entries, October 19-November 5, 1840, Ibid.
[12] JRV to Mother, November 13, 1840, John Rogers Vinton Letters, Notes: Correspondence (1836-1842), IRCML.
[13] Ibid.
[14] Journal entry, December 24, 1840, John Rogers Vinton Diaries: Journal I (1838-1841), PPL.
[15] JRV to Lt. R. [Randolph] Ridgely, Adjutant, December 25, 1840, John Rogers Vinton Letters, Notes: Letterbook (1839-1841), IRCML.
[16] Journal entries, January 1-12, 31, 1841, John Rogers Vinton Diaries: Journal I (1838-1841), PPL.

[17] JRV to Mother, January 8, 1841, John Rogers Vinton Letters, Notes: Correspondence (1836-1842), IRCML.
[18] Ibid.
[19] Ibid.
[20] JRV to Lt. Col. [William] Gates, January 27, 1841, John Rogers Vinton Letters, Notes: Letterbook (1839-1841), IRCML.
[21] JRV to Mother, February 17, 1841, John Rogers Vinton Letters, Notes: Correspondence (1836-1842), IRCML.
[22] JRV to Lt. Col. [William] Gates, March 17, 1841, John Rogers Vinton Letters, Notes: Letterbook (1839-1841), IRCML.
[23] JRV to Mother, March 21, 1841, John Rogers Vinton Letters, Notes: Correspondence (1836-1842), IRCML.
[24] JRV to Mother, April 3, 1841, Ibid.
[25] Col. William Jenkins Worth, 1st Lieutenant, 23rd Infantry (1813), Captain (1814), transferred to 2nd Infantry (1815) and to 1st Artillery (1821), Major Ordnance (1832), Colonel, 8th Infantry (1838). Brevets for gallant and distinguished conduct at battles of Chippewa and Niagara (1814), for gallantry and highly distinguished services as commander of forces in the war against the Florida Indians (1842), for gallant and meritorious conduct in several conflicts at Monterey, Mexico including presentation of a sword for gallant and good conduct in the storming of Monterey (1847). Heitman, *Historical Register,* 1061.
[26] JRV to Mother, June 16, 1841, John Rogers Vinton Letters, Notes: Correspondence (1836-1842), IRCML.

Chapter 15

[1] JRV to Mother, July 14, 1841, John Rogers Vinton Letters, Notes: Correspondence (1836-1842), IRCML.
[2] JRV to [unknown] and to W. [William] L. McClintock, July 20, 1841, John Rogers Vinton Letters, Notes: Letterbook (1839-1841), IRCML.
[3] JRV to Maj. S. [Samuel] Cooper, July 29, 1841, Ibid.
[4] JRV to Maj. S. [Samuel] Cooper, July 20, 1841, Ibid.
[5] JRV to Mother, August 2, 1841, John Rogers Vinton Letters, Notes: Correspondence (1836-1842), IRCML.
[6] JRV to Mother, August 12, 1841, Ibid.
[7] Dr. Richard Weightman, Post Surgeon (1818), Assistant Surgeon (1821). Heitman, *Historical Register,* 1014. For more on Weightman, see John Bemrose, *Reminiscences of the Second Seminole War*, University of Tampa Press, 2001.
[8] JRV to Mother, August 2, 1841, John Rogers Vinton Letters, Notes: Correspondence (1836-1842), IRCML; AGO. Returns from U.S. Military Posts, 1800-1916, M-617, roll #97 (New Smyrna, FL), NA; Heitman, *Historical Register,* 1014.
[9] JRV to Mother, August 28, 1841, John Rogers Vinton Letters, Notes: Correspondence (1836-1842), IRCML.
[10] JRV to Mother, September 30, 1841, Ibid.
[11] Ibid.
[12] JRV to Mother, October 11, 1841, Ibid.
[13] JRV to Mother, October 31, 1841, Ibid.
[14] Capt. Daniel D. Tompkins, Cadet (1814), 3rd Lieutenant Ordnance (1820), 2nd Lieutenant, 2nd Artillery in reorganization of the Army to rank from 1820 (1821), transferred to 1st Artillery (1821), 1st Lieutenant, 1st Artillery (1825), Captain (1835-1846), Captain, Staff—Assistant Quartermaster (1838), Major, Staff—Quartermaster (1842), Lieutenant Colonel, Staff—Department Quartermaster General (1851), Colonel, Staff—Assistant Quartermaster General (1856), Depot

Quartermaster at NY City during Rebellion of the Seceding States (1861-63). Brevets for gallant and meritorious conduct in war against the Florida Indians (1836) and in prosecution of the war with Mexico (1848). Heitman, *Historical Register,* 965; Cullum, *Biographical Register,* 1: 251-252.

[15] Capt. Justin Dimick, Cadet (1814), 2nd Lieutenant, Light Artillery (1819), 2nd Lieutenant, 1st Artillery in reorganization of the Army (1821), 1st Lieutenant, 1st Artillery (1824), Brevet Captain (1834), Captain (1835), Major (1850), Lieutenant Colonel, 2nd Artillery (1857), Colonel, 1st Artillery (1861), Brevet Brigadier General (1865). Brevets for gallant and meritorious conduct in war against the Florida Indians (1836) and Battles of Contreras, Churubusco, Chapultepec, Mexico (1847). Heitman, *Historical Register,* 374; Cullum, *Biographcial Register,* 1: 213-214.

[16] Capt. William B. Davidson, Cadet (1814), 3rd Lieutenant Ordnance (1815), 2nd Lieutenant (1813), transferred to 1st Artillery then 3rd Artillery (1821), 1st Lieutenant (1825), Captain (1838). Heitman, *Historical Register,* 356; Cullum, *Biographical Register,* 1: 143-144.

[17] JRV to friend [unknown], October 31, 1841, John Rogers Vinton Letters, Notes: Letterbook (1841-1843), IRCML.

[18] JRV to Mother, October 31, 1841, John Rogers Vinton Letters, Notes: Correspondence (1836-1842), IRCML.

[19] Lt. Francis Octavus Wyse, Cadet (1833), 2nd Lieutenant, Artillery (1837), 1st Lieutenant (1838), Captain (1847), Major, 4th Artillery (1861), Lieutenant Colonel (1861), resigned (1863), Lieutenant Colonel, 4th Art (1879). Brevet for gallant and meritorious conduct at Calabosa River, Mexico (1847), Heitman, *Historical Register,* 1065.

[20] Captain Richard Dean Arden Wade, 2nd Lieutenant, Corps. Artillery (1820), transferred to 7th Infantry (1821) and 3rd Artillery (1822), 1st Lieutenant (1828), Captain (1840). Brevets for gallantry and successful service in the war against the Florida Indians (1841) and for gallantry and meritorious conduct at Molino del Rey, Mexico (1847). Heitman, *Historical Register,* 991.

[21] JRV to Maj. T. [Thomas] Childs, November 6, 1841, John Rogers Vinton Letters, Notes: Letterbook (1841-1843), IRCML.

[22] Lt. William Hunter Churchill, Cadet (1836); 2nd Lieutenant, 3rd Artillery, 1 July 1840; 1st Lieutenant, 27 June 1843; brevet Captain, 9 May 1846 for gallantry and distinguished service in the battles of Palo Alto and Resaca de la Palma Tex; Captain, Asst. QM, 3 Mar 1847. Heitman, *Historical Register,*301; Cullum, *Biographical Register,* 3: 135.

[23] JRV to Maj. T. [Thomas] Childs, November 6, 1841, John Rogers Vinton Letters, Notes: Letterbook (1841-1843), IRCML.

[24] JRV to Major [Thomas] Childs, November 12, 1841, Ibid.

[25] Capt. Martin Burke, 2nd Lieutenant, 8th Infantry (1820), transferred to 1st Infantry (1821) and 3rd Artllery (1823), 1st Lieutenant (1828), Captain (1838), Major, 2nd Artillery (1856), Lieutenant Colonel, 3rd Artillery (1861), Brevet Brigadier General. (1865). Brevets for gallantry and meritorious conduct at Contreras, Churubusco, and Molino del Rey, Mexico (1847). Heitman, *Historical Register,* 263.

[26] JRV to Maj. [Thomas] Childs, November 14, 1841, John Rogers Vinton Letters, Notes: Letterbook (1841-1843), IRCML.

[27] The attack on the Mandarin settlement, on the east bank of the St. Johns River approx. 35 miles NW of St. Augustine, was committed by a band of Seminole warriors led by Halleck Tustenuggee on December 20, 1841, killing four whites and looting and burning two buildings. Mahon, *Second Seminole War,* 305.

[28] JRV to Lt. [George] Taylor, January 11 1842, John Rogers Vinton Letters, Notes: Letterbook (1841-1843), IRCML.

[29] JRV to Mother, January 27, 1842, John Rogers Vinton Letters, Notes: Correspondence (1836-1842), IRCML.

Chapter 16

[1] Billy Bowlegs (Holata Micco), leader of the Seminoles at the end of the Second and during the Third Seminole Wars, immigrated to the Indian Territory in Oklahoma in May 1858, joined Union forces in Kansas and appointed Captain of an Indian regiment during the Civil War, reportedly died of smallpox in the fall of 1864. Porter, "Billy Bowlegs in the Seminole Wars," 219; Porter, "Billy Bowlegs in the Civil War," 392, 397-400.
[2] Sprague, *Florida War,* 526-548.
[3] JRV to John T. Sprague, February 6, 1842, John Rogers Vinton Letters, Notes: Letterbook (1841-1843), IRCML.
[4] JRV to Adjutant General [Roger] Jones, March 8, 1842, Ibid.
[5] Dr. Hamilton S. Hawkins, Assistant Surgeon (1824), Major Surgeon (1836). Heitman, *Historical Register,* 513.
[6] JRV to Mother, March 17, 1842, John Rogers Vinton Letters, Notes: Correspondence (1836-1842), IRCML.
[7] JRV to Mother, April 2, 1842, Ibid.
[8] JRV to Mother, April 28, 1842, Ibid.
[9] Mary Vinton to Francis Vinton, May 19, 1842, Francis Vinton Papers, MS 68306a, CHS.
[10] Wilentz, *Rise of American Democracy,* 539-540.
[11] Schantz, *Piety in Providence,* 214.
[12] Ibid., 216.
[13] Ibid.
[14] Wilentz, *Rise of American Democracy,* 541.
[15] JRV to Mother, June 28, 1842, Vinton Family Papers, MS 60090, CHS.
[16] Wilentz, *Rise of American Democracy,* 541-545.
[17] JRV to Francis Vinton, July 16, 1842, Francis Vinton Papers, MS 68306a, CHS.
[18] JRV to Francis Vinton, July 28, 1842, Ibid.
[19] JRV to Mother, August 23, 1842, Vinton Family Papers, MS 60090, CHS.
[20] JRV to Mother, September 17, 1842, Ibid.
[21] Moses Brown Ives (1794-1857), prominent Rhode Island businessman, held interests in Providence textile manufacturing firm of Brown & Ives, President of Providence Bank, trustee of Brown University and treasurer of Butler Hospital for the Insane. Historical note, accessed November 13, 2016, http://www.rihs.org/mssinv/Mss509.HTM.
[22] Dr. Francis Wayland (1796-1865), President of Brown University in Providence (1827-1855). Biography, accessed November 13, 2016, http://www.brown.edu/Administration/News_Bureau/Databases/Encyclopedia/search.php?serial=W0110.
[23] JRV to Mother, September 9, 1842, Vinton Family Papers, MS 60090, CHS.

Chapter 17

[1] JRV to Helena, November 11, 1842, John Rogers Vinton Letters, Notes: Correspondence (1836-1842), IRCML.
[2] Lt. Richard Pindell Hammond, Cadet (1837), 2nd Lieutenant, 3rd Artillery (1841), 1st Lieutenant, Artillery (1846). Brevets for gallant and meritorious conduct at Cerro Gordo, Contreras and Churubusco, Mexico (1847). Heitman, *Historical Register,* 495; Cullum, *Biographical Register,* 2: 17-18.
[3] Lt. Braxton Bragg, Cadet (1833), 2nd Lieutenant, 3rd Artillery (1837), 1st Lieutenant (1838), Captain (1846); Brevet Captain for gallant and distinguished conduct in the defense of Ft. Brown, Texas (1846); Major for gallant conduct in several conflicts at Monterey, Mexico (1846) and Lt. Col. for gallant and meritorious conduct in the battle of Buena Vista, Mexico (1847); General C.S.A. war (1861-1865). Heitman, *Historical Register,* 240; Cullum, *Biographical Register,* 1: 663-664.
[4] JRV to Francis Vinton, November 13, 1842, Francis Vinton Papers, MS 68306a, CHS.

[5] JRV to Honorable. Ab'r Dupont, Mayor of St. Augustine, November 28, 1842, John Rogers Vinton Letters, Notes: Letterbook (1841-1843), IRCML.

[6] John Lee Williams (1775-1856) was a Florida attorney, a member of the commission that selected Tallahassee as the site for the Territorial Capital, asst. adjutant general of the Florida Militia under Joseph Hernandez. Williams authored *A View of West Florida* (1827) and *The Territory of Florida* (1837). After retiring, he spent his remaining years travelling throughout Florida and working on a revised edition of *The Territory of Florida.* Thrapp, *Encyclopedia of Frontier Biography* , III: 1572; Cusick, "Lost Manuscript Comes to Light," 4.

[7] JRV to Jn. [John] Lee Williams, Esq., December 10, 1842, John Rogers Vinton Letters, Notes: Correspondence (1836-1842), IRCML.

[8] Lt. John Fulton Reynolds, Cadet (1837), Bvt. 2nd Lieutenant, 3rd Artillery & 2nd Lieutenant. (1841), 1st Lieutenant, 3rd Artillery (1846), Captain (1855), Lieutenant Colonel 14th Infantry (1861), Brig. General Vols. (1861), Major General Vols. (1862), Colonel, 5th Infantry (1863). Brevets for gallant and meritorious conduct at Monterey, Mexico (1846) and Buena Vista, Mexico (1847). Heitman, *Historical Register,* 825; Cullum, *Biographical Register,* 2: 22-23.

[9] JRV to [unknown], December 29, 1842, John Rogers Vinton Letters, Notes: Letterbook (1841-1843), IRCML.

[10] JRV to Mother, January 13, January 1843, John Rogers Vinton Letters, Notes: Correspondence (1836-1842), IRCML.

[11] Lt. Col. Ethan Allen Hitchcock, Cadet (1814), 3rd Lieutenant Corps of Artillery (1817), 2nd Lieutenant and 1st Lieutenant, 8th Infantry (1818), 1st Lieutenant, 1st Infantry in reorganization of the Army (1821), Captain, 1st Infantry (1824), Major, 8th Infantry (1838), Lieutenant Colonel, 3rd Infantry (1842), Colonel, 2nd Infantry (1851), Major General Volunteers (1862). Brevets for gallant and meritorious conduct at Contreras, Churubusco and Molino Del Rey, Mexico (1847). Heitman, *Historical Register,* 532; Cullum, *Biographical Register,* 1: 167-168.

[12] JRV to Mother, February 10, 1843, John Rogers Vinton Letters, Notes: Correspondence (1836-1842), IRCML.

[13] JRV to Lt. [Braxton] Bragg, February 13, 1843, John Rogers Vinton Letters, Notes: Letterbook (1841-1843), IRCML.

[14] JRV to Mother, March 6, 1843, John Rogers Vinton Letters, Notes: Correspondence (1836-1842), IRCML.

Chapter 18

[1] Lt. George Henry Talcott, Cadet (1827), 2nd Lieutenant, 3rd Artillery (1831), 1st Lieutenant (1836), 1st Lieutenant, Ordnance (1838), Major Voltigeurs (1847), Captain, Ordnance (1847). Brevets for gallant conduct in the war against the Florida Indians (1835) and gallant and meritorious conduct at Molino Del Rey, Mexico (1847). Heitman, *Historical Register,* 943; Cullum, *Biographical Register,* 1: 474-475.

[2] JRV to Adjutant General R. [Roger] Jones, April 1, 1843, John Rogers Vinton Letters, Notes: Letterbook (1841-1843), IRCML.

[3] JRV to Adjutant General [Roger Jones], April 6, 1843, Ibid; AGO, Returns from U.S. Military Posts, 1800-1916, M-617, roll #55 (Augusta Arsenal , GA), NA.

[4] JRV to Mother, February 2, 1844, John Rogers Vinton Papers, box 1, RLDU.

[5] JRV to Mother, February 19, 1844, Ibid.

[6] JRV to Mother, February 19 and March 23, 1844, Ibid.

[7] JRV to LuLu, March 7, 1844, Ibid.

[8] JRV to Mother, April 25, 1844, Ibid.

[9] JRV to Mother, March 23, 1844, Ibid.

[10] JRV to Mother, May 11, 1844, Ibid.

[11] JRV to Mother, July 15, 1844, Ibid.

[12] JRV to Helena, July 21, 1844, Ibid.
[13] JRV to Mother, August 12, 1844, Ibid.
[14] JRV to Helena, August 25, 1844, Ibid.
[15] JRV to Mother, September 21, 1844, Ibid.
[16] Ibid.
[17] JRV to Mother, October 17, 1844, Ibid.
[18] Frank Laurens to LuLu, October 29, 1844, Ibid.
[19] JRV to Mother, December 5, 1844, Ibid.
[20] JRV to Mother, December 23, 1844, Ibid.
[21] JRV to Mother, December 23, 1844, Ibid.
[22] Frank Laurens and JRV to Mother, January 11, 1845, Ibid.
[23] Thought to be Timothy Copp, born (1820), graduated at D.C. (1843), and died while teaching at Augusta, GA (March 28, 1845). Lancaster, *History of Gilmanton,* 253.
[24] Frank Laurens to Helena and JRV to Daughters, April 5, 1845, Ibid.
[25] JRV to LuLu, April 6, 1845, Ibid.
[26] JRV to Mother, May 15, 1845, Ibid.
[27] Ibid.
[28] JRV to LuLu, November 9, 1846, Ibid.
[29] AGO. Returns from U.S. Military Posts, 1800-1916, M-617, roll #55 (Augusta Arsenal, GA), NA.
[30] JRV to Mother, May 15, 1845, John Rogers Vinton Papers, box 1, RLDU.
[31] Lt. Roswell Sabin Ripley, Cadet (1839), 2nd Lieutenant, 3rd Artillery (1843), 2nd Lieutenant, 2nd Artillery (1846), 1st Lieutenant (1847). Brevets for gallant and meritorious conduct at Cerro Gordo (1847) and Chapultepec, Mexico (1847). Heitman, *Historical Register,* 832; Cullum, *Biographical Register,* 2: 76-77.
[32] Journal entries, May 17 and 18, 1845, John Rogers Vinton Diaries: Journal III (1846-1847), PPL.
[33] Journal entry, May 26, 1845, Ibid.
[34] Dr. Henry Hegner Steiner, Assistant Surgeon (1839), resigned (1852), Surgeon C.S.A. War (1861-1865). Heitman, *Historical Register,* 920.
[35] Journal entry, May 27, 1845, John Rogers Vinton Diaries: Journal III (1846-1847), PPL.
[36] JRV to Mother, May 31, 1845, John Rogers Vinton Papers, box 1, RLDU.
[37] JRV to Mother, August 3, 1845, Ibid; Journal entries, June 20-July 15, 1845, John Rogers Vinton Diaries: Journal III (1846-1847), PPL.
[38] JRV to Mother, August 9, 1845, John Rogers Vinton Papers, box 1, RLDU.
[39] Lt. William Tecumseh Sherman, Cadet (1836), 2nd Lieutenant, 3rd Artillery (1840), 1st Lieutenant (1841), Captain C. S. (1850), resigned (1853), Colonel, 13th Infantry (1861), Brigadier General Volunteers (1861), Major General Volunteers (1862-1864), Brigadier General (1863), Major General (1864), Lieutenant General (1866), General (1869), Commander-in-Chief of the Army (1869-1883). Brevet gallant and meritorious service in California during War with Mexico (1848), thanks of Congress for gallant and arduous services in relief of Army of the Cumberland, gallantry and heroism in battle of Chattanooga, gallantry and good conduct in campaign from Chattanooga to Atlanta, and capturing Savannah (1864). Heitman, *Historical Register,* 882.
[40] Journal entry, August 27, 1845, John Rogers Vinton Diaries: Journal III (1846-1847), PPL.
[41] Sherman, *Memoirs of Gen. W. T. Sherman,* 1: 32.
[42] Journal entry, August 31, 1845, John Rogers Vinton Diaries: Journal III (1846-1847), PPL.
[43] JRV to Mother, July 3, 1845, John Rogers Vinton Papers, box 1, RLDU.
[44] JRV to Helena, August 16, 1845, Ibid.
[45] Frank Laurens to Grandmother, November 1, 1845, Ibid.
[46] JRV to Mother, November 6, 1845, Ibid.

[47] JRV to Mother, November 13, 1845, Ibid.
[48] Journal entries, October 3, 9, 21 and December 3, 30, 1845, John Rogers Vinton Diaries: Journal III (1846-1847), PPL; AGO. Returns from U.S. Military Posts, 1800-1916, M-617, roll #55 (Augusta Arsenal, GA), NA; Court of Inquiry: F. A. Wyse vs. Capt. J. R. Vinton, United States Army, Journal (1846), ID 343, United States Military Academy Library, Special Collections and Archives Division.
[49] JRV to Mother, February 26 and March 10, 1846, John Rogers Vinton Papers, box 1, RLDU.
[50] Journal entries, February 17-March 24, 1845, John Rogers Vinton Diaries: Journal III (1846-1847), PPL.
[51] JRV to Mother, April 18, 1846, John Rogers Vinton Papers, box 1, RLDU.
[52] JRV to Mother, May 11, 1846, Ibid.
[53] Ibid.
[54] Journal entries, May 7 and 13, 1846, John Rogers Vinton Diaries: Journal III (1846-1847), PPL.
[55] Journal entry, May 14, 1846, Ibid.
[56] JRV to Francis Vinton, May 14, 1846, Francis Vinton Papers, MS 68306a, CHS.
[57] Journal entry, May 23, 1846, John Rogers Vinton Diaries: Journal III (1846-1847), PPL.
[58] JRV to Francis Vinton, May 23, 1846, Francis Vinton Papers, MS 68306a, CHS.
[59] JRV to Mother, June 11, 1846, John Rogers Vinton Papers, box 1, RLDU.
[60] Journal entries, May 26-29, 1846, John Rogers Vinton Diaries: Journal III (1846-1847), PPL.

Chapter 19

[1] Journal entries, May 30-June 2, 1846, John Rogers Vinton Diaries: Journal III (1846-1847), PPL.
[2] Journal entries, June 11-30, 1846, Ibid.
[3] Journal entries, July 8-14, 1846, Ibid.
[4] JRV to Mother, July 18, 1846, John Rogers Vinton Papers, box 1, RLDU.
[5] Ibid.
[6] Journal entries, July 17-23, 1846, John Rogers Vinton Diaries: Journal III (1846-1847), PPL.
[7] JRV to Mother, July 27, 1846, John Rogers Vinton Papers, box 1, RLDU.
[8] Journal entries, July 28-31, 1846, John Rogers Vinton Diaries: Journal III (1846-1847), PPL.
[9] JRV to Mother, August 7, 1846, John Rogers Vinton Papers, box 1, RLDU.
[10] Valentin Gomez Farias, Vice President and Acting President during the presidency of General Santa Anna (1833-1834), President (1846-1847). Biography, accessed November 13, 2016, https://www.tshaonline.org/handbook/online/articles/fgo06.
[11]Journal entry, August 19, 1846, John Rogers Vinton Diaries: Journal III (1846-1847), PPL.
[12] Journal entries, August 22, 26 and September 9, 1846, Ibid.
[13] Brig. Gen. David Emanuel Twiggs, Captain, 8th Infantry (1812), Major, 28th Infantry (1814), honorable discharge (1815), reinstated as Captain, 7th Infantry (1815) with Brevet of Major from 1814, transferred to 1st Infantry (1821), Major (1825), Lieutenant Colonel, 4th Infantry (1831), Colonel, 2nd Dragoons (1836), Brigadier General (1846), Major General, C.S.A. War (1861-1865). Brevet for gallant and meritorious conduct in conflicts at Monterey, Mexico (1846) and presentation of a sword for gallantry and good conduct in storming Monterey (1847). Heitman, *Historical Register,* 976.
[14] JRV to Mother, August 25, 1846, John Rogers Vinton Papers, box 1, RLDU.
[15] Journal entries, September 13-20, 1846, John Rogers Vinton Diaries: Journal III (1846-1847), PPL; general information on the Battle of Monterrey from John S. D. Eisenhower, *So Far from God: The U. S War With Mexico, 1846-1848.* (Norman: University of Oklahoma Press, 2000), 127-151.
[16] Eisenhower, *So Far from God,* 131.
[17] Ibid., 133.
[18] Ibid., 133-139.

[19] Thomas Staniford, Ensign, 11th Infantry (1812), 2nd Lieutenant (1813), R. Paymaster (1813-1814), 1st Lieutenant (1814), Adjutant Paymaster General (1814-1815), retained as 1st Lieutenant,. 6th Inf. (1815), R. Adjutant (1819-1820), Captain (1820), transferred to 2nd Infantry (1821), Brevet Major (1830), transferred to 8th Infantry (1838), Major, 4th Infantry (1839), transferred to 5th Infantry (1845), Lieutenant Colonel, 8th Infantry (1846), Colonel, 3rd Infantry (1852). Brevets for gallant and meritorious conduct at Palo Alto and Resaca de la Palma, TX (1846) and Monterey, Mexico (1846). Heitman, *Historical Register,* 915.

[20] Journal entry, September 22, 1846, John Rogers Vinton Diaries: Journal III (1846-1847), PPL.

[21] Senator Albert Collins Greene, Rhode Island, House speaker (1821-25), Attorney General of RI (1825-43), State Senate (1843-44, 1851-52), U.S. Senate (1845-51), House of Representatives (1857). United States Congress. *Biographical Directory,* 1234.

[22] Capt. John Benjamin Scott, Cadet (1817), 2nd Lieutenant, 4th Artillery (1821), 1st Lieutenant (1827), Captain (1841), Major,. 3rd Artillery (1857). Brevet for gallant conduct at Palo Alto and Resaca-de-la-Palma, TX (1846). Heitman, *Historical Register,* 869; Cullum, *Biographical Register,* 1: 270-271.

[23] Capt. Samuel Hamilton Walker, Captain Texas mounted rangers, (1846), Lieutenant Colonel (1846), honorably mustered out (1846), Captain Mounted rifle (1846). Heitman, *Historical Register,* 997.

[24] Capt. Albert Gallatin Blanchard, Cadet (1825), 2nd Lieutenant, 3rd Infantry (1829), 2nd Lieutenant, 3rd Infantry (1833), 1st Lieutenant (1836), resigned (1840), Captain LA Volunteers. (1846), Major, 12th Infantry (1847), Brigadier General C. S. A. War (1861-1865). Heitman, *Historical Register,* 224; Cullum, *Biographical Register,* 1: 439.

[25] Lt. George Washington Ayers, Cadet (1837), 2nd Lieutenant, 3rd Artillery (1841), 1st Lieutenant (1845). Brevet for gallant conduct in several conflicts at Monterey, Mexico (1846). Heitman, *Historical Register,* 177; Cullum, *Biographical Register,* 2: 11.

[26] Capt. James Voty Bomford, Cadet (1828), 2nd Lieutenant, 2nd Infantry (1832), 2nd Lieutenant (1834), 1st Lieutenant, 8th Infantry (1838), R. Adjutant (1838-1839), Captain (1845), Major, 6th Infantry (1860), Lieutenant Colonel, 16th Infantry (1862), Colonel, 8th Infantry (1864), Brevet Brigadier General (1865). Brevets for gallant and meritorious conduct at Contreras and Churubusco, Mexico (1847), Molino Del Rey, Mexico (1847), battle of Perryville, KY (1862). Heitman, *Historical Register,* 229; Cullum, *Biographical Register,* 1: 524-525 .

[27] Capt. William Chapman, Cadet (1827), 2nd Lieutenant (1831), 2nd Lieutenant (1833), 1st Lieutenant (1836), Captain (1845), Brevet Major (1847), Brevet Lieutenant Colonel (1847), Major (1861), Lieutenant Colonel (1862), Brevet Colonel (1862). Heitman, *Historical Register,* 296; Cullum, *Biographical Register,* 1:483-484.

[28] Capt. Moses Emery Merrill, Cadet (1822), 2nd Lieutenant, 5th Infantry (1826), 1st Lieutenant (1833), Captain (1837). Heitman, *Historical Register,* 705; Cullum, *Biographical Register,* 1: 382-383.

[29] Lt. Edmund Bradford, Cadet (1833), 2nd Lieutenant, 4th Artillery (1837), 1st Lieutenant (1841), resigned (1849), Major Adjutant Inspector General, C. S. A. War (1861-1865), Heitman, *Historical Register,* 237; Cullum, *Biographical Register,* 1: 674-675.

[30] Lt. Joseph Francis Farry, Cadet (1841), 2nd Lieutenant, 3rd Artillery (1846), 1st Lieutenant (1847), Heitman, *Historical Register U.S. Army,* 414; Cullum, *Biographical Register,* 2: 121-122.

[31] Capt. James Duncan, Cadet (1831), 2nd Lieutenant, 2nd Artillery (1834), 1st Lieutenant (1836), Captain (1846-1849), Col,. Staff—Inspector Gen. (1849). Brevets for gallant conduct at Palo Alto, TX (1846), gallant and highly distinguished conduct at Resaca-de-la-Palma, TX (1846), and for gallant and meritorious conduct at Monterey, MX (1846). Heitman, *Historical Register,* 387; Cullum, *Biographical Register,* 1: 569-570.

[32] JRV to Hon. A. (Albert) C. Greene, December 10, 1846, Vinton Family Papers, 1803-1868, MS 60090, CHS; extract from Memorandum of the Operations of the 2nd Division of the Army against Monterey, 21st, 22d, 23d September 1846, John Rogers Vinton Papers, box 1, RLDU.

[33] Capt. A. G. Blanchard to Frank Vinton, December 5, 1846, Ibid.
[34] Journal entry, September 23, 1846, John Rogers Vinton Diaries: Journal III (1846-1847), PPL.
[35] Journal entries, September 24 and 25, 1846, Ibid.
[36] Journal entry, September 26 & 27, 1846, Ibid.
[37] JRV to Rev. R. Park, October 3, 1846, Francis Vinton Papers, MS 68306a, CHS.
[38] Gen. Pedro de Ampudia (1803-1868), Mexican general. Biography, access November 13, 2016, https://www.tshaonline.org/handbook/online/articles/fam05.
[39] JRV to Mother, October 6, 1846, John Rogers Vinton Papers, box 1, RLDU.
[40] JRV to Mother, October 6, 1846, Ibid.
[41] JRV to Mother, October 12, 1846, Ibid.
[42] Maj. Gen. Robert Patterson, Captain., Lieutenant Colonel and Colonel, 2nd PA Militia, (1812-1813), 1st Lieutenant, 22nd Infantry (1813), transferred to 32nd Infantry (1813), Captain Adjutant Quartermaster General (1813-1814), Captain, 32nd Infantry (1814), honorable discharge (1815), Major General Volunteers (1846), honorable discharge (1848), Major General PA Volunteers (1861). Heitman, *Historical Register,* 775.
[43] Journal entry, November 17, 1846, John Rogers Vinton Diaries: Journal III (1846-1847), PPL.
[44] Journal entries, November 3 and 6, 1846, Ibid.
[45] Journal entries, October 13-November 11, 1846, Ibid.; JRV to Mother, November 19, 1846, John Rogers Vinton Papers, box 1, RLDU.
[46] Journal entries, November 13-17, 1846, John Rogers Vinton Diaries: Journal III (1846-1847), PPL.
[47] JRV to Mother, November 19, 1846, John Rogers Vinton Papers, box 1, RLDU.

Chapter 20

[1] Journal entries, January 8-24, 1847, John Rogers Vinton Diaries: Journal III (1846-1847), PPL.
[2] Journal entry, January 26, 1847, Ibid.
[3] General information on the Battle of Veracruz from Eisenhower, *So Far from God,* 253-265.
[4] JRV to Mother, January 25, 1847, John Rogers Vinton Papers, box 1, RLDU.
[5] Eisenhower, *So Far from God,* 255.
[6] Roman historian Caius Sallustius Crispus, 86 b.c.-34 b.c.
[7] Cousin, probably daughter Elizabeth (1835-1904) of Hammond, named after his sister Elizabeth. After the death of Hammond's wife Pamela in 1845, the children seem to have been sent to various schools, and in earlier letters, Lillie seems to be a little younger than LuLu (1832-1891). Mary Vinton to LuLu, February 19, 1848, Vinton Family Papers, MS 60090, CHS; Vinton, *Vinton Memorial,* 284-285.
[8] LuLu to JRV, February 4, 1847, Vinton Family Papers, MS 60090, CHS.
[9] Journal entries, February 14-21, 1847, John Rogers Vinton Diaries: Journal III (1846-1847), PPL.
[10] JRV to Mother, February 27, 1847, John Rogers Vinton Papers, box 1, RLDU.
[11] Journal entries, February 21-March 1, 1847, John Rogers Vinton Diaries: Journal III (1846-1847), PPL
[12] Journal entry, March 1, 1847, Ibid.
[13] Mary Vinton to Helena, March 1, 1847, Vinton Family Papers, MS 60090, CHS.
[14] Journal entries, March 2-8, 1847, John Rogers Vinton Diaries: Journal III (1846-1847), PPL.
[15] JRV to [Rev.] Park, March 9, 1847, John Rogers Vinton Papers, box 1, RLDU.
[16] Journal entry, March 9, 1847, John Rogers Vinton Diaries: Journal III (1846-1847), PPL.
[17] Eisenhower, *So Far from God,* 259.
[18] Maj. Edmund Kirby, was married to Eliza, sister of Hammond's wife Pamela, an Ensign, 4th Inf. (1812), 3rd Lieutenant (1813), 2nd Lieutenant (1813), R. Adjutant. (1813-1815), transferred to Corps Artillery then to 5th Infantry (1815), 1st Lieutenant (1817), R. Adjutant (1816-1819), trans-

ferred to 2nd Artillery then 1st Artillery (1821), Captain (1824), Major Paymaster (1824). Brevets for gallant and meritorious conduct at Contreras and Churubusco and at Chapultepec, Mexico (1847). Heitman, *Historical Register,* 603; Cullum, *Biographical Register,* 2: 526-527.

[19] Major Kirby to Hammond Vinton, March 22, 1847, John Rogers Vinton Papers, box 1, RLDU.

[20] General Scott in a dispatch from before the walls of Veracruz, John Rogers Vinton Diaries: Journal III (1846-1847), PPL.

[21] Lt. Col. Joseph Eccleston Johnston, Cadet (1825), 2nd Lieutenant, 4th Artillery (1829), 1st Lieutenant (1836), Resigned (1837), reappointed 1st Lieutenant Corps of Topographical Engineers (1838), Captain, Corps Topographical Engineers (1846), Lieutenant Colonel, Voltigeurs (1847), disbanded Lieutenant Colonel, Voltigeurs and reinstated to original rank as Captain Topographical Engineers (1848), Lieutenant Colonel, 1st Cavalry (1855-1860), Brig. Gen, Staff—Quartermaster General (1860). Brevets for gallant and meritorious conduct at Cerro Gordo and Chapultepec, Mexico (1847). Heitman, *Historical Register,* 578; Cullum, *Biographical Register,* 1: 427-529.

[22] Maj. E. Kirby to Hammond Vinton, March 22 & 23, 1847, John Rogers Vinton Papers, box 1, RLDU.

[23] Maj. Martin Scott, 2nd Lieutenant, 26th Infantry. (1814), 1st Lieutenant (1814), honorable discharge (1815), 2nd Lieutenant, Rifle (1818), 1st Lieutenant (1819), transferred to 5th Infantry (1821), Captain (1828), Major (1846). Brevets for gallant conduct at Palo Alto and Resaca de la Palma, TX (1846), and for gallant and meritorious conduct in several conflicts at Monterey, Mexico (1846). Heitman, *Historical Register,* 869.

[24] Lt. Stephen Clegg Rowan, naval officer, played an active role in the Mexican War by leading the landing party that captured San Diego and operations in California. Biography, accessed November 14, 2016, http://www.ibiblio.org/hyperwar/OnlineLibrary/photos/pers-us/uspers-r/s-rowan.htm.

[25] Lt. Charles Pomroy Stone, Cadet (1841), 2nd Lieutenant, Ordnance (1845), 2nd Lieutenant (1847), 1st Lieutenant (1853), Colonel, Staff—Inspector General D.C. Volunteers (1861), Colonel, 14th Infantry (1861), Brigadier General Volunteers (1861). Brevets for gallant and meritorious conduct at Molino Del Rey and Chapultepec, Mexico (1847). Heitman, *Historical Register,* 928-929; Cullum, *Biographical Register,* 2: 117-118.

[26] Maj. E. Kirby to Hammond Vinton, March 28, 1847, John Rogers Vinton Papers, box 1, RLDU.

[27] Eisenhower, *So Far from God,* 264, 342.

[28] Mary Vinton to Helena, May 15, 1847, Vinton Family Papers, MS 60090, CHS.

[29] Mary Vinton to LuLu, May 17, 1847, Ibid.

[30] Mary Vinton to Helena, July 21, 1847, Ibid.

[31] Mary Vinton to Helena, February 17, 1848, Ibid.

[32] John Rogers Vinton appointed his brothers Francis and Alexander guardians of his children. Estate of John Rogers Vinton. Will and Testament of John R. Vinton, Probate Record No. A6743, Providence City Hall, County Clerk; Vinton, *Vinton Memorial,* 206; Passport Application No. 15.141 for Helena L. Vinton, United States Passport Applications, 1795-1925, M-1372, roll #59, NA; United States Federal Census, 1860 and 1870; *Journal of the Eighty-Eighth Annual Convention of the Protestant Episcopal Church,* 25, 90; *Rhode Island Marriages, 1724-1916*; United States Bureau of Education, *Report of the Commissioner of Education,* 409.

[33] *Massachusetts, Marriages, 1695-1910; United States Federal Census*, 1860; Porter, "Picturesque Pomfret," 11; Hoppin, "The Hoppin Family," 9, (typescript) CS 71.H795 1937, RIHS.

[34] Cullum, *Biographical Register,* 2: 424-425.

[35] Ibid; historical notes of the School of Mines Records at Columbia University Libraries, accessed November 14, 2016, http://findingaids.cul.columbia.edu/ead/nnc-ua/ldpd_5801754/summary;

Francis Laurens Vinton's obituary, accessed November 14, 2016, http://localhistory.morrisville.edu/sites/unitinfo/vinton-43.html.

Appendix

[1] The Vinton Obsequies, May 11, 1848, Miscellaneous Manuscript Collection, 1703-2004, Mss Group 20, box 1, folder 7, University of Rhode Island, Special Collections; *Providence Daily Journal,* May 11, 1848.

[2] *Providence Daily Journal,* May 11, 1848; Nilla is the penname of Abby Allin of Pomfret, Connecticut, author of *Home Ballads: a Book for New Englanders,* and contributor of several periodicals. Allibone, *Dictionary of English Literature and British and American Authors,* 1:55.

[3] Journal entry, January 11, 1828, John Rogers Vinton Private Journal No. V, Item 062, UDL; digital image, accessed November 14, 2016, http://www.lib.udel.edu/ud/spec/findaids/pdf/mss0097_0062.pdf.

Bibliography

Manuscripts

Hoppin, Louise Clare. "The Hoppin Family: Sketches from Memory, October 1937." (typescript) CS 71.H795 1937. Rhode Island Historical Society, Special Collections, Providence, Rhode Island.

Vinton. Family Papers (1803-1868), MS 60090. Connecticut Historical Society, Hartford, Connecticut.

Vinton, Francis. Papers (1825-1846), MS 68306a. Connecticut Historical Society, Hartford, Connecticut.

Vinton, John Rogers. Diaries: Contains Journal I (1839-1841), Journal III (1846-1847). Miscellaneous Manuscripts. Providence Public Library, Special Collections, Providence, Rhode Island. Digital images available at http://hub.provlib.org/special-collections/.

-----. Estate of. Will and Testament of John R. Vinton, Probate Record No. A6743. Providence City Hall, County Clerk, Providence, Rhode Island.

-----. Letters, Notes: Contains Correspondence (1836-1842), Letter Book I (1836-1838), Letter Book 2 (1839-1841), Letter Book 3 (1841-1843), and Journal (April 10-June 8, 1838). Microform, Duke University PhotoReproduction Service, 1985, (same as John Rogers Vinton Papers, roll #2, David M. Rubenstein Rare Book & Manuscript Library, Duke University, Durham, North Carolina). Indian River County Main Library, Archive Center and Genealogy Department, Vero Beach, Florida.

-----. Papers (1814-1861), Microfilm 293-01-2, roll #1: Contains Journals (1817-1819) and (1827-1828). David M. Rubenstein Rare Book & Manuscript Library, Duke University, Durham, North Carolina.

-----. Papers, box 1 (1844-1847). David M. Rubenstein Rare Book & Manuscript Library, Duke University, Durham, North Carolina.

-----. Private Journal No. V (September 20, 1827 to March 22, 1828), MSS 097, Item 062. Special Collections, University of Delaware Library, Newark, Delaware. Digital image available at http://www.lib.udel.edu/ud/spec/findaids/pdf/mss0097_0062.pdf.

-----. The Vinton Obsequies, May 11, 1848. Miscellaneous Manuscript Collection, 1703-2004, Mss Group 20, box 1, folder 7, University of Rhode Island, Special Collections, Kingston, Rhode Island. Also published in *Providence Daily Journal,* May 11, 1848.

Public Documents and Public Records

Adjutant General's Office. Letters Received, Main Series, 1822-1860. RG 94, National Archives (NA). Microcopy No. M-567, roll 152.

-----. Returns from U.S. Military Posts, 1800-1916. RG 94, NA. Microcopy No. M-617, rolls 55, 97, 197, 792, 851, 958, and 1456.

-----. United States Military Academy Cadet Application Papers, 1805-1866. RG 94, NA. Microcopy No. M-688, roll 3.

American State Papers: Indian Affairs. 2 vols. Washington, D.C.: Gales and Seaton, 1832-61.

Arnold, James N. *Vital Record of Rhode Island, 1636-1850, first series, births, marriages and deaths: a family register for the people.* Providence, R.I.: Narragansett Historical Publishing Co., 1895.

Court of Inquiry: F. A. Wyse vs. Capt. J. R. Vinton. United States Army, Journal (1846), ID 343, United States Military Academy Library, Special Collections and Archives Division, West Point, New York.

Cullum, George W., comp. *Biographical Register of the Officers and Graduates of the U. S. Military Academy.* 3 vols. New York: Houghton, Mifflin and Co., 1891.

Drake, Samuel Adams. *History of Middlesex County, Massachusetts, Containing Carefully Prepared Histories of Every City and Town in the County, by Well-Known Writers; and a General History of the County, From the Earliest to the Present Time.* 2 vols. Boston: Estes and Lauriat, 1880.

Heitman, Francis R. *Historical Register and Dictionary of the United States Army, From its Organization, September 29, 1789, to March 2, 1903.* Urbana, IL: University of Illinois Press, 1965.

Lanman, Charles. *Biographical Annals of the Civil Government of the United States.* 2nd ed. New York: J. M. Morrison, 1887.

Massachusetts, Marriages, 1695-1910.

Massachusetts Soldiers and Sailors of the Revolutionary War: a compilation from the Archives. 17 vols. Boston: Wright & Potter Printing Co., 1896-1908.

-----. *Town and Vital Records, 1620-1988.*

New England Historical and Genealogical Register. Vol. 35. Boston: New England Historic Genealogical Society, 1881.

New England Historical and Genealogical Register and Antiquarian Journal. Vol. 25. Boston: New England Historic Genealogical Society, 1871.

Passengers Who Arrived in the United States September 1821-December 1823. Baltimore: Genealogical Publishing Co., Inc., reprinted with permission for Clearfield Company, Inc., 2005.

Providence Directory, Containing Names of the Inhabitants, Their Occupations, Places of Business, and Dwelling-Houses. Providence: Brown & Danforth, 1824.

Report of the Commissioner of Education for the Year 1885-'86. Washington, D.C.: Government Printing Office, 1887.

Rhode Island Marriages, 1724-1916.

United States Bureau of Education. Department of the Interior. *Report of the Commissioner of Education for the Year 1885-'86.* Washington, DC: Government Printing Office, 1887.

United States City Directories, 1821-1989.

United States Congress. *Biographical Directory of the American Congress, 1774-1961, the Continental Congress and the Congress of the United States.* Washington, D.C.: Governmental Printing Office, 1961.

-----. House. *Document No. 127,* 19th Cong., 2d sess. (1827), "Message from the President of the United States Transmitting Copies of Communications of the Governor of Georgia and Lieut. Vinton, to the Secretary of War, March 2, 1827."

-----. House. *Report No. 98*, 19th Cong., 2d sess. (1827), "Report of the Select Committee of the House of Representatives, to Which Were Referred the Message of the President U.S. of the 5th and 8th February, and 2d March 1827, with Accompanying Documents and a Report and Resolutions of the Legislature of Georgia.

United States Federal Census, 1820, 1830, 1860, and 1870.

United States Federal Judiciary. *The Federal Cases, Comprising Cases Argued and Determined in the Circuit and District Courts of the United States From the Earliest Times to the Beginning of the Federal Report, Arranged Alphabetically By the Titles of the Cases and Numbered Consecutively.* Book 28: *U.S. v. Sweeney-Waling, Case No. 16,426 to Case No. 17,059.* St Paul: West Publishing Co., 1896.

United States Passport Applications, 1795-1925. RG 59, General Records of the Department of State, 1756-1993, NA. Microcopy No. M-1372, roll 59.

Vital Records of Medford, Massachusetts, to the Year 1850. Boston: New England Historic Genealogical Society, 1907.

Newspapers and Periodicals

Army and Navy Chronicle. 13 vols. Washington: Benjamin Homans, 1835-1842.

New-York Times, 1873.

Providence Daily Journal, 1848.

Secondary Sources

Allibone, S. (Samuel) Austin. *A Critical Dictionary of English Literature and British and American Authors, Living and Deceased, From the Earliest Accounts to the Latter Half of the Nineteenth Century, Containing Over Forty-Six Thousand Articles (Authors), with Forty Indexes of Subjects.* 3 vols. Philadelphia: J. B. Lippincott, 1872.

American Church Silver of the Seventeenth and Eighteenth Centuries: With a Few Pieces of Domestic Plate Exhibited at the Museum of Fine Arts, July to December, 1911. Boston: Museum of Fine Arts, 1911.

Bayles, Richard M., ed. *History of Providence County, Rhode Island.* 2 vols. New York: W. W. Preston & Co., 1891.

Bemrose, John. *Reminiscences of the Second Seminole War.* Tampa, Florida: University of Tampa Press, 2001.

Biographical Cyclopedia of Representative Men of Rhode Island. Providence: National Giographical Publishing Co., 1881.

Bishop, J. Leander. *A History of American Manufacturers from 1608-1860.* 2 vols. Philadelphia: Edward Young & Company, 1864.

Bockelman, Charles W. *Six Columns and Fort New Smyrna.* Daytona Beach, Florida: Halifax Historical Society, 1985.

Bonner, James C. "Journal of a Mission to Georgia in 1827," *The Georgia Historical Quarterly* 44, no. 1 (March 1960): 74-84.

Brown, Harry Glenn, and Maude O. Brown. *A Directory of Printing, Publishing, Bookselling & Allied Trades in Rhode Island to 1865.* New York: New York Public Library, 1958.

Buker, George E. *Swamp Sailors in the Second Seminole War.* Gainesville: University Press of Florida, 1997.

Carlton, Hiram, ed. *Genealogy and Family History of the State of Vermont.* 2 vols. New York: The Lewis Publishing Co., 1903.

Carroll, Francis M. *A Good and Wise Measure: The Search for the Canadian-American Boundary, 1783-1842.* Canada: University of Toronto Press, 2001.

Cole, Hugh A. "Pleyel's 'Masonic Dirge,'—Or Is It?" *The Illinois Lodge of Research* 8, no. 1 (August 1996): 29-30.

Cooper, Wendy A., and Tara L. Gleason, "A Different Rhode Island Block-and-Shell Story: Providence Provenances and Pitch-Pediments." *American Furniture* (1999): 162-208.

Crackel, Theodore J. *West Point: A Bicentennial History.* Lawrence: University Press of Kansas, 2002.

Cusick, James. "After 150 Years, a Lost Manuscript Comes to Light," *Chapter One.* Gainesville: George A. Smathers Libraries, University of Florida (Summer 2003): 1-8.

Dana, Richard H. *Memoir: Major John R. Vinton, U.S.A., Who fell at Vera Cruz, March 22, 1847.* Newport, RI: Davis and Pitman, Printers, 1878.

Eisenhower, John S. D. *So Far from God: The U.S. War With Mexico, 1846-1848.* Norman: University of Oklahoma Press, 2000.

Flynt, Henry N., and Martha Gandy Fales. *The Heritage Foundation Collection of Silver With Biographical Sketches of New England Silversmiths, 1625-1825.* Old Deerfield, MA: Heritage Foundation, 1968.

Gray, Ralph D., and Michael A. Morrison, eds. *New Perspectives on the Early Republic: Essays From the Journal of the Early Republic, 1981-1991.* Illinois: Board of Trustees of the University of Illinois, 1994.

Greene, Welcome Arnold. *The Providence Plantations for Two Hundred and Fifty Years.* Providence: J. A. & R. A. Reid, Publishers and Printers, 1886.

Guthrie, Charles S. "Author of Funeral Dirge," *The Northern Light* 14, no. 5 (November 1983): 12-13, 18.

Hargreaves, Mary W. M. and James F. Hopkins, eds. *The Papers of Henry Clay.* Vol. 6. *Secretary of State 1827*. Kentucky: University Press of Kentucky, 1981.

Hurd, Charles Edwin, ed. *New England Library of Genealogy and Personal History: Contains Genealogy and History of Representative Citizens of the Commonwealth of Massachusetts.* Boston: New England Historical Publishing Co., 1902.

Johnson, Rossiter, and John Howard Brown, eds. *The Twentieth Century Biographical Dictionary of Notable Americans.* Vol. 5. *Habb-Izard.* Boston: Biographical Society, 1904.

Journal of the Eighty-Eighth Annual Convention of the Protestant Episcopal Church in the Diocese of Connecticut. Hartford, CT: Church Press, 1872.

Kane, Sharyn and Richard Keeton. *Fort Benning: The Land and the People.* Fort Benning: United States Army Infantry Center, 1998.

Lancaster, Daniel. *The History of Gilmanton, Embracing the Proprietary, Civil, Literary, Ecclesiastical, Biographical, Genealogical, and Miscellaneous History.* Gilmanton: Alfred Prescott, 1845.

Littell, E. *Littell's Living Age.* Vol. XIII. Boston: E. Littell & Company, 1847.

Mahon, John K. *History of the Second Seminole War, 1835-1842.* Rev. ed. Gainesville: University of Florida Press, 1992.

Memorial of St. Mark's Church in-the-Bowery. New York: Thomas Whittaker, 1899.

Missall, John and Mary Lou. *The Seminole Wars: America's Longest Indian Conflict.* Gainesville: University Press of Florida, 2004.

Morris, John D. *Sword of the Border: Major General Jacob Jennings Brown 1775-1828.* Kent, Ohio: Kent State University Press, 2000.

Mueller, Edward A. "Steamboat Activity in Florida During the Second Seminole Indian War." *Florida Historical Quarterly* 64, no. 4 (April 1986): 407-431.

National Cyclopaedia of American Biography. 63 vols. New York: James T. White, 1907.

Pappas, George S. *To the Point: The United States Military Academy, 1802-1902.* Westport, Connecticut: Praeger Publishers, 1993.

Porter, John Addison. "Picturesque Pomfret." *The Connecticut Quarterly* 2, no. 1 (Jan., Feb., March 1896): 3-24.

Porter, Kenneth. "Billy Bowlegs (Holata Micco) in the Seminole Wars." *Florida Historical Quarterly* 45, no. 3 (January 1967): 219-242.

-----. "Billy Bowlegs (Holata Micco) in the Civil War." *Florida Historical Quarterly* 45, no. 4 (April 1967): 391-401.

Remini, Robert V. *John Quincy Adams.* New York: Times Books, 2002.

-----. *Daniel Webster: The Man and His Time.* New York: W. W. Norton, 1997.

Rothwell, Richard P., and Raymond, Rossiter W., eds., "Editorial: Death of Francis Laurens Vinton." *The Engineering and Mining Journal.* Vol. 28. *July to December, 1879.* New York: Scientific Publishing Co., 1879.

Rugg, Henry W. *History of Freemasonry in Rhode Island.* Providence: E. L Freeman & Son, 1895.

Schantz, Mark. *Piety in Providence: Class Dimensions of Religious Experience in Antebellum Rhode Island.* Ithaca, New York: University Press, 2000.

Sherman, William Tecumseh. *Memoirs of Gen. W. T. Sherman, Written by Himself,* with an Appendix by James G. Blaine. Vol. 1. 4th ed., New York: Charles L. Webster, 1891.

Smith, J. V. C., ed. *Boston Medical and Surgical Journal.* Vol. XLV. Boston: David Clapp, Publisher, 1852.

Sprague, John T. *The Origin, Progress and Conclusion of the Florida War.* A Reproduction of the 1848 Edition with an Introduction by John K. Mahon. Tampa: University of Tampa Press, 2000.

Stone, Edwin M. *The Life and Recollections of John Howland, Late President of the Rhode Island Historical Society.* Providence: George H. Whitney, 1857.

Thrapp, Dan L. *Encyclopedia of Frontier Biography.* III. Reprint, (Lincoln: University of Nebraska Press, 1991.

Transactions of the Rhode Island Medical Society. Vol. 3. Providence: Rhode Island Medical Society, 1883.

Troup, Gov. G. M. "Letter to Secretary of War James Barbour dated Feb. 17, 1827." *The Examiner, and Journal of Political Economy* 2 (Feb. 4, 1835): 209-224.

Vinton, John Adams. *The Vinton Memorial, Comprising a Genealogy of the Descendants of John Vinton of Lynn, 1648. Boston:* S. K. Whipple, 1858.

Watson, Samuel J. *Peacekeepers and Conquerors: The Army Officer Corps on the American Frontier, 1821-1846.* Lawrence, Kansas: University Press of Kansas, 2013.

West, Patsy, "Abiaka, or Sam Jones, in Context: The Mikasuki Ethnogenesis through the Third Seminole War." *Florida Historical Quarterly* 94, no. 3 (Winter 2016): 366-410.

Westgate, Alice W. A., comp. *Mayflower Families Through Five Generations: Descendants of the Pilgrims Who Landed at Plymouth, Mass., 1 December 1620.* 23 vols. Plymouth: General Society of Mayflower Descendants, 2000.

Whicher, John. "Letter to Fraternity Brother Joseph Fort Newton re: David Vinton including excerpts from the Proceedings of the Grand Lodges of North Carolina and Rhode Island, and the minutes of Mount Vernon Lodge No 4 of Providence, Rhode Island." *The Builder Magazine* 3, no. 1 (January 1917): 110-115.

Wilentz, Sean. *The Rise of American Democracy: Jefferson to Lincoln.* New York: W. W. Norton, 2005.

Woodward, Thomas S. *Woodward's Reminiscenses of the Creek, or Muscogee Indians, Contained in Letters to Friends in Georgia and Alabama.* Montgomery, AL: Barrett & Wimbish, 1859.

Index